THE EARL

A History of Urban Society in Europe
Edited by Robert Tittler

FIRST VOLUME TO BE PUBLISHED

The Early Modern City, 1450–1750
Christopher R. Friedrichs

The Early Modern City 1450–1750

CHRISTOPHER R. FRIEDRICHS

Longman
London and New York

Longman Group UK Limited,
Longman House, Burnt Mill,
Harlow, Essex CM20 2JE, England
and Associated Companies throughout the world.

*Published in the United States of America
by Longman Publishing, New York*

First published 1995

ISBN 0 582 01321 6 CSD
ISBN 0 582 01320 8 PPR

British Library Cataloguing-in-Publication Data

A catalogue record for this book is
available from the British Library

Library of Congress Cataloging-in-Publication Data

Friedrichs, Christopher R., 1947–
The early modern city, 1450–1750 / Christopher R. Friedrichs.
p. cm. — (A history of urban society in Europe)
Includes bibliographical references (p.) and index.
ISBN 0–582–01321–6. — ISBN 0–582–01320–8 (pbk.)
I. Title. II. Series.
HT131.F75 1994
612.8′6—dc20 94–21545
CIP

Set by 5 in 10 on 12pt Bembo
Produced by Longman Singapore Publishers (Pte) Ltd.
Printed in Singapore.

Contents

List of Figures and Tables

Editor's Preface

The four volumes of this series are designed to provide a descriptive and interpretive introduction to European Urban Society from the Middle Ages to the present century. The series emerged from a concern that the rapidly burgeoning interest in European Urban History had begun to outstrip the materials available to teach it effectively. It is my hope that these volumes will provide the best possible resource for that purpose, for the serious general reader, and for the historian or history student who requires a scholarly and accessible guide to the issues at hand. Every effort has been made to ensure volumes which are well-written and clear as well as scholarly: authors were selected on the basis of their writing ability as well as their scholarship.

If there is a bias to the project, it is that some considerable degree of comprehension be achieved in geographic coverage as well as subject matter, and that comparisons to non-European urban societies be incorporated where appropriate. The series will thus not simply dwell on the familiar examples of urban life in the great cities of Europe, but also in the less familiar and more remote. Though we aim to consider the wide and general themes implicit in the subject at hand, we also hope not to lose sight of the common men and women who occupied the dwellings, plied their trades and walked the streets.

This undertaking did not come about by random chance, nor was it by any means conceived solely by the series editor. Well before individual authors were commissioned, extensive efforts were undertaken to survey the requirements of scholars active in research and teaching European Urban History in all periods. I am grateful to Charles Tilly, Miriam Chrisman, William Hubbard, Janet Roebuck,

Maryanne Kowaleski, Derk Visser, Josef Konvitz, Michael P. Weber, Laurie Nussdorfer, Penelope Corfield and Tony Sutcliffe, as well as of the authors themselves, whose comments and concerns have been extremely valuable in shaping the series.

Robert Tittler, Montreal

Acknowledgements

This book attempts to distil something of what I have learned over many years of reading, writing and teaching about the early modern city. It would be impossible to mention by name all of those friends and colleagues who have contributed over the years to my thinking about this topic. But I do wish to acknowledge the help of four individuals who specifically assisted me in the preparation of this book. In the first place I must thank Robert Tittler for inviting me to write the book, for offering much useful advice along the way, and for reading the manuscript very carefully once it was completed. I am also grateful to my friends John Fudge and Gordon DesBrisay for critically reading drafts of the manuscript. Finally, I am deeply grateful to my wife, Rhoda Lange Friedrichs, for reading each chapter as it was completed and for generous amounts of encouragement and advice. All of these people offered numerous thoughtful comments about the text. I have gratefully adopted many of their suggestions and stoutly resisted some others. The final product is very much my own.

In an indirect way this undertaking also owes much to the inspiration of two great teachers with whom I studied long ago at Princeton University: Lawrence Stone and Theodore K. Rabb. Neither of them is a specialist in urban history, nor would either of them agree with everything that is said in these pages about the nature of early modern society. But most of what I know about how to look at early modern European history goes back to what I learned from these two teachers, and for that I remain very grateful.

A Note to the Reader

This is a book about cities and towns in early modern Europe. One might think that this is a perfectly straightforward statement, but in fact most of these terms require some clarification.

Some European languages have one principal word to describe an urban community, such as *ville* in French or *Stadt* in German. English, by contrast, has two: city and town. North American usage tends to favour 'city' except when the community is very small; British usage tends to favour 'town' except when the community is very large. But the distinction is never a precise one. In this book the terms city and town are used interchangeably.

'Early modern' is also problematic. Unlike 'medieval', which most people readily understand, the term 'early modern' has not achieved general currency. Historians use this phrase to refer to the period of European history which extends from the end of the middle ages to the beginning of truly modern times in the epoch of the French and Industrial Revolutions. Historians do not agree on the exact limits of the early modern era, but it always includes the sixteenth and seventeenth centuries and usually includes something on either side. In this book the early modern era is defined as the period from 1450 to 1750.

Even 'Europe' creates difficulties. Modern politicians find it hard to define exactly what constitutes Europe; historians can scarcely be blamed for finding it no easier. In this book Europe is understood to correspond to the region encompassed, at the start of early modern times, by the Church of Rome. This includes all of western and central Europe and some of eastern Europe, but it excludes Russia and the Ottoman Empire – lands whose social and political structures set them sharply apart from the region which, at the beginning of early modern times, could still be identified as 'Latin Christendom'.

Introduction
A Way of Living

INTRODUCTION
A Way of Living

Historians – like many other people – have often tried to imagine what it might have been like to visit a European city in the early modern era. Many a description of some city in the sixteenth or seventeenth century begins with a colourful evocation of what the community must have seemed like to the traveller arriving from afar. Approaching the city by land – perhaps in a wagon or on horseback, but more likely trudging along on foot – the traveller would first have seen, far in the distance, the highest church spire of the city. Gradually more and more steeples, towers and rooftops would have become visible, along with the city's stout walls and towered gates. Having passed a cluster of outbuildings on the city's edge, the traveller would now have had to get through the nearest gate complex, answering the watchman's queries or passing an inspection of goods. Once inside the city itself, the traveller would have jostled along some crowded street, first through an outer zone of smaller houses and walled gardens, past increasingly substantial dwellings and through a market square or two, to reach eventually the town centre with its grand merchant homes, public buildings and lofty churches.

This is not, however, how the average town-dweller of early modern times generally experienced his or her own community. For the inhabitant of any city normally approaches the city from within, stepping across the threshold of his or her home right into the bustling street. Let us try to imagine, then, how somebody in one European city of the sixteenth century might have experienced her own immediate environment. Let us walk, for a few moments, with Margareta Toll through her neighbourhood in the German town of Munich one day in the late sixteenth century.

The communal records of Munich for Thursday, 1 April 1574,

note that a linen-weaver named Georg Toll and his wife Margareta purchased a corner house on the Sendlinger Gasse, a major street in the southern part of town leading towards one of the city gates.[1] Since Georg and Margareta Toll owned no other houses in Munich in 1574, one may safely assume that they occupied this newly purchased house as their own dwelling and place of work. Suppose that Margareta Toll now stepped out into the Sendlinger Gasse to look over her new neighbourhood – what would she have seen? Stretching southward from her new home was a long row of attached houses, most of them two- or three-storey buildings with extensive attic space under their high sloping roofs. The house right next door was owned by Peter Schnabel, occupation unrecorded, who came from the village of Bogenhausen just outside Munich. The next house belonged, as of 1570, to the flour-dealer Ulrich Planckh and his second wife Barbara. Next door was a house owned by Martin Khirein, a weaver of heavy woollens. Then came a house owned by the baker Wolfgang Hagen, an immigrant from the village of Eching north of Munich. The next house – a higher, narrower building than most on the street – had just been purchased by a stonemason and his wife. The house after that had belonged to a flour-dealer as of 1572; by 1575 it had been purchased at an auction by a wealthy member of the Munich council. The adjacent house also underwent a change in ownership between about 1572 and 1575, from a linen-weaver to a turner. The next house was owned by a linen-weaver, the one after that by a wool-weaver. Then came a large building, formerly two houses which had been remodelled into one by their current owners, a family of beer-brewers. The next four houses were owned by fine-cloth weavers. The last house, at the end of the row, belonged to members of a family named Weiss; when Hans Weiss died in 1574 his widow bought out the children's share of the house before she remarried.

By now Margareta would have been at the corner of the Henkersgasse – Hangman's Lane. Looking down to her left, Margareta would have spotted the small city-owned house in which the city executioner lived. Contact with the executioner or his family was always to be avoided in a German city of early modern times, since even casual relations with such 'dishonoured' folk could bring disgrace to your own family or even your whole guild. So unless she had pressing business that would require her to walk down Hangman's Lane,

1. *Häuserbuch der Stadt München*, 4: 392; the following passage is based on 4: 28, 393–419.

Margareta would more likely have stayed in the bustling environs of the Sendlinger Gate, turned right towards the small St Peter's churchyard – or headed back up her own street to return home.

We could of course accompany Margareta Toll on more walks through the city of Munich. We could go up the Sendlinger Gasse in the other direction, towards the city centre, arriving soon at Munich's great marketplace and continuing towards the palace of the Bavarian dukes at the north end of the city. Or we could turn left from the marketplace to inspect Munich's greatest church, the Liebfrauenkirche, and enter the zone of high-walled cloisters along the city's western edge. But even a short walk down one street has already taught us something about the social fabric of an early modern city. We see that such a street would be inhabited by people from a mixture of occupations, though there might be some clustering of particular crafts – in this case weaving. We note that both men and women could own and purchase houses. And we note that property frequently changed hands, often by purchase either within families or between non-relatives.

Yet how do we know all these things about Margareta Toll's neighbourhood? Like most men and women in early modern Europe, Margareta left no records in her own hand to tell us of herself or her neighbours. But there is plenty of evidence. The physical description of the Sendlinger Gasse comes partly from a remarkable primary source – a painstakingly detailed wooden scale model of the entire city of Munich prepared by an artisan named Jacob Sandtner in 1572. The information about specific houses was established by a team of local historians, who worked for decades to reconstruct from property records in the city archives the ownership history of every house in the inner-city zone of Munich.[2]

Such an undertaking normally requires teamwork. But sometimes one historian, studying a particular locality in a limited time period, can singlehandedly reconstruct an entire urban neighbourhood. This has been done, for example, for the Boroughside district of Southwark just south of London Bridge during the early seventeenth century. From Jeremy Boulton's study of this London suburb, we know something about almost every house in the Boroughside district in 1622.[3] Walking south from London Bridge along the High Street, to our right we would have seen a long row of butcher shops,

2. Erdmannsdorfer, *Bürgerhaus in München*, 43–6 and plates 2–6, 13–14, 18–20, 70, 93; *Häuserbuch*, passim.
3. Boulton, *Neighbourhood and Society*, 175–92.

broken only occasionally by other food shops or the home of a tailor or shoemaker. There were practical reasons for clustering all the slaughtering activity so close together, as this would help to confine the unavoidable noise and stench to one area. To our left, however, we would have seen a greater variety of shops: beginning at the Hospital Gate corner, for example, we would have passed a saddler, a grocer, a barber-surgeon, an ironmonger, another grocer, a vintner, two more grocers, another ironmonger, a linen-draper and a turner before reaching a house occupied by two gentlemen too wealthy to practise a specific trade. Almost all these households on the High Street were headed by men, and most of them were relatively well-to-do – or at least rich enough to contribute to the weekly poor-rate to assist their humbler neighbours. If, however, we turned from the broad High Street into one of the narrow alleyways leading off it, we would find a different picture. In little Horsehead Alley, for example, there were over sixty households; most of them were headed by tailors, shoemakers and other male artisans, but over a dozen were headed by widows or single women. Of these sixty households, only nine could afford to contribute to the poor-rate, while over twice as many received charity instead.

Even this brief excursion through the Boroughside suggests some distinct features of urban life. As in most European cities of the early modern era, rich and poor lived in close proximity – but the rich were more likely to be found on a major thoroughfare, especially one bustling with commercial activity, while the poor were more heavily concentrated in smaller back streets. Most households were headed by men; those headed by women were more likely to be impoverished. A variety of trades were practised in the neighbourhood, although – in striking contrast to the Sendlinger Gasse in Munich – there were hardly any weavers in the Boroughside.

Historical research has made it possible to reconstruct what we might see if we could walk through these streets, and many others like them, in early modern Europe. In a few cases, we have an actual record of somebody's movements through the streets of an early modern town – above all, perhaps, in the uniquely detailed diary kept by Samuel Pepys, an English naval administrator of the late seventeenth century. Pepys's diary, covering the years 1660 to 1669, was published in the nineteenth century and for generations readers have followed the author as he moved through London by coach, by boat or on foot in his inexhaustible pursuit of business and pleasure.[4]

4. The definitive edition is Pepys, *Diary*, ed. by Latham and Matthews.

Private letters, travel accounts, diaries – and there are many, though few are as detailed as Pepys's – are invaluable sources of information about the nature of urban life in early modern Europe, but they answer only the questions their own authors considered important at the time. We know much, for example, about Pepys's own house in Seething Lane on Tower Hill – but we know almost nothing about his neighbours. For all his curiosity, Samuel Pepys did not produce an occupational profile of his neighbourhood, or record how many men and women on his street lived in comfort or distress. To find out about things like this, modern social historians have moved beyond the evidence produced by individual observers, valuable as it often is, to undertake the systematic assessment of municipal records, church records and similar documents which make possible an ever fuller picture of early modern urban life.

Every city is distinct, of course, and this was as true in the early modern era as it is today. Munich was different from Southwark; indeed, Southwark was different from the City of London just across the river Thames. It is important to know and understand the ways in which cities differed from each other. But it is just as important to realize that European cities of the early modern era belonged to a common urban civilization. Towns on the outer fringes of the European continent – in Russia, along the steppe frontier, in most of the Balkan peninsula – were not fully part of this particular civilization. But from Aberdeen on the North Sea to Dubrovnik on the Adriatic, from Lisbon on the Atlantic to Tallinn on the Gulf of Finland, the towns and cities of western, central and much of eastern Europe during the early modern epoch had remarkably much in common. This book will explore the social history of towns and cities across this vast area during the three hundred years from the mid-fifteenth to the mid-eighteenth century. In doing so, we will never lose sight of the many ways in which cities could differ from each other. But we shall emphasize instead what they had in common. In doing so, this book hopes to recapture something of the collective experience of the men, women and children who lived in the European city of the early modern era. Somewhere between 100 million and 200 million human beings lived part or all of their lives in European cities between 1450 and 1750. This book will try to tell their story.

To learn something about the life and death, the work and play, the hopes and fears of human beings in past generations would, perhaps, be enough for many readers. But the historian always hopes to do more – to put what has been learned about individual or collective experiences into the framework of some larger effort to understand the dynamics of past society. This, too, is one of the objectives of this book.

A framework of explanation, however, is not something on which all historians can agree. Today in particular this is the case, for one of the central concepts around which our understanding of the European past has been based is increasingly being called into question. It is therefore important to know something about this concept and its implications.

For well over a generation the central idea around which most people constructed their understanding of European social history – and of the place of the city within it – has had to do with the theory of modernization. This is the notion that the broad currents of European social history must best be understood as a transition from a traditional, largely agrarian and 'underdeveloped' society to the modern industrial and 'developed' society with which we are familiar today. Traditional society, in this view, was static, deferential and strongly religious; powerful local elites dominated a vast, largely illiterate population engaged in unchanging and inelastic economic activity. By contrast, a modern society is seen as dynamic, mobile, heavily secular and at least potentially democratic; a fully literate population relates to political life on the national level and engages in economic activity geared to constant expansion and growth.[5] The transition from traditional to modern society is described as an interactive process in which advances in any one sphere of life contributed to changes in every other; the transition may have been irregular and even stalled at times, but eventually enough changes took place to make the onset of modernization irreversible. These transforming changes, we have been taught, first took place in northwestern Europe and then spread gradually to the rest of Europe, to North America and eventually to other parts of the world.

The concept of modernization owes much to even earlier concepts of long-term social change. It owes something, for example, to the view of Max Weber, the great social theorist who emphasized the advent of 'rationality' as a key step in the evolution towards modern societies. It owes even more, however, to Marxism. Though modernization theory was created, to some extent, as an alternative to the Marxist description of social evolution, the two theories actually have much in common. The movement from 'traditional' to 'modern'

5. cf. Black, *Dynamics of Modernization*, 9–26; see also Wrigley, 'Process of Modernization', 48–55.

society echoes the classic Marxist concept of a transition from feudal to capitalist society. As originally formulated by Karl Marx and Friedrich Engels, Marxism attributed a central role to the European city of late medieval and early modern times – for it was in the city that a new class and a new system of economic relations emerged. The class was the bourgeoisie; the system it created was capitalism. In time, according to the classic view, bourgeois capitalism overthrew the old feudal order and came to dominate every aspect of economic, political and social life. This view has always had its critics, of course – including neo-Marxists who give more emphasis than Marx and Engels themselves did to the capitalist transformation of agricultural relations. But the basic conceptual framework has remained remarkably durable. So, more recently, has modernization theory.

What all this implies for the history of the city is a deep-seated, often unconscious tendency to search the records of urban history for evidence of the onset of modern conditions. It is only natural, perhaps, in studying the rich variety of social and economic changes in any particular city, to focus on those events which seem to betoken a significant shift towards modernity. The literature about European cities in the early modern era is in fact full of descriptions of landmark events when some crucial shift towards the modern allegedly took place.

Yet this tendency can in fact be highly misleading. Certainly the early modern city experienced countless changes – many of which will be explored in detail in the pages to come. But these changes were by no means all unilinear, leading systematically from pre-modern to modern conditions. Some, in fact, can only be described as regressive. To take but one example: the massive and systematic persecution of women who were accused of being witches was a highly innovative development in the sixteenth century. Both the ideology that lay behind the witch-craze and the way in which it was conducted represented a clear case of dramatic change as against the previous centuries. But 'modern' as it was in its day, the European witch-craze was not the direct antecedent of any contemporary aspect of gender relations. It was instead a developmental dead end.

In fact, the entire emphasis on change in the early modern city can be misleading. For in many of its most important aspects, the early modern city remained remarkably unchanged during the era covered by this book. This is a point that needs emphasis, for it runs strongly against the grain of most recent studies of the early modern town. To be sure, there are historians who emphasize the immobility and lack of innovation in early modern Europe – but by and large their emphasis is on rural society. The city, by contrast, is normally seen as a centre of innovation and creativity. And so it is. Yet the truly creative and transforming epochs in the history of the European city took place not during the early modern era, but before and after it. It was in fact during the last few centuries of the middle ages that the physical form of the European city and its institutional framework were developed. The basic relationship of the city to the state, the internal organization of urban life, the role of the guilds and the church, the very pattern of streets and buildings – all these things were firmly in place by 1450. Of course the early modern era was an age of dramatic movements in European history: the Reformation and Counter-Reformation, the growth of European contact with other continents, the development of new techniques of capitalism, the theory and practice of absolutism, the revolutions in physics and astronomy. There were specific changes in cities as well, particularly in those cities closely linked to the princely and royal courts of western and central Europe. Many towns grew substantially in size, and some new towns were founded. But the impact of all these changes on the everyday life and routine of most city-dwellers was, as we shall see, relatively small. Despite all that had happened, the basic styles of work and worship, love and leisure, birth and death in the European city of 1750 were much the same as they had been three centuries before. It was the nineteenth century, not the early modern era, that radically transformed the European city in its appearance and, more importantly, in its social and economic life.

From this point of view it might be suggested that the very term 'early modern' is not entirely apt for the period covered by this book. Some historians even prefer to write of the 'post-medieval' city.[6] In fact there are good reasons to stick to standard usage in referring to the period from the mid-fifteenth to the mid-eighteenth century as the early modern era.[7] But this does not bind us to a ceaseless search for the onset of the 'modern' in every aspect of urban life. One of the wisest students of European village life has recently warned historians to avoid reducing the history of any one community to 'an instance of a stage in the process of modernization'. For when this is done, David Sabean argues, 'attention is turned away from the dynamics of social relations in a particular society to a grand narrative of human

6. e.g. Spiess, *Braunschweig im Nachmittelalter*, 1: 6n.
7. cf. the discussion in de Vries, *European Urbanization*, 3–10.

progress. Each new study recodes its findings to fit an objectified story already known to the observer.'[8]

The same of course applies to the early modern city. To force what we know about the early modern city into a 'grand narrative of human progress' is to ignore much of what was most interesting and significant about the way that human beings lived in that era. When Margareta Toll moved to the Sendlinger Gasse in 1574, or Samuel Pepys took a coach to Whitehall in 1665, they were not searching for modern times – they were looking, as all humans do, for ways to make their own lives successful and meaningful for themselves and their families. And they did so in ways that would, in many respects, make perfect sense to us.

Of course the social norms of urban life in early modern times differed massively from those of today. Patterns of family life, work, leisure, politics, religious expression, and of course the very look and feel of the city itself have little in common with today's world. But this book does not accept the widespread argument that these obvious differences are accounted for by some deeper difference between human nature in early modern times and human nature today. To say that people were more religious, or less worldly, or more deferential, or less able to plan ahead, or more violent, or less affectionate towards their children than people today – these and countless other statements of a similar kind imply that there was some fundamental variation in mental structure between people then and people now. This is not true. Men and women of the sixteenth and seventeenth centuries were motivated by much the same mixture of values and emotions as motivate people today: they were ambitious and altruistic, optimistic and pessimistic, devout and impious, assertive and passive, spontaneous and deliberate. But they operated in a different framework. What made this framework different from ours was, above all, one thing: limited technology in certain key areas of activity. And this in turn was due largely to the lack of information about certain specific topics – particularly a number of physical, chemical and biological processes whose workings are taken for granted today.

This does not mean that people in early modern times lacked scientific information or technological skills. Far from it. Indeed, many of the products of medieval and early modern cities – from cathedrals to cloth, from cannons to clocks – were the result of enormously complex technical processes, developed over centuries of

8. Sabean, *Property, Production, and Family*, 9.

trial and error. But early modern life was burdened by technical and scientific limitations of enormous consequence. Power sources were meagre. Almost all power had to be generated by human or animal muscles, for the use of inanimate power was extremely limited. This in turn had implications for the way in which products were manufactured, the way in which buildings were constructed and the way in which people and goods were transported. Communications were slow. Information could travel no faster than the wind at sea or the fastest horse by land. It was hard to make things very hot. This restricted what could be done with metals. It was hard to make things very cold. This prevented people from preserving most foods. Control of pain was extremely limited. Surgical intervention beyond a few outer millimetres of the human body was virtually impossible. The role of bacteria in human biology was not understood. Antibiotic medications were not available. All these factors contributed to creating an entirely different age-distribution of illness and mortality than the one we are used to today. This in turn had significant implications for relations within families and attitudes about life, death and the hereafter.

Of course there were important changes in scientific knowledge during the early modern era. But most of these changes were in the areas of physics and astronomy, and their impact on everyday life was quite limited before the later eighteenth century. There were striking technological developments as well. The early modern era opened with the invention of gunpowder and printing: both changed the way in which cities interacted with the surrounding world and the way in which city-dwellers interacted with each other. But neither fundamentally altered the institutional structure or value system of European urban life. Only the massive scientific and technological transformations of the nineteenth century would change all that.

In short, this book will not attempt to fit the early modern city into some broader pattern of progress or modernization. Instead, it will approach urban society of early modern times on its own terms, showing how men and women in an environment of limited resources tried to shape and reshape the physical and institutional heritage of the European city to cope with the challenges of their day and meet their own needs and aspirations. Every attempt to understand human society, however, must take account of some basic analytical principles. It may be useful therefore to keep in mind two fundamental concepts which can contribute to the understanding of urban society. One is the concept of community. The other is the notion of power.

For some social historians, community is the more important of these concepts. Such historians look in past societies for evidence of shared goals, conflict resolution and social stability. For others, the key concept is power, as revealed by patterns of exploitation and domination. But in fact the questions these historians ask often overlap. How effectively did cities as a whole function in meeting the needs of their inhabitants? How did sub-communities or groups within each city do so? Did cities offer a satisfying life to most of their inhabitants, or only to a small minority who exploited all the rest? To what extent was the success of some individuals or groups dependent on the domination, repression or exclusion of others? Was urban society of the early modern era an arena of opportunity and participation, or an arena of conflict and domination?

The answers to all these questions are shaped above all by one simple fact: no human community is made up of equals. Inequality is the fundamental truth of the human condition. But every community includes numerous overlapping axes of inequality, for each individual belongs to a multiplicity of groups. Determining which of these groups is most significant for the lives of individuals is often the most challenging problem in any form of social analysis.

In trying to understand the social organization of the early modern city, modern sociologists and social historians have followed the lead of early modern city-dwellers themselves by putting the primary emphasis on groups identified by economic and political function. City-dwellers of the sixteenth and seventeenth centuries envisioned their communities as being made up of such groups as the rich and the poor, patricians and commons, merchants and craftsmen, citizens and outsiders – with most of these groups being subdivided into numerous smaller groups. Modern social historians, drawing on data and conceptual models unavailable to people in early modern times, have refined, elaborated and corrected the traditional models for understanding the social, economic and political hierarchies of cities in the early modern era. But they still emphasize social groupings that would have been comprehended by contemporaries.

There are of course many other groups to which people could belong which overlapped with these well-known socio-economic categories. People in the early modern city lived in distinct neighbourhoods, wards or parishes. In some cities the inhabitants were divided into religious or, more rarely, ethnic sub-groups. And of course everyone belonged to a family and network of kin.

But two other categories to which all humans belong also deserve emphasis because, unlike many other social groupings, they so often form the basis for the consistent, even universal domination of one group of people by another.

The first is age. In early modern society, as in our own, children were consistently dominated by adults. This domination could be harsh and brutal or it could be what we call paternalistic – though it is not without significance that the conventional term for nurturing domination is 'paternalism' rather than 'maternalism'. Either way, the domination of children by adults was total. But it was also temporary. About half of all children in the early modern city eventually survived into adulthood. As adults most of them, though not all, were released from subjection and many themselves eventually participated in the domination of the next generation of children.

The second category is, of course, gender. Unlike age, gender is permanent. In early modern cities, roles and distinctions based on gender were universal, as was the domination of females by males. This does not mean, of course, that all males exerted domination over all females. The male servant did not give orders to the female patrician – quite the contrary. But within any marriage, within any household, and more broadly within any single social group, adult males exerted unquestioned authority over females. This authority was not unlimited. Laws and social custom granted some powers and many protections to women. A few women even managed to stretch the bounds of social custom to exert more power than was usual for females of their social situation. At certain points in the life-cycle, notably widowhood, and within certain institutions, such as convents, women could exert powers that echoed and mimicked those of men. But even in those cases there were limits. And women were systematically excluded from certain aspects of urban life. Women participated, for example, in almost every sphere of economic activity – but they were rigorously excluded from participation in urban government and politics. In short, gender was a permanent distinction which cut through every other social or economic grouping in the early modern city.

Every individual human who lived in the early modern city belonged, then, to a multiplicity of social identities: age, gender, family, neighbourhood, occupation, civic status and religion. Some aspects of identity were immutable, some could be easily changed, some could be lost and some could be acquired. The city was in many ways an arena in which individuals attempted to shape their personal fates within often rigid constraints of custom, law and social expectation. The tensions between individual, group and communal needs and aspirations lay at the heart of all social interactions in the early modern city.

To understand the early modern city, however, we must begin by looking at its physical form, a form largely inherited from the middle ages though modified in some crucial respects during the sixteenth and seventeenth centuries. We must then look at the political, religious, economic and biological systems which shaped and bounded urban life in early modern Europe. These themes will occupy Part One of this book. Having thus established the basic parameters of urban life, in Part Two we will turn to the inhabitants of these cities, seeing them above all in terms of the multiplicity of social groups to which they belonged. Finally, in Part Three, we will see how cities functioned in times of tranquility and in times of stress, asking ourselves how the exercise of power and the pursuit of collective goals interacted in shaping the rhythms and eruptions of urban life.

This book is not about the 'way of life' in early modern cities. A way of life is something individuals or families self-consciously shape for themselves in response to some ideal of how they wish to live. Some people had the means to do so in the early modern city – but only very few. Most people could respond only to circumstances, making the best of limited opportunities. The history of urban society in the early modern era is the collective history of countless people who struggled to survive, to achieve some security in this life or confidence in the next, perhaps even to rise above their fellows or help their children to do so. They did all this within the limited confines of a world not yet affected by the dazzling technological transformations of the nineteenth and twentieth centuries. This book is about their way of making the most of early modern urban society. It is a book, then, not about their way of life, but about their way of living.

PART ONE

The City in Context

CHAPTER ONE

Boundaries and Buildings

For much of the seventeenth century, Paris was the largest city in Europe. Almost half a million people lived and worked in Paris, said their prayers in the city's churches and chapels, elbowed their way through its old crowded streets, or promenaded down its new esplanades. Some Parisians slept out of doors or died miserably in one of the city's great charity hospitals. Others spent their days in the salons of aristocratic *hôtels*, talking of the latest news from Fontainebleau or Versailles. Most Parisians lived and laboured in the high houses that lined the city's countless streets. All of them knew that they dwelt in one of the great urban centres of Europe.[1]

Zell am Harmersbach was also a city. Prettily situated on a stream in the German Black Forest, Zell never had more than a thousand inhabitants. The community was poorer in early modern times than some of the surrounding agricultural villages; prosperous peasants ignored with impunity their obligation to pay taxes which the city was supposed to collect. Yet there was no doubt of the community's urban credentials, for Zell enjoyed the confirmed and recognized status of a Free and Imperial City of the Holy Roman Empire.[2]

Zell was an extreme case, of course – but so was Paris. Few cities in early modern Europe were quite as small as the urban hamlet on the Harmersbach, and few were as large as Paris. These two cities, however, suggest the full range of sizes within which European cities fell.

1. The estimated population of Paris rose from 220,000 in 1600 to 430,000 in 1650 and 510,000 in 1700: De Vries, *European Urbanization*, 275. For descriptions of seventeenth-century Paris, see Bernard, *Emerging City*, and Ranum, *Paris*.
2. Kähni, 'Reichsstädte der Ortenau', 59.

Demographic information of the kind we take for granted today is not available for the early modern era; the first national censuses of the modern type were undertaken only after the late eighteenth century. Through the painstaking collation of local records, however, historians have been able to arrive at reliable estimates of population for many towns and cities. According to one recent estimate, in the year 1500 there were over 150 cities in western and central Europe with populations of 10,000 or more; by 1750 there were over 250 cities of that size.[3] But there were also thousands of smaller urban communities. It is always difficult to draw the exact dividing-line between cities and towns on the one hand and mere markets and villages on the other.[4] Certainly population was not the only factor. To many people in early modern Europe, what really distinguished a city or town from other communities was not its size or function but its possession of specific political and economic privileges. Cities as small as Zell were rare, but Europe was dotted with urban places of only 2,000 to 3,000 inhabitants which were still true cities, with political privileges and economic activities that clearly distinguished them from the neighbouring villages.

The populations of cities rarely remained constant. A few cities declined during the early modern period. The great Spanish city of Toledo, for example, dropped from about 50,000 in 1600 to less than half as much a hundred years later. But the general trend was strongly in the other direction, for taken as a whole the early modern era was an epoch of considerable urban growth.[5] A few cities of metropolitan rank emerged. The greatest city in Europe in 1500 was probably Naples, with a population of about 150,000. By the early seventeenth century Naples had been overtaken by Paris, but then Paris in turn was overtaken by London, whose population reached almost 700,000 in 1750.[6] The great metropolitan centres had a huge social and cultural impact on other communities. According to one famous estimate, one out of every six adults in seventeenth-century England lived in London at some point in his or her life.[7] Yet there were only a few cities of such magnitude. By one count in 1750 some

3. De Vries, *Urbanization*, 33. Higher estimates are provided by Bairoch *et al.*, *Population*, 270–1, but here as elsewhere I have followed de Vries's more conservative estimates.
4. cf. the discussion in Jones, *Towns and Cities*, 1–12, and Patten, *English Towns*, 21–8.
5. De Vries, *Urbanization*, passim; for Toledo, 278.
6. ibid., appendix 1.
7. Wrigley, 'A Simple Model', 49.

3 million people in western or central Europe lived in 16 cities with more than 80,000 inhabitants – but almost 6 million lived in 245 cities whose population fell between 10,000 and 80,000.[8] Millions more lived in thousands of smaller cities and towns. Even after three centuries of urban growth, cities of small to medium size still harboured the vast majority of European town-dwellers.

To be sure, the inhabitants of all cities still made up only a small portion – something like 15 per cent – of the total European population in early modern times. But the impact of cities was enormous. Tens of thousands of villagers migrated to cities every year; millions more had at least intermittent contact with urban life through markets, fairs and temporary employment. Few Europeans lived more than a day's walk from some city or other. Even those villagers – and they must have been few – who had never set foot in a city were affected by administrative and economic structures organized and controlled by people in the nearest urban centre. Cities were important to almost every European.

I

Most people, no matter where they live, know intuitively what a city is. Yet formally to define the term is notoriously difficult. Few theorists can claim to have improved on the observation made by Max Weber, awkward though it may sound in English: 'The many definitions of the city have only one element in common: namely that the city consists simply of a collection of one or more separate dwellings but is a relatively closed settlement'.[9] This, after all, is how people first experience the city: long before they become conscious of its distinct economic or administrative functions, they perceive the city as a physical place, an assembly of buildings and other structures which differ in character, in size, and above all in the density of their concentration from what would be found in smaller communities. So before we can explore how men and women actually lived in European cities of the early modern era, we must know something of the physical environment in which they lived out their lives.

The most distinctly urban feature of the early modern city was the outer wall. Even villages could have churches, marketplaces, public buildings and houses – but by and large only a city would have a wall. To be sure, not every city had a wall, and not every walled community was a city. But the correlation was remarkably high. It

8. The calculation is based, with some rounding-off, on the data in de Vries, *Urbanization*, 34.
9. Weber, *The City*, 65.

is hard for people today to capture any sense of the size and ubiquity of city walls in early modern Europe. Only a few European cities – mostly small ones – still have their walls intact. Far more often, just a few metres of the old wall still visible behind modern houses or a gate tower hindering the traffic on a busy street will receive the visitor's fleeting notice on his or her way to the cathedral or museum. Yet in early modern times, the wall was almost a city's dominant architectonic feature.

Indeed, the term 'wall' is hardly sufficient to suggest the size and solidity of urban fortifications. The basic wall system for almost any city was a product of the middle ages, but throughout the early modern era urban fortifications were lavishly expanded and strengthened. Many cities, already girdled by one massive wall, received an additional perimeter of bastions linked by new walls in the sixteenth or seventeenth century.[10] Access to the city was possible only through perpetually guarded gates, many of which were surmounted by high towers from which watchmen could survey the flow of traffic for miles in any direction.

City walls obviously had a military function. A walled city was almost impossible to take by storm; an enemy army would normally have to negotiate its way into the city or initiate a siege, hoping to starve the inhabitants into submission. But the wall had other functions as well, for the system of fortifications had come into being largely to give city officials some control over the flow of goods and people in and out of their community. Access to the city was deliberately made difficult. Consider, for example, how travellers had to enter Frankfurt am Main in the seventeenth century. Arriving, say, from the southwest, they would first enter a fenced enclosure. Passing the pikeman posted there, they then took a wooden bridge across the city's outer moat and went through a stone gate into the bastion ring. Turning sharply left, the travellers continued along the bastion wall, past numerous soldiers, till they reached the next wooden bridge. After crossing the second moat, they went through yet another small stone gateway. Now at last they stood before one of the actual gate towers of Frankfurt, where of course a watchman stood to ask questions or check papers. Permitted to pass through the great arched entry of the gate tower, the travellers were finally inside the city itself and free to go about their business.[11]

10. Stoob, 'Stadtbefestigung'.
11. This is based on the highly detailed plan of Frankfurt by Matthäus Merian, as revised *c.* 1682; the plan is reproduced in Bothe, *Geschichte der Stadt Frankfurt*, 446.

Of course the system of control was far from flawless. On busy days the throng of people, animals and vehicles coursing through the gates might be difficult to regulate, and many an unwelcome visitor was able to slip through. Schemes to control the traffic more tightly were liable to backfire. When an outbreak of bubonic plague was reported in the environs of Barcelona in 1650, the authorities' usual concerns about unwanted beggars and untaxed goods were compounded by their added fear of infected travellers. To maintain a closer watch on arrivals, the officials closed all but two of the city gates – but, as a contemporary diarist reported, 'as the Angel Gate is so narrow and so many carts and mules and people had to enter, there was little room for the guards, and it became so crowded that it was easier to break the rules'. Within a few days, the other gates were reopened.[12]

In actual fact, walls offered little protection from the seemingly endless stream of unwelcome vagrants who drifted from the countryside into the cities. But the importance of the walls was as much psychological as practical. In 1634 the magistrates of Nîmes in southern France became alarmed when it appeared that some small walls around the city might be torn down to provide building materials for an aqueduct. Painting a grim falling-dominoes scenario, the magistrates warned that this small act of plunder would lead, step by step, to the depopulation of the whole city,

> inasmuch as the little walls serve as a reinforcement for the big walls, so that once they have been torn down indubitably the big walls will collapse and by those means the city . . . will be exposed to entry by every sort of person and the clergy, magistrates, merchants and other inhabitants will be unable to stay.[13]

Not every city had a wall, nor did every city that had one maintain it carefully. In England, which had not experienced a foreign invasion for centuries, city walls were often neglected – though their importance was quickly rediscovered during the civil wars of the mid-seventeenth century. A few cities, of course, had no need of walls at all. The most spectacular case of an unwalled city was Venice, which lay on a group of islands far out in the Venetian lagoon, defended from all attacks by one of the greatest navies in Europe. Other cities might have benefited from fortifications but had never been granted permission to construct any. Debrecen, whose population of about

12. Amelang, *Journal of the Plague Year*, 34.
13. Teisseyre-Sallmann, 'Urbanisme et société', 979.

10,000 made it the largest urban centre in early modern Hungary, was technically only a market rather than a city until 1693 – and it was surrounded by a fence, not a proper wall. The merchants of Debrecen were the richest town-dwellers in Hungary, but their unprotected community, located in a perpetually tense border region, was vulnerable to ceaseless financial demands from regional princes and marauding soldiers.[14]

Some cities lost their walls for political reasons. The English town of Gloucester, for example, was forced to tear down its wall in the 1660s as a result of having supported the wrong side in the recent civil war.[15] Similarly, when Louis XIV seized control of the Alsatian town of Colmar in 1673, he ordered that the city's fortifications be destroyed. Bitter citizens complained that the city was now 'open to all to come and go, like a village', or had become nothing more than an 'urban village' itself. But the king's purpose was to assert the power of his regime, not to undermine the routine control of goods and travellers; within a few years a new, smaller wall was erected.[16] Indeed, throughout the seventeenth century the conquest of a city was as likely to lead to a strengthening of its fortifications as it was to lead to the opposite. After conquering the Flemish town of Lille in 1667, for example, Louis XIV immediately ordered the construction of a massive citadel connected to the city's bastion ring – partly to protect the city from reconquest and partly, it seems, to intimidate the inhabitants themselves.[17]

The city wall normally enclosed the built-up areas of the community. But the city's legal boundary customarily extended for some distance beyond the actual walls. A few buildings – mills, chapels, convents, hospices – could always be found outside the walls. Some cities also had built-up suburbs or *faubourgs* outside the walls. In the middle ages it had been customary from time to time to build new walls to accommodate urban growth, and in many cities this continued to be done in the early modern era. In cities which experienced rapid urbanization, however, this was not possible. London, which underwent the most spectacular growth of any major city in early modern Europe, is the paradigmatic case. In 1500 London was still contained within its medieval walls; the administrative centre at Westminster a few miles upriver was a

14. Zimányi, 'Entwicklung der Städte Ungarns', 138.
15. Clark, 'Civic Leaders of Gloucester', 322.
16. Rathgeber, *Colmar und Ludwig XIV*, 38, 66, 69, 110.
17. Lottin, *Chavatte*, 167.

completely separate community. By the end of the sixteenth century, however, there were extensive settlements beyond the walls of London. Growth continued in all directions, and by 1750 London had become a vast urban agglomeration. The City of London was still a compact, clearly defined area at the centre of the metropolis, but the outer districts formed a dizzying tapestry of archaic boundaries and overlapping jurisdictions. It was centuries since anyone had worried about enclosing all of London within a single wall.

But London and the other great metropolitan centres were exceptions. Most cities retained their walls and gates until the end of the eighteenth century. In many places, however, there was increasing negligence in maintaining the fortifications. The outer ring of bastion walls built in the seventeenth century proved of little tactical value and their upkeep was often slipshod. Then even the integrity of the basic city walls began to be threatened. Little openings and doorways appeared in the walls and were quietly tolerated by the authorities. In the late eighteenth century, city walls suddenly came to be seen as impediments to urban growth, aesthetic form and the flow of traffic. Within two generations in city after city the walls were razed and parks and promenades were laid out in their place. But the idea that traffic should move in and out of a city without any impediment was still too much for the average European to swallow. Frankfurt am Main well illustrates the point. In 1804 the demolitions began and within a matter of years the once mighty walls of Frankfurt were totally gone. But on the major roads, where imposing city gateways had once served to channel movement in and out of the city, there now stood little guardhouses and metal gates. Not until 1846 did these last faint echoes of the walled city of Frankfurt finally disappear.[18]

II

Everyone has some mental image of the topography of the medieval or early modern city: a densely congested network of narrow, winding streets lined with high house fronts, a pattern relieved only occasionally by open squares and marketplaces. The image is not inaccurate, but it can be misleading. Most cities had considerable amounts of green space, even within the walls: there was no shortage of pleasure gardens, market gardens and orchards, not to mention other open areas like cemeteries and workyards. But the gardens were private spaces, behind houses or enclosed by walls, generally

18. Pehl. *Als die Frankfurter*, 77–91.

inaccessible to anyone but their owners or those who worked there. Public activity took place in the streets and marketplaces, or outside the city gates. The open spaces just beyond the walls were often available for recreational activity – but they, too, could be threatened by urban growth as fields and meadows were converted into sites of intense cultivation, organized leisure, or additional housing. John Stow, the topographer of late sixteenth-century London, complained bitterly about what had happened in his own lifetime to the district beyond London's northern wall, where the 'pleasant fields, very commodious for citizens therein to walk, shoot, and otherwise to recreate and refresh their dulled spirits in the sweet and wholesome air' had recently turned into 'a continual building throughout, of garden-houses and small cottages; and the fields on either side be turned into garden-plots, tenter yards, bowling alleys, and such like'.[19]

The basic street plan of almost every European city was a product of the middle ages, and once it was laid down the plan normally proved remarkably resistant to change. Only entirely new cities could ignore the constraints imposed by past construction. Early modern Europeans were quite alert to the potential attractiveness of straight streets and broad vistas: the 'ideal cities' of Renaissance theorists like Antonio Filarete or Francesco di Giorgio Martini almost always involved a rectangular grid or a pattern of identical straight avenues radiating from a central square.[20] A few cities were even constructed along such lines. The most flawlessly realized ideal city was probably the Venetian military outpost of Palma Nuova, which was founded in 1593 and still looks from above like a page torn from Filarete's textbook. The town of Freudenstadt, established by the duke of Württemberg in 1599, had rows of houses aligned evenly around the central market in a series of ever larger perfect squares.[21] When a Polish magnate founded Zamość in the late sixteenth century he commissioned an Italian architect to design the entire city; the result, predictably enough, was an almost flawless grid with impressive sightlines.[22] Similar concepts formed the basis for a handful of other cities as well.

Such designs, however, could hardly ever be imposed on existing built-up cities. Property owners, ranging from richly endowed

19. Stow, *Survey of London*, 116; this passage is discussed in Rappaport, *Worlds within Worlds*, 65.
20. For some examples, see Burke, *Towns in the Making*, 72–8.
21. Deiseroth, 'Fürstliche Stadtgründungen', 46; see also plates 6 and 25.
22. Kalinowski, *City Development*, 37–8.

institutions down to modest householders, were likely to resist any proposal to realign streets if it meant impinging on their land. Even the popes of the sixteenth century were thwarted in their attempts to run a system of straight avenues through the densely inhabited heart of Rome; great axial boulevards could be built only on the outskirts.[23] Nor did the sudden destruction of a city centre by fire routinely clear the way to significant changes in urban topography. It could happen, of course: when much of Stockholm burned down in 1625, the Swedish king insisted on redesigning the inner city to eliminate a cluster of small dark alleys and provide for a major new thoroughfare.[24] But this was hardly the norm. When the heart of London was destroyed by fire in 1666, numerous proposals were offered to reconstruct the city on elegant new lines. But any such plans would have required massive schemes for compensating landlords or redistributing property. In the end some realignments were made, a few streets were widened, and less flammable building materials were mandated – but major changes in the layout of the city proved impossible to realize.[25] When, to take another example, two-thirds of the German town of Schwäbisch Hall went up in flames in 1728, the authorities did succeed in straightening out one main street which ran from the market square down to the river – but everything else stayed the same.[26]

None of this means, of course, that city centres remained completely unaltered. Property was constantly changing hands in early modern cities, and every now and then a new owner would tear down an existing dwelling to put a newer, more ostentatious building in its place. New public buildings were constructed and old ones were extended. Occasionally a whole group of dwellings would be razed and new structures erected. Or a vacant area within the city might be developed. In 1605, for example, King Henri IV of France decreed that a neglected royal tournament-ground in northeastern Paris – an area which was being used as a horse-market – should be transformed into an architecturally integrated residential square. Lots were granted to royal officeholders or other wealthy Parisians who promised to build elegant matching townhouses linked by a continuous arcade in conformity with a predetermined plan. One

23. Girouard, *Cities and People*, 121–3.
24. Roberts, *Gustavus Adolphus*, 1: 487–8; Råberg, 'Development of Stockholm', 14.
25. Rasmussen, *London*, 99–122; Reddaway, *Rebuilding of London*, 31–199 passim.
26. Krüger, *Schwäbisch Hall*, 79–80.

side of the square was initially used for silk-workshops, but these were soon relocated elsewhere so that all four sides could present a pleasingly coordinated appearance.[27] The resulting Place Royale, which was completed by 1612 and soon became a highly fashionable address, has long been praised by historians as a masterpiece of urban planning – and rightly so. But it came into being only because the ground concerned was a vacant tract held by a single owner, in this case the crown. Without this advantage, even the most energetic king would have had trouble putting such plans in place. For by and large, in Paris as elsewhere, once the city core was built up it became highly resistant to topographical change.

It was in the undeveloped districts outside the city wall that more dramatic changes could take place. Fields and gardens outside the walls were occasionally transformed into formal parks and promenades where well-dressed members of the public were permitted to stroll. Entire new neighbourhoods were established as well. Where no previous pattern of houses existed, it was easier to lay out a rectangular grid of wide streets which approximated the Renaissance ideals of city planning. Many a European city thus acquired elegant new districts adjacent to the old crowded centre. Up to the mid-seventeenth century, for example, Aix-en-Provence retained its conventional medieval appearance. But in 1646 the archbishop of Aix – whose brother, conveniently, was the chief minister of France – obtained the king's permission to create an entirely new district to the south of the old city. A major stretch of wall was razed and new walls were constructed further south to enclose a neighbourhood of wide, straight streets which soon came to be lined with spacious homes. Where the old southern wall of Aix had run, between the old city and the new neighbourhood, there was now a broad tree-lined avenue – the grandest public space in Aix.[28]

What happened once in Aix-en-Provence happened over and over in a metropolis like London. Throughout the seventeenth and eighteenth centuries, tracts of land outside the City – typically former monastery lands which had been acquired by secular owners – were developed into tracts or squares with elegant homes suitable for rental by prosperous tenants.[29] As in Aix, such developments normally required royal permission; traditionally the conversion of open land to housing had been discouraged in London – but in fact permission was rarely

27. Ballon, *Paris of Henry IV*, 57–113.
28. Kettering, *Judicial Politics*, 24–6.
29. Stone, 'Residential Development'.

denied. And once an elegant quarter like Covent Garden or what became Bloomsbury Square went up, it was soon surrounded by less carefully planned infill settlements.

Many new districts, in fact, developed in a much more haphazard way. In certain parts of London, for example, growth was almost completely uncontrolled – especially in areas east of the city and south of the Thames where the old ribbon development along major roads and down the riverfront increasingly gave way to a vast agglomeration of suburban tenements. Ramshackle dwellings were often thrown up by squatters who tried to avoid paying any rent to the landholders. But increasingly in the seventeenth century, landlords would forestall such intrusions by building orderly rows of houses to be rented out.[30]

Some cities experienced no physical expansion at all. In many cases, the area enclosed by the city walls proved ample for a stable or even declining population. In other cases, the population grew but there was nobody with sufficient interest, incentive or influence to orchestrate the systematic development of a new district. In such places the density of population within the walls would steadily increase as existing dwellings were subdivided or new buildings were squeezed into alleys and courtyards. Suburban growth, if it occurred at all, was spotty and uncontrolled.

Walls and streets were the two main elements of urban topography imposed by human design on the physical environment. But a third element was provided by waterways and canals. Almost every city, of course, had grown up either alongside a river or near a body of water. Often river water had been diverted to supply a network of waterways around and through the city. Where the terrain permitted, a moat might encircle the walls to improve the city's defensive posture. And often marshy areas had been drained and streams regulated so as to form a series of canals. These waterways served a variety of purposes. Many urban industries, such as the manufacture of textiles, leather or paper, required ready access to water for their technical processes.[31] And a canal often served as a source of drinking water or a convenient place to flush away wastes. In some cities – as in parts of the Netherlands, where settlements had emerged behind massive dikes on marshy land below sea level – there might be a vast and intricate network of canals, traversed in turn by bridges which linked an equally complex system of streets and roads.

30. Power, 'East London Housing', 238–42.
31. Guillerme, *Age of Water*, 95–8, 149–62.

Only in Venice, however, did the system of canals completely dominate the city's topography, reducing the streets to little more than pedestrian pavements. There was a reason for this, of course. Venice was the only major city in Europe which could be reached from the surrounding country exclusively by water. There was little point in ferrying horses and wheeled vehicles across the lagoon to Venice when goods and people could be moved around the city just as efficiently by boat. The priority given to canal traffic was signalled by the construction of increasingly high arched bridges with steps, easy for boats to pass under but impossible for anything but two-legged pedestrians to pass over. By the early modern period, as a result, horses and wheeled vehicles had virtually disappeared from Venice.[32] In terms of topography, Venice was thus unique. Yet in many ways it was regarded by educated Europeans as the ultimate embodiment of what a city could or should be. Its constitution, its economic system, its cultural activity were all richly admired – and so was its capacity, throughout the early modern period, to defend itself from attack. For Europeans always respected a city with strong and successful defensive walls, even if the walls were made of water.

III

The modern urban geographer is apt to look at the spatial organization of cities in terms of functional zones, to determine where commercial, industrial, residential, recreational and other activities are primarily situated. The functional differentiation of modern urban space is powerfully reinforced by the zoning practices of most cities in the western world, under which certain activities are specifically restricted to particular districts or neighbourhoods.

The functional differentiation of urban space was by no means unknown to the early modern city. Some patterns evolved informally; others were specifically enforced. In many cities, for example, there were particular districts in which the wealthiest and most influential inhabitants preferred to live. Traditionally the favoured district had always been right in the centre of town, near the major marketplaces, though beginning in the seventeenth century the development of elegant new residential tracts occasionally modified this pattern. In many cities, certain productive activities were confined to specific neighbourhoods. Sometimes there were practical reasons for this related to the nature of the productive process itself: tanning, for example, required running water, so tanners were almost always

32. Morris, *Venice*, 68–9.

consigned to some neighbourhood near a river or stream. Some other activities might be restricted to specific districts or even removed to areas outside the city walls because of offensive odours or the danger of fire.

Generally, however, trades were dispersed throughout the entire city.[33] The functional differentiation of urban space was limited by the fact that residential, commercial and productive activities normally took place in very close proximity. Household production accounted for a vast amount of the economic activity in every European city. It would be misleading to think that all work was done in people's homes; in fact, one of the important insights of recent research in urban social history is the extent to which people in early modern cities, even married men and women, had to seek employment or income outside their own households. Yet the domestic workshop did remain, throughout the early modern period, the most important locus of productive activity. This meant that the spatial differentiation into residential and productive zones which generally characterizes modern cities would have been pointless in the early modern town.

In any case, for many inhabitants of an early modern city, the most important form of spatial differentiation was not functional but was instead jurisdictional. Even within the walls, many cities had specific zones which did not fall under the control of the city government. Many of these enclaves' 'liberties' and 'immunities' belonged to a monastery, convent, hospital, cathedral or other ecclesiastical institution. Some, especially in Protestant cities after the Reformation, no longer belonged to the church, but the special privileges which had been granted centuries before continued to apply. Other enclaves were purely secular: many cities, for example, had a castle precinct which stood under the direct control of the ruler or some regional lord. Some of these special zones were clearly demarcated by walls and gates; others were easily accessible to all. But no matter how they had come into being and how they were distinguished from the rest of the city, these privileged areas were a constant irritant to municipal authorities, whose ability to control economic activity or even to enforce criminal laws in the enclaves was strictly limited.

The northern English city of York well illustrates the variety of such enclaves which could coexist in one relatively small community. There were two secular liberties in York. The castle and its grounds were controlled by the high sheriff of the county of York. There was also a small building in the middle of town called Davy Hall.

33. Cramer, 'Gewerbegasse'.

Formerly a jail for poachers in a nearby forest, by the sixteenth century this building had come to be owned by a wealthy family which permitted certain poor shoemakers, who were forbidden to work in York itself, to practise their trade under its roof. There were also numerous liberties of ecclesiastical origin: some were eliminated in the 1530s, during the Reformation, and two – a hospital and an abbey – were taken over by officials of the crown. But the most important enclave continued to be run by officials of the church until the nineteenth century. This was the cathedral close, where the dean and canons of York Minster ran their own judicial system and permitted craftsmen to operate in defiance of city rules. Just how far beyond the immediate cathedral precincts the liberty extended, however, was a sore point over which the dean and the city authorities continued to squabble for centuries.[34]

Great cities like Paris and London had dozens of 'sanctuaries' and liberties of this general sort.[35] And similar enclaves could be found in cities of almost every size in many parts of Europe. City officials and guild masters were constantly struggling against these special districts, trying to draw the enclaves under a more unified control. But many of the enclaves succeeded in retaining their special privileges throughout the early modern era. Though only some of these districts were physically demarcated, everyone was aware of their exact location. It was convenient to know which yard you should enter or which street you should cross if you wanted to avoid arrest by the city beadle or planned to sell your wares in defiance of the guild. For the invisible lines that crisscrossed many an early modern town divided the community into zones that were, at times, very functional indeed.

IV

Nature provided the setting: some cities were situated on flat terrain, some developed on sloping ground above a river or shore, a few nestled beneath an imposing hill topped by a fortress. Walls, streets and canals were the key elements of the city's infrastructure. But above all, a city was a collection of buildings, public and private. To understand something of the way in which early modern town-dwellers used and reshaped their physical surroundings, we must first know something about the urban building stock at the end of the

34. Palliser, *Tudor York*, 88–90.
35. Bernard, *Emerging City*, 127–9; Archer, *Pursuit of Stability*, 234–5; Pearl, *London and the Outbreak*, 23–31.

middle ages.[36] Then we can see to what extent and in what ways things changed in the early modern era.

Among public buildings the most prominent ones were generally ecclesiastical in nature. With only rare exceptions, churches were the largest buildings in any city at the beginning of the early modern era. Their spires and steeples dominated the skyline. If the city was the seat of a bishop – and there were about 500 bishops in early modern Europe – the most important church in town would be a cathedral. But a church did not have to be a cathedral to dominate the cityscape. Most urban churches were parish churches, serving the religious needs of a particular neighbourhood. Some parishes were large – a few, in fact, encompassed whole cities – but most covered only a small part of the city. Yet the size of a parish church had little to do with the size of the parish itself. Part of the very purpose of a church, after all, was to inspire a sense of awe in worshippers and visitors, and this was done, wherever possible, by the effective use of high interior spaces.

Churches were not the only ecclesiastical buildings in the city. At the beginning of the early modern period, almost every European city was also dotted with building complexes occupied by members of religious orders. The vows taken by monks and nuns generally involved some degree of seclusion from the surrounding world, so the interior of a monastery or convent would remain forbidden to the inquisitive outsider. But most such institutions also operated a church which was open to all – indeed, some monastic churches served as the standard place of worship for inhabitants of the neighbourhood or members of some craft or trade. Religious inspiration or obligation had led to the construction of numerous other buildings as well, from small chapels to hospices and hostels.

Of course there was no shortage of major secular buildings as well. Some cities had a castle which had once been or continued to be the seat of some prince or ruler. Some castles, as in Nuremberg or Salzburg, were dramatically located on a high slope or hill overlooking the community; others, as in London or Ghent, were situated along a river or canal at the city's edge. Only cities of great strategic or administrative importance were likely to have castles. But every city by the end of the middle ages had a number of public buildings specifically designed to meet the political and economic needs of the city-dwellers themselves.

36. For a useful typology of medieval urban buildings, see Meckseper, *Kleine Kunstgeschichte*, 89–246.

The largest of these were often devoted to the administration of city government. These included such grandiose establishments as the doge's palace in Venice, the Palazzo Vecchio in Florence, or the great town halls of Brussels and Bruges with their soaring belfries. But many other cities had more modest town halls at the end of the fifteenth century. The town hall could in fact be overshadowed by other municipal buildings. The regulation of commerce had emerged in the middle ages as one of the chief functions of urban government, and this was reflected in the construction of huge facilities for the sale, transfer, inspection or storage of commercial goods. The massive cloth hall of Breslau, where dry goods, leatherware and other items were exchanged, was vastly bigger than the adjacent town hall. Sometimes one building combined commercial and administrative functions. In the great town hall of Torun in Poland, the ground floor housed the cloth hall and other commercial facilities while the next storey held the council chamber and civic offices.[37] Some English town halls were built on pillars, so that magistrates could meet on the first floor while market activities took place in the covered space below.[38]

Another critical obligation of urban governments – the guarantee of a sufficient supply of food for the population – was manifested by the existence of municipal mills in most cities and granaries in many. And there were quasi-public buildings as well, reflecting the importance of the associational life that had emerged in all medieval cities by the end of the middle ages: these included the meeting-halls of individual guilds and, especially in Germany, dance halls and drinking clubs for members of the social elite.

All these public or semi-public buildings were of immense importance to the life of a pre-modern city. Many of them have survived to the modern day and many others, destroyed by neglect or war, have been painstakingly reconstructed. The modern tourist, guidebook in hand, will rightfully savour them all, from the three-starred cathedral or town hall down to the one-starred mill or chapel. But Weber was right when he reduced his preliminary definition of the city to little more than a 'collection of dwellings'. For the great majority of buildings in a late medieval city were in fact not public buildings at all, but houses.

As in any modern city, houses varied tremendously in size and durability, reflecting the relative wealth of their original builders or

37. ibid., 174–7; Gruber, *Gestalt der deutschen Stadt*, 104–7.
38. Tittler, *Architecture and Power*, 25–33.

subsequent owners. Some urban domiciles went beyond mere houses: nobles who lived in the city or merchants who aspired to noble status might well occupy miniature urban palaces. But such buildings were rare. Most of the housing stock of an urban community consisted of a continuum of dwellings, all built in accordance with local conventions but vastly different in size. One must not assume that any one house was always occupied by a single household or family. Subdivision and multiple occupancy were common.

House design varied across Europe. Local custom powerfully influenced the appearance and layout of buildings. A few characteristics, however, were common to houses in most of Europe. Houses were generally built in rows, with little or no space between them and fronting directly on to the street. Houses were hardly ever more than four or five storeys high, but differences in width and depth were common. Large houses might have an interior courtyard or a yard or garden to the rear. The ground floor would most likely include a workshop and probably a kitchen. The higher floors would have rooms in which families lived and slept. Cellars and attics were used for storage or for accommodating servants or tenants. Glass windows were still a luxury; wooden shutters were the norm.

This, then, was the basic repertory of urban building forms inherited from the middle ages. Of course the building process is always dynamic, and throughout the early modern era new buildings went up and old ones were extended, remodelled or converted to new purposes. New architectural forms and, to a lesser extent, new methods of construction were developed. More and more major buildings were designed in accordance with foreign architectural styles: Italian models were increasingly copied north of the Alps. Some building complexes, such as shipyards, grew larger than they had ever been in medieval times. Significant innovations emerged in military architecture, as bastions and citadels came to ring the periphery of some major cities. Yet the basic categories of urban building types remained relatively constant during the early modern era. The traditionalism of economic and administrative systems and the absence of sweeping technological change diminished the likelihood of fundamental innovations within the cities. In fact it was not until the nineteenth century that radically new types of urban structures – factories, railways, department stores and the like – were introduced in European cities on a massive scale.

The stock of ecclesiastical structures in the European city certainly did undergo some important changes during the early modern era. The basic parish system remained in force all over Europe, but in cities where the Protestant Reformation was adopted during the sixteenth century monasteries and convents were suddenly closed down. Their inhabitants were usually thrust back into the mainstream of secular life, and the buildings were quickly put to other uses. In countries that remained Catholic, however, monasteries and convents flourished. Indeed, they became ever more prominent parts of the urban landscape as new religious orders were founded and new houses and churches were erected to serve their purposes.

In Protestant and Catholic countries alike, the construction or, more often, reconstruction of church buildings continued throughout the early modern period. Two of Europe's most important churches were rebuilt in a grandiose new form: the papal basilica of St Peter's in Rome and, following the fire of 1666, St Paul's cathedral in London. All over Europe new churches were founded and old ones embellished. But even so, the pace of ecclesiastical construction fell behind medieval precedents. Especially in high-growth cities like London or Paris, the construction of new churches never kept up with the rate of expansion; new districts invariably had fewer churches per capita than the old city centres.[39] Sometimes ecclesiastical construction came to a dead stop. Work on the great cathedral of Cologne was suspended in the sixteenth century, leaving the central nave unbuilt and a huge crane perched atop an unfinished steeple. For over 300 years the crane remained in place, becoming a virtual symbol of the city itself, until construction of the cathedral was resumed and completed in the nineteenth century.

There was more innovation in secular construction. The greatest urban secular buildings of the middle ages had been the castles that served as centres of royal or princely power. But the traditional urban castle, a defensible fortress which could also serve as a judicial and administrative centre, was increasingly irrelevant to the new concept of protecting the entire city with an outer ring of bastions. A few castles, like the Tower of London, retained their defensive integrity. Many others were permitted to decay or lose their military significance. Some, like the Louvre in Paris, were converted into palaces.

The urban palace was, in fact, far more characteristic of the early modern era. Like the erstwhile castles, true palaces were found chiefly in those cities which had a resident ruler or prince. Many palaces grew ever larger during the early modern era, usually in a series of uncoordinated accretions as successive rulers would add a wing

39. Kaplow, *Names of Kings*, 122; Rudé, *Hanoverian London*, 101–4.

here or a section there. Awkwardly crammed between city walls on one side and built-up areas on the other, the urban palace was often more impressive in its parts than as a whole. In the seventeenth and eighteenth centuries, princes increasingly despaired of turning their urban palaces into the grandiose and unified buildings of which they and their advisors dreamed – so it became ever more common for rulers to command the construction of new, architecturally integral palaces in parklands far beyond the urban core.

In any case, only a handful of European cities ever had a princely palace in their midst or on their outskirts. The extension of old city halls or construction of elaborate new ones represented a much more common theme of European urban history throughout the early modern era.[40] Sometimes the old mixed-use halls of medieval times were replicated in a modern architectural guise: in Dublin, for example, the new baroque 'Thorsel' of the 1670s had an open arcade below and a courtroom, the municipal offices and premises for the merchants' guild and the royal exchange above.[41] In some cities, the construction of a grand town hall assumed an importance for civic self-representation which echoed the effort and energy traditionally devoted to the erection of churches. In the mid-seventeenth century, for example, the city of Amsterdam constructed a new town hall so grandiose that it serves today as a royal palace. Pious members of the civic elite, who were hostile to the construction of so lavish a secular building, insisted that a neighbouring church which was then being rebuilt should at least be given a spire which would be higher than the city hall's cupola. But the spire was never completed and the city hall totally dominated Amsterdam's main square.[42]

Some new types of public and quasi-public buildings emerged. Evolving economic practices occasionally required new facilities. Great halls for the storage or exchange of goods remained important, but new buildings were needed for the systematic transfer of more abstract instruments of wealth. This accounts for the erection of such buildings as the Royal Exchange in London in the late sixteenth century or the Bourse of Amsterdam in the early seventeenth. New patterns of leisure also had an impact. Commercial theatres emerged.

40. For important German examples, see Hitchcock, *German Renaissance Architecture*, 62–4, 120–1, 182–98, 293–300, 321–6; for the full extent of town hall construction in early modern England, see Tittler, *Architecture and Power*, 160–8, and Borsay, *Urban Renaissance*, 325–8.
41. Craig, *Dublin*, 47–8.
42. Schama, *Embarrassment of Riches*, 116–19; see also Fremantle, *Baroque Town Hall*.

So did coffee houses. Changing forms of interaction among members of the social elite required new structures, such as the 'assembly rooms' which became popular in early eighteenth-century England.[43] Other new buildings reflected an expansion in the responsibilities of municipal governments. In the middle ages, most schools, almshouses and hospitals were run by members of the clergy in buildings operated by the church. During the early modern period, secular governments became increasingly involved in the administration of such institutions, and this often led to the construction of new municipal schools, hospitals, orphanages and workhouses.

There is little doubt that public buildings, broadly defined, increased in number during the early modern era. A study of twelve towns in northern England shows that the average number of public buildings per town rose from four in 1600 to over seven in 1700 and twenty in 1800.[44] This pattern may have been replicated in many other communities. Yet even so, in every city, private houses continued to be the dominant building form. Of course the distinction between public and domestic structures was not an absolute one. A transitional form was provided by inns, taverns and alehouses – 'public houses' in terms of function and accessibility, but private in that they were normally inhabited by families that owned or managed them. Inns were normally larger than ordinary dwellings. But they were never as big as the grandest private homes in major cities. As in medieval times, throughout the early modern era those who could afford it – or were able to convince builders and creditors that they could afford it – constructed lavish palatial homes. Forms and styles changed, as the heavy stonework of late fifteenth-century *hôtels* and *palazzi* gave way to the ornamented masonry of neoclassical or baroque façades. But the function of these domestic palaces – to awe and impress – remained little changed.

The same continuity of function applied all the more to the conventional houses which lined street after street in every European town. The basic purposes and spatial organization of urban housing underwent no dramatic transformation in the early modern period, as long as the domestic workshop remained the basis of most urban production. But the housing stock of early modern cities was constantly undergoing a process of change. Not only were new houses built, but also existing ones were remodelled or extended: an upper floor might be added, an annexe installed, rooms divided or

43. Borsay, *Urban Renaissance*, 150–62.
44. ibid., 104, citing an unpublished thesis by K. Grady.

combined. The stately street façade of many an urban house often gave no hint of the jumbled warren of extensions, passageways, courtyards and sheds that lay to the rear. Even the formal residential squares that became increasingly popular from the seventeenth century onward imposed far more uniformity on the front of the houses than on the interior and the gardens that lay behind.[45]

There was certainly a steady increment of amenities. Occasionally an upgrading of building materials or techniques would be mandated, typically after a fire. In addition, certain luxuries became increasingly commonplace. In early sixteenth-century York, for example, glass windows were still regarded as movable furnishings which could be transferred from one house to another by gift or sale. Eventually, however, houseowners insisted that panes of glass be installed as permanent fixtures.[46] Many houses were remodelled or refurbished to reflect changes in taste or convenience. But much urban housing remained spartan, dense and crowded.

Much is known about the physical layout of houses in early modern Europe. Countless early modern houses survived to the late nineteenth or early twentieth century, when scholars began to take an interest in the history of domestic architecture and made careful records and photographs. A few such houses are even extant today, though recapturing how they looked in early modern times is a matter more of urban archaeology than mere photography. Some house-plans have survived from early modern times; by the seventeenth century architects began to issue books of stock plans, and occasionally architectural sketches and drawings were made in connection with property inventories or building permits.[47] Yet none of this evidence tells us much about the actual use of domestic space. Except for the workshop and, usually, the kitchen, the disposition of rooms was not functionally rigid. The critical distinction, at least in northern countries, was between those rooms which had a hearth or stove and those that did not. In German houses one always distinguished between a heated *Stube* and an unheated *Kammer*; the warmer room would be used for as many activities as possible. Sleeping-space was rarely segregated. Beds could be found in almost any room of the house, including, at times, the workshop.[48]

45. cf. Ballon, *Paris of Henry IV*, 103–10, 150–7, and figs 171–4.
46. Palliser, *Tudor York*, 35–6.
47. Ranum, *Paris*, 102–4; Brown, 'Continuity and Change'; Kastner, 'Bürgerliches Wohnen', 206–31.
48. Brown, 'Continuity and Change', 578–80.

Above all, one must never assume that a single house was occupied by a single household. Records from Innsbruck in 1603 show that, on average, every household had about four inhabitants but every house had about twelve – so an average house could have contained three households.[49] In early seventeenth-century Augsburg, 70 per cent of all families listed in the tax records lived in houses which contained four or more households.[50] Some houses were actually constructed as tenements, with multiple occupancy in mind. But more often, the use of domestic space simply underwent a constant process of reallocation as the house itself was remodelled or the families who occupied it changed in size or wealth. In many towns, even modest craftsmen owned their own houses – though the house could be encumbered with debts and some parts might have to be sublet to others. But much urban property was owned by landlords or by institutions and the rental of homes, even by the well-to-do, was entirely customary.

V

Although as a rule we know little about the overall use of space in early modern houses, occasionally it is possible for historians to reconstruct in remarkable detail the exact contents of each room in a particular household at a specific moment in time. This is due chiefly to the survival of a particular kind of source: an inventory of all the goods present in a person's house at the time of his or her marriage or death. Local practices varied; only some communities required inventories, and sometimes they were quite perfunctory. But from time to time one comes across inventories so detailed that they tell us more about the contents of a particular dwelling than we may know about our own homes.

Let us see, then, what one historian found when he used such an inventory to explore the home of Euphrosina Burkhart in the German town of Augsburg in the summer of the year 1600.[51] Euphrosina's husband Matthes, a butcher, had just died, leaving behind substantial debts – which may be one reason why the city officials conducted such a very thorough listing of the household's goods.

The dwelling occupied by the Burkharts consisted of four distinct spaces: a room with a hearth which served as the kitchen and main living area, an unheated room, an attic and a shed. There was no shop, since Matthes did his butchering at a city slaughterhouse and sold the

49. Mathis, *Bevölkerungsstruktur*, 22–7.
50. Roeck, *Stadt in Krieg und Frieden*, 1: 492.
51. ibid., 1: 387–9.

meat at a stand on the marketplace. His work tools were not included in the inventory. But everything else he or his wife owned was.

The kitchen had a cooking hearth, a chopping-block, a small wall-cabinet and an old oak table; the table had a drawer in which the officials found a mirror, an old tablecloth, eight spoons and a few other items. There were only two chairs. Cooking was done on a tripod placed in the hearth; there were fourteen pans, six pots, six ladles and two big knives. For consuming ordinary meals the Burkharts had at their disposal ten wooden plates, one glass serving-plate, eight wooden spoons, four metal spoons and ten glasses – but no forks or small knives. The kitchen also had a handful of containers for storing food and a wooden tub for washing up.

The unheated room was used chiefly for sleeping and for storage of linen. There was an oak bedstead – with a canopy, a straw-filled mattress and a blanket – along with a crib and a stool. The room also had an oak cabinet, two cupboards, four cases and two chests, all crammed with clothing, linen and other textile goods. The couple's personal treasures amounted to a handful of silver buttons, some coins, a locket and the wreath and bouquet from their wedding.

The attic contained a spare bed without a canopy, a child's bed, some straw mattresses, a pitchfork, some other tools and one outdated calendar. But above all, the attic was used to store the couple's collection of copperware and tinware: twelve tankards, nineteen bowls, six meat plates, five basins, one salt box and a few other items, altogether weighing a total of 81 pounds. There were also some vessels made of brass and tinplated clay, and eleven 'old plates'. We can assume that most of these items were rarely, if ever, used in the kitchen; they were a form of investment, available to be pawned or sold if the need arose. The tiny shed was used to store a few additional, less valuable items: an old armchair (possibly too broken to use but too cherished to discard), some bowls, a shovel, an additional pitchfork and a cage for poultry.

This, then, was what Euphrosina and Matthes Burkhart owned at the time of Matthes's death. We cannot know how typical their household was in a formal sense, but the size and contents of their home were certainly representative of the material environment of working people in sixteenth- and seventeenth-century Europe. Evidence from early modern Bordeaux confirms this impression: a recent study of a hundred inventories from the households of servants, labourers and poorer artisans between 1515 and 1675 shows that almost every such household had at least one bed and one or more storage chests, most had a table, more than half had benches, but fewer had chairs. There was some improvement in the course of the seventeenth century – the proportion of households in this social milieu that had chairs, for example, rose from less than one-third in the sixteenth century to over half by 1675. But there was no radical change.[52]

We need not know the exact number of stools or chairs in an artisan household, however, to recognize from examples like these that the physical artifacts with which people were surrounded in early modern homes were sufficiently limited in number so as never to be taken for granted. All of the furniture, tools, utensils, tableware and linen used by these people had been made by hand. Not all the things they owned were needed for everyday living – many objects were clearly preserved as a form of investment or security for hard times – but none was considered superfluous. Broken furniture and tools were saved, just in case. Before the age of mass production, labour imparted value to each manufactured object in a way which Karl Marx still understood but we, except in theory, no longer can. Recycling was taken for granted.[53] The waste-disposal problem in early modern cities – and there certainly was one – had chiefly to do with the removal of body wastes and animal remains, not, as today, with the disposal of manufactured goods.

VI

Such, then, was the physical environment in which early modern town-dwellers lived. Great walls girdled their communities, making the act of entering or leaving town a deliberate experience. Narrow house-lined streets predominated, but the pattern was occasionally broken by open market squares or the broad boulevards of new districts. Great public buildings were found in every larger city, but most were accessible only to those who had business to transact. For most townspeople, churches and taverns were no doubt the most frequently visited public indoor spaces. Houses were variable in size and structure, their interior spaces flexible in use and function. Material goods were carefully assembled and preserved; how much people owned obviously had something to do with their wealth, but the distinction between luxuries and necessities was not always an obvious one. For Euphrosina Burkhart it was clearly more important to keep twelve tankards and nineteen bowls in her attic than to pick up some additional chairs for her kitchen. There was, as we shall see, much want in the early modern city – but there was little waste.

52. Dinges, *Stadtarmut in Bordeaux*, 165–239 passim, 533–4.
53. cf. ibid., 223.

CHAPTER TWO

City and State

One day in June of the year 1613, the old German town of Worms on the Rhine received two most distinguished visitors. The 16-year-old Prince-Elector of the Palatinate, Frederick V, and his new bride, Princess Elizabeth of England, together with a great retinue of followers, were passing through Worms. Promptly at 12 noon the prince and his retinue arrived in the city. A delegation of local officials assembled to greet the prince, and the city's chief legal advisor, Johann Jacob Buntz, made a formal speech of welcome. Lavish presents were given: the prince received a goodly quantity of wine, vintage 1610, and twenty-five measures of oats in sacks embossed with the city's arms. The princess received a silver tankard and wash-basin. When the ceremony was over Frederick and his retinue left Worms to continue their way southward to the princely capital at Heidelberg.[1]

Ceremonies like this took place time and again in early modern Europe. The annals of countless cities are replete with accounts of such visits: the assembling of craftsmen or schoolchildren in the market square, the speech of welcome by Mr Recorder or the city's Syndic, the bestowal or, perhaps, exchange of gifts, the gracious reply from princely lips – all these are stock themes of these accounts. Yet each such event had its own special dimensions.

Frederick V, for example, was more than just a neighbouring prince to whom routine courtesy had to be shown, for he had a distinct political relationship to Worms. Yet he was not the city's overlord, for Worms, like about eighty other cities in Germany, acknowledged only the Holy Roman Emperor himself as its true overlord. Worms also

1. Stadtarchiv Worms, 1B 8a: Zorn-Meixnersche Chronik, folio 254v.

had a 'municipal lord', the bishop of Worms, who not only controlled the cathedral precincts but also had certain rights in the rest of the city. The Elector of the Palatinate, however, was the 'protective lord' of Worms. What that title meant had been spelled out in a treaty, valid for sixty years, which one of Frederick's predecessors had imposed on Worms in 1581 – a treaty under which, for example, the prince could put up to 500 soldiers in Worms any time he wanted.[2] Yet the power relationship was not entirely one-sided: the highly practical gifts of wine and grain given to Frederick were none-too-subtle demonstrations of the town's economic strength. The fact that the grain sacks were embossed with the city's emblems was a reminder that the city, though acknowledging Frederick as protective lord, also stood under the authority of the Emperor. Behind the polite exchanges of a festive summer day lay a wealth of symbols which were surely understood by all.

I

Every European city was part of a larger political system. Almost every city, moreover, was subordinate to some higher political entity. Cities had grown and prospered in the middle ages largely because of economic and political privileges which were granted to them by the leaders of the larger political order. But in return cities provided important political and economic services to that order. In fact there was a constant give-and-take between the city and other elements of the political system.

This was as true in early modern times as it had been in the middle ages. To be sure, much is said in historical writing about the 'centralizing state' to which cities supposedly lost their power in the early modern era. But the concept of a zero-sum relation between city and state, in which the power gained by one side was lost by the other, has little to do with the realities of urban and national politics in early modern Europe. It exaggerates both the degree of autonomy which cities had enjoyed during the middle ages and the extent to which cities lost that autonomy in early modern times. Even worse, it fosters the impression that the central state was the only significant counterweight to urban autonomy, when in fact the political order almost always included a variety of influential magnates and regional institutions which could have as much impact on the city as any organs of government on the national level. And, finally, it de-emphasizes the fact that in some parts of Europe the city

2. Friedrichs, 'Uprising in Worms', 94–5.

itself could be a state, ruling over villages or even smaller cities while at the same time deferring to some higher authority within the larger political system.

The term 'state' is unavoidable in discussing the political organization of early modern Europe, but it is not without some ambiguity. The national monarchies of western and northern Europe – Spain, Portugal, France, England, Scotland, Sweden and Denmark – approximated states as the term is now understood. But at the beginning of the early modern period most of these realms were still undergoing a process of political integration. Spain, for example, actually consisted of half a dozen separate kingdoms, each with its own laws and political traditions. Even France included provinces which had only recently come under the control of the crown and still retained considerable autonomy. Moving eastward the situation became yet more complex. The Holy Roman Empire, which took up most of central Europe, consisted of hundreds of distinct territories whose princes ruled with considerable independence yet scrupulously acknowledged the overlordship of the Holy Roman Emperor. The Emperor himself was a major territorial prince, ruling lands both inside and outside the borders of the Empire. He was also the recognized overlord of about eighty imperial cities in various parts of Germany. In eastern Europe, kingdoms were large but royal authority was generally weak; in some regions, noble magnates were virtual rulers in their own right. In Italy the forms of political authority were also diverse; princely states and the territories of the pope took up large parts of the peninsula, while city-states, ruled by municipal elites, occupied the rest.

In order to understand how cities were embedded in the larger political order, however, it is best to begin by looking not at the various kinds of states but at the cities themselves. To be even more exact, we must understand where power was located on the urban level before we can see how that power interacted with other sources of authority.

Most cities in early modern Europe were governed not by individuals but by collective bodies: by a senate, a city council, or a group of interlocking councils. Sometimes the structure of conciliar government was highly complex, confusing to contemporaries and even more confusing to modern historians. Take, for example, the much-studied case of Strasbourg in the sixteenth century. Strasbourg had a Senate of thirty members, whose main function was to serve as the city court. There was also a Council of Thirteen, chiefly concerned with military and external affairs, and a Council of Fifteen to deal with internal affairs. A few Senate members sat on each of these councils. Executive authority was vested in an *Ammeister*, who served for a one-year term, but there were also four *Stettmeister* – senators who served in rotation as figurehead rulers of the city. Legislative authority was concentrated in a body known as the 'Senate-and-Twenty-One', consisting of the Senate, the Thirteen, the Fifteen, and a few other members. This awkwardly named group was the actual magistracy of Strasbourg, the true embodiment of civic authority.[3]

Virtually every city in Europe had some variation on this conciliar system. Sometimes the structure of interlocking councils was even more complex, as in many Italian cities. But it could be simpler. In sixteenth-century York, for example, the council had two distinct parts: a small inner group of twelve aldermen who handled much of the decision-making, and a larger group of twenty-four who never met independently but, when added to the aldermen, made up the full city council.[4] In many towns one or two men would be singled out, usually for a term of office but sometimes for life, to represent the authority and dignity of the city in public. These men – mayors, consuls, *Bürgermeister* and the like – often had special responsibilities. But they were not executives in the modern sense, for they always ruled closely in conjunction with the council. Even the grandest civic official in Europe, the doge of Venice, who was elected for life and counted himself the equal of princes, was sharply circumscribed in his actual exercise of political power.

Every city's constitutional tradition was unique, at least in some respects. But it is easy to identify three basic and interrelated features which were common to the constitutional structure of cities all across early modern Europe. First, as already noted, urban authority was collective. Occasionally a single strongman would try to seize control of the community, but such episodes were rare and usually short-lived. Power was exercised jointly by a group. Second, membership in this group was by election or selection, not by heredity. The procedures for selection to a senate or council varied enormously from one city to the next. Sometimes council members represented specific neighbourhoods or guilds, sometimes they were chosen by complex practices that permitted some popular input, often they were simply appointed by the existing councils themselves. Occasionally the city's overlord had a major hand in selecting members. But the guiding principle was always the same: that new members were chosen from

3. Brady, *Ruling Class, Regime and Reformation*, 163–6; the figure of twenty-one excluded those members of the Thirteen or Fifteen who were already Senators. See also Ford, *Strasbourg in Transition*, 12–13.
4. Palliser, *Tudor York*, 61–7.

among a pool of potentially eligible candidates. Certainly it might help to come from a well-known family, and sometimes seats on a ruling body were informally reserved for the brother or son of a previous member. In a few cities it even became possible for a magistrate to resign his office in favour of a chosen successor, who might be a relative.[5] But this was generally regarded as a distortion of the proper method for choosing council members. Heredity was never a formal, legally recognized basis for obtaining civic office.

This fact, in turn, contributed to the third distinctive feature of urban constitutions. Political power was completely gendered: only men could participate in governing the city. The way power was conferred in cities thus differed significantly from the way it could be transmitted in the larger political order. Authority in noble and ruling houses was passed on by inheritance; males were favoured, but in the absence of male heirs, in many parts of Europe women could and did inherit authority. Whenever the elective or selective principle applied, however, women were excluded. If power was to be granted to somebody drawn from a pool of candidates, the pool would include only men, since men were thought by virtue of their gender to be more fit to govern. The sole exception would be a situation in which only women could be considered. This might be the case, for example, when a convent elected its abbess. But it was never the case when a city's rulers were chosen. The distinction between power transmitted by inheritance and power conferred by election or selection is thus crucial to understanding the nature of urban government in early modern Europe. England was governed by two queens in the sixteenth century – but nobody would have expected a woman to sit on the council of even the smallest town.

The men who occupied these council positions had no mean opinion of their own importance. They expected deference and obedience and were prepared to punish harshly anyone who showed too little of either. In a famous confrontation with a delegation of citizens in 1602, the mayor of Hamburg, Dietrich vom Holte, let loose a sweeping definition of the council's powers:

> Even if the ruling authority were godless, tyrannical and greedy, even so it would be inappropriate for the subjects to rise up and set themselves against it; they should instead regard it as a punishment by the Almighty, which the subjects had brought down upon themselves by their sins.[6]

5. Diefendorf, *Paris City Councillors*, 14–16; Hiltpold, 'Noble Status', 23–4.
6. Bolland, *Senat und Bürgerschaft*, 29; see also Brunner, 'Souveränitätsproblem', 345.

The political philosophy embodied by this statement was a familiar one in the early seventeenth century, especially in Protestant circles, reflecting as it did a customary elaboration of St Paul's injunction that all must obey 'the powers that be'.[7] What is striking here is the willingness to apply that concept not only to kings and princes but to city councils as well.

Yet in actual fact the power of any city council was subject to significant constraints. For the authority of the council was held in check by forces both from above and from below.

In the first place, the council was almost always held to be politically accountable to a specific group within the community: the citizens. The members of this group – the freemen, burgesses, *bourgeois, Bürger, vecinos, cives* or the like – constituted the city's political community, the persons on whose behalf the council was understood to rule. The citizenry never encompassed the entire population of the community; it was often a relatively select group, though in some towns it might be sufficiently broad to include most of the householding craftsmen. Only men were full citizens; women might hold the title but never participated openly in the community's organized political life.

What it actually meant for a man to be a member of this political community, however, could vary from one town to the next. City government was normally structured so as to fulfil two essentially incompatible objectives. On the one hand, it was assumed that authority and decision-making should be in the hands of a small, reliable core of responsible men, sufficiently prosperous to be able to take time off from work to engage in the often time-consuming minutiae of civic administration. On the other hand, the entire body of citizens had to be reassured that their voices would be heard and their interests taken into account. Out of this tension, common to all urban communities, there had arisen a considerable range of constitutional forms. None of them, however, involved the direct election of civic leaders by the ordinary citizens.

Every city had its own, often highly elaborate system for selecting new members of the city council. The procedures were normally designed, however, not to maximize participation in the political system but to ensure the selection of candidates deemed suitable by the existing elites. Thus the council often played the major role in filling any vacancies in its own ranks. In some cities, especially in southern Europe, there were special provisions to eliminate favouritism and nepotism in the electoral procedures. In Aix-en-Provence, for example,

7. Romans 13:1–2.

a nominating committee consisting of current and recent holders of the highest civic offices would draw up a list of a hundred suitable candidates; thirty names would then be drawn by lot from an urn, and these thirty men would serve a two-year term on the council.[8] In Venice, where even the nominating committees themselves were chosen by lot, a further protection against any manipulation of the results was provided by having a young boy pull names out of the urn. Even the boy had to be randomly selected: just before the election of a doge, a member of one of the city's councils would step outside and pick the first boy he saw milling about the Piazza San Marco to serve as *ballotino* for the next few years.[9] But this was as close as any ordinary Venetian ever got to participating in the electoral system; the actual process was restricted to the male members of Venice's noble families.

There were other towns in which, as in Venice, council membership was limited to specific families, but in most cities any male citizen was at least theoretically eligible for elevation to the council. In many cities certain council seats were reserved for representatives of specific neighbourhoods, or members of particular guilds or occupational groups. But this did not always mean that the guilds or neighbourhoods concerned would freely choose their representatives; often the council members themselves decided who would fill the designated seats. And in countless other cities, especially in northern Europe, vacancies were filled by simple, unconstrained co-optation of new members by the existing councillors.

In some parts of Europe – notably England and Germany – a city might also have a 'large' or 'common' council which was regarded as speaking for the broader group of citizens. Its members might represent specific constituencies within the community – guilds, wards or parishes – or they could simply be appointed by the senior council from the citizenry at large. This great council would be summoned on special occasions to hear important announcements or lend support in times of war or crisis. In England it might even participate in the system of indirect elections by making some nominations for higher offices. But the large council hardly ever took any independent political initiative.

Sometimes an even larger group was assembled: the entire body of citizens. In certain cities, all male citizens were summoned from time to time to hear announcements or to renew their oaths of loyalty to

8. Kettering, *Judicial Politics*, 41–2.
9. Muir, *Civic Ritual*, 279.

the city. An oath-day, when and if it occurred, was a solemn occasion: in Augsburg a citizen was severely punished in 1590 for staying home to work during the oath-taking.[10] But such events were rare.

Even the fullest descending pyramid of participation could not disguise the fact that real power was exercised only at the very top. The oligarchical character of urban government in early modern Europe was as obvious to contemporaries as it is to us. But this does not mean that citizens played no role in urban politics. If they appear to us as powerless or passive it is only because, guided by modern assumptions about the nature of democratic government, we insist on looking for contested elections or a formal system of checks and balances. In fact historians are increasingly aware that much of the real political activity by ordinary citizens in the early modern town took place in the framework of organizations other than the city-wide organs of government. Guilds, parishes, wards, militia companies, religious confraternities – these were the organizations through which citizens often had the greatest opportunity not only to participate in decision-making but also to influence the policies of the city council. The individual citizen might appear before the council only as a humble supplicant asking, say, for a tax abatement or permission to open a new business. But the collective interest group to which he belonged could exert considerably more pressure.

When truly vital issues were at stake, moreover, the citizens often threw deference to the winds and became politically active. The normally quiescent large council might suddenly voice strong opinions, or a committee of citizens could be formed to press aggressively for some new policy or change of direction. Citizens and magistrates alike knew that such confrontations always had the potential to spill over into violent conflict – and there was always the possibility that if the magistrates were too high-handed, exactly that would happen. The political power of the citizens normally remained latent, but the magistrates could never completely ignore it. When mayor vom Holte of Hamburg made his celebrated remark about the need for total obedience, he was immediately challenged by the president of the council of parish representatives – who happened to be his own brother Jürgen. Far from setting itself above the citizens, Jürgen declared, the council should be linked more closely to them, since it was from within the body of citizens that the members of the council were called to serve as the government.[11] Similar views

10. Roeck, *Stadt in Krieg und Frieden*, 1: 211.
11. Bolland, *Senat und Bürgerschaft*, 29.

found expression from time to time, usually in moments of crisis or duress, in cities all over Europe during the early modern era.

Thus the council's freedom of action was always held in check from below. But it was also constrained from above. For while the magistrates were accountable to the citizens, they derived their political authority from the dominant elites of the larger political order. What normally set a city legally apart from other communities was that it had been granted certain privileges. There was scarcely a city in Europe which had not received such privileges from some specific source of higher authority – be it a king or duke, a bishop, an ecclesiastical institution, a noble seigneur, or quite possibly a combination of these. The sources of privileges could vary substantially from one region to another. Only one-third of the cities in seventeenth-century Poland were communities which had received their privileges from a reigning prince and thus stood under the ruler's own authority; the rest were 'private towns' controlled by noble or ecclesiastical lords.[12] In western Europe, by contrast, privileges were far more likely to have come from the ruling prince. The body of persons to whom the privileges had been granted could also vary from place to place. In principle the recipients might well encompass the entire collectivity of citizens. But in practice it was almost always the city council which derived and sustained its political legitimacy from a grant of privileges.

These privileges were not abstract rights. They took the form of very concrete grants of permission – to hold a fair twice a year, to have a market once a week, to build a new wall, to charge tolls on the bridge, to try certain cases, to impose certain fines. Each new right had been the product of specific negotiations and circumstances. And each grant of privilege was confirmed in a distinct and separate charter. The small town of Winchester in southern England treasured a total of thirty-three charters, granted by various rulers from Henry II in the twelfth century to George III in the eighteenth.[13] Some larger cities accumulated hundreds of charters. Each time a new ruler came to power the city would seek confirmation of all its existing privileges and, perhaps, a few new ones as well – all for a stiff price, of course.

The charters were normally kept under tight security in a tower or other stronghold somewhere in the heart of the city. The physical preservation of these documents was often a matter of high urgency

12. Bogucka, 'Entwicklungswege', 180–1.
13. Atkinson, *Elizabethan Winchester*, 48.

for the magistrates – for if the charters were lost, there might be no way to confirm the rights concerned. It could never be assumed that even the most powerful royal house kept a permanent archive of the charters its members had issued.[14] When, for example, around the year 1500 the Holy Roman Emperor Maximilian I expressed some scepticism about whether one of his predecessors had really granted the city of Worms as many rights as the magistrates claimed, a delegation from the city had to visit the Emperor in person and show him the actual charter of 1348 before he was convinced. A century later the same issue arose again: this time Maximilian's great-great-grandson, the Emperor Matthias, had to be persuaded that the charter really existed, though he was willing to settle for a certified copy.[15]

Of course it was easy for a ruler and his advisors to claim ignorance of the terms of some antiquated privilege. But they never forgot which cities were dependent on them, and they never doubted their right to be deeply involved in the city's affairs. A city could have hundreds of charters all carefully catalogued and zealously preserved in the belfry of the town hall, but no charter gave a city unlimited freedom. It is true that a handful of European cities – notably in northern Italy and Switzerland – had managed to escape their dependence on any higher authorities by the end of the middle ages. Most of the Italian cities which had done so, however, soon fell under the control of some other prince or some neighbouring city, leaving only a few which were truly autonomous. To be sure, in those few cities which remained independent the political elites were immensely proud of this fact: the doge of Venice, for example, appeared in public ceremonies under an umbrella which symbolized his claim to be equal in political rank to the Holy Roman Emperor and the pope.[16] The concept of a sovereign city was thus known and available to the people who thought about such things in early modern times. But it was irrelevant to all but a tiny list of communities. Most urban elites – and most rulers – took for granted that cities were part of a larger political system. The challenge for everyone concerned was to derive the greatest possible benefits from this situation.

A conventional model holds that during the later middle ages, when rulers were weak and highly dependent on cities for funds, the cities acquired privileges which gave them increasing independence, while in early modern times, as rulers strove for greater power

14. For the case of Spain, see Nader, *Liberty in Absolutist Spain*, 72–3.
15. Friedrichs, 'Uprising in Worms', 100, 122.
16. Muir, *Civic Ritual*, 115–16.

and acquired more resources for enforcing their will, cities steadily lost their autonomy. This formula may be useful as a way of comprehending the issues involved, but it has little to do with the actual situation. Rulers continued to grant charters with new privileges whenever it seemed politically or financially expedient to do so. Throughout the sixteenth and seventeenth century, for example, the Spanish crown granted hundreds of villages charters that released them from subordination to larger municipalities and made them independent towns.[17] Countless towns received new charters, confirming old rights or offering new ones, throughout the early modern period. Yet at the same time, all over Europe, rulers would revoke, override or simply ignore urban privileges when the cities concerned had incurred their anger or seemed too weak to resist.

Sometimes the intervention by rulers involved a show of military force. Frustrated by a city's refusal to pay taxes, incensed by its religious policies, angry because it had supported the opposite side in a civil war, or offended because the municipal leaders refused to swear an oath of allegience, a ruler might arrive with an army in hope of forcing the city into submission. It is true that some such attacks failed. In 1686 the king of Denmark laid siege to Hamburg in hope of enforcing a long-dormant claim to sovereignty over the city. Supported by other princes who had their own reasons for wanting to restrain Danish expansion, Hamburg successfully resisted the king's attempt.[18] Usually, however, a direct show of force was fully successful. Indeed, a city's resistance was likely to crumble once the prince and his army showed up on the scene, as happened when the Emperor Charles V arrived with 5,000 soldiers to punish the town of Ghent for a long-simmering rebellion in 1540.[19] Sometimes a real siege was necessary, as proved to be the case before the Protestant stronghold of La Rochelle fell to the king of France in 1628, or before Erfurt was reduced to obedience by the archbishop of Mainz in 1664, or before Braunschweig would accept direct rule by the duke of Braunschweig-Wolfenbüttel in 1671. The result was generally the same no matter how long it took: once the city had been forced to submit, charters would be revoked, fines levied, fortifications levelled, old magistrates dismissed and new ones installed.

All these episodes, and others like them, made a profound impression on contemporaries. But their significance should not be exaggerated.

17. Nader, *Liberty*, 1–4.
18. Schramm, *Neun Generationen*, 1: 85–8.
19. Brandi, *Emperor Charles V*, 426–30.

Armed intervention was hardly representative of the normal interaction between rulers and cities. Certainly it transpired often enough that a new ruler wanted, for practical fiscal reasons or for abstract political ones, to assert his prerogatives more aggressively than his predecessors had. But normally the civic elite knew exactly how to read such signals and they accommodated the ruler's wishes in such a way that a crisis would never arise.

Sometimes the ruler's power was embodied by the presence of one of his own officials right in the city. In most of the major cities of Castile, for example, an official appointed by the crown – the *corregidor* – sat with the city council and guided its decision-making. To make sure that this official would remain loyal to the king and not become too cosy with the local elite, he would be rotated out of the city and sent to a new posting after just a few years.[20] The Spanish *corregidor* was unusual only in that he actually sat on the council and led its discussions. A city could also have a set of royal officials distinct from but parallel to the municipal ones, as in Paris where the royal officers of the *prévôté de Paris* operated quite independently from the city council; their jurisdictions overlapped, but this was such a common feature of government in the early modern era that few contemporaries would have considered it worthy of comment.

Of course the ruler's authority might also be represented by an official whose competence extended beyond the municipality itself – by a military commandant, for example, or by regional officials such as the lord lieutenant or sheriff of the shire in England or the provincial governor or *intendant* in France. Nor did a ruler even need a permanent representative to make sure that his or her wishes were known to the inhabitants of the city. A messenger or special commissioner could do the job just as well. And much of the time the city council could be expected to know with very little prompting what was expected of the community.

In most cases the ruler's chief interest was fiscal. Many of the city's privileges were predicated on the direct or implied assurance that taxes and loans would be provided at regular intervals. The magistrates might gripe about the extent of the financial demands, but taxes were inevitable and their main concern was often a different one: to retain control over the machinery of revenue collection. In most cities it was the council, not the state officials, who maintained the records, determined the rates, collected the payments and punished delinquents. But the state's demands set the pace.

20. Elliott, *Imperial Spain*, 92–4; cf. Hiltpold, 'Noble Status', 22–3.

Taxation practices in sixteenth-century Paris well illustrate the way in which municipal governments could respond to fiscal pressure while trying to preserve some fragments of their administrative autonomy. Well-established privileges had long exempted the inhabitants of Paris from the payment of direct taxes to the crown. Yet by the sixteenth century the crown repeatedly found it necessary to extract exactly such taxes from the city on an emergency basis. The royal council would issue a decree, the municipal officials would respond with a protest, the crown would slightly reduce the sum demanded, and city officials would then begin apportioning the tax among the citizens. To sustain the legal fiction that this was a one-time-only emergency tax, however, as soon as all the revenues were collected the city officials would ostentatiously burn the tax rolls. Soon afterward the entire cycle would begin anew.[21]

Towns often sought strength in numbers. Wherever there were national, territorial or provincial parliaments, the towns were sure to be represented, and their delegates often took a leading role in resisting new or excessive taxation. Towns also formed special organizations to protect their interests. In Scotland, for example, the Convention of Royal Burghs met regularly in the late sixteenth and early seventeenth century to develop coordinated policies and apportion taxes fairly; in 1590 the convention voted to punish any town which entered into tax negotiations with the crown before consulting all the other members.[22] In the short run, solidarity among cities could certainly limit or moderate the demands of the higher authorities. In the long run, however, few towns could escape or evade the relentless fiscal pressure posed by rulers all over Europe.

But the extraction of taxes and other kinds of income was only one aspect of the state's involvement with the city. Reports of public disorder or religious dissidence, rumours of political disloyalty, fears of open rebellion or concern about an impending invasion – motives like these would quickly stimulate rulers or their councillors into demanding information or action. The level and timing of state involvement was irregular and unpredictable: a long period during which the city council heard little from the higher authorities might suddenly be followed by a cycle of heavy intervention and involvement. For urban autonomy was never absolute or permanent. Freedom from interference was an indication of temporary equilibrium,

21. Diefendorf, *Paris City Councillors*, 24–6.
22. Lynch, 'Crown and the Burghs', 61–2, 77n.

a sign that the ruler was at that particular point in no position to expect or extort any more from the community than it currently provided.

Even the most venerable privileges were only conditional. The procedures for selecting council members and other civic officials might have been confirmed in one charter after another – but this would hardly deter a ruler from interfering with elections. Paris is a good example. The major municipal officials – the *prévôt des marchands* and the four *échevins* – were selected by a typically convoluted process involving chiefly their fellow-magistrates. The crown had reserved the right to approve and install the officials thus elected – but this was not enough for some French kings, who would overrule the results and install the runner-up or announce in advance who should be chosen.[23] It is not surprising, of course, that the kings of France should have taken such an interest in the affairs of their own capital, but smaller cities were by no means immune from interference, especially when the citizens themselves started quarrelling about election results. When the Scottish burgh of Perth fell into turmoil in the mid-sixteenth century, the queen-regent of Scotland tried to settle things by dictating a new list of council members. As it happened, this did not end the troubles – but nobody doubted her right to try.[24]

Often, in fact, rulers would not be content with changing specific election results but would revamp the entire municipal constitution. Sometimes, of course, the city's own officials lobbied for a new charter to revise procedures they found too unwieldy or too open to popular influence. But the initiative could also come from above. The most spectacular instance of this was undertaken between 1548 and 1552 by the Holy Roman Emperor Charles V, acting in his capacity as direct overlord of the free imperial cities of Germany. Angered by the reluctance of town councils in which guilds were represented to support him in his struggles against the Protestant religion, Charles ordered twenty-seven imperial cities in southern Germany not only to install new, more cooperative council members but also to revise completely their constitutional procedures.[25] Yet in fact this kind of thing could happen to almost any city. In 1597 King Henri IV of France decided to reorganize the government of Amiens, a strategically located city which had failed to offer him support during the recent civil wars. The city council, which for centuries had consisted of twenty-four members, was summarily reduced to seven

23. Diefendorf, *Paris City Councillors*, 19–22; Bernard, *Emerging City*, 32–3.
24. Verschuur, 'Merchants and Craftsmen', 45.
25. Naujoks, *Kaiser Karl V. und die Zunftverfassung*, 1–31, 335–46.

and placed under the supervision of four new municipal councillors chosen by the king or royal governor. The position of mayor was abolished and replaced by a mere 'first councilman', appointed by the king. The council, stripped of most of its judicial authority and control of civil defence, was reduced to keeping order in the community and trying misdemeanours; part of the civic revenue was diverted directly to a fund for building new fortifications to be controlled by the crown. The city elite knew that Henri IV would not change his mind, but once his successor was on the throne they pleaded desperately for a restoration of the traditional mayoralty and control of the diverted revenues. Their complaints got nowhere, and the new constitution promulgated in 1597 remained in force.[26]

It is certainly true that during the early modern era, especially in the seventeenth century, some rulers or their advisors began to regard the role of their cities in a new light. Influenced by the concept of 'social discipline' or guided by a vision of the 'well-ordered police state', these rulers began to perceive their cities not only as sources of revenue or reservoirs of military manpower, but also as integral parts of a coherent social order whose energies could be harnessed to become more rational and productive.[27] To this end some rulers tried to impose standardized systems of urban administration on their cities or insisted that councils enforce specific uniform policies in regulating the economic affairs of their communities. Sometimes these rulers elicited genuine cooperation from the local elites. Traditionally urban councils had regarded any interference from above as a burden to be accommodated if it could not be fended off, but in many cities the magistrates now decided that their own interests were better served not by struggling to defend urban liberties but by functioning willingly as agents of the prince's will.[28]

Yet one must never exaggerate the extent to which urban governments were subordinated to state control. Even in France, whose kings and their advisors had virtually pioneered the concept of absolutism, practice often lagged far behind theory. Louis XIV's appointment of a lieutenant-general of police for the city of Paris in 1667 is generally taken as a landmark in the extension of royal control over municipal affairs, especially since the same office was subsequently established in many other cities.[29] The new lieutenant-general was given extensive powers over streets and markets and his

26. Deyon, *Amiens*, 430–2.
27. For a useful overview, see Raeff, *Well-Ordered Police State*.
28. For a striking illustration of this process, see Mörke, 'Der gewollte Weg'.
29. Bernard, *Emerging City*, 39–46; see also Benedict, 'French Cities', 33–5.

appointment had a noticeable impact on life in the French capital. But his position was really an expanded version of the old *prévôt de Paris*; the rival municipal government headed by the *prévôt des marchands* remained in office and continued to control municipal finances.[30] Sometimes measures which seemed to involve the imposition of tighter controls turned out, on closer inspection, to be little more than a new means of solving the old problem of squeezing money from the cities. In 1692, for example, the crown ordered the establishment of the new office of mayor in almost all the major towns of France. Like most new offices in France during the *ancien régime*, this position was for sale – and it easily attracted buyers, since it offered social status and exemption from taxes. Though the new mayors had few duties, the existing magistrates resented the imposition of this office – so the crown then offered cities the option of buying back the position and leaving it vacant.[31] Soon the crown began to sell a host of other municipal offices, most of which, once sold, could also be bought back and eliminated by the city officials.[32] In short, the crown's purpose was primarily fiscal, not administrative.

II

It was hard enough for urban magistrates to deal with the demands and designs of the state. But often the state was not the only higher authority with claims on the city's obedience or allegiance. Frequently, for example, the bishop of the diocese in which the city was located claimed authority over various aspects of city life – especially, of course, if the city in question was the bishop's own episcopal seat. Not only would the cathedral precincts form an exempt area from which the magistrates' authority was excluded, but also the bishop almost invariably expected to be consulted about the city's policies in general. The magistrates might count themselves fortunate if the bishop's interests were confined to areas of traditional concern to the church, such as the organization of schools and charitable institutions.

The city normally also had to deal with the interests and demands of influential noblemen from the surrounding region. There was always abundant cause for friction between the city and the regional nobles; if nothing else, the question of just how far the city's own territory and authority extended beyond the walls could generate issues that were

30. Bernard, *Emerging City*, 47–55.
31. The process is well illustrated by Schneider, *Public Life in Toulouse*, 280.
32. Benedict, 'French Cities', 34–5.

rich in possibilities for conflict. Some regional nobles tried to get involved in factional politics in the city, or came into town to recruit armed retainers. Of course the municipal authorities were bound to object if any of their citizens were to bear arms for a regional noble or gentleman.[33] But the contacts with neighbouring magnates were not always hostile: the civic elite might also cultivate relations with the regional lords in order to have allies with connections to the court. Frequently some members of the municipal elite themselves had estates in the surrounding countryside: this could lead to alliances and intermarriages – or to hostility and resentment. Either way, the political power of the regional nobility could never be overlooked.

An even more delicate problem for the municipal leaders arose when different persons or institutions claimed – often with equally valid reason – to be speaking or acting on behalf of the king or overlord. This became a familiar situation in seventeenth-century France, when municipal leaders might have to deal simultaneously with a provincial governor and a royal *intendant*, or maybe even two different *intendants* – both duly appointed by the king, but quite possibly bitter rivals who were pursuing conflicting political agendas.[34] On top of this, in most of France's leading cities there was also a *parlement*. Though primarily a court of law, the *parlement* invariably functioned as well as an additional source of local authority, issuing orders and injunctions to regulate the city's affairs whenever the judges felt that municipal officials had been remiss.

All this underscores one basic fact: to posit a simple polarity between 'city' and 'state' would overlook the variety and mutability of real political issues as experienced by municipal authorities in early modern Europe. Urban magistrates were engaged in a constant struggle to maintain their own power by dealing effectively with the demands and claims generated by various elements in the broader political arena. Though the impulse to defend 'urban liberties' was authentic, excessive zeal could backfire. The traditional rights of the city had more than symbolic value, but they were never absolute; experience showed only too clearly that the most cherished privileges and charters could be revoked or ignored. Deference, delay and diplomacy might do more for the city than outright defiance.

All of this was made more complicated by the fact that different groups within the community itself might have very different notions of where the city's ultimate interests lay. Only in panegyrical pamphlets,

33. See for example Dyer, *City of Worcester*, 212–13.
34. cf. the case described by Beik, 'Two Intendants'.

allegorical paintings or idealistic sermons was the city likely to be depicted as a unified whole; on sober reflection everyone recognized that the community included numerous groups whose economic, social or familial interests might clash sharply with each other. To harmonize these different interests and prevent factional conflict from getting out of hand was a major obligation of urban government.

The magistrates themselves were never a completely unified group, and their own motives were often suspect. It was only too obvious that membership in the governing elite provided ample opportunities for economic or social gain. But high public office in the early modern city was also a burden – one which, in fact, despite all the prestige it conveyed, some candidates tried to evade or had to be forced to accept.[35] For these were the men upon whom everyone – from the distant royal council to the insistent beggar on the city hall steps – relied to satisfy their various needs or demands. Every now and then a generation of visionary leaders might come to the fore in urban politics and some great project or reform might be carried through to a successful conclusion. But this was rare. Normally urban government was something far less dramatic: a constant attempt to maintain a modicum of public order while trying to satisfy the conflicting claims of various constituencies both within and beyond the high walls of the city.

35. cf. Phythian-Adams, *Desolation of a City*, 250–2.

CHAPTER THREE

City and Church

The holiest person in the Spanish town of Avila in the mid-sixteenth century was an illiterate woman named Mari Díaz. Originally from a nearby village, Mari Díaz had moved to Avila in the 1530s not only to seek work but also to pursue a religious vision. Though she never became a nun – presumably her parents were not rich enough to provide the customary dowry – Mari Díaz became widely known for her unique blend of austerity, piety and practical advice. By the 1560s she was living permanently in a tiny chamber next to the main altar of the great church of San Millán. Clad in rags, subsisting on one meal a day, Mari Díaz spent hours at prayer, interrupting her devotions only to dispense her wisdom to the admirers of every social rank who thronged to visit her tiny enclosure. When she died in November 1572, the authorities ordered magnificent funeral rites which lasted for nine days.[1]

Just a few weeks before her death, religious passions of a very different sort had gripped an even greater European city. After ten frustrating years of religious and civil war, the king of France had ordered the assassination of Protestant leaders gathered in Paris. What may first have been envisioned as a limited strike against political enemies soon turned into a bloodbath as undisciplined soldiers and hostile neighbours massacred Protestant inhabitants of every district in Paris.[2] Nor were Protestants the only victims. According to one contemporary, amidst all the bloodshed and confusion some Catholic priests were murdered as well – by cynical co-religionists eager to create vacancies in a few well-paid church positions.[3]

1. Bilinkoff, *Avila*, 97–105.
2. Diefendorf, *Beneath the Cross*, 93–106, 159–75.
3. Coudy, *Huguenot Wars*, 204.

There were few living saints in early modern towns, and few religious massacres. Yet the life of Mari Díaz and the Massacre of St Bartholemew's Eve were only extreme manifestations of an all-pervasive aspect of early modern urban life. For of all the many elements which bound the men and women of the early modern city into a common civilization, nothing was more central or enduring than their membership in the Christian church and their commitment to the Christian religion.

Not every inhabitant of an early modern city was necessarily a Christian. Some cities had small Jewish communities. In the cities of Mediterranean Europe there were often Muslims. A few African slaves or travellers from distant lands who lived in Europe may have adhered to other religious traditions. These groups, especially the Jews and Muslims, fascinated and disturbed the Christians of Europe and sometimes evoked vicious spasms of alarm or antipathy. But their actual numbers were miniscule. The population of early modern Europe was overwhelmingly Christian.

What made people Christians was not their common adherence to a single body of religious beliefs, nor was it their common participation in a single pattern of religious practice. These aspects of Christianity were already enormously varied at the end of the middle ages and became even more so during the early modern era. What made all these people Christians was a single ritual, normally performed within days or even hours of a person's birth: the sacrament of baptism. It was baptism that defined an individual as a member of the church and subjected him or her to a set of specific religious obligations. Some people fulfilled these obligations well; many others did so poorly. Countless people engaged, sometimes unknowingly, in religious practices that ran counter to the formal teachings of Christianity. But all remained members of the church.

To many historians, the single most important theme of European history during the early modern era has to do with the occurrence and consequences of the Protestant and Catholic Reformations of the sixteenth century. Certainly the breakup of the Roman church as it had existed throughout the middle ages and the emergence of Protestant and Catholic forms of Christianity had a profound impact on countless aspects of political, social and cultural life – and cities in particular were caught up in these changes. Yet the importance of the Reformation era must not obscure the fact that even before the sixteenth century, Christianity had been characterized by enormous variety and subject to constant change. Indeed, in many ways the events of the Reformation era are best understood as extreme manifestations of a constant, cyclical pattern in the history of the church. Relatively stable beliefs and institutions would suddenly be challenged by religious zealots, usually members of the clergy, who were convinced that the church as an institution or the practice of Christian life needed a dramatic change in direction. As a rule the church would either crush these challenges or absorb and normalize them. In the early sixteenth century, however, neither approach proved successful. The result was a sudden burst of religious upheaval – a dramatic, invigorating process in which the cities of Europe played a central part. But this brief episode of disruption and dissent soon gave way to the establishment of new Protestant churches modelled to a larger extent than their founders cared to admit on the Roman church from which they had broken away. These churches too began to experience the customary process of challenge from within. They reacted by and large in the traditional ways.

All this, as we shall see, had a profound impact on the religious life of the European city. But the great changes which we shall trace must not obscure some equally important constants. In 1750, as in 1450, the rhythm of weekly worship, the role of the church in regulating major life-cycle events and the influence of the clergy in defining standards of communal behaviour were still familiar patterns in every European city. In some towns, especially in northern Europe, minority churches and sects were tolerated in a way that would not have been possible in 1450. There were even some in 1750 who believed that a meaningful life could be lived outside the framework of Christian tradition. But their numbers were miniscule and their influence was small. The established church – Catholic or Protestant – was still a profoundly influential institution in every European city at the end of the early modern era.

The church derived much of its power from its intricate links to the state. Of course the history of Christianity is studded with dramatic episodes of conflict between religious and secular leaders. But these struggles, significant as they were, must still be understood as episodes of readjustment or reallocation of authority within the ruling power structure. Both before and after the Reformation era, secular and religious leaders ultimately depended on each other to reinforce their authority.

Power within the church was strongly gender-linked. In the medieval church and the Catholic church which emerged from it, all could pray and do good works, but only male priests could administer the crucial rituals – the sacraments – which stood at the heart of Christian practice. The Protestant churches denied the sacramental power of the priest, but their ministry was as completely masculine as the Catholic priesthood had ever been. Public preaching was, with the rarest exceptions, forbidden to women by Protestants and Catholics alike. Specific religious roles were of course assigned to women, especially in the Catholic tradition, but female devotion was always supposed to remain subject to male guidance and enclosed by the walls of a cloister or home. Guided by her bishop and her confessor, Mari Díaz was encouraged to impart inspiration or discreet advice from her tiny booth under the altar of San Millán. She never could have been seen at the altar itself – or heard from the pulpit.

I

To appreciate the pervasive role of the church in urban life in early modern Europe, one must keep in mind the central beliefs and practices of the Christian religion as they had evolved during the middle ages. The starting-point is easy: the doctrine that human nature is fundamentally inclined to evil. All humans deserved punishment, if not on earth then in the afterlife, for the sins they committed. Yet divine intervention, as embodied in Jesus, had opened up for some humans the possibility of salvation. On this much, all forms of Christianity were in agreement. But which people would be saved and to what extent could they themselves contribute to their own salvation? If salvation were available only to a select few, there would be scant encouragement for the great mass of people to modify their sinful behaviour. If, however, salvation were unstintingly granted to all, this too would make any modification of earthly behaviour irrelevant. Medieval theology therefore generally endorsed the view that salvation was available not to all but at least to many – specifically, to those who repented of the sins they committed and participated in the central rituals of the faith.

Here, of course, is where the church came in. For according to medieval doctrine only those rituals duly administered by the church's own priests had saving power. Only a priest could offer the repentant sinner valid assurance that his or her sins were forgiven. And only a priest could conduct the mass, the act of worship which was held to celebrate the miraculous transformation of bread and wine into the body and blood of Christ. Priests, like all humans, were sinners. But the priest was only a vessel. As long as he was properly ordained and conducted the rituals properly, his acts had religious force. This doctrine, more than any other, accounted for the enormous power the church acquired in the course of the middle ages. Priests, bishops – even the pope himself – could be steeped in sin, fully accountable to God for their personal failings. Yet their religious acts were always valid. Nobody had any excuse for looking beyond the church in search of spiritual aid. The church, and only the church, held the keys to salvation.

The priesthood was the central institution of the medieval church. Priests had to be males and were supposed to remain celibate – though only the former rule was strictly enforced. The church also included a vast number of monastic foundations, both for men and for women. Monks and nuns were pledged to poverty and celibacy, but their institutions often commanded great wealth. The initial gifts of land or rents normally made when a monastery or convent was founded would be supplemented by dowries from the parents of newly admitted inmates. From time to time some inspired soul would press for the establishment of a new religious order, devoted to a higher level of religious dedication or more rigorous observation of the rule of poverty. But within a generation or two the new order would settle into the traditional routines of monastic life. A European city of the late middle ages might thus be host to a number of different orders – Benedictines, Augustinians, Carmelites, Dominicans, Franciscans and more – each with its own house and gardens within the city and extensive landholdings without.

Christianity was formally monotheistic. The mystery of the Trinity, postulating God as three beings in one, was beyond the comprehension of many average Christians. Medieval devotional life, in any case, was centred less on God than on the Virgin Mary and the innumerable saints. Much like pagan deities, the saints were assigned individual portfolios; specific occupations, ailments, enterprises and localities, and parishes all had their own patron saints. In formal theology, saints could only be asked to intercede with God. But the veneration of saints often bordered on outright worship.

Some popular beliefs and practices diverged even more radically from the formal teachings of the medieval church. Priests themselves were often confused about the finer points of theology – and the theologians who presumably did understand the finer points were often engaged in bitter doctrinal disputes. But none of this shook the fundamental authority of the church as an institution which provided a framework for religious belief and practice that enveloped all of Europe at the close of the middle ages.

II

The pre-Reformation church was universal, but it took special forms in the urban setting. Above all, of course, there was the sheer multiplicity of ecclesiastical institutions and clerical personnel in the city. A village normally had a single church, manned by a single priest who might well be shared with another parish. But the city could have numerous parish churches, monastic foundations, chapels and charitable institutions. Members of the clergy abounded. The rare censuses that survive from some German cities of the mid-fifteenth century indicate that one of every fifty inhabitants might be a member of the clergy. Nuremberg, for example, had 20,219 inhabitants in 1450, of whom 446 were clerics.[4]

Only priests could administer the sacraments, but all clerical persons, men and women alike, were clearly distinguished from other members of the community. The final vows taken by priest or members of religious orders were permanent. Attached to clerical status were specific privileges, such as exemption from municipal taxes or the right to be tried in church courts. Ecclesiastical institutions, as religious corporations, also enjoyed extensive privileges, many of which were a source of constant irritation to municipal leaders.

Yet the division between lay and clerical members of urban society must not be exaggerated. There was a constant interpenetration of the religious and secular spheres. Members of the clergy were involved in every aspect of urban life – but laypeople also had a vast influence over the affairs of the church. Some ecclesiastical institutions had property from which they derived a steady income, but growth and expansion depended on further gifts from the pious. Donations and bequests were crucial to the functioning of many churches and chapels. We stand today in awe before the most visible of such donations – the magnificent altarpieces commissioned by donors who would ask to be painted praying reverently before the Virgin or a favourite saint. But the priest of the late middle ages was likely to be more interested in another type of bequest: a will leaving payment for any number of masses to be celebrated for the soul of the deceased. Such a bequest could keep a priest busy – and paid – for a long time to come.

Clerical appointments were by no means always internal matters for officials of the church. By old tradition, those who had originally founded any particular church normally had the right to name its personnel – unless in the meantime they had sold or given this right to somebody else. The power to appoint the priests or other clergy of any particular church or chapel was thus as likely to be held by a secular dignitary as by any ecclesiastic.

4. Endres, 'Sozialstruktur', 194. In 1459 Nördlingen had a population of 5,295, of whom 80 were clerics and their underlings: Dorner, *Steuern*, 94–100.

Let us take a close look at the array of churches in the north German town of Braunschweig in the late fifteenth or early sixteenth century, just before the Reformation.[5] This can help us grasp both the variety of ecclesiastical establishments that might be found in a single town and the interpenetration of lay and clerical control that was so typical of European cities.

The greatest house of worship in Braunschweig was the collegiate church of St Blasius in the centre of town. The church had eighteen canons and almost fifty humbler vicars, all of whom were appointed by the dukes of Braunschweig. In theory the canons were expected to participate in time-consuming religious rituals, but their income came chiefly from rents of houses and land and much of their time was spent in administering these properties. There was also a second, much smaller collegiate church, St Cyriacus, whose twelve canons were likewise named by the dukes.

Braunschweig had seven parish churches. The largest was the church of St Martin, with twenty altars and a staff of almost forty priests who owed their appointments to the city council. The council also named the priests for two other parishes, but the remaining four parish churches each had a different patron: the duke, the two collegiate churches, and the local Benedictine monastery. Yet even in the churches where it had no control over appointments, the city council kept a viligant watch to make sure that money donated by citizens was properly used. It was only too likely, after all, that an altar-priest who had been paid for saying hundreds of masses might start getting slipshod. One had to keep an eye on things.

There were four religious houses in the city. The most important one was the Benedictine abbey of St Aegidius, which had scarcely twenty monks but also a substantial number of lay brothers who performed menial chores and cultivated the abbey's vast lands outside the city. The dukes had originally been the abbey's patrons, but by the end of the middle ages the city council had come to control the appointment of new monks. The second most important foundation was the Cistercian convent of the Holy Cross, with about forty nuns, most of them daughters of local citizens. The abbess shared her authority with a male provost installed by the city council to supervise the convent's economic affairs and provide priestly services. In addition, Braunschweig had houses for Franciscan and Dominican friars. These were modest establishments: since friars, in contrast to monks and nuns, were supposed to live from charitable donations

5. Spiess, *Braunschweig*, 2: 622–9, 636–63.

instead of agricultural activity, the friaries had no property to speak of.

This hardly exhausts the list of ecclesiastical establishments in Braunschweig. There were numerous hospitals, including one for lepers, and about half a dozen chapels. In most cases the city council was heavily involved in the appointment of priests or the administration of funds for these institutions.

In almost every European city of the fifteenth or early sixteenth century one would have found a similar variety of religious establishments. 'The church', after all, was not a single hierarchical institution but a vast network of separate corporate bodies, each with its own rights and customs. Many of these ecclesiastical corporations had extensive landholdings and collected revenues from property both within and beyond the city walls. The exact degree to which secular authorities in the city were involved in the affairs of these various ecclesiastical institutions would differ from place to place. In many towns, for example, bishops had much more control of church appointments than was the case in Braunschweig. But nowhere was the church a self-contained organization detached from the rest of urban society.

For just this reason, of course, many a city was burdened by a history of conflict between secular and ecclesiastical authorities. Usually these disputes were jurisdictional in character: clerical tax exemptions and property rights could lead to endless friction between church officials and the municipal government. Nor were these the only manifestations of ill-feeling on the official level. Anti-clericalism was rife: priests and monks were constantly being mocked and criticized for keeping concubines, evading their duties, and regarding their appointments as nothing more than sources of income. Clerics were regarded in much the same way that lawyers were – as members of a profession which, though undeniably necessary, offered all too many opportunities for self-promotion. The church as an institution controlled the keys to salvation, but the clergy as individuals had no monopoly on spirituality. Most members of the clergy, after all, had entered religious careers not due to any personal vocation but because they had been placed there by their parents. Many laypeople were far more devout than the priests to whom they whispered their confessions or before whom they knelt to partake of the sacrament.

Lay participation in religious life was not confined to worship in church or passive reception of sacraments. Much of the dynamism of religious life in European cities of the late middle ages was provided by lay confraternities, or religious brotherhoods.[6] These were predominantly but not exclusively masculine organizations. Some confraternities were volunteer groups, made up of members who had freely chosen to join together in pursuit of a holier life. More often confraternities overlapped or coincided with the membership of particular guilds; sometimes, in fact, guild and confraternity intermeshed so closely as to form a single unit. Mutual aid was important, especially *post mortem*: staging impressive funeral processions for deceased members was often one of the brotherhood's major functions. But a lot of confraternal energy was also directed outward: confraternities operated hospitals, comforted prisoners, or tried to rehabilitate prostitutes. Some of their activities also provided gratifying opportunities for public recognition and display. Dressed in their distinctive robes or costumes, members of the confraternities would join in the great religious processions which routinely wound through city streets on major holidays or in times of communal celebration or distress.

The initiative for public religious rituals often came from the political authorities. Civic processions were frequently instituted by the magistrates, but even when they were undertaken to celebrate or commemorate purely secular events – military victories, for example – the processions almost always had a religious component and typically ended up in a church.[7] On the other hand, even a purely religious event could be shaped by lay leaders to give it powerful secular overtones. In the late middle ages all over Europe the annual feast of Corpus Christi was observed by staging huge processions to escort the Host – the consecrated wafer of bread which was understood to be the body of Christ – through city streets. In many towns the procession was accompanied or followed by religious pageants or plays staged by individual guilds or confraternities, usually under the overall direction of the municipal government. The original impulse behind this solemn festival was entirely religious, but a political message sometimes got embedded in the Corpus Christi observances. In fact a celebration of the Body of Christ lent itself aptly indeed to the objectives of magistrates who wanted to enhance communal solidarity by making all citizens feel like indispensable parts of the 'social body' – a body whose head or heart, of course, was

6. For a useful overview, see Black, *Confraternities*; see also Flynn, *Sacred Charity*, esp. chs 1–2.
7. e.g. Muir, *Civic Ritual*, 212–19.

embodied by the mayor or council.[8] Religion was always a powerful asset for municipal rulers.

At the same time, however, the clergy constantly strove to extend its control over religious initiatives of the laity. Clerics were always nervous when men or women tried to meet on their own to pray, worship or even just engage in good works without formal spiritual guidance. The clergy were also concerned, of course, to maintain religious discipline in the confraternities and prevent the brothers from getting lax or drifting into taverns after their devotions. But there were also times when the clerical authorities had to do exactly the opposite: to tone down excesses of religious zeal. In Italy, for example, some confraternities had to be warned not to overdo the custom of penitential self-flagellation – or at least to practise it only in private.[9]

The ecclesiastical authorities always tended to be wary of excessive enthusiasm; a steady, predictable level of devotion normally suited them better. But spiritual impulses are hard to control, and laypeople often put their own stamp on the pattern of religious expression. Preaching in particular was popular with the laity, who never minded being rebuked for their own sins as long as the preacher took care to criticize misconduct among his fellow clerics as well. Often a preacher owed his very appointment to members of the laity. In Strasbourg, for example, a group of wealthy citizens put up the money in 1478 to lure the most famous preacher in the Rhineland, Johann Geiler von Kaysersberg, away from his position in Freiburg to serve as a preacher in their city's cathedral. Though he strictly defended both the doctrines and the privileges of the church, Geiler was unstinting in his condemnation of the moral failings of clergymen and laity alike. His sermons were wildly popular.[10]

In fact preaching could have a profoundly transforming impact on urban life – though the impact was not always permanent. The most spectacular instance of this was provided by the career of Girolamo Savonarola in Florence during the 1490s. Savonarola owed his position in Florence to the Medici, the family which dominated the city's political life for most of the fifteenth century. In 1490 Lorenzo de Medici arranged for Savonarola to be named prior of the convent of San Marco, which the Medici had long supported

8. James, 'Ritual, Drama and the Social Body'; for discussion of a more blatantly political exploitation of the Corpus Christi ritual, see Muir, *Civic Ritual*, 228–30.
9. Black, *Confraternities*, 100–3.
10. Abray, *People's Reformation*, 25, 28–9; see also Chrisman, *Strasbourg and the Reform*, 68–78.

and controlled. Initially Savonarola's powerful sermons followed the traditional lines of moralist preaching: the end was nigh – the day of judgement near at hand – but there was still time for sinners to repent and earn a place in heaven. The rich in particular would be punished unless they renounced their avarice and remembered their duty to the poor. Soon, however, the political situation in Florence was transformed. Lorenzo died in 1492. His son Piero, who hoped to succeed his father as the city's unofficial ruler, was soon discredited by his inept handling of the political crisis that erupted when the king of France invaded Italy in 1494. Piero was driven from Florence, and the citizens turned to their most celebrated preacher for moral and political guidance. Of course Savonarola continued to demand repentance and personal reform. But as modern research has shown, his message now underwent a subtle but significant reorientation, for he began to absorb into his sermons some of the traditional themes of Florentine political discourse which emphasized the city's unique history and destiny.[11] The end, it now seemed, was not quite so near after all. In fact Florence would first emerge as a New Jerusalem, blessed by prosperity and leading all of Italy in a process of moral and political regeneration – if only its citizens would mend their ways, become more self-disciplined, and govern themselves for the benefit of all. The constitution had already been revised right after the Medici left, but Savonarola also demanded the kinds of changes in behaviour typically promoted by religious fundamentalists: young women were to appear in public more modestly dressed, with their faces veiled; adultery, fornication and sodomy were to be eliminated; riotous games and festivals were to be replaced by solemn religious processions.[12] Some of this actually happened. Yet like most episodes of religious enthusiasm, the Savonarolan impulse soon died down, especially as the promised growth of power and prosperity showed no signs of emerging. In fact Florence was beset by political troubles and the pope himself turned against the city, eventually decreeing Savonarola's excommunication. In 1498 Savonarola was arrested and tried as a heretic; soon he was hanged and his body was burnt in the main square of Florence. The city went back to politics as usual.

Meanwhile, far to the north, Geiler von Kaysersberg – the 'German Savonarola' in some modern textbooks – faced no comparable difficulties. Though he attacked the council of Strasbourg for its violation of church privileges, nothing he said went dangerously beyond

11. Weinstein, *Savonarola*, 97–9, 132–3, 138–47.
12. ibid., 171, 271–2.

the customary give-and-take between lay and clerical leaders. His greatest impact was on personal lives, not on the community as a whole. He died in 1510, honoured and esteemed after thirty years of preaching which had deeply inspired the people of Strasbourg without appreciably changing the communal way of life.

III

The Protestant Reformation began in 1517 in a city: Wittenberg, a small university town in the electoral duchy of Saxony. Its first and strongest appeal was to urban men and women. But to look for an 'urban' component in the thought of Martin Luther would be to stretch the facts. Luther was concerned with a strictly theological question which had perplexed Christian thinkers for over a thousand years: to what extent, if at all, could human acts or human will contribute to a person's own prospects of salvation? No Luther was needed, of course, simply to condemn the degeneration of religious practice that had become so evident in the late middle ages. Serious theologians agreed that no amount of good works – whether acts of charity, endowment of masses or repetition of prayers – could alone contribute to a person's salvation; the true contrition of a repentant heart had to be part of the process. But Luther went further than all his predecessors when he insisted that even the most heartfelt contrition was also a mere 'work' and thus no more efficacious than the crassest attempt to buy one's way into heaven. Salvation came exclusively from faith – and faith was entirely a gift from God, granted for God's unfathomable reasons to the undeserving sinner. To many of Luther's contemporaries, this doctrine seemed intensely liberating. The church and its priests, they were told, did not have the keys to salvation after all – only God did, and his dispositions could not be influenced by any human action. The burden and expense of participating in the vast system of rituals imposed by the medieval church appeared to be based on a faulty premise.

Luther never envisioned that churches as such should be abolished. The faith given by God was channelled to humans chiefly through the propagation of the divine word, and clergymen would still be needed to read, expound and explain the Scriptures. But Luther denied the unique sacral status of the priesthood. There was no basis for celibacy – which, in any case, countless priests had violated; the pastor should get married like everyone else and settle down to a useful life of preaching and teaching. Two sacraments would be retained: baptism to establish membership in the Christian community and holy communion to sustain it. Preaching should be expanded and more schools organized. But clerical institutions which did not primarily serve to spread the word of God – notably monasteries and convents – would no longer be needed.

The first enthusiasts for Luther's doctrines were, like Luther himself, members of the clergy. So were his bitterest enemies – beginning, of course, with the pope himself. But the conflict soon spread from within the ranks of the clergy to other sectors of society. Within a decade Lutheran concepts were familiar subjects of debate among educated laypeople all over Europe. A clear demarcation rapidly arose between Catholics, who continued to accept the authority of the ecclesiastical structure headed by the pope, and Protestants, who did not. Yet the Protestant movement itself was soon fractured into separate denominations. Some, like those who denied the authority of Scripture or the importance of infant baptism, were bitterly opposed by Luther and his followers. Others, like adherents of the Reformed or Calvinist tradition which spread from Switzerland northward, functioned in uneasy coexistence with the predominantly German Lutherans. By contrast, the Catholic church – though itself divided between less adventurous traditionalists and those committed to internal renewal and reform – remained united under papal authority.

There is no question that the appeal of Protestantism lay more in the implications of its doctrines than in its fundamental premises. The Protestant rejection of the priesthood and abolition of monastic life drew on a strong tradition of anti-clericalism which had long flourished in full compatibility with sincere religiosity. But only the most courageous souls could wholly comprehend the stark doctrine that the soul's destiny lay entirely with God and all human will was irrelevant. No doubt many early Protestants assumed that their very decision to adopt the new faith was in itself an indication that God had predisposed them for eventual salvation. The willed act of becoming Protestant could thus be interpreted as the consequence of a divine decree.

In any case, it was always only a select group of people who had to make a conscious decision in favour of one faith or another. For the overwhelming majority of men and women in sixteenth-century Europe, the choice between Protestantism or Catholicism was eventually determined by their political rulers. Secular leaders were entirely used to being heavily involved in the affairs of the church. So if the church, as it now seemed, was itself divided as to the legitimacy of its traditional institutions, it was only natural for secular rulers to intervene. Ultimately the acceptance or rejection of the Reformation was a political decision. Often the urban magistrates themselves had to determine what faith the inhabitants of their community would practise. But the distribution of political authority was frequently ambiguous, and even where it was not, the decision-making process was often subject to intense and conflicting pressures.

All across Europe urban populations were caught up in the initial excitement of the Reformation debate and urban leaders were rapidly pressed to take a stand. Nowhere was this more evident than in central Europe, where the lines of political authority were particularly unclear. Within a few years of the first articulation of Luther's doctrines, almost every city in Germany or Switzerland had a small cluster of clerical or lay enthusiasts who pressed for the adoption of Protestant principles. Support often came from the ranks of householding artisans, among whom anti-clericalism was strong and personal connections to the ecclesiastical hierarchy were weak. Urban magistrates were initially more hesitant to adopt Protestant ideas. Kinship and tradition often linked them to the monasteries and convents which the Reformers wanted to close; in addition, the magistrates were gravely concerned about how the city's overlord would react to religious changes. Yet many magistrates accepted the argument that their community's political and even spiritual welfare required a uniformity of religious allegiance. And the often intense pressure from below could not be ignored.

In the south German city of Ulm in 1530 the city council conducted a formal poll of all guild members and other adult male heads of households, who represented about 10 per cent of the city's total population. The council itself leaned towards Protestantism, but the voters were encouraged to speak their minds freely. Of the 1,865 votes cast and recorded, 1,621 were in favour of the Reformation and 243 were against. Only one nervous voter, a baker, refused to take a clear stand – the scrutineers recorded that 'he will support the mayor and council; we could not get anything else out of him'. The outcome of the poll settled the issue for the magistrates: within a few months the Catholic mass was replaced by Protestant forms of worship and the city closed down its monastic houses.[13]

The formal mechanism by which the citizenry of Ulm was consulted was unusual. But it was by no means rare for urban magistrates, in dealing with a matter of such grave consequence for the city's well-being, to be guided by the wishes of the community. Effective governance normally required some responsiveness to the council's

13. Specker, *Ulm*, 115–26.

core constituency of established male householders. The final decision, however, always lay with the authorities.

The process was not always smooth. In many cities in which the Reformation was introduced, there remained a cluster of inhabitants loyal to the old church – while there were others who felt the authorities had not gone far enough in their reforms. Quiet dissidents might be left in peace, but those who expressed their views too openly ran the risk of prosecution or even execution. Nor was the Reformation settlement always permanent. Many south German imperial cities – including Ulm – first became Protestant in the 1520s and 1530s despite the objections of their overlord, the Emperor Charles V. Then, after the Emperor's military victory over his Protestant opponents in the late 1540s, Catholic worship was re-introduced in these cities. But this lasted only a few years, until the next turn of the political wheel made possible a Protestant restoration.

Everywhere, in fact, the acceptance or rejection of new religious forms was a political question whose resolution ultimately depended on the attitude of secular leaders. Under the guidance of the great reformer John Calvin, the town of Geneva was said to have become, in John Knox's famous phrase, 'the most perfect school of Christ that ever was in the earth since the days of the Apostles'.[14] But the Genevan Reformation was in fact closely linked to the city's revolt against the political authority of the local bishop who was, in turn, a client of the dukes of Savoy. Despite Calvin's huge influence elsewhere in Europe, his reforms in Geneva could be carried out only with the assent of the magistrates, who were never content to agree supinely to all the measures he hoped to implement.[15]

All over Europe, in fact, magistrates during the Reformation era confronted conflicting pressures from inside and outside their communities. Sometimes members of the citizenry pressed for religious reforms while officials of the state demanded the repression of Protestantism. But the reverse was equally possible: the state could mandate reform while citizens tried to remain loyal to the traditional church. Nor was state policy itself necessarily constant or consistent. In England urban magistrates had to adapt to four radical shifts in religious orientation in less than thirty years. In the 1530s Henry VIII broke with the pope, asserted his religious supremacy and dissolved monasteries all over England, while still trying to preserve many

14. McNeill, *Calvinism*, 178.
15. Monter, *Calvin's Geneva*, 29–122.

traditional doctrines. Beginning in 1547, under his son Edward VI, a thoroughgoing Reformation on the continental model was introduced. When Edward's sister Mary became queen in 1553, Catholicism was restored. Five years later Elizabeth I re-established the Church of England on a Protestant basis. Each change required new local arrangements which urban magistrates were expected to implement.

The assumption that political leaders were entitled to determine religious policy was, in fact, so deep-seated in the sixteenth century – in England as elsewhere – that most magistrates and citizens could adapt to these changes with relative ease. To be sure, each shift in the tide invariably left a small residue of religious zealots who could not abandon the open expression of their faith and either had to go into exile or face martyrdom at home. Most town-dwellers, however, were more pragmatic in their response. In the northern English town of York, for example, a nostalgic loyalty to the traditional church remained strong and the accession of Mary I was generally welcomed. But the magistrates were cautious. When ordered to celebrate their city's return to the papal fold, the council worded their proclamation vaguely, thanking God in general terms for his 'mercifulness now and all times'. Many citizens were equally prudent. One shrewd benefactor bequeathed a sumptuous priestly vestment to a local chapel but specified that the garment should revert to his family if the use of such robes went out of fashion again. Another left funds to endow Catholic-style prayers for the dead – but they were to be continued only as long as the laws of the realm would not deem such practices 'superstitious or ungodly'. Such attitudes were by no means uncommon.[16]

Prudence and caution could, however, give way to short-lived bursts of passionate religious feeling, often tinged with violence. Such episodes of intense collective religiosity had, after all, long been a feature of European life. Now they received a powerful new impetus from the events of the Reformation.

Frequently it was preaching which triggered religious violence. Medieval preachers had generally directed religious energy inward, inspiring their hearers to pinnacles of penitential self-denial. Some medieval preaching, however, had stirred up hostility against alien religious groups: in the late middle ages, for example, in many communities a cycle of virulent anti-semitic preaching led to the persecution or banishment of the Jews. When a fundamental division arose within Christendom in the sixteenth century, new targets for

16. Palliser, *Tudor York*, 241–3.

incendiary preaching obviously lay close at hand. In the summer of 1566, for example, Calvinist preachers launched a great campaign of religious agitation in the Netherlands – an area already unsettled by political resentment against the regime of the king of Spain, who also ruled the Low Countries. The preachers' attacks against Catholic practices such as the veneration of saints unleashed a wave of iconoclastic activity: in town after town, small bands of committed Protestants – aided, in a few cases, by hired thugs – invaded churches to destroy statues and other images.[17] These disturbances helped to precipitate the long conflict known as the revolt of the Netherlands, but the actual wave of rioting lasted only a few weeks. It would scarcely have lasted even as long as that were it not for the helplessness of urban magistrates who received neither military support nor clear instructions from the royal government.[18]

Religious riots, like all riots, were normally short-lived, their energy spent in any one place within a matter of days. Where governments were weak, however, there could emerge a cycle of recurrent riots in which each outburst of violence contributed to resentments that would feed the next outbreak. Nowhere was this more obviously the case than in France during the civil wars of the late sixteenth century. For almost forty years, from 1562 to 1598, religious conflicts between Catholics and Protestants were reinforced and sustained by the political struggle of great noble factions whose competition rendered the monarchy almost helpless. Individual towns were also divided into Protestant and Catholic factions; often the municipal elite was religiously split. In the absence of effective mechanisms for establishing and defending an official religious settlement, groups of Catholic or Protestant citizens would consider themselves justified in imposing their own solutions, at least on a short-term basis. Inflamed preaching often precipitated rioting – as did religious processions and festivities, conspicuous events which the other side often considered offensive. Protestants and Catholics were equally likely to launch the violence, but the actual character of religious brutality could take on different forms which subtly reflected theological differences between the confessions. Protestant mobs were most inclined to attack the Catholics' devotional images and ritual objects, whose veneration they regarded as idolatry. When Protestant brutality extended to persons, the victims were likely to be members of the Catholic clergy, whose claims to unique sacral status were so

17. Parker, *Dutch Revolt*, 72–9.
18. ibid., 79–81.

offensive to the Protestant mind. Catholics, by contrast, were willing to attack Protestants of any age or calling, for in their view every adherent of the false creed had contributed equally to undermining the age-old unity of the church.[19]

Sacked churches, murdered priests and disembowelled babies all made a huge impression on contemporaries. The details were recorded in martyrologies which circulated among members of each confession, shaping and reinforcing their religious allegiances. But accounts of confessional violence can distort our perception of the real character of urban religion in sixteenth- and seventeenth-century Europe. For every instance of religious violence in European towns, in fact, there were many more cases in which religious passions were kept from boiling over. Even in France at the height of the civil wars, there were towns in which Catholic and Protestant magistrates ignored their religious differences in order to work together on some other project, such as reorganizing educational institutions or protecting the town as a whole from military occupation.[20] In many towns with an established religion, especially in central and northwestern Europe, inhabitants with divergent religious views were quietly tolerated so long as they kept to themselves and confined their worship to private homes. In late sixteenth-century Strasbourg the Lutheran clergy persistently pressed the city council to impose precise professions of faith on the citizens – but the magistrates insisted that adherence to a few basic tenets would be quite sufficient. Religious dissidents were tolerated if they remained quiet; only if they became too obvious would they be banished. Yet even in Strasbourg there were limits. In 1569 a drunken soldier muttered that Christ would not have been crucified unless he had done something to deserve it. This was unacceptable. The soldier was arrested, tried and beheaded.[21]

Everywhere the main concern of the magistrates was to have a single official church that would at least encompass all but the most stubborn members of the community. Yet it was possible for Catholicism and Protestantism to be openly practised in a single state – though without being precisely equal in status. By the Edict of Nantes, which brought the French civil wars to a close in 1598, Protestantism was formally recognized as a minority religion, and its adherents were permitted to occupy over 100 towns as their own strongholds. There were also some cities in Europe in which

19. Davis, *Society and Culture*, 152–87.
20. cf. Konnert, 'Urban Values'.
21. Abray, *People's Reformation*, 175–85, 194.

members of different religious groups could worship openly in separate churches. Under the Peace of Augsburg of 1555, the rulers of princely states and imperial cities throughout the Holy Roman Empire had been assured of the right to determine whether their subjects would be Catholic or Lutheran. In a few imperial cities – including Augsburg itself – the political balance made it impossible to impose a single faith. Though relations between the two confessions in such cities always remained troubled, both Catholics and Protestants maintained churches and worshipped freely in public. It was even possible for services of two confessions to take place in the same church building. This unusual situation emerged in the imperial city of Wetzlar. The great collegiate church of Wetzlar was also used as the city's main parish church; according to arrangements carefully negotiated in the course of the middle ages, the canons worshipped in the choir while the parishioners worshipped, at different hours, in the nave. During the Reformation Wetzlar became Protestant, but neither the city nor the chapter would relinquish its rights to the church. Out of the ensuing stalemate emerged a pattern of staggered services which persists to the present day, with the Catholic mass celebrated in the choir as of old and Protestant services conducted in the nave.[22]

Of course such anomalies were rare. By the end of the sixteenth century, in fact, the basic pattern of religious allegiances had largely been settled, and the great majority of town-dwellers in Europe were likely to dwell, work and worship only in proximity to people of their own faith. In Spain and Italy, religious non-conformity had been sternly repressed and urban populations were overwhelmingly Catholic. In the Lutheran lands of the Baltic region, monoconfessional towns were equally prevalent. Across the rest of Europe, depending on the choices made by local or national rulers, towns were predominantly Catholic or Protestant but minority groups might attempt to follow their own creeds with varying degress of furtiveness.

Certainly there were distinct differences in the texture of religious life in Catholic and Protestant towns. In Catholic towns, above all, the sheer numbers of resident clergy were always larger than in Protestant communities of a comparable size. The great movement of religious revival and reform known as the Catholic Reformation stimulated the founding of new and more ascetic or more militant religious orders: Theatines, Ursulines, Capuchins and above all Jesuits were added to the existing array of monks, nuns and friars. Religious processions continued to course through the streets of every Catholic

22. Schoenwerk, *Wetzlar*, 208–9, 224–7.

city. Confraternities were as vital as ever, though their composition had begun to change: brotherhoods based on membership in a guild lost some of their importance as the clergy encouraged the formation of new confraternies whose members were expected to join solely as an expression of religious devotion. The veneration of ritual objects continued to shape everyday life, and not only in the confined spaces of churches and chapels. As the priest and his acolytes hurried through the streets of a Catholic town to administer the sacrament to a dying parishioner, every passer-by genuflected before the consecrated wafer.

The Protestant town had fewer clergy. Monastic institutions disappeared: some of the religious had been driven from their cloisters at the height of the Reformation; more left willingly or let themselves be pensioned off; a few were permitted to linger on in their decaying abbeys until they died off. By the end of the sixteenth century all were gone, their monasteries and convents long since converted to other uses. Sometimes cathedral chapters and collegiate churches continued to function, especially if the canons were from well-connected families. But they normally had little impact on the life of the community. The variety of physical venues for religious expression typical of Catholic towns was not maintained in Protestant communities. Protestant religious life was generally confined to home and parish church. The church buildings themselves were often more spare, reflecting the Protestant distrust of images and other physical aids to devotion. Street-corner shrines and chapels disappeared. Confraternities were disbanded. The traditional cycle of saints' days and religious festivals was scaled down or even reduced to the simple alternation of sabbath and weekdays. The very streets lost much of their religious coloration. The huge religious processions that remained so typical of Catholic religiosity had no place in the Protestant scheme of indoor devotion. In lieu of the old array of male and female religious in their white, grey, brown and black robes, there was now only the company of pastors in their sober black.

These differences in ecclesiastical organization and devotional style meant that the more tangible aspects of religious life in Protestant and Catholic towns had little in common. But this must not obscure the fact that the role of religious authorities remained largely constant despite confessional differences. In Protestant and Catholic towns alike, religion could offer consolation to the weak, but the church as an institution remained an instrument of power for the strong. This power was always exercised in close collaboration with the secular authorities: jurisdictional quarrels, which were common enough, never undermined the shared commitment by clerical and secular officials to maintain public order and deference for superior authority. The structure of power-sharing differed, of course. In Reformed communities pastors and laymen sat together on consistories which determined crucial aspects of church policy and judged cases of irreligious or immoral behaviour. Elsewhere the formal structures of ecclesiastical and secular authority tended to remain more discrete. But everywhere in Europe it was ultimately the state which determined the form of worship and the rights of the church. Even the Inquisition, the uniquely powerful instrument by which the Catholic hierarchy attempted to suppress religious non-conformity, could operate effectively only where the state authorities concurred. Clerical deference towards political authority was never absolute: political policies might be criticized, and a few bold theologians – Protestant and Catholic alike – defended the theory that conscience could, in extreme cases, justify resistance to a tyrannical ruler. But such declarations were risky and rare. What normally came from the pulpit was a prayer for the ruler and a reminder that governmental authority was ordained by God.

Nothing that happened in the sixteenth century undermined the fundamentally masculine aspect of power in the church. This is important to emphasize, because some historians have speculated as to whether the Protestant Reformation was a liberating experience for women, especially in cities.[23] Certainly many individual women – like men – were caught up in the initial excitement of the Reformation, and shared in the sense of liberation from the ritualized burdens of the late medieval church. Some specific categories of women experienced a significant change in their personal status as a result of the Protestant rejection of monastic life and clerical celibacy. For nuns who had been placed unwillingly in the convent, the Reformation offered freedom. But for every nun who welcomed the chance to abandon the cloister, there were others who balked at leaving a cherished way of life in which they had experienced some measure of autonomy. Women who had lived with priests as their concubines were now permitted to marry their menfolk – but their status was still cloudy and their children might still be regarded as illegitimate.[24]

The Reformation certainly encouraged religious devotion among women – but so had the old church. Even more than Catholicism, Protestantism emphasized that religious leadership by females should

23. Davis, *Society and Culture*, 65–95; see also Ozment, *When Fathers Ruled*, 9–25.
24. Roper, *Holy Household*, 19–20.

be confined to the household. The few women who attempted to preach in public were sternly repressed by the Protestant authorities. Indeed, by eliminating celibacy and virginity as religious ideals, Protestantism sharply reduced the varieties of religious expression available to women. The Reformation's emphasis on home and family meant there was no role in Protestantism for a Mari Díaz, who had in fact resisted an offer of marriage so as to remain celibate and pursue her personal vocation. Certainly the Reformation as a whole was in no sense a liberating movement for women. But then again, it was scarcely liberating for men either. After the first great flush of intense enthusiasm, Protestantism simply became a different model for the organization and expression of religious values. Protestants were exposed more intensively than Catholics to the words of Scripture, but they were scarcely encouraged to draw their own conclusions. In 1521, at the Diet of Worms, Martin Luther had rejected the authority of popes and church councils in favour of the voice of his own conscience, held 'captive to the Word of God'.[25] But this was never intended as encouragement for ordinary people to put forward their private interpretations of Scripture. In fact, once the new churches were established, generations of Protestant children were subjected to thorough instruction, often by means of Luther's own Shorter Catechism, so that all would know exactly what the word of God meant and how they should apply it in their daily lives.[26]

IV

The religious balance that had evolved by the late sixteenth century did not remain static. In France the special political rights of Protestants were eliminated in the 1620s and their remaining religious rights were destroyed by Louis XIV half a century later. Behind the revocation of the Edict of Nantes in 1685 lay the king's determination to make his realm religiously homogeneous. Yet at the same time, ironically enough, other policies of the French crown had precisely the opposite effect: the step-by-step detachment of most of Alsace and Lorraine from the Holy Roman Empire and the integration of these territories into the French kingdom required, at times, the promise that existing religious rights would be honoured. Thus cities like Colmar and Strasbourg became predominantly Protestant enclaves within Catholic France.

During the first half of the seventeenth century, Protestantism

25. Bainton, *Here I Stand*, 185.
26. Strauss, *Luther's House of Learning*, esp. part 2.

was crushed in some parts of the Holy Roman Empire, especially in those areas directly ruled by ardently Catholic princes such as the rulers of Bavaria. The Habsburgs did likewise in most of the lands under their direct control, such as Austria and Bohemia. Yet attempts by the Habsurg Emperors to exploit their imperial status to promote Catholicism in the Empire as a whole were less successful. The peace of Augsburg had established that the religious complexion of each principality or imperial city would be determined by its ruler. There was no shortage of ambiguous cases that led to legal disputes or armed conflict. The Thirty Years War which began in 1618 involved countless attempts to redraw the religious map of central Europe. Yet the Peace of Westphalia which brought the war to a close in 1648 confirmed the basic principle laid down almost a century earlier: the Empire continued to be a patchwork of Catholic and Protestant territories.

Some of the most violent religious conflicts of the seventeenth century were in fact not between the Protestants and Catholics but among Protestants themselves. In England the Elizabethan settlement of 1558 began to unravel as various groups within the church not only pursued new styles of personal devotion which drew strongly on the Reformed tradition but also demanded a form of public worship and structures of religious organization which the leadership of the English church could not accept. The Puritans, to use an inevitable if adequate term, hoped to rid the English church of what they perceived as remnants of Catholicism, including the existence of bishops. For the first four decades of the seventeenth century most Puritans continued to function within the Church of England. Occasionally they secured control of specific parishes, but more often they maintained a formal membership in existing parishes while also attending separate services which offered preaching and worship in the style they preferred. This awkward situation broke down in the 1640s when England was plunged into a civil war from which a coalition of forces including most of the major Puritan groups emerged victorious. But the republican system of government established by Oliver Cromwell in 1649, which in fact amounted to rule by a single religious faction, was ultimately unable to sustain its authority. The restoration of royal government in 1660 brought back the Church of England, bishops and all. Those who tried to remain faithful to Puritan traditions were now reduced to non-conformists subject to punishments and penalties.

All these conflicts on the national or international level could have a profound impact on the religious life of individual towns. Where, as in England, different tendencies within Protestantism were often encompassed within a single community, control of the municipal government might shift between religious factions in direct or indirect response to developments on the national level. This, in turn, would lead to changes in the organization of religious life to which most, though never all, of the inhabitants would quietly accede. On the continent some communities faced an even starker choice: pressure to convert from one major confession to the other. By the seventeenth century the distinctions between Protestantism and Catholicism had hardened to the point where conversions from one faith to the other were strongly resisted, and the attempt was usually avoided. But where the reversal of a community's religious pattern was attempted with sufficient pressure, it could certainly succeed.

The small town of Amberg, capital of the Upper Palatinate in southern Germany, was a case in point. Previously ruled by the Protestant prince of the Palatinate, this region was acquired by the ardently Catholic duke of Bavaria in the early phases of the Thirty Years War. In 1628, once his legal claim to the region had been secured, the Bavarian ruler ordered all inhabitants of the region to convert within half a year. If they refused, they were to emigrate from the Upper Palatinate – an alternative that would have been unwelcome at any time and even more unpalatable in the midst of war. Once the decree had been issued, the head of each family in Amberg was polled as to the household's intention. The results were mixed: 172 families agreed to convert, 245 families refused, and 299 families said they needed more time to consider. There is little doubt that most of the waverers eventually came around. One member of the city council, Georg Pöck, unburdened himself with particular candour. He did not want to emigrate simply for religious reasons, he said. He had been attending Catholic sermons and did not find them objectionable. There were, however, still some points he wanted to have explained. In any case he did not want to become known as the first council member to convert – but if the city's mayors led the way, he would be willing to accommodate. Two of the city's *Bürgermeister* stoutly refused to abandon their ancestral faith. But a third one assured the duke's officials that he had long been studying Catholic books in secret, and though he was still unclear on some points of doctine he was more than willing to convert. So he did – and so did Pöck.[27]

27. Ambronn and Fuchs, *Oberpfalz*, 41–8.

Choices like these, when they had to be made, were never easy and could indeed be agonizing. But the need for such decisions also became increasingly rare. By the end of the seventeenth century, the overwhelming majority of European towns had long since settled into an established religious identity. Many communities – especially Protestant ones – harboured religious minorities, but the fundamental religious complexion of a town was firmly fixed. Indeed, the differences in character between Protestant and Catholic communities, already evident by the end of the sixteenth century, were elaborated and hardened in the course of the next hundred years.

We can grasp these differences more clearly if we take a close look at the religious life of two communities – one Catholic, one Protestant – towards the end of the seventeenth century. The towns we shall examine are the Catholic city of Lille, on the northern frontier of France, and the Protestant town of Aberdeen, on the northeast coast of Scotland.[28]

Both towns experienced major political upheavals in the course of the seventeenth century. Lille, which lay in the Spanish Netherlands, was conquered by the French in 1667 and rapidly incorporated into the French kingdom. The new regime, however, did not bring about any major religious changes. Indeed, when the city submitted to the French, one clause in the formal articles of surrender specifically promised that Catholicism would be preserved and 'liberty of conscience would not be permitted'. The most immediate religious impact of the French victories in 1667 was that now the king of France would appoint the bishop of Tournai in whose diocese Lille lay.

Aberdeen's political history in these years was also unsettled. Scotland, though a separate kingdom, had shared a common ruler with England since 1603 and was deeply involved in the political upheavals which eventually culminated in the execution of King Charles I. Much of the tension, of course, related to religious issues. Since 1560 the Church of Scotland had been run on presbyterian lines which accorded laymen a major role in church government. The Stuart kings had superimposed bishops on this system, but in 1638, over royal objections, the Scottish bishops were deposed. The civil wars soon followed. During the 1640s Aberdeen was repeatedly captured and recaptured by rival armies; in the 1650s it was occupied by English troops of the Cromwellian regime.

28. The material in the following paragraphs is based on Lottin, *Chavatte*, esp. 199–258, and DesBrisay, 'Authority and Discipline', esp. ch. 5.

Meanwhile the Aberdeen church had fallen under the control of a rigidly Presbyterian faction. The restoration of the monarchy in 1660 brought about the re-establishment of bishops in Scotland – but only for thirty years, until the Revolution of 1688–89 swept bishops away again and restored the Presbyterian system once and for all. Yet throughout this period, whether under the episcopal or the Presbyterian system, it was the city council that really ran the church in Aberdeen. The council not only paid the ministers' salaries but appointed them as well – though between 1660 and 1690 the bishop had to confirm the appointments.

To serve the religious needs of its 7,500 inhabitants, Aberdeen was supposed to have four ministers. At times, in fact, the city had only two or three. Aberdeen was an unpopular posting and many ministers declined the job. Nor did the city always try aggressively to fill the vacancies, for it was cheaper to hire village pastors or theology students as substitute ministers at lower wages. Some additional religious leadership, however, was provided by the professors of divinity at the two colleges which made up the small university of Aberdeen. And of course much religious life was centred on the home. Domestic prayers and Bible reading were encouraged in the Protestant tradition and in some homes, no doubt, they were ardently practiced.

Lille was much larger than Aberdeen. Its population in the late seventeenth century was about 45,000. To meet the inhabitants' spiritual needs, the city had a large number of religious personnel – at least 1,200, in fact. In 1695 the city's seven parish churches had 213 priests, chaplains and other clerics. There were about thirty monasteries, nunneries and other religious houses in Lille, with well over 1,000 inmates. Only some of the monks and nuns lived entirely cloistered lives. Nuns were often involved in charitable activity. Members of the male religious orders were highly conspicuous in the community, preaching sermons, hearing confessions and helping organize the ever-popular processions in honour of Mary and the saints.

Formal religious life in Aberdeen, as in most Protestant towns, offered much less variety. Many of the ministers were vigorous controversialists, a fact which must have been reflected in their sermons. Yet even when Presbyterian-minded ministers were ousted in favour of episcopal ones or vice versa, the actual form of Sunday services remained almost unchanged. An important element of religious diversity, however, was provided by the presence of two important minority groups. For over a century Aberdeen had housed a small and generally quiescent Catholic community. From time to time, reminded of the Catholic presence, the town's ministers would agitate for a campaign of repression – but the magistrates invariably dragged their feet. The Catholics of Aberdeen had protectors among some of the powerful gentlemen of the surrounding countryside whom the magistrates were loath to antagonize. Beginning in the 1660s, however, a second religious minority emerged in Aberdeen: the Quakers. Though an offshoot of Protestantism, Quakers challenged the fundamental assumptions of Protestant thought by relegating the importance of Scripture behind the guidance of a personal 'inner light'. The Quakers' rejection of all forms of social hierarchy – including their famous refusal to tip their hats to any social superior – was alarming to clergy and magistrates alike. Thus the Quakers were far more aggressively persecuted than Catholics in late seventeenth-century Aberdeen. In the 1670s a struggle erupted over the Quakers' attempt to establish a separate burial ground, as this, in the magistrates' eyes, would imply a recognition of the Quakers' status as a distinct religious community. Over the course of five years, the bodies of seven Quakers were exhumed from the illegal burial ground and reinterred in the official churchyard. Living Quakers were persecuted with scarely less vigour.

Sectarian divisions of this sort were unknown in Lille. The only Protestants ever seen in the city were occasional mercenary soldiers, and sustained attempts were even made to convert them. But the solid Catholicism of the community did not imply any lack of diversity in belief or practice; nothing, in fact, could be more misleading than an image of Catholicism as a monolithic religion whose members all took their cue from Rome. Nor were religious disputes confined only to the clergy, for members of the laity often followed theological debates with avid interest. Over the centuries, for example, Catholic thinkers had engaged in repeated controversies about the immaculate conception of the Virgin Mary. When the Franciscan Recollects won a new round of debates on the doctrine against the Dominicans in 1665, their success was seen as a cause for celebration among those inhabitants of Lille who were particularly devoted to the cult of the Virgin. A grand procession was held and a new Confraternity of the Immaculate Conception was organized. In the 1670s the new bishop of Tournai, an eminent churchman deeply influenced by the austere Jansenist movement, tried to impose more controls on the ever-popular friars, whom he considered inadequately trained, and warned his flock against excessive reliance on prayers to Mary and the saints. His pastoral letters, however, were received with widespread resistance in Lille. Dedication to the popular tradition of religious expression was visibly stronger than respect for the ecclesiastical hierarchy.

In fact laypeople were deeply involved in organizing the religious life of both communities. Not only were ministers appointed by the city council in Aberdeen, but also crucial decisions were made by the kirk-session, which included both the ministers and a large number of laymen, including many of the magistrates. Though the kirk-session was in fact a consistory on the Calvinist model, it remained in force throughout the years when the Church of Scotland included the very unCalvinistic office of bishops. The kirk-session was chiefly concerned to impose 'godly discipline' on the community, both indirectly, by distributing charitable relief to those it considered worthy, and directly, by punishing those visibly guilty of sin – especially transgressions of a sexual nature.

In Lille sin was handled by the clergy alone: as in all Catholic communities, parishioners were to confess at regular intervals and were granted absolution by the priest. But laymen were deeply involved in aspects of church administration: magistrates controlled the use of church buildings in the city, regulated the number of clerics who could settle in Lille, and supervised the educational and welfare institutions which were staffed by members of the clergy. In addition each parish had a board of churchwardens appointed by the magistrates to maintain the church building and manage the parish budget.

Purely religious initiatives often came from the parishioners themselves. In 1669 a group of gardeners and other poor inhabitants of the parish of Saint Sauveur took up a collection to found a new confraternity in honour of St Paulinus of Nola, who was regarded as the patron saint of gardeners. In 1685, after fifteen years of successful operation, the confraternity decided to enhance its status by securing an appropriate relic. With considerable effort, a suitable object was obtained from Rome and in July 1686 a week's worth of solemn ceremonies in the church of Saint Sauveur celebrated the safe arrival of the thigh bone of St Paulinus. It was a moment of glowing pride for the poor parishioners – mostly gardeners or their friends from equally humble occupations – whose own efforts had, in their eyes, successfully enhanced the sanctity of their parish and their city.

This would never have happened in Aberdeen, of course. By the late seventeenth century, the divergence of devotional styles which had already sharply distinguished Protestant and Catholic communities soon after the Reformation had become, if anything, even more pronounced. Yet there was much that bound the inhabitants of these two cities, and indeed all European towns of the seventeenth century, into a common pattern. Above all there was the central importance of religion in the life of the community. Priests and ministers alike might fulminate against their parishioners' irreverent attitudes or their ignorance of doctrine or their tendency to slip into taverns during hours of worship, but nowhere before the eighteenth century would one have found any more than a handful of people for whom the Christian religion was not a fundamental aspect of their identity. Everywhere, in fact, people considered religion something much too important to be left to the clergy. Municipal authorities were as eager in the seventeenth century as they had been two centuries earlier to influence or control church policies and clerical appointments. Even humbler sections of the laity always included some people whose religious devotion matched or even exceeded that of the most ardent clerics. In Protestant communities there was always the allure of alternative denominations or breakaway sects. In Catholic communities contact with alternative religions was rare and fraught with danger, but the dominant religion itself offered countless opportunities for men and women to shape their own devotional style.

The major focus of organized religious life was always the parish. A few marginal people – immigrants, vagrants, beggars or members of religious sects – certainly escaped the attention of the parish authorities. In a few of the most rapidly expanding cities of Europe, by the early eighteenth century, the number of people who fell outside the purview of the parish system may have slowly increased. But in European urban life as a whole, cases like these were still highly anomalous. For most townspeople in Europe, throughout the early modern period the most important influence on their system of values was always the Christian religion and the most important institution in their everyday lives was always the church.

CHAPTER FOUR

Production and Exchange

Few people in seventeenth-century London can have been quite so obsessed with religion as Nehemiah Wallington of Philpot Lane in the parish of St Leonard's Eastcheap. Wallington was one of the 'godly', someone who exemplified in extreme form the intense spirituality of the Puritan movement. In the course of his lifetime – he died in 1658, at the age of 60 – Wallington composed about 20,000 pages of spiritual meditations which he collected in fifty handwritten notebooks. From the few volumes which survive today, we know that he spent hours every day in prayer, reading and reflection. But these were stolen moments. For Nehemiah Wallington passed most of his time – typically about twelve hours a day – in his workshop, plying his trade. Wallington was a turner, who earned a living by making chair legs, tool handles, bowls and other rounded wooden objects on a lathe. He hated his work and, not surprisingly, he was not very good at it. He garbled his accounts, got cheated by journeymen, fell into debt – but he never stopped working.[1]

In his obsessive religiosity, Wallington was unusual – in some ways he had more in common with a Mari Díaz than with most of his own contemporaries in seventeenth-century London. But in other ways he was entirely typical of his age. For the men and women of the early modern town passed most of their waking hours earning a living – or trying to do so. The range of different income-generating activities in the early modern city was huge. Some work – like Wallington's – was carried out as part of an organized trade whose practices were closely controlled by law and custom. Much other work was irregular and unregulated. But only a small number of people could

1. Seaver, *Wallington's World*, 1–13, 112–42.

support themselves without having to engage, six days a week, for decade after decade, in physically demanding labour in the houses, shops, streets and markets of the early modern city.

Economic activity in the city took place within the framework of a European economic system whose basic parameters were fully developed by the end of the middle ages. This system was never static, of course. Some crucial transformations took place during the early modern era: new types of commercial undertakings emerged, new ways of organizing labour or producing goods were pioneered, new products were created and marketed. But at the same time, many important aspects of the European economic system remained remarkably stable until the end of the eighteenth century. And many of these more conservative aspects of economic life related specifically to the city.

As in many societies, there were obvious differences between the predominant forms of urban and rural activity. Villages were naturally engaged more extensively in primary-sector production of agricultural goods, while urban production centred more strongly on secondary-sector manufacture of finished goods. But this distinction was never absolute: agricultural products were grown in cities, and crafted goods were produced in villages. In fact a more significant distinction between the urban and rural economies had to do with something else: the relative importance of exchange transactions in the two settings.

The steady expansion of market relations in the rural economy is an important theme in the history of early modern Europe. The commercialization of rural life was especially apparent in north-western Europe, but no region was quite untouched. Yet even so, in most of Europe until the end of the *ancien régime* the dominant type of transaction in the rural economy was something that might best be described as appropriation: the unremunerated transfer of a large portion of the agricultural product or its monetary equivalent from the primary producers to more powerful members of society.[2] These transfers – in the form of dues to a seigneur, rent to a landlord, repayments to a creditor, tithes to the church or taxes to the state – were so strongly rooted in tradition and so firmly upheld by law that they only rarely had to be secured by force.[3] Not everything produced

2. 'Appropriation' is an important concept in Marxist thought (where it is closely related to 'surplus extraction'), but the term is used here in a broader sense and not as a technical usage of Marxist analysis.
3. cf. Goubert, *Ancien Régime*, 122–34.

in the rural community was, of course, transferred in this manner. A certain portion of agricultural product was always withheld by the peasant producer to sustain his or her household and to provide seed for the coming year. Furthermore, even after all obligations were met, there was sometimes a surplus that could be conveyed to the market. But the appropriation of a large part of the agricultural product by those with social power was always a fundamental aspect of rural life.

The urban economy was different. Of course appropriation of product affected cities as well – though it could cut both ways. The urban economy lost wealth through appropriation, notably in the form of taxes or forced loans levied by the state; but on the other hand, urban landlords and creditors were among those who gained wealth through appropriation from the rural economy. Yet what primarily distinguished the urban from the rural economy was the fact that so many more of the goods produced within the city were transferred not by appropriation but by exchange. By this we mean the transfer of goods, services or labour in return for something else of value, usually in the form of money. Unlike appropriation – which involves an uneven transfer founded on an acute imbalance of power – exchange normally involves a considerable element of mutual advantage for both partners. Of course exchange in the early modern city, as in our own society, was never completely free, never subject only to what we would call the laws of the marketplace. Custom, tradition, regulation by the authorities, and occasionally even coercion played a role in setting prices and determining the conditions under which goods, services or labour could be sold. But even so, exchange transactions which responded to market conditions were fundamental to the urban economy and involved a large part of the urban population. Of course exchange relations existed in the rural economy as well. But in much of rural Europe it was chiefly the beneficiaries of the system of appropriation – the seigneurs, landlords or creditors – who participated significantly in the market economy. In the city many more people did.

This had long been the case. Most European cities had been granted the right to hold markets at an early stage in their history. This, in turn, had stimulated the development of an economic system in which exchange as a whole played a fundamental role. The right of the primary producer in the urban economy to sell his own product, though occasionally undermined in practice, remained one of the most cherished principles of European urban life until the end of the *ancien régime*. Of course not all who laboured in the city were understood to hold this right: it pertained above all to the male heads of households. Subordinate members of the household – family members, journeymen, apprentices and servants – primarily supported the master's work. At times a master's wife might be engaged in separate economic activities, but her income was generally used to sustain the household as a whole. The economically autonomous household, headed by a master or his widow, was the core institution of urban society. Ineffectual as he was, Nehemiah Wallington remained an independent craftsman and shopkeeper all his life, buying raw materials and a few finished goods from chapmen, making implements on the lathe, and retailing his wares to the small stream of customers who chanced into his shop. He was, in fact, the archetypal economic actor of the early modern city, representing a way of working and earning a living which remained remarkably stable for centuries on end.

I

Both the types of goods made in the city and the methods by which they were produced remained highly constant throughout the early modern period. This was not for any lack of interest in new products or new methods of production. The potential benefits of technological change were often recognized. Some new techniques were, in fact, introduced, in fields as varied as stocking-knitting, ribbon-making and the manufacture of nails.[4] In most fields of urban production, however, it proved impossible to move significantly beyond the technological level that had already been reached by the end of the middle ages. The reason was simple: most of what could be done with the existing sources of power – human and animal muscles, water flow and wind – had to a large extent already been discovered and applied.

Technological innovation did occur in a few significant fields. The movable-type technology of printing pioneered by Johannes Gutenberg in the mid-fifteenth century suddenly created a more easily reproducible form of written text. The ensuing diffusion of things to read and resulting increase in the demand for reading skills unquestionably contributed to the steady growth of literacy, especially in cities.[5] A second significant area of innovation involved a series of refinements in the use of gunpowder, which made possible the simultaneous creation of more powerful and more portable instruments of firepower – from ever more effective cannons down

4. De Vries, *Economy of Europe*, 90–4.
5. See Houston, *Literacy*, esp. 137–45.

to muskets, rifles and revolvers. This not only affected the way in which warfare was conducted, but also changed the way in which cities were designed: the new bastion rings which began to girdle European cities in the sixteenth century were a response to the development of cannons against which traditional city walls offered little effective defence.[6] A third area of continuing innovation had to do with shipbuilding. Steady improvements in construction and design led to the development of ever larger and more seaworthy vessels. As an industry, of course, shipbuilding was confined to coastal cities. But improvements in the seagoing capacity of Portuguese, Spanish, Dutch, English, French and Scandinavian ships, along with firearms, facilitated both the European conquest of the Americas and the European incursion into Asian trading networks – all of which had substantial effects on the economy of the continent as a whole.

Of these three crucial areas of technological innovation, however, only one – firepower – involved the exploitation of a new source of energy. And even this had its limits: gunpowder could be effectively harnessed in no other way than to permit the swift projection of missiles. Printing, like handwriting, was still based on human muscle power. And ships continued to depend on wind; even the most impressively crafted vessels could be idle for weeks if the winds were blowing in the wrong direction. Until steam power came to be systematically used in the later eighteenth century, the technology of production in Europe was largely based on principles that had become firmly established by the end of the middle ages.

Not only the methods of production but also the list of goods produced and type of work done in cities remained relatively stable during the early modern era. Of course new products came on to the market: printed matter, firearms, wigs. Useful instruments were developed: watches, telescopes, microscopes. There was constant innovation in the production of luxury goods. Meanwhile other products, such as armour, gradually disappeared. Individual communities often experienced dramatic shifts as the demand for certain goods collapsed and interest in other products emerged. But in the European urban economy taken as a whole the basic range of goods and services remained relatively unchanged.

Throughout the early modern era, four major spheres of activity occupied the overwhelming majority of urban producers: the processing of foodstuffs into consumable food; the manufacture of cloth and leather goods; the construction of houses and other buildings;

6. Parker, *Military Revolution*, 7–24.

and the making of tools and household objects. Each of these sectors, however, had countless sub-categories, for urban production was highly specialized. In many fields of production – especially in the textile industry – the process of manufacture was divided among numerous artisanal groups, each of which was responsible for completing one stage in the sequence of production. Take woollen textiles, for example: between the time it was sheared off a sheep and the time it finally draped a human body, the wool had to be combed or carded, spun, woven, fulled, dyed, dressed and tailored. Each one of these processes occupied different workers, who operated autonomously on their own premises and applied the long-established techniques of their own craft.[7] Some of these workers – notably the spinners – might be rural. Most of them were urban and determined to keep it that way.

For not only technical processes but also the organization of production tended to remain highly resistant to change during the early modern era. This was due largely to the role of two powerful institutions which structured production: the household and the guild. Both had functions that were more than economic, but their economic role was always fundamental – and their impact was generally conservative.

The household was the more fluid of these institutions, for its composition constantly underwent alteration due to life-cycle changes and accidents of birth and death. In most households a primary craft or trade was firmly entrenched, but often the household could not support its needs exclusively through the production and sale of a single type of product. Supplementary income might be secured by individual members of the household – often women – who engaged in retail activity or worked in service occupations. A craftsman's wife was expected to assist her husband in running his shop and supervising the servants. Yet at the same time she might sell foodstuffs from door to door, operate a market stall, make piecework goods at home, or work as a midwife.[8] Thus the members of, say, a weaver's household might well live by more than weaving alone. But that part of their activity which involved weaving itself would be significantly governed by the traditions and prescriptions of the guild. And the guild was usually a powerful retardant of change.

The guild system was one of the great creations of European

7. Well described by Deyon, *Amiens*, 179–92, and, with minor differences, by Gutmann, *Modern Economy*, 22–6.
8. Swanson, 'Craft Guilds'; Wiesner, *Working Women*, esp. 134–42.

medieval civilization.[9] The exact origins and initial purposes of the guilds are still subjects of conjecture and debate. By the end of the middle ages, however, guilds were firmly entrenched in virtually every European city. The details of guild structure and the precise range of guild activities varied enormously across the map of Europe. But some important features were almost universal, especially among those guilds which incorporated members of the artisanal crafts. Each guild normally linked together all the male masters who made a particular product or purveyed a particular service. One major purpose of the guild was to provide a framework for training new members by regulating each man's progression from apprentice to journeyman and then – in some cases – to independent master with a household of his own. Another key function was to enforce consistent standards of quality. But a major objective of almost every guild was also to protect the economic viability of its members, not only by controlling the admission of new masters but also by preventing non-members from engaging in production processes over which the guild claimed exclusive rights. Such aims could be achieved only in collaboration with the municipal government. In some towns the guilds participated directly in government through representation on the city council; in other places they were firmly excluded from a formal role in governing. Some city councils were far more beholden to guilds than others. But everywhere the guilds constituted powerful interest groups whose concerns could not be overlooked.

Many guilds engaged in periodic rituals to give public expression to the ideals of mutuality and solidarity among their members, and most guilds endorsed the notion of equal opportunity and economic autonomy for all masters. Yet the very tenacity with which guilds sometimes promoted these ideals reflected the fact that equality and autonomy were constantly being threatened by economic realities.

In the first place, the economic autonomy of the masters could be undermined by an oversupply of labour. Sometimes there were simply too many masters. But in addition, guild monopolies were often challenged by outsiders – interlopers who offered the same goods or services at a lower price. Illegal competition which arose within the town itself could usually be crushed by appealing to the municipal authorities. But rival craftsmen beyond the city walls were often harder to control – especially since they often worked for

9. For two recent surveys, the first stressing theory and the second stressing practice, see Black, *Guilds and Civil Society*, and Mackenney, *Tradesmen and Traders*.

powerful merchants or entrepreneurs who found villagers to be a cheaper and more flexible source of labour. The struggle against rural competition and other forms of rival labour was, in fact, a recurrent theme of guild history throughout the early modern era.[10] Inevitably the struggle led guilds to defend traditional practices with increased tenacity.

But economic autonomy could also be undermined by inadequate demand. A master's independence, after all, was most easily preserved if he could buy his raw materials and sell the finished product at consistent prices and at a steady pace, week after week, year after year. If demand slackened or collapsed, however, he might have to sell his goods at a loss and buy a new batch of supplies on credit – a situation that could rapidly drive him into economic dependence on someone with more capital or better commercial contacts. The main beneficiaries of this process were often the city's own merchants. Of course the merchants themselves had corporate organizations – their own guilds, in fact – but their interests were often thoroughly at odds with those of the craftsmen. Naturally it was the merchants who repeatedly pressed for the modification or elimination of restrictions championed by the craft guilds.

Yet guild solidarity could also be threatened by differences among the masters themselves. Only in theory were all members equal. In actual fact, accidents of marriage or inheritance or even simple differences in ability might lead to huge variations in wealth among the masters. Often the ensuing tensions led to conflicts which could not be settled within the guild but had to be thrust before the municipal authorities for adjudication. Rich masters would lobby for the right to produce more goods, introduce new products, or hire more workers. Poor masters would oppose innovation and insist that all guildsmen must be treated the same.

The fronts could change from time to time. Rich masters might side with their poorer brethren to protect guild traditions – or they might join with merchants in favouring innovation. But the fundamental issues were usually clear to all: economic freedom, favoured by the rich, would increase the output of the community as a whole while plunging poorer masters into economic dependency; restrictions and limitations, favoured by the poor, would promote greater equality but reduce total output. The magistrates generally struggled to find compromise solutions that would pacify all parties. But this merely

10. For a vivid example, see Poni, 'Norms and Disputes', 84–92.

pushed the problem temporarily aside. Sooner or later, the same issues might arise again.

The recurrent, almost cyclical nature of these problems is well illustrated by the case of Lille. During the 1560s, the authorities in Lille struggled mightily to satisfy competing interests in the light-cloth industry. Entrepreneurs were bending the existing rules by setting up large-scale weaving operations which used semi-skilled labour. To the fully trained masters, this was unfair competition. The magistrates eventually upheld the strict rules for admission to mastership and permitted no more than six looms in any one shop – so that, as the guild leaders demanded, 'everyone can have the means of earning a living without the least being crushed and oppressed by the advance of the most powerful'.[11] But a century later the magistrates were still grappling with the same issues. Early in the 1660s, certain rich masters and merchants introduced a new style of cloth which, they argued, was not covered by the established rules – so they tried to set up shops with more than six looms, operated by semi-skilled workers. Of course the established members of the weaving craft protested bitterly. After years of conflict, the magistrates reaffirmed the traditional rules but permitted certain exemptions – a compromise against which the weavers protested so violently that their agitation had to be suppressed by arrests and punishment.[12] The need to use force was, of course, a symptom of ineffective political management. But the fundamental tension between guild traditionalism and entrepreneurial pressures for deregulation was a recurrent structural problem of the urban economy – one that was played out in countless cities of the early modern era.

A final source of instability, however, could arise from within the artisanal household itself, in the potential for conflict between masters and their own journeymen. In theory all journeymen were supposed to be trained and socialized in anticipation of eventually becoming masters themselves. In fact many remained paid labourers throughout their careers. Blocked mobility and frustrated expectations inevitably led to tensions which undermined the solidarity of the craft as a whole. Often the journeymen formed organizations of their own to promote their interests, assist members in distress and organize work stoppages when any of them had been mistreated.[13] It was

11. DuPlessis, *Lille*, 108–14.
12. Lottin, *Chavatte*, 86–94.
13. Davis, 'Trade Union'; Farr, *Hands of Honor*, 64–75.

inevitable that whenever a substantial number of journeymen in any given trade saw their chances of advancement to mastership blocked, a more strained relationship was bound to emerge between them and their masters. Some historians have tended to regard this development as the product of a particular epoch or even as a specific landmark in the transition from pre-modern to modern forms of economic organization. Yet there is no agreement as to when this process took place. One historian traces it back to the fourteenth century; another places it predominantly in the eighteenth.[14] In fact journeymen's organizations were almost as old as the guild system itself. In central Europe these organizations date back at least to the fourteenth century; by the early fifteenth they had become so powerful in some parts of Germany that city governments banded together to block their activities.[15] In French towns *compagnonnages* were well organized by the sixteenth century and continued to function until the end of the *ancien régime*. But this did not mean journeymen were always a source of instability. When economic conditions were more favourable, relations could become more harmonious. Friction between journeyman and masters was not the product of a specific historical epoch; it was a recurrent structural problem inherent in the character of the guild system itself. And even when hostilities were acute, masters and journeymen continued to share powerful common interests: both groups might find their livelihood equally threatened by untrained workers or technical innovations. All members of a traditional craft were bound together by a strong incentive to preserve intact the customary forms of urban production.

Of course there were times when an enterprising merchant did succeed in restructuring the organization of production. Occasionally such an entrepreneur would succeed in concentrating previously separated stages of a production process in one shop under his full control. Ever since the middle ages, moreover, entrepreneurs in some cities had been able to introduce the putting-out system, under which previously independent masters were, in effect, reduced to hired hands using their own tools to work on materials owned by the merchant.[16] The putting-out system – also known as the domestic or *Verlag* system – was particularly prevalent in the textile trade, but in fact it could emerge in any field in which raw materials were hard to get and demand for the finished product was irregular and

14. Rice, *Foundations*, 48–9; Shorter, 'History of Work', 13.
15. Schulz, *Handwerksgesellen*, 68–97.
16. Furger, *Zum Verlagssystem*, esp. 1–75.

unpredictable. In sixteenth-century Nuremberg, for example, much of the metal-working and weapons industry was organized on the putting-out basis.[17] But as a whole such developments remained relatively rare in the early modern city – largely because they provoked such stout resistance from the masters and the guilds. Even in cities where economic conditions seemed ideal for the introduction of this system, it did not always get a footing. In the early seventeenth century, for example, the city of Augsburg had some of the poorest weavers and some of the richest merchants in Europe – a situation that almost invited the establishment of the putting-out system. Yet the laws which forbade *Verlag* in textile production were firmly upheld, except in the marginal field of silk-weaving.[18] Instead of fighting such entrenched forces within the city, many entrepreneurs found it easier to organize the putting-out system in the countryside, using the unskilled labour of peasant households. As a result some of the most dramatic changes in the organization of production – changes which eventually laid the groundwork for the development of disciplined factory labour in the industrial revolution – took place not in cities but in rural areas, where there were no urban guilds and municipal regulations to hinder the entrepreneur.[19] To the economic historian, the guild system and the guild mentality may look like obstacles to economic progress. To the social historian, however, they may look more like mechanisms for preserving a system under which adult male householders could continue to regard themselves, despite all differences in wealth, as sharing a common relationship to the means and methods of production.

II

Urban forms of production, then, remained highly conservative during the early modern era. It is when we turn our attention from production to another great economic function of the city – exchange – that we find more significant transformations. These changes were, of course, part of a broad European pattern. Both the geographical scope and the sheer volume of European trade expanded substantially – though not uninterruptedly – between 1450 and 1750. New ways of extending credit and organizing commercial activity were developed. The national state came to play a far more active role in organizing the economy and creating conditions to encourage investment. These and other developments have convinced many historians to see the early

17. Aubin, 'Formen und Verbreitung', 635–7.
18. Clasen, *Augsburger Weber*, 330–2.
19. Gutmann, *Modern Economy*, 63–7, 90–6.

modern era as an epoch of crucial transformation in the European economy.

Yet the basic mechanisms of exchange in the European urban economy had already been established by 1450. By the end of the middle ages the city had become firmly established as the locus for three different levels of exchange: local, regional and long-distance. Obviously the distinctions between these three levels were not always rigid. But each level had a distinct character. Local exchange was closely linked to production: to a large extent it was supposed to be handled by the primary producers themselves, with much of the activity taking place in their own shops. Regional exchange operated through the city's weekly or even more frequent markets, to which produce and other goods from the countryside could be bought and from which goods destined for distribution throughout the region were sold. Such markets could still involve direct participation by primary producers, selling their own wares or purchasing the supplies they needed. This was not the case, however, at the third level of exchange: long-distance trade. Here the primary producer was, at best, involved at only one end of the transaction.

Long-distance trade, the most risky but potentially the most profitable form of exchange, was facilitated by the great urban fairs which took place once or twice a year in certain cities – times at which goods from afar could be traded and, almost more importantly, contacts could be made and accounts could be settled. But the real key to the system was still the individual merchant. The basic premise of long-distance trade was, after all, quite simple: the merchant hoped to profit from the differential between the lower value of the goods at the point of source and their higher value at point of sale. But trade was associated with significant risks: uncertain supply, unreliable transportation and unpredictable demand. Centuries of experience had shown that the opportunities for profit were sufficiently high to make the risks worth facing. Even so, many merchants preferred to spread the risk by entering into partnerships, often limited to the duration of a particular venture: thus different merchants would pool some of their resources to finance the enterprise and would share the profits, if there were any, in proportion to what they had put in. Of course the stage at which merchants themselves had to travel personally to procure goods and accompany them back to the market had, by 1450, long since been superseded. Major merchants worked through agents, factors and middlemen.

The economy of cities had become thoroughly monetarized by the end of the middle ages. This does not just mean that goods, services and labour were normally paid for in cash. More importantly, it means that virtually all transactions were assigned a monetary value, even if no cash actually changed hands. The coins in actual circulation all over Europe were enormously varied in their provenance and metallic content. But major transactions were often recorded in a standardized money of account, against which exchange rates for specific currencies would be calculated. Long-distance trade was facilitated by letters of exchange: payment for goods might be made not in cash but with a letter promising reimbursement to the bearer in local funds from the purchaser's agent in a distant city.

By the late fifteenth century there were banks in many European cities, especially in the Low Countries in Italy.[20] They differed from modern banks, which make profits by accepting deposits on which they offer interest and then lending money out at even higher rates of interest. This simple system was rare in the late middle ages, less for economic than for theological reasons. Profits as such were considered morally acceptable, as long as they were generated in a venture which involved the risk of failure – but the church condemned the simple taking of interest at predetermined rates as the sin of usury. Thus banks normally did not engage in straightforward interest transactions. They could, however, perform numerous services for their customers – such as accepting deposits or extending loans with the understanding that a monetary 'gift' would express the recipient's gratitude for the use of the funds.[21] In particular, banks could make profits from foreign exchange transactions – which, being risky, were morally acceptable. These profits, in turn, might be used to finance new commercial ventures. The very emphasis on foreign exchange meant that some of the biggest banking operations, such as the great Medici bank of fifteenth-century Florence, had vast international connections.

The pursuit of profit emboldened merchants in the later middle ages to invest in ventures of enormous geographic scope. In the 1440s, for example, merchants from Dubrovnik in Dalmatia travelled to England and back – a round trip of over a year – in pursuit of woollen cloth to be sold in the Balkan hinterlands or the Levant.[22] This was, as it turned out, an adventure that was not often repeated: much more cloth came into Dubrovnik from Italy. But trade over vast distances could become entirely regularized. By the mid-fifteenth

20. Goldthwaite, 'Local Banking' and 'Medici Bank'.
21. Goldthwaite, 'Local Banking', 31–7.
22. Carter, *Dubrovnik*, 260.

century trade between southern France and the Baltic sea was so well organized that in 1468 a total of sixty ships arrived in Danzig carrying cargoes of salt and wine from French Atlantic ports.[23] The great seafaring achievements of the following centuries, which brought European ships to Asia and the Americas, built on a firmly established tradition of extensive voyaging within European waters.

Despite these foundations, however, there is no question that the three centuries from 1450 to 1750 brought about major changes both in the volume and in the methods of exchange in the European economy. These changes are often described in terms of the spread of capitalism; indeed, it is almost impossible for a historian to discuss the early modern economy without some reference to this concept. Yet it has proved quite impossible for historians to agree on what they actually mean by this intensely evocative term. To some, capitalism is simply the pursuit of profit. To others, following Max Weber, it is the pursuit of profit in a regular and rational manner, characterized by the application of strategies for maximizing gain by systematic reinvestment. Historians in the Marxist tradition define capitalism in specific terms as a mode of production in which the increased concentration of capital gives one class ever more control of the means by which goods are produced.[24] Yet to other analysts, capitalism is little more than a vague synonym for economic development.[25] To enter the lists and produce yet another definition would not be very useful. For in fact what is really important is not to specify what capitalism in the early modern era was, but to make clear what it was not.

In the first place, by any definition, capitalism was not an exclusively urban phenomenon. Whether understood as acquisitive profit-seeking or as control of the means of production, capitalist enterprise at any given point in the early modern era was as important in agriculture as in other sectors of the economy. Second, whatever it was, capitalist enterprise had little or nothing to do with competition.[26] Certainly merchants who wanted to maximize profits could be ruthless in their dealings with other sectors of society; as we have seen, some merchants were only too willing to impinge on the rights of guild artisans. But among themselves, the same merchants were more likely to make agreements and form cartels than to compete openly for a share of the same market. Once a group of merchants had secured monopoly rights, they would fight to uphold their collective

23. Fudge, 'Foodstuffs in Northern Europe', 30.
24. For a classic restatement of the Marxist view, see Hilton,'Capitalism'.
25. Miskimin, *Economy*, 63–4.
26. Goldthwaite, 'Medici Bank'.

privileges against all outsiders – but the monopoly was collective, not individual. Third, capitalism was in no way antagonistic to state involvement in the economy. On the contrary, entrepreneurs normally looked to the state to grant them the privileges they needed to uphold their economic interests. The economic monopoly enjoyed by many a merchant cartel came not from outperforming rivals in the marketplace but from a charter graciously granted by political authority – in return, of course, for direct payments or promises of financial support. In the words of one astute student of the early modern merchant community, 'the fear of competition and the preoccupation with protection that characterize the guild mentality also guided the actions of the big entrepreneurs'.[27] As in most epochs, people looked to the state to create conditions favourable to economic activity – especially their own.

People in the early modern city could hardly have been conscious of the spread of capitalism – after all, the very concept is a modern one, dating to the late nineteenth century. But they may have noted some changes in the way economic life was organized. The old ways of doing business never disappeared. But they were supplemented by new, less personal methods in the deployment of capital.

Consider first how business was done in the sixteenth century. In 1546, two businessmen in the Italian town of Lucca, Bonaventure Michaeli and Girolamo Arnolfini, organized a new 'company' whose purpose was to conduct trade with the French city of Lyon. Michaeli and Arnolfini each contributed a stake of 6,000 écus to the venture, and they collected another 21,000 écus from six other investors. Two of the investors were appointed as 'governors' of the company, to run its affairs on a day-to-day basis. The company was not a permanent undertaking; it was a partnership which would last for five years, at which point any profits would be distributed to the participants in accordance with the size of each investor's stake, except that the two 'governors' would receive a larger share in return for their services.[28] In short, this was a company based on investment, but two of the investors were actively engaged in running its affairs.

In 1570, the merchant Thomas Faure of Lyon founded a company to deal in silks and carry on trade with the city of Milan for a period of four years. Faure put up all the capital but the company's operations would be handled entirely by another merchant, Benoît Joyet. Joyet contributed no capital, only his time and skill. In return for this he

27. Jeannin, *Merchants*, 60.
28. Gascon, *Grand commerce*, 1: 280–1.

would be paid an annual fee to cover actual expenses, such as the rental of premises and wages for subordinates – but he was also promised a substantial incentive payment: when the company's books were wound up in 1574, Joyet would receive one-quarter of the profits.[29] Here there was a sharper separation between the investor who put up the capital and the agent who ran the operation – but we can assume that Faure, as the sole owner of the company, took an active interest in the affairs of the firm.

Both of these companies were still entirely typical of the style of sixteenth-century business operations. Even the largest enterprises were often conglomerations of specific, more limited ventures. The great English commercial organizations of the sixteenth century – the Merchant Adventurers and other 'regulated companies' – were really privileged cartels consisting of individual merchants who conducted overseas trade on their own while relying on the influence of the company to fend off any interference from interlopers. The first real innovations in business organization began in the late sixteenth or seventeenth century, when joint-stock companies were established.[30] The first of these companies were organized in the Netherlands, to engage in trade in the Americas or the East Indies. Like the earlier regulated companies, these new enterprises relied on charters from the political authorities to maintain their monopoly rights. But because of the large amount of capital needed to launch major overseas ventures and the long time-lag that might ensue before profits could be generated, the Dutch East India Company and other such organizations were turned into permanent, open-ended businesses. Individual investors would purchase shares in the company and would receive profit dividends not when the company was wound up – since that, in fact, would never happen – but at periodic intervals. Dividends became a source of income to investors who thus had only the most abstract relationship to the affairs of the company itself. Indeed, the original investors' shares of stock could be sold to others and resold further through the new medium of the stock exchange.

The joint-stock companies of the seventeenth century represented an important step in the direction of less personalized forms of investment, making it possible for people to make capital available for enterprises in which they played no active part. These companies became particularly important in western Europe – notably in Holland itself, where investment in such ventures was especially widespread.

29. ibid., 1: 289.
30. Supple, 'Nature of Enterprise', 436–47.

Yet it may be seeing things too much from the perspective of Dutch history to argue, as one historian does, that 'the novelty of the great chartered trading companies could have escaped no one living in seventeenth-century Europe'.[31] Few Europeans would have had occasion to learn of the existence, let alone the importance, of this new type of permanent economic enterprise which existed apart from those who invested in it. Even the traditional time-limited 'company' was a rarity in smaller towns. To most Europeans, a merchant was a man – or, more rarely, a woman – who ran a family-based operation, receiving goods from afar for local resale and shipping local products to a larger town to be sold.

Economic changes which many more Europeans, especially in towns, would have noticed involved the steady expansion of credit and the increasing openness with which interest could be charged. Theologians – Catholic and Protestant alike – continued to condemn the charging of interest until deep into the seventeenth century. But their strictures had ever less impact on everyday life. Secular authorities were less concerned by now to forbid usury than to prevent excessive interest charges by specifying a reasonable rate. Interest was charged with ever less embarrassment by pawnbrokers and moneylenders, who often played a crucial role in advancing small-scale credit. But the collapse of traditional strictures against usury also meant that banks could operate with increasing directness as institutions which offered interest to depositors and charged interest to lenders.

Credit as a whole expanded during the early modern era – not only due to private economic activity, but also due to government initiatives. States and cities alike vastly expanded the medieval practice of offering annuities: in return for a cash payment, the government would make annual payments to the creditor. Sometimes royal and municipal officials worked together, as in the sixteenth century when the French crown forced the city of Paris to act as its agent in selling bonds known as *rentes sur l'hôtel de ville*. The cash payments went right to the king, who promised to reimburse the Paris city hall for the annuity payments it would disburse every year.[32] Bonds of this sort were hardly a blue-chip investment, since at times royal governments were unable to keep up their payments. But for many town-dwellers, government bonds were part of a broader investment package which

31. De Vries, *Economy of Europe*, 131–2.
32. Diefendorf, *Paris City Councillors*, 26–9.

also included revenue from mortgage payments and annuities on loans extended to private borrowers.

A related development which profoundly affected urban Europeans, even when they did not fully comprehend it, was the growth in the money supply. As in many economic systems, the money supply grew in more than one way. Most concretely, there was an increase in the actual amount of coinage in circulation – especially in the sixteenth century, when silver from central European mines and then from the Spanish-controlled mines of South America got converted into coins which spread across Europe. But the money supply was also increased through the expansion of credit. Throughout the early modern era, new means were constantly being devised to facilitate commerce by reducing the need for cash. Merchants began, for example, to endorse letters of exchange, passing them from one bearer to the next until they were finally cashed in. This, in effect, made the letter into a temporary form of paper money. Expedients of this sort, each of which contributed to expanding the money supply, eventually culminated in the practice of issuing bank-notes. The Bank of England, for example, was chartered in 1694 and immediately put into circulation notes that were payable on demand. In theory this was a risky practice, since the bank issued notes far in excess of its actual deposits. But since the English government was pledged to making regular interest payments on the money it borrowed from the bank, the bank-notes were considered to be backed not only by the meagre contents of the bank's own vaults but also by the government itself. So the notes remained in circulation, increasing the supply of money.

Generally when the money supply expands at a rate corresponding to the rate of economic growth – thus accommodating the needs created by an increased number of transactions – there will be no significant impact on prices. When, however, the money supply grows more quickly than the economy, prices will rise. Exactly this may have happened in the sixteenth century.[33] This was a period of population growth in Europe, accompanied by a general expansion of economic activity. But it was also a period when the European economy was hit by inflationary pressures that drove prices steadily upward. The exact extent of what used to be called the 'price revolution' of the sixteenth century has been almost impossible for historians to calculate: local conditions varied, and different commodities fared differently even in the same place. Nor

33. cf. Chabert, 'Price Revolution'.

have economists arrived at any consensus about the ultimate causes of the inflationary trend.[34] But there is little doubt that an increase in the money supply – both through the influx of new coins and through the rapid expansion of credit – played some part in the process. The seventeenth century, by contrast, was a period of slight contraction in the European economy. There was probably some levelling-off of the money supply. There was certainly a tendency for prices to rise more slowly, if at all.

Most contemporaries were only dimly aware of these long-term trends. They were far more sensitive to sudden short-term changes – especially in the realm of prices. For long-term developments were far less disturbing to most people than the sudden episodes of drastic price increase which erupted at unpredictable intervals throughout the early modern period. Sometimes these episodes could be traced to specific manipulations of the currency. In 1542, for example, the English crown began debasing the currency, calling in old coins and minting a larger supply of new ones at the same face value but with less silver content. This may have helped the government in the short run to pay its outstanding bills. Within a few years, however, prices for some commodities had doubled in London.[35] An even more drastic cycle of currency manipulations affected Germany in the early seventeenth century: once some princely states started debasing their currency, the neighbouring ones had to follow suit. By the early 1620s, prices were rising in an uncontrollable spiral. Eventually the entire monetary system started to collapse and governments were forced to put their currencies on an entirely new footing.[36] Yet inflationary spirals due to monetary factors were still relatively rare compared to the catastrophic price-rises that could be triggered by sudden disparities between supply and demand, especially with respect to foodstuffs. When harvests failed, bread prices might double, triple or quadruple within a matter of months. In a world of carefully regulated economies, the law of supply and demand operated most ruthlessly precisely where people were most vulnerable: government officials accustomed to supervising economic affairs in painstaking detail could be rendered helpless where it mattered most, since any attempt to decree lower prices might simply reduce the supply even further. This was the kind of economic crisis which European town-dwellers of the early modern era dreaded more than any other – and with every good reason.

34. For a useful overview, see Miskimin, *Economy*, 35–46.
35. Rappaport, *Worlds within Worlds*, 132–5.
36. Kindleberger, 'Economic Crisis'.

III

One of the most spectacular developments in European history of the early modern era was the expansion of economic contacts with other continents. Of course European expansion was not an exclusively economic phenomenon.[37] Politics and religion were important among the factors that impelled Europeans to venture overseas. Even intellectual curiosity and a sheer sense of adventure were not irrelevant. But the dominant motive was the pursuit of economic gain.

The pattern of European contact varied sharply from one part of the globe to another. In the western hemisphere, where even the well-organized empires of central and south America were unable to withstand the Europeans' military superiority, contact generally took the form of sheer conquest. In Asia, where the Europeans confronted powerful local regimes, their incursions took the form of trading posts and small, localized conquests. In Africa the Europeans were chiefly concerned to take over the existing slave trade, vastly expanding its scope and brutalizing its methods to provide labour for the plantations of the western hemisphere.

Most of the transoceanic ventures required the stimulus and support of national governments. Even if princes did not invest heavily themselves in the ventures, they granted monopoly rights and military support to those who did. But the basis for European expansion was the participation of countless individual people as investors and as members of the overseas expeditions. In this way the process of economic expansion came to have an impact on countless European communities, including many which were far removed from the main centres of activity.

Consider, for example, the career of Piero Strozzi of Florence.[38] Born in 1483, Piero belonged to a well-known family of merchants. As a youth he was sent, like his brothers, on trading ventures to France, but in 1509 he decided to seek his fortune in overseas trade. Florence as such played no part in the transoceanic trade, so – like many other Italians – Piero headed for one of the Atlantic kingdoms. Armed with a small financial stake provided with some reluctance by his family, Piero signed up with a Portuguese expedition to India. After a brief diversion when his ship was commandeered to help in the Portuguese conquest of Goa, Piero Strozzi began to travel up and down the Indian coast, trading in spices and jewels and parlaying his initial stake into a growing fortune. He remained closely

37. cf. Rabb, 'Expansion of Europe'.
38. Subrahmanyam, 'Piero Strozzi'.

in touch with his family and friends in Florence, occasionally shipping consignments of jewels, but he constantly postponed his expected return home. When he died in India around 1523, Piero was said to be fabulously wealthy. Attempts by his brother to retrieve his fortune were evidently fruitless – but tales of his wealth may have lain behind the decision made by other members of the Strozzi clan in later decades to head for the Indies in search of wealth.

In the centuries that followed, tens of thousands of men like Piero Strozzi set out from Europe, hoping to become rich overseas as traders, soldiers or settlers. A few returned wealthy, but many others came back with nothing to show for their efforts or never even made it home. Many Europeans settled overseas, especially in the Americas. But many of the beneficiaries of European expansion were people who never left Europe at all. In the seventeenth and eighteenth centuries there were increasingly many opportunities for passive investment in overseas ventures. These undertakings involved high risks – but also, for some, high gains. Many a European city, especially along the Atlantic seaboard, prospered as a result of overseas trade. Some of this wealth was even derived from the carriage of goods which never even touched Europe: by the eighteenth century, merchants in cities like Nantes, Bristol and Liverpool grew rich from the Atlantic slave trade, which involved the transfer of captives from Africa directly to the West Indies or other parts of the Americas.

Overseas trade provided an important stimulus for the European economy of the early modern era. But overseas exports and imports were always overshadowed by the volume of local, regional and even long-distance trade within Europe itself.[39] Extensive overland transport along Europe's inadequate roads was often prohibitively expensive, except for lightweight items or for livestock, which could transport itself on the hoof before being slaughtered. But transport by river-barge and coastal shipping from one port to another were central to the European economy. The importance of such trade is easier to appreciate if one takes into account that much of it dealt not with luxury items or goods of optional consumption but with indispensable foodstuffs. There were many European cities whose inhabitants could not be sustained solely by the produce of the immediate hinterland but depended instead on long-distance supply. Grain from Prussia and Poland, channelled through Danzig and other Baltic ports, was regularly shipped to cities along the Atlantic seaboard. In the 1590s, when there were widespread harvest failures

39. For a useful overview, see Glamann, 'Patterns of Trade'.

in the Mediterranean region, Baltic grain was even shipped to Italy to be sold in Florence, Venice and other cities.[40]

The relative importance of extra- and intra-European products is suggested by records of the goods shipped from the Atlantic seaboard ports to the great German city of Hamburg in the late seventeenth century. Significant amounts of sugar and tobacco from the Americas arrived in Hamburg, mostly via Portugal. But these products were greatly exceeded in value by items produced within Europe itself – notably raisins, figs, currants, lemons, wine and other non-perishable foodstuffs which originated in Spain, Portugal and Italy.[41] In fact the basic patterns of shipping between different parts of the continent were already in place long before the first Portuguese and Spanish ships ventured overseas – and they continued to account for the most important aspects of long-distance trade in Europe throughout the early modern era.

IV

Any economic system is a framework to organize the exploitation of resources and the production and distribution of commodities. The character of the system is normally determined by social and political elites, who have an interest both in maximizing output and in perpetuating inequality – goals which, though not entirely compatible, can often be effectively reconciled. Every system offers individuals certain economic choices while imposing many constraints – but the rigidity of the constraints and, correspondingly, the range of choices can vary substantially. On the whole, the early modern city offered its inhabitants a greater range of economic choices than would have been the case in most European villages. But town-dwellers of every social level were also subject to powerful constraints which sharply limited their economic options.

A man like Piero Strozzi enjoyed a freedom of choice that was rare indeed in early modern society. This resulted from an accident of birth. Piero belonged to a moderately prosperous family of merchants who were accustomed to travelling abroad in pursuit of wealth and fortune. Piero's own cousins from the richer branch of his clan might have found it harder to do what he did: the main line of the Strozzi had a prominent position in Florentine society which each generation would have been expected to uphold.[42] Even Piero's father was not

40. ibid., 221–2.
41. Newman, 'Hamburg', 58–63.
42. On the main branch of the family, see Goldthwaite, *Private Wealth*, 31–107.

enthused about his son's decision to head for the Indies – but Piero did have brothers who followed the more traditional path of seeking patrons and business opportunities somewhat closer to home. So their father agreed to let Piero go and advanced a sum which, as we have seen, was parlayed into substantial – if evanescent – wealth in the Indies.

Nehemiah Wallington's choices were much more circumscribed – not because he lacked advantages of birth, but due to his own personality. Nehemiah's father was a prosperous and respected member of the company of turners, well able to help his sons get launched in life. But Nehemiah himself suffered from an incapacitating passivity in any sphere of life other than religion. Although fathers normally played an influential role in their sons' career choices, Nehemiah's case was extreme: he became a master turner with a shop of his own at the early age of 22, but only because his father made all the arrangements.[43] For the rest of his life Nehemiah depended heavily on his father and his older brother to help him manage his affairs.

Yet despite his lack of personal initiative, Nehemiah Wallington still had the opportunity to make his own choices and enjoyed a degree of economic autonomy that set him apart from the great majority of people in the early modern city. Countless other town-dwellers reached adulthood with neither the inherited property nor the family connections that could help to provide economic security or at least a range of options. With muscle power as their only capital, people like these could choose only between work as domestic servants or as hired labourers – if such employment was even available. Even people with some financial resources were often limited to certain careers on account of their religion, ethnicity, illegitimate birth or servile status.

A far more universal constraint, however, related to gender. Within any particular social group, the range of economic options was normally far greater for men than for women. Deep-seated assumptions about gender structured every aspect of economic life. The right of women to inherit and transmit property was fundamental – but whenever possible, it was assumed that a man, normally the woman's father or husband, should actually administer the property concerned. Nobody believed, of course, that women should not work. But the forms of labour were gender-specific. Retail sales were normally considered a suitable activity for women, as were certain kinds of supervised handwork. But skilled labour that involved the

43. Seaver, *Wallington's World*, 115–16.

organization of the production process or completion of finished articles was generally reserved for men.[44] In short, within any given social milieu, women were always subject to more constraints than men.

Some women broke through these constraints. The fact that women had an unquestioned right to inherit and transmit property emboldened some wealthy wives to get more involved in deciding how their property was to be used. The knowledge that women's labour was so obviously indispensable for the survival of most households encouraged some wives to assume a more direct role in running the production process. But these were anomalies. Single women and widows had more freedom of action than married women. But the image of the widow who could relish her economic independence after decades of bondage to her father and husband applies, at best, to only a handful of women. Certainly a wealthy widow could be well positioned to make autonomous economic decisions.[45] But most women suffered economically when their husbands died. A widow might retrieve her own dowry, but she normally inherited only part of her husband's wealth, as the rest went to his children. And her opportunities for continuing to make a living were sharply circumscribed by conventions about what kind of work was acceptable for women to do. In most cities, in fact, households headed by women were on average substantially poorer than those headed by men.

Individual economic choices and opportunities, then, were powerfully structured by birth. But they were also structured by death. The timely or untimely death of parents, siblings, uncles, aunts, spouses – even children – could profoundly affect an individual's economic situation. Death could remove an indispensable source of economic support – or it could clear the way to a useful inheritance. Every man or woman in the early modern city tried to make a living within the context of an economic system whose most basic characteristics remained relatively unchanged throughout the early modern period. How successfully he or she did so certainly depended in part on personal qualities of skill, character or imagination. But success or failure was also, to a large part, determined by demographic accidents. To the average town-dweller in early modern Europe, the conquest of the Americas was much less important in shaping everyday life than the unfathomable mysteries of birth, survival, illness and death.

44. Roper, *Holy Household*, 40–9.
45. Diefendorf, *Paris City Councillors*, 285–8.

CHAPTER FIVE
Life and Death

Lienhard Romig was a tanner in the German city of Schwäbisch Hall. Born in Ansbach in 1504, Romig had settled in Schwäbisch Hall in 1529, presumably after spending some years on the road as a journeyman. Romig did well in his adopted city, eventually becoming one of the twenty-five richest citizens. When he died in 1589, his heirs commissioned a memorial painting for the city's main church, showing Romig and his entire family posed devoutly in prayer. Here one can see the venerable tanner with his 5 wives, his 16 children, and – kneeling gingerly on the branches of a great family tree – his 125 grandchildren and 30 great-grandchildren. Nearby in the church hangs a similar tablet for Marie Firnhaber, who died in 1647. It shows Marie and her deceased husband Peter with their 15 children and 105 grandchildren.[1]

It was a point of pride in Schwäbisch Hall to produce a large number of descendants. When the octogenarian Katharine Bratz, née Wagner, died in 1691, her pastor noted that 'by her fecundity, she added ninety-one people to the world' – specifically sixteen children, thirty-six grandchildren, thirty-eight great-grandchildren and one great-great-grandchild.[2] What he neglected to mention, however, was how many of them were still living. Yet there is no doubt that a large number would have died by then. Indeed, if we look closely at the memorial tablet for Lienhard Romig, we would see in it not so much a celebration of life as a commemoration of death: about half of the portraits are embellished with a skull to show who had died before the aged patriarch. Lienhard's first wife, Amalia, had died in

1. Wunder, *Bürger*, 53–4, 177, 204–5 (plates 7 and 8), 282, 285, 290.
2. ibid., 177.

1547 after giving birth to eleven children; his second wife, Sibylle, produced five more before her death in 1554. Two more wives predeceased Lienhard, as did six of his children and almost half of the further descendants. Marie Firnhaber's experience was comparable: one of her children died in infancy, three in childhood, six others in adulthood before their mother. Many of her 105 grandchildren predeceased her as well.

Lienhard Romig and Marie Firnhaber were not 'typical' of their times, for no single individuals ever are. But they did live out their lives in the context of a distinct demographic system, a pattern of population and family dynamics that characterized the society of early modern Europe as a whole. Some characteristics of this system have always been recognized. Everyone knows that in pre-modern times women often bore more children than is customary in modern western society. Everyone realizes that death was far less age-specific than it is today. But a real understanding of the population dynamics of early modern Europe is a product of relatively recent times. Important advances in European historical demography, especially since the 1950s and 1960s, have given historians a much more precise apprehension of the patterns of life and death so vividly suggested by the memorial tablets of a Lienhard Romig or a Marie Firnhaber.[3]

I

Countless different records have been exploited in the study of early modern European historical demography, but one type of source stands out as uniquely important. Beginning in the course of the sixteenth century, in many parts of Europe it was required of the priest or pastor to record every baptism, marriage and funeral performed in his parish. Thousands upon thousands of parish registers were thus duly compiled and preserved in churches all over Europe. For a long time these books were of interest chiefly to genealogists and ancestor-hunters, but eventually this vast stock of records attracted the interest of historical demographers. The difficulties of extracting useful information from these sources can readily be imagined. Many registers have been lost, and even those that survive are of varying quality: some priests and pastors were meticulous record-keepers, others were careless or slovenly. Even the most complete registers do not always provide complete vital statistics. Some births were not followed by a baptism, especially if the baby died too soon; some deaths were not followed by a proper funeral, particularly in

3. A good introduction is still provided by Wrigley, *Population and History*.

times of war or crisis. A few communities had inhabitants whose members would never appear in a church register: Jews, for example, or members of certain Christian sects. Yet despite such anomalies, the best-preserved registers have provided historians with a useful record of the approximate number of births, marriages and deaths in parishes all over Europe. Many demographers have gone far beyond mere counting, devising sophisticated techniques to compensate for inadequacies in the data. Some detailed registers have been used to reconstruct the history of entire families so as to determine the ages at which people married, the number of children they had and the intervals at which they had them, and the age at which people died. When enough families can be 'reconstituted', the dynamics of family life in a past community become increasingly visible.

Some crucial data will always remain conjectural. This is particularly the case with demographic rates, which specify, among other things, how many births and deaths occurred per year for every thousand members of a population. In 1990, for example, the birth rate in Great Britain was about fourteen per thousand; the death rate was about eleven. Such rates are easy to determine when not only the total number of births and deaths but also the total size of the population is known. The latter figure, however, is exactly what is generally missing in early modern Europe. Real national censuses were unknown until the early nineteenth century, and even for individual communities, reliable head-counts are very rare. Many apparent censuses were undertaken – but on closer inspection they usually turn out to give the total number of taxpayers or households, not individuals. Most estimates of a community's population are in fact extrapolations from the known number of households.

Information is often more complete for villages than for cities. A village normally constituted a single parish, so all the inhabitants would be encompassed by a single register. A city generally included numerous parishes, and not all registers have necessarily survived. Cities also had more people who were likely to fall between the cracks of parish registration: immigrants, vagrants and members of religious minorities. Yet even so, there is enough information from cities in various parts of Europe to give a clear picture of urban demographic norms. Obviously no two cities were quite alike, but certain patterns were characteristic of a broad range of European communities from the late middle ages until sometime in the eighteenth century. Inevitably one must illustrate these patterns by looking at specific cities, but such cases can tell us a lot about the demographic character of early modern cities as a whole.

Figure 5.1 Baptisms, burials and weddings in Esslingen, 1571–1750

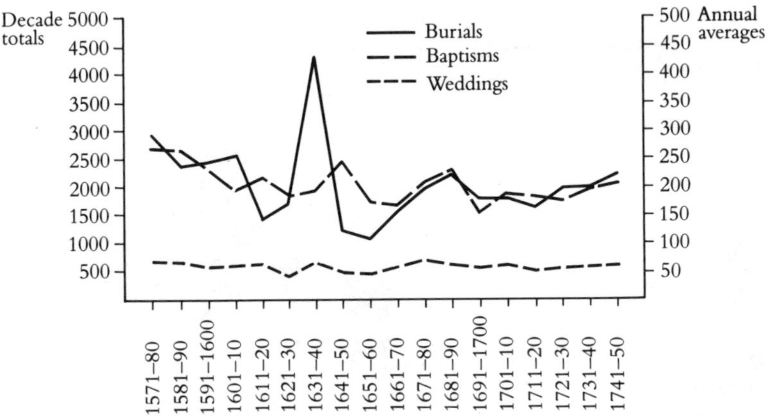

Source: Data from Schraitle, 'Bevölkerungsentwicklung Esslingens'

II

We may begin by looking closely at one well-documented community – the south German town of Esslingen, where parish registers were introduced in the 1560s.[4] Figure 5.1 gives the total number of baptisms, burials and marriages for each decade from 1570 to 1750. These are raw data; for example, the burial register included both local inhabitants and outsiders who happened to die in Esslingen.[5] But even so, these figures give us a clear sense of the basic demographic trends in this early modern town.

Start with weddings. In each decade, there were between 450 and 700 weddings; thus, on average, in any given year 45–70 new married households were established. Now look at baptisms. Here the totals were less constant than for weddings, ranging between 1,500 and 2,700 per decade, or an average of 150–270 a year. Next, consider burials. In many decades, especially after the mid-seventeenth century, the number of burials closely matched the number of baptisms, suggesting a period of demographic equilibrium. But in some periods the totals sharply diverge – especially in the 1630s, when a total of 4,281 burials were recorded, as against 1,854 baptisms.

4. The following figures are based on the tables in Schraitle, 'Bevölkerungsentwicklung', 94–105.
5. From 1660 on, the burial figures were increased by inclusion of burials of stillborn babies, which totalled roughly ten per year: ibid., 100–2.

Table 5.1 Baptisms, burials and weddings in Esslingen, 1631–40

Year	*Baptisms*	*Burials*	*Weddings*
1631	207	145	35
1632	170	137	60
1633	173	171	39
1634	268	598	37
1635	177	1,985	46
1636	162	113	237
1637	149	156	63
1638	204	656	67
1639	195	234	61
1640	211	86	48
Decade total	1,916	4,281	693
Decade average	192	428	69

Source: Adapted from Schraitle, 'Bevölkerungsentwicklung Esslingens', 94, 99, 104

Let us take a closer look at the figures for that particular decade. As Table 5.1 shows, the annual number of baptisms between 1631 and 1640 showed considerable variation, from a high of 268 to a low of 149. But these variations were trivial when compared to the burial figures. Only 137 people were buried in 1632. But the figure rose to almost 600 in 1634 and to triple that number the year after that. For two years burials dropped, but in 1638 more than 650 were buried.

Historians know that an excess of burials over baptisms on such a scale indicates the occurrence of a demographic crisis.[6] Such a crisis could be caused by a major shortage of food, by a massive onset of epidemic disease – or by a combination of both. The crises of the 1630s in Esslingen were certainly compounded by social disruptions caused by the Thirty Years War: throughout the 1630s, the Swabian region of Germany in which Esslingen lay was the scene of constant military activity, and the city was often full of refugees from villages which had been occupied or destroyed by undisciplined soldiers. What the refugees found in Esslingen in 1634, however, was not relief or safety but a major outbreak of the most dreaded disease in early modern Europe: the bubonic plague.

The 2,583 people whose burials were recorded in 1634 and 1635

6. For classic discussions of demographic crises in early modern times, see Meuvret, 'Demographic Crisis', and Goubert, *Beauvais et le Beauvaisis*, 1: 45–59.

may not even have encompassed the total number of people who died in Esslingen As elsewhere in times of acute crisis, vagrants, refugees and even a few local inhabitants may have been buried in anonymous graves without proper funerals. This certainly happened during the less acute but still serious crisis of 1638, when the number of anonymous burials was specifically noted. Of the 656 people who were buried in that year, only 297 were known to the minister and listed by name. As for the rest, the parish register noted only that 'according to the list of payments made to the gravedigger, this year there were 359 from the orphanage or the hospice or found dead in the streets, whose names were not recorded'.[7]

Yet drastic as it might be, a demographic crisis was almost always followed by a cycle of communal recovery. This, too, is apparent from Table 5.1. In 1635, the worst year of the crisis, only 46 marriages were recorded. But the following year there were 237 weddings. It is easy to imagine why. The plague had created a vast pool of widows and widowers. Now the survivors began to reconstitute their households by finding new partners. Some local widows and widowers must have married each other. But a crisis of this magnitude would also have created marital opportunities for journeymen, servants or immigrants who until then might have had scant hopes of entering the marriage market. People like this were well positioned to move into the vacancies created by a demographic crisis.

A fivefold increase in the number of weddings – even though only a temporary phenomenon – was bound to have an impact on births. Baptisms dropped sharply in the second year of the crisis and the years immediately after it, no doubt reflecting both a decline in sexual activity during the plague and the elimination of potential parents. But in 1638 there was a sharp increase in baptisms: by now the great burst of post-crisis marriages had begun to have an effect. The trend for increased baptisms continued into the following decade.

That the 1630s were a period of demographic crisis in Esslingen would have been obvious from even the quickest glance at the decennial figures presented in Figure 5.1. But now consider a decade during which baptisms and burials appeared to be balanced. During the 1590s, Esslingen had an average of 232 baptisms and 246 burials a year – a difference of only 14. Yet Figure 5.2 shows that these averages mask a sharp short-term increase in burials, which began rising in 1593 and reached a peak of 620 in 1594. The following year there

7. Schraitle, 'Bevölkerungsentwicklung', 82.

Figure 5.2 Baptisms, burials and weddings in Esslingen, 1591–1600

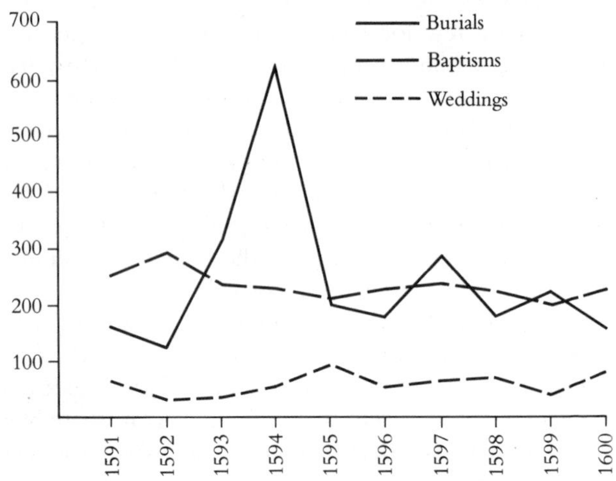

Source: Data from Schraitle, 'Bevölkerungsentwicklung Esslingens'

was a noticeable increase in marriages and the year after that one can observe a slight increase in baptisms. In short, Esslingen in the early 1590s experienced all the signs of a classic demographic crisis and recovery. There were comparable crises in 1576, 1585 and 1610.

Esslingen is worth looking at not because it was unique but because it was so typical of European cities of the early modern era. The pattern by which a rough parity between births and deaths was interrupted by periodic cycles of sudden crisis and slow recovery can be detected in countless cities. At some point or other after the mid-seventeenth century, however, the crises tended to become less acute. In Esslingen no major demographic crises occurred after 1650, though there was an echo in 1694 when deaths exceeded births by about 200. Yet in some parts of Europe the crisis pattern continued to recur until the mid-eighteenth century.

The vulnerability of early modern town-dwellers to this kind of crisis brings us to the fundamental point about any demographic system. Population dynamics always reflect the tension between factors over which humans have some control – notably births, marriages, immigration and emigration – and other factors over which they have little or none, notably illness and death. The relative balance between willed and unwilled factors is a large part of what characterizes one demographic system and makes it different from another.

Let us start with births. It was, after all, primarily through an adequate rate of births that a community could overcome the impact of demographic crises. The frequency of births within any human population is never entirely controlled by willed choices, but even so, it is linked to a whole array of conscious decisions. To start with, in the early modern town birth was strongly correlated with marriage. Much sexual activity certainly took place outside marriage, but most babies were born to married parents.

The proportion of children whose parents were not married is often easy to calculate from the parish registers, because pastors in most cities made a special note of illegitimate births – sometimes even by keeping a separate list or by writing the names in red ink or upside down or by drawing a hand with a pointing finger in the margin.[8] Consider the evidence from eight London parishes whose population history between 1540 and 1650 has been studied in detail; in seven of these parishes, the percentage of illegitimate births varied between 0.6 and 2.6 per cent; only in one did the illegitimacy rate rise higher, to 4.3 per cent.[9] In Strasbourg between 1560 and 1650, the rate scarcely exceeded 1 per cent; in the German town of Mainz between 1600 and 1780 illegitimacy never rose above 3 per cent.[10] Such rates were widely typical, at least until the mid-eighteenth century. There is certainly more evidence, in some communities, of children having been conceived by parents who were still single – but in most such cases, by the time the child was actually born the parents had got married.

Virtually all births in the early modern city, then, took place within marriage. This means, of course, that the age at which women first married could assume great demographic importance: whether women started having children at 15 or at 25 would have a significant impact on the birth rate. In some traditional cultures, marriages are arranged by parents, with the groom having little and the bride even less to say about the matter. In societies of this sort, girls are often given in marriage soon after they reach sexual maturity. This pattern may have prevailed in medieval Europe – but it was no longer the norm in early modern times.[11] Some women,

8. cf. Rödel, *Mainz*, 15; Kintz, *Société strasbourgeoise*, 214.
9. Finlay, *Population and Metropolis*, 149.
10. Kintz, *Société strasbourgeoise*, 214; Rödel, *Mainz*, 169.
11. The distinct character of the 'European marriage pattern' was first emphasized by Hajnal, 'Marriage Patterns'.

especially from aristocratic families, were pressured into marriage in their teenage years. But such cases were rare among the vast majority of the European population. The exact age at which women married in European cities is often difficult to determine, for the bride's age was hardly ever entered in the register, but for some cities historians have been able to determine ages through family reconstitutions. The evidence from the sixteenth to the eighteenth century always tends to show the same thing: though teenage brides were not unknown, women normally got married in their early to mid-twenties.[12]

Once they were married, women started having children, early and often. Some married women, of course, never gave birth. But among the vast majority who did, the first child was born, in about half of all cases, within a year of the wedding. Subsequent children might be born about two years apart – though the intervals tended to get progressively longer as the mother got older.[13] The cycle would be broken, of course, if either parent died. In order to determine how many children a woman would normally have had if death did not intervene, family reconstitution studies usually isolate demographically 'complete' marriages, in which both parents survived until the woman can be assumed to have reached menopause. Cases of women who married at 20 and gave birth fifteen or more times before reaching their late forties are certainly documented. Few women were quite so fecund, of course, and the later a woman married, the fewer children she was likely to have. But the number of children born to women who had 'complete' marriages was still very high: in some cities, the average total for such cases was about eight births in the course of a marriage.[14]

Obviously the frequency of births varied enormously from one woman to the next. But demographers look at groups, not individuals. In doing so, they have noted that urban women appear, on average, to have given birth slightly more often than village women. In some cities, moreover, women who lived in richer neighbourhoods showed a tendency for shorter intervals between births than women in poorer districts.[15] There are many possible explanations for these differences – but the most important factor was probably related to the practice of wet-nursing. Peasant women and poorer urban women always

12. e.g. Finlay, *Population and Metropolis*, 137; Deyon, *Amiens*, 36; Kintz, *Société strasbourgeoise*, 198; Rödel, *Mainz*, 261–3.
13. e.g. Turrel, *Bourg en Bresse*, 220–2; Finlay, *Population and Metropolis*, 134–6; Deyon, *Amiens*, 36–7; Rödel, *Mainz*, 289–94; François, *Koblenz*, 27.
14. Rödel, *Mainz*, 266–70; Turrel, *Bourg en Bresse*, 225–6.
15. Rödel, *Mainz*, 267–8; Finlay, *Population and Metropolis*, 142–8.

breast-fed their own babies. But women of greater means often sent their babies out to neighbouring villages to be nursed by peasant women. This practice had an obvious biological impact, since lactation tends to retard conception. The women who were no longer nursing their own babies were thus likely to conceive again more rapidly.

The detailed study of birth intervals has revealed that in certain communities at some point in the early modern era the average time-span between one birth and another might start getting longer. In the German town of Giessen, for example, the average interval got noticeably longer in the late seventeenth century – though the trend lasted for only a generation or so.[16] Such evidence of lengthened birth intervals inevitably raises the question of whether some form of birth control was being practised. Certainly the concept of birth control was widely known, and strong condemnations by the church did not discourage people from discussing or occasionally even attempting it. Yet it would have been almost impossible for early modern Europeans to develop sophisticated means of contraception, since the mechanics of conception itself were so poorly understood. Until the eighteenth century, after all, it was widely believed that a woman was most likely to conceive immediately after her menstrual period.[17] It was widely recognized, however, that lactation reduced the likelihood of conception – and its effectiveness as a deterrent was enhanced by a traditional taboo against sexual relations with a nursing mother. The taboo was not absolute – but it could be exploited, along with prolonged nursing, by a mother who wanted to postpone the next pregnancy without openly flouting the religious prohibitions on birth control. In this sense there could have been an element of family planning. But eventually the baby would be weaned, or it would die, and sexual relations would resume. Soon another baby would be on the way. For most of the evidence from early modern cities strongly suggests that once she got married the average woman went on getting pregnant and giving birth until her husband died, or she died, or the possibility of further pregnancies was ended by illness or menopause. Amalia Romig of Schwäbisch Hall had eleven children during the approximately eighteen years of her marriage – a new baby, on average, about every nineteen months. This placed her on the high end of the fertility scale – but her experience was still entirely normal for women of the early modern city.

16. Imhof, 'Demographische Stadtstrukturen', 223–6.
17. McLaren, *Reproductive Rituals*, 70–1.

A society in which a couple whose marriage lasted to the end of the wife's fertile years might well have eight children was obviously very different from our own. It is typically estimated that the birth rate in early modern cities ranged between thirty and forty per thousand – which is roughly triple the rate that prevails in many western countries today.[18] This high birth rate, however, was offset by levels of mortality which were also much higher than those of the modern west. To understand the population dynamics of an early modern town, then, we must not only look at the frequency with which lives were started, but also determine how and why they came to end.

III

Death in modern society is highly age-specific. People can die at any age, but the likelihood of dying increases drastically, year by year, as people move into their sixties and seventies. In early modern times, by contrast, death was distributed broadly across the entire age spectrum. Exact information about ages at death is not always easy to come by, but some parish registers recorded ages at death, or divided burials into broad age categories. The specific ages given cannot always be considered reliable – but the broader categories usually are: after all, even the most heedless pastor still knew if he was burying an infant, a child or an adult.

Consider some evidence from the German town of Nördlingen. In the hundred years from 1621 to 1720, the parish registers recorded the deaths of 23,744 residents of the community. These can be broken down into three broad categories which make clear where the highest mortality took place:

Burials of Nördlingen residents, 1621–1720[19]

Infants (up to 1 year)	11,038	(46.5%)
Children (1–12 years)	3,012	(12.7%)
Adolescents and adults	9,694	(40.8%)

In short, almost half of all residents who were buried during this century were infants – and children as a whole accounted for almost two-thirds of all burials. Infant mortality seems to have been unusually high in Nördlingen, but the overall proportion of child

18. Rödel, *Mainz*, 152–3; Kintz, *Société strasbourgeoise*, 233–6; François, *Koblenz*, 26–7.
19. Friedrichs, *Urban Society*, 306–8. Travellers and other non-residents who died in the city are not included in these totals.

burials was by no means exceptional. In seventeenth- and eighteenth-century Mainz, for example, roughly half of those buried were children under the age of 10.[20] In various parishes of Amiens between 1665 and 1725, children under the age of 15 normally accounted for 50–60 per cent of all burials.[21] In early eighteenth-century Giessen, 25 per cent were infants and another 28 per cent were aged from 1 to 15.[22]

All this makes amply clear that infant and child mortality was a central feature of the demographic system of early modern towns. Demographers warn that in the absence of information about the total population and age structure of the communities concerned, figures like these cannot be taken to give the exact dimensions of child mortality. There are ways, however, to make a more precise estimate of the ages at which a representative group of urban people died. This has been done, for example, by using the data produced by family reconstitutions in Geneva. The Genevan registers are a particularly impressive source, not only because of their completeness but also because deaths were recorded not by a clergyman but by a surgeon, appointed by the city to investigate each case and report the particulars. Even the Genevan records, of course, do not include information about people who left the city and died elsewhere, but enough full lives have been reconstituted to make possible an unusually precise estimate of the ages at which children born in Geneva died – or, to put it another way, how long they survived.

Table 5.2 records the survival rate of children born to Genevan couples who married between 1625 and 1684.[23] Of every 1,000 children born alive – stillborn children are not included – only 736 would still be living a year after their birth. Ten years after birth, less than half of the original 1,000 would be living. By age 50, just over a quarter would still be alive; by age 80, only 28 of the original group were living.

The risk of death, as indicated by the 'mortality quotient', was clearly very different for various age groups. In the first year of life, over a quarter of all Genevan children – 264 per 1,000 – could be expected to die. Of the 736 who would reach their first birthday, a total of 185 – or 251 per 1,000 – would die in the next four years. The following years were less dangerous. The risks of dying were lowest

20. Rödel, *Mainz*, 201–6.
21. Deyon, *Amiens*, 40; in one parish in 1665–7 the proportion reached 66 per cent.
22. Imhof, 'Auswertung', 212: data for Giessen, 1701–50.
23. Perrenoud, 'L'Inégalité sociale', 230–1.

Table 5.2 Estimated survival rate of children born in Geneva to parents married between 1625 and 1684 (Base: 1,000)

Age	*Number still alive*	*Number of deaths in next period*	*Mortality quotient (per thousand)*
0	1,000	264	264
1	736	185	251
5	551	64	116
10	487	49	101
20	438	50	114
30	388	62	160
40	326	66	202
50	260	78	300
60	182	78	429
70	104	76	731
80	28	26	929
90	2	2	1,000
100	0	—	—

Source: Adapted from Perrenoud, 'L'Inégalité sociale', 230–1

for people in their teens – only one-tenth of those who reached age 10 would be gone by age 20. But after that the risk of dying would go up again, rising steadily with every passing decade.

These figures are not universal constants. Even in Geneva there were significant variations. It has been shown, for example, that the rate of infant mortality was substantially lower for rich families than for poor ones.[24] There was also change over time: by the mid-eighteenth century, mortality for infants under 1 year had dropped to a rate of just under 200 per 1,000. This was a significant change, but it certainly did not yet represent any breakthrough to a demographic system of the modern kind. Of any 1,000 children born in Geneva between 1745 and 1770, more than 400 would still die before reaching their twentieth birthday.[25] In Geneva, as in every European city, a high rate of infant and child mortality remained a fundamental feature of the demographic system throughout the early modern era.

The distinctive age-distribution of death in the early modern city reflected the fact that the predominant causes of mortality were

24. ibid., 232–6.
25. Perrenoud, 'La Mortalité', 219–21.

entirely different from those that prevail in our own society. In modern western countries roughly two-thirds of all deaths are caused either by cardiovascular diseases or by cancer – diseases which are strongly associated with ageing. Such medical conditions were by no means unknown in early modern Europe. But the major causes of death were entirely different.

Early modern Europeans, like all people, were fascinated by diseases and death. Medical textbooks and treatises abounded. Many specific cases were exhaustively described, and we know in detail about the death agonies of many prominent people and some obscure ones. Major epidemics gave rise to extensive reports in books, diaries and letters. But systematic information about the relative importance of various causes of death is hard to establish. There were very few towns in which the cause of each death was routinely recorded. In Geneva the city-appointed surgeon provided this information, and in London periodic bills of mortality specified the total number of deaths from various causes. But even when such information exists, it often reports what modern medicine would regard as symptoms rather than diseases. The bills of mortality, for example, show that many Londoners died of clearly defined ailments like smallpox or the bubonic plague – but others were reported as dying of 'agues' and 'fevers' whose origins can scarcely be determined.[26]

We do, however, have a general picture of what caused death in early modern towns. Certainly many Europeans died of degenerative diseases of ageing or the gradual malfunctioning of vital organs. Numerous people, for example, were afflicted by kidney or bladder stones, which could cause a victim decades of distress before resulting in complications which finally dispatched the patient. People died of strokes and other sudden failures of the circulatory system. There were fatal accidents and acts of violence. As in any society, the list of medical and social conditions that terminated human lives was long indeed. But there is little doubt that for the great majority of early modern Europeans the causes of death all fell under one general heading: infectious disease.

Most of these infections were caused by micro-organisms whose very existence was unknown to anyone in early modern times. Viruses caused smallpox and influenza. Rickettsia caused typhus. Bacteria led to dysentery, tuberculosis, syphilis, puerperal fever, bubonic plague and other often fatal ailments. We know today not only which microbe causes each of these diseases but also how it is

26. Appleby, 'Nutrition and Disease', 6–8; Forbes, *Chronicle*, 86–118.

normally transmitted, whether by direct human exposure, through contaminated water, via human wastes – or by contact with animals. The bubonic plague, for example, is chiefly a disease of rodents, but the bacillus is transferred from rats to humans by fleas. The people of early modern Europe recognized that infectious diseases were often contagious – but, lacking any concept of microscopic living organisms, they never understood the exact means of transmission.

What they did know was how greatly these diseases varied in their symptoms and their severity. Some infections could afflict the patient for years before he or she finally succumbed; others ran a short, sharp course. Some offered a greater chance of survival than others. Some were endemic throughout the year. Others recurred chiefly during a particular season. Yet others were epidemic, disappearing for years and then breaking out anew. Of all the epidemic diseases, none was more fearsome than the bubonic plague.

A brief look at some statistics from London will show us why. From the bills of mortality – a flawed but still instructive source – we can see how many deaths were attributed to five major types of infectious conditions in the mid-seventeenth century. In the late 1650s and early 1660s the main killers were consumption – which chiefly denoted tuberculosis – and fevers which were probably due mainly to influenza. Next in importance came smallpox and typhus. From 1657 to 1664, the bubonic plague killed an average of fourteen people a year in London. In 1665, it killed almost 70,000.[27]

Table 5.3 Major infectious causes of death in London, 1657–65

	1657–1664 (annual average)	1665
Consumption (Tuberculosis)	3,368	4,808
'Fevers'	2,213	5,257
Smallpox	847	655
Typhus	178	1,929
Bubonic Plague	14	68,596

Source: Adapted from Appleby, 'Nutrition and Disease', 20

27. Appleby, 'Nutrition and Disease', 18, argues that some of the deaths attributed to other diseases were actually from the plague, which would push the total well over 70,000. By contrast, Slack, *Impact of Plague*, 151, gives a somewhat lower total figure.

In terms of total deaths, the epidemic of 1665 was the most severe visitation of bubonic plague in early modern London. It was also to prove the last one – but nobody knew that at the time. For centuries, in fact, periodic outbreaks of the bubonic plague had been a fact of life in almost every European city, and the impact of the disease could be devastating. London itself had been severely hit by the plague in 1563, 1593, 1603 and 1625, with smaller outbreaks in many other years. The plague and other diseases in 1665 may have killed over 17 per cent of the city's inhabitants; in some of the previous plague years almost a quarter of the population may have been eliminated.[28] The impact on other communities was sometimes even greater. The little German town of Uelzen had two major outbreaks of the plague in the sixteenth century; the epidemic of 1597, which claimed 510 lives, wiped out about one-third of the city's population.[29]

Outbreaks of the bubonic plague normally reached a peak in the late summer and early autumn, presumably because this was the time of year when rats and fleas were most numerous or active. Once infected, a human had but modest hopes of survival – most victims began to experience fever and swellings within a matter of days and died within a week. The contagious nature of the plague was always recognized, but the role of animals in transmitting the disease was not, so public health measures to stop the spread of the plague focused only on reducing human contact: plague victims were confined to special hospitals or locked into their own houses; the bodies and bedding of the dead were rapidly disposed of; travel to and from plague-infested cities was forbidden. These measures were not totally irrelevant, since a small number of cases were caused by human contact, but they had little impact on overall mortality. The best personal strategy for avoiding the plague was to leave town – and quickly, before travel restrictions were imposed.

Once infected, a person of any age, gender or social status was equally likely to die. But many studies have shown that the rate of plague deaths was higher in poorer urban neighbourhoods or in less well-to-do households.[30] This was because poor people confronted a greater risk of being infected in the first place. They had fewer opportunities than rich people to leave town at the beginning of an epidemic – and their smaller and shabbier dwellings were more likely

28. Slack, *Impact of Plague*, 145–51.
29. Woehlkens. *Pest und Ruhr*, 78–83.
30. Slack, *Impact of Plague*, 111–43, 151–69; Deyon, *Amiens*, 17–25; Dinges, *Stadtarmut in Bordeaux*, 113–14; but Woehlkens, *Pest und Ruhr*, 83–7, shows only a slightly lower rate of plague deaths among the richest households.

to be infested with rats. Sometimes the social distinctions among plague victims can even be traced within a single district: in the Christ Church parish of Bristol, for example, the incidence of plague was higher in the crowded back alleys than in the prosperous houses of Wine and Broad Streets.[31]

Sometime after 1670 the bubonic plague suddenly disappeared from western and central Europe; a last anomalous outbreak in the early 1720s was confined to Marseille and other cities of southern France. The reasons for the disappearance of plague are still being debated, but it seems likely that ecological and zoological factors were more important than any form of human intervention.

During its heyday the bubonic plague was, on the whole, the most important cause of demographic crisis in the European city. But sometimes other diseases could prove equally serious. In London, for example, a great outbreak of influenza in 1557 and 1558 may have rivalled the worst episodes of plague.[32] Epidemic outbreaks of dysentery and smallpox could also reach crisis proportions. And demographic crises could also result from food shortages due to harvest failures. Cities had some protection against irregularities in the food supply, since municipal governments often maintained emergency stores of grain. But a major harvest failure could well have repercussions that even the best-stocked city could not evade. Wartime conditions which disrupted the normal patterns of procurement could sharply aggravate a shortage in the food supply. Occasionally a drastic increase in the price of grain or bread was dramatically paralleled by a sharp increase in the number of burials.[33] Except in the most extreme cases, lack of food was usually not the direct cause of death – but acute malnutrition undoubtedly lowered resistance to the various infections that actually carried people off in the course of a subsistence crisis.

Mortality during such crises was often increased by the presence of half-starved outsiders. Whereas an epidemic typically drove rich people out of the city, a subsistence crisis would drive poor people into it.[34] For the city was often perceived as a place of refuge: in wartime, desperate peasants headed for the protection of the town walls; in famines, they came to the city in search of bread, work or charity. Often they found instead nothing but privation, illness and death. Their presence in the city aggravated the food shortages, their

31. Slack, *Impact of Plague*, 123–6.
32. Rappaport, *Worlds within Worlds*, 71.
33. e.g. Deyon, *Amiens*, 498.
34. cf. Rödel, *Mainz*, 221–2.

debility contributed to the spread of disease – and their deaths swelled the total number of burials in the city.

Demographic crises did not end with the disappearance of the plague. In England the crises faded away, but on the continent periodic episodes of atypically high mortality were still the norm deep into the eighteenth century. But this in turn was part of a larger scheme of things. For as of 1750, long-established demographic patterns – and the expectations they created about life and death – still continued to predominate in most European cities.

IV

Over the long run, in most cities of early modern Europe, the number of deaths tended to exceed the number of births. Even if, for a number of years, the birth totals were higher, the tremendous mortality of crisis years generally pushed the long-term death totals far over the birth levels. This fact has been recognized for a long time – indeed, thoughtful observers of the seventeenth and eighteenth centuries were aware of this imbalance, and they arrived at a conclusion which modern historians have almost universally endorsed: that only a constant flow of immigration made it possible for cities to grow, or even maintain their existing size.[35] 'Without a constant contribution from outside, the city seems incapable of developing or even surviving. It cannot live and cannot progress except in relation to the rural world, which constitutes its demographic reserve' – so we are told with regard to seventeenth-century Amiens.[36] A similar argument can be found in countless other works.

This assumption, however, has not gone completely unchallenged. It has in fact been argued that the immigrants themselves accounted for the surplus of deaths in the early modern city. Most immigrants arrived as young adults, and many of them never married and never had children in the city. The unmarried immigrants thus contributed only to the number of deaths, not births. If their deaths are discounted, it has been suggested, the 'native' families would show a surplus of births over deaths.[37] This line of argument has been firmly rejected by some historical demographers and given respectful consideration by others.[38] But in fact the issue may never be completely resolved – for the data are simply not sufficient to answer the question.

35. The development and widespread acceptance of this thesis are surveyed in De Vries, *European Urbanization*, 179–82.
36. Deyon, *Amiens*, 42.
37. Sharlin, 'Natural Decrease'.
38. e.g. for the former, Finlay, 'Natural Decrease'; for the latter, De Vries, *European Urbanization*, 182–98.

This is not to say that only little is known about immigrants to the early modern city. In fact there is a vast amount of information about urban immigrants – but only those in certain categories. Some immigrants were regarded as being much more desirable than others. Those with skills or money were welcomed to the town as new citizens or marriage partners for local residents. Careful records were kept about newcomers who married, became citizens or began practising a trade. Some towns also maintained a register of males who were inscribed as apprentices or journeymen – some of whom eventually succeeded in becoming citizens and craft masters. Information about 'desirable' immigrants thus abounds. We also know much about the very least welcome immigrants – the vagrants or beggars who were apprehended and, in many cases, banished from the town as petty thieves or social undesirables. The administrative or criminal proceedings that preceded their punishment often generated a substantial amount of paperwork. We know least about the broad middle group of immigrants: the men and women who came to town to work as journeymen, hired hands, day-labourers, maidservants or the like. This large group of people – who contracted no marriages, paid no taxes and – in most cases – committed no crimes, left the fewest traces, sometimes appearing in the local records only once: when they were buried. More systematic information about this group of immigrants would make possible a more definite assessment of the demographic impact of immigration as a whole.

A classic study of migrants in the towns of southeastern England posits the distinction between 'betterment' migrants who came to town with skills and resources, confidently anticipating further social advance, and 'subsistence' migrants who owned nothing and turned up in desperate hopes of finding work or bread.[39] The distinction is a fundamental one, but of course not all immigrants can be easily assigned to either category: the experiences and intentions of many newcomers must have fallen between these two clear poles.

It must also be remembered that there were also many emigrants from every early modern town – and emigrants generally left even fewer traces than immigrants. Here again, the fullest information normally pertains to a small group of prominent cases. Many German towns, for example, levied a stiff 'leaving tax' on citizens who moved to other cities. Such cases were fully recorded. But most emigrants probably left during adolescence without their departures being formally noted. Males in particular were likely to depart in their

39. Clark, 'Migrant'.

youth – perhaps to gain experience as journeymen, perhaps merely to seek their fortunes as soldiers or servants in more promising communities. A few always returned home, but many died or settled down elsewhere.

Nor was immigration always undirectional. Many men and women came to the city, worked for some years, and eventually returned to their native town or village. It has been estimated, for example, that in the mid-sixteenth century, almost nine out of every ten young men who signed up as apprentices in London were immigrants from outside the city. Yet only about 40 per cent of them finished out their seven-year terms and stayed on in London. Since it is not likely that more than 10–20 per cent of a group of young men would have died during a seven-year period, the remaining 40–50 per cent must have left London before their terms were up, in many cases probably returning to their home towns.[40] In London, as in all cities, the immigrants' own intentions were by no means uniform. Of course many immigrants came to the city with every intention of staying there, and did so. Some no doubt arrived hoping to stay but left when no permanent prospects emerged – while others planned to work in the city for just a few years but ended up staying for good.

All this makes it almost impossible to quantify immigration flows as a whole. But everywhere we look in early modern Europe we are struck by evidence of the large number of migrants whose presence is apparent in the city. This is suggested, for example, by a recent study of 2,000 church-court depositions by men and women from various provincial towns in late seventeenth-century England. These men and women had nothing in common other than the accident of having been summoned as witnesses before various ecclesiastical courts. But before they could give any evidence, they had to provide some information about their life histories. Well over half mentioned that they had originally lived elsewhere and had moved – typically in their early twenties – to the town in which they now lived.[41]

Marriage records also suggest the importance of immigration for urban life. A study of marriage contracts in late sixteenth-century Aix-en-Provence shows that, among brides and grooms for whom a place of origin is specified, roughly half came from outside the city.[42] In seventeenth-century Nördlingen, the proportion of marriages

40. Rappaport, *Worlds within Worlds*, 76–7, 311–14.
41. Souden, 'Migrants', 134–42.
42. Dolan, 'Artisans', 179–80.

involving outsiders was smaller: about one-fifth of all brides in the seventeenth century and an even lower percentage of grooms originated outside the community. But if the number of immigrants in Nördlingen was smaller than in some other towns, their role in the community was still significant: about 20 per cent of all the men who were enrolled as householding citizens in seventeenth-century Nördlingen had immigrated. More than half of them, moreover, came from beyond the city's immediate hinterland. If we could tabulate the number of men who came to the city as labourers and servants, we would surely find that most of these men came from nearby villages. But the immigrant males who were admitted to citizenship – 'betterment migrants' *par excellence* – were mostly of urban stock. Some arrived with families, but a majority of them came to Nördlingen as bachelors and were given permission to marry in the city and settle down.[43] Unlike sons of citizens, who were automatically entitled to be enrolled, the immigrants had to prove that they had sufficient training and financial security to deserve being granted citizenship. Selective admissions policies by the urban elite thus guaranteed the community a supply of new inhabitants whose presence would be economically advantageous: throughout the seventeenth century, citizens who had immigrated to Nördlingen tended to be wealthier, on average, than those who were natives.[44]

Examples like these cannot solve any debates about the overall demographic impact of immigration on the early modern city. But they do remind us that immigration was a fundamental fact of urban life all over Europe. The exact proportion of immigrants among urban populations in early modern Europe may always remain elusive, precisely because 'immigration' is a term which covers many different forms of social behaviour. But everywhere we look, we see cities full of migrants from near and far – male and female, rich and poor, skilled and unskilled.

Schwäbisch Hall was no different from any other city in this respect. There was no shortage of wealthy immigrants like Lienhard Romig, who came as a young man from Ansbach, or Marie Firnhaber, who had arrived in Schwäbisch Hall as the widow Marie Busch from Heilbronn. They certainly had a demographic impact on the city – as we have seen, between the two of them they lived to see 291 descendants born in the city. But to get a fuller sense of the character of inter-urban migration in early modern Europe, we should also

43. Friedrichs, *Urban Society*, 53–66.
44. Friedrichs, 'Immigration'.

consider the life of Catharina Ickermann, who died in Schwäbisch Hall without ever having married or given birth. Here is her entry. from the burial register for 1 February 1695:

> Catharina, legitimate daughter of the late Bartholomaus Ickermann, shoemaker, and his wife Catharina Firckin, was born about 97 years ago in Perleberg in the New Mark of the Electorate of Brandenburg, and was given holy baptism, raised as a Christian and sent to church and school; after the death of her beloved parents at fifteen years of age she went into service and worked in an inn in Weissenburg, an hour from Perleberg, for twenty years; then in Hamburg at a confectioner's for ten years; then in Königsberg in Prussia for Herr Johann Adam Hocheicher for ten years; then in Bünincken in Württemberg and in Wimpfen for ten years; and then here for the late Herr Josias Hocheicher for 28 years and for Herr Sigelin, innkeeper at the sign of the Eagle, for four years, always serving well, honestly and industriously, until some time ago she found herself unwell and stayed in bed and the day before yesterday passed away between 5 and 6 in the morning.[45]

Catharina Ickermann's odyssey was not a sequence of random travels; once she had started to work for the Hocheicher family, she remained in their service while they themselves moved all over Germany. Her last employer, in fact, was married to the granddaughter of the man she had worked for in Königsberg.[46] But masters and servant alike illustrate the extent to which migration could shape personal lives and reshape urban populations in early modern Europe.

45. Wunder, *Bürger*, 174–5.
46. ibid., 175.

PART TWO

The City as a Social Arena

CHAPTER SIX

Work and Status

Life is a struggle – a constant attempt to make the most of one's condition, to improve one's lot, to provide for one's own future and, in many cases, for that of one's family. This is true of all people, at all times. In the struggle for a secure and meaningful life, men and women exploit any number of available resources. Intelligence and health always help. Communal support may compensate for the lack of either or both. But the most important resources on which people draw are generally derived from the two great spheres of human experience and identity: work and family.

We may begin with work. For most adults in most human societies, work is the unavoidable precondition for the economic security to which all aspire. Of course different types of work yield vastly different rewards. Yet people are highly constrained in choosing the work they perform. What kind of work people do is partly determined by the opportunities available within the economic system of their society. But it is also heavily controlled by such factors as age, gender, family background and social status. This is true today, but it was even more powerfully true in early modern times. So in order to understand the role of work in the early modern city, we must begin by looking at the overall structure of social organization.

I

As in every human society, the fundamental characteristic of urban social structure in early modern times was inequality: some individuals exercised more power, commanded more respect or controlled more resources than others. This much is easy to grasp. But to describe convincingly the actual structure of social inequality in any particular setting is a daunting task. Almost every attempt to describe social structure starts from the premise that each human society has a vertical hierarchy or 'ladder' of power and prestige, and every individual has a specific place on that ladder. Of course no society is really made up of a single hierarchy: there is always a complex pattern of intermingled chutes and ladders, and any person can occupy a multiplicity of 'social positions'. Yet there is an inevitable tendency to reduce the complexity of social structure by positing, at least in theory, a single primary 'ladder' of social positions.

In modern western societies, the concept of a social hierarchy competes with a democratic ideology according to which each adult person is legally and formally equal. Nobody doubts the existence of a social hierarchy. But in the absence of any formal differences in personal status, some other attribute – typically occupation – will be taken to indicate where a person stands on the invisible ladder of status. One familiar modern assumption posits that those who perform 'white-collar' work are socially superior to those engaged in 'blue-collar' occupations. Schematic approaches like this undergo frequent revision as the economic rewards associated with various types of work undergo change. But two aspects remain constant. First, in modern societies occupation is normally taken as the chief determinant of social status. Second, as in almost all human societies, rank is normally determined by masculine activity or prestige – for women and children are assumed to share the social status of the adult male head of their family.

Early modern Europeans also had a formal ideology of human equality – but it applied only to the afterlife. All individuals would ultimately stand as equals before God, their chances of salvation or damnation completely unaffected by differences in worldly rank. But down on earth no such principles applied. God himself had ordained human inequality as a fundamental fact of life. Everyone stood somewhere on the great ladder of status – and everyone should know his or her position.

This principle was so widely expounded by lay and clerical leaders alike that most people in early modern Europe must have taken it for granted. Yet to apply this idea in practice often proved difficult. Even in a single community, it was hard to assign every inhabitant to an undisputed locus on the ladder of status. Of course merchants stood above craftsmen, masters above servants, men above women. But the details were less obvious.

In many cities, laborious efforts were undertaken to establish a distinct hierarchy of social ranks. In some communities the distinction between different ranks was reinforced by sumptuary ordinances which specified exactly what articles of clothing or items of adornment could be worn by members of each social group. A shadow of this principle survives today in the visible distinctions among military uniforms and academic robes; in early modern cities it was entirely customary to specify that only people of a particular social rank could wear silk or satin or line their collars with fur. But such regulations merely reflected the broader assumption that urban inhabitants were divided into graduated ranks.

In 1621 the magistrates of Frankfurt am Main issued a new ordinance which refined previous practice by dividing the city's inhabitants into five legal 'orders'.[1] The first order consisted chiefly of the city's old patrician families who claimed quasi-noble status. Next came non-patrician members of the city council, along with other 'distinguished' citizens and merchants. The third order consisted of 'distinguished' retailers and members of the legal profession. Then came common retailers and all craftspeople – a vastly larger category than the first three orders combined. The fifth order encompassed unskilled labourers and everyone else. The ordinance was revised twice, partly to specify more precisely just what made a merchant or other citizen 'distinguished' enough to belong to the second order. In 1671 this group was described more precisely as those engaged in wholesale or banking activities. In 1731 the category was revised again; now merchants and others could belong to the second order if they met a specific wealth requirement.[2] But no amount of tinkering could ever succeed in squeezing the rich social variety of a city like Frankfurt into the strait-jacket of five arbitrary categories. Ethnic and religious distinctions complicated the social structure. Frankfurt was predominantly Lutheran; Calvinists and Catholics, though often quite wealthy, were denied full political rights and would not normally have been accepted into the higher social ranks. And the city's many Jewish inhabitants were not included in any of the five orders.

In countless European cities, formal or informal attempts were undertaken to divide the inhabitants into a series of graduated ranks. These ranking systems, however, served different purposes and reflected different concerns. In Venice only three ranks really mattered: the inhabitants were divided into a small group of *nobeli*, a scarcely larger group of *cittadini*, and a vast number of *popolani*.[3] In the French town of Beauvais, by contrast, the community was divided

1. Soliday, *Community in Conflict*, 62–3.
2. ibid., 61–5.
3. Cowan, *Urban Patriciate*, 51.

for political purposes into no fewer than thirty-one corporate groups: the first six consisted chiefly of civic officials and professionals; the remaining twenty-five were made up of various occupational clusters, beginning with the great cloth merchants and descending downward to the agricultural labourers.[4] Neither scheme adequately reflected social realities. The Venetian system glossed over the substantial distinctions which could exist among the plebeians; the Beauvais scheme implied more rigid differences than could have existed in fact. Most urban Europeans, if asked to describe the social structure of their own communities, might have come up with a scheme much along the lines established in Frankfurt. At the top, in larger cities, were those who claimed noble status. Then came the highest officeholders and wealthy inhabitants who lived off rents or other permanent revenues. Next were the major wholesale merchants, followed by lesser merchants, innkeepers, retailers and the like. Then came the great mass of artisans, ranging from goldsmiths and other prestigious craftsmen downward towards the weavers and shoemakers. Unskilled labourers, servants, and unemployed or unemployable people occupied the bottom ranks. Women were assumed to share the social rank of their husbands or fathers.

The Frankfurt system of ranks was characteristic of urban self-perception in its mixture of criteria based on family, office, occupation and wealth. Membership in the first order was essentially genetic. The fourth and fifth orders, by contrast, were based chiefly on occupation. But the qualifications for membership in the second and third orders were not determined by any single criterion. Wealth, for example, could modify status rankings based on occupation: sufficient riches could boost a merchant from the third into the second order, while a retailer moved up one rank if his establishment was considered sufficiently solid.

The entire concept of social rankings, after all, was never intended to prevent social mobility – it was supposed only to control and regulate it. It is true that in some major cities membership in the very highest social rank – the patriciate of Frankfurt, say, or the nobility of Venice – was extremely restricted. But even here some newcomers eventually gained admission. In fact no city had a rigid caste system. Sufficient wealth, perhaps combined with a strategic marriage, almost always made it possible to move up the social ladder. Downward mobility, of course, was equally common. Members of the very highest social ranks enjoyed some protection

4. Goubert, *Beauvais et le Beauvaisis*, 1: 266–8.

from the consequences of a loss in wealth: while most charity was relentlessly public, confidential assistance might be extended to decayed members of the social elite, for the hierarchical system itself would be undermined if people of high social status were seen to be openly dependent on public assistance.[5] But in the middle ranks of the social structure, the risks of slipping visibly down the social ladder were always as great as the chances of moving up.

Most attempts to describe the social structure of an early modern city start from the top down. Yet this can be a misleading perspective, for the social elite was the sector whose composition was most likely to differ from one community to the next. A more useful way to conceptualize the society of the early modern city may be to begin at the centre – with the great core group of householding families, the people who produced goods or were engaged in the endless round of petty economic exchanges that characterized the urban economy. To join this core group of householding families was the dream of many: every young journeyman or maidservant must have hoped, at some point, to have a shop, home and family of his or her own. Among those who already belonged to the group of householding families, many had to struggle just to stay within the group. But there were others who struggled just as hard to leave this group, aspiring to rise up into the lower ranks of the social elite.

In some parts of Europe membership in this core group of householding families was closely linked to the right of citizenship. This was certainly the norm in the Germanic regions of central Europe, where it was customary for a young man to marry, set up an independent household and start exercising his duties as a citizen all at once. Only the son of a citizen had an automatic claim to this status; all others had to apply for admission – a situation that gave municipal authorities a considerable degree of control over family formation and economic activity. In most English towns, at least until the seventeenth century, nobody could operate an autonomous economic activity unless he – or more rarely she – had obtained the freedom of the city by inheritance, purchase or successful completion of an apprenticeship. Outsiders who wanted to trade in the city could do so only by selling to or buying from a local freeman. But the link between citizenship and economic autonomy was not universal. In France, for example, the status of municipal *bourgeois* was generally more exclusive than in England or Germany – but formal membership

5. e.g. Martz, *Poverty and Welfare*, 202, 206; Perry, *Gender and Disorder*, 175; Pullan, *Rich and Poor*, 229.

in the political community was not required for the exercise of one's rights as a master of the craft.

What the core group of householding families did have in common almost everywhere in Europe was this: their lives were centred on work, and their work, in turn, was structured by the guild system. Of course guilds were not uniform in the way they functioned. In some towns they acted with a high degree of independence, influencing or even controlling the municipal political institutions. In other towns exactly the reverse applied: the municipal government closely regulated and supervised the guilds. Some guilds were strictly limited to those who engaged in a single craft; other guilds encompassed masters who performed related but not identical work. Some guilds had broad religious and social functions; others did not. But everywhere the work performed in artisanal households was shaped and structured by the traditions and regulations of the guild system. In some English towns, by the early eighteenth century the guilds had given up the attempt to exercise any meaningful control over economic life; a few even dissolved.[6] But everywhere else in Europe the guild system and the values it represented remained a powerful force right to the end of the *ancien régime*.

The central values promoted by the guild system were familiar all over Europe. Membership in the guild was to be restricted, so that not too many people would compete in the same market. Complete equality was never envisioned, but each guild master was entitled to a fair opportunity to earn a living as the head of an autonomous unit of production. All guild members shared a collective responsibility to uphold traditional standards of production and norms of personal conduct, for the disgrace of any one would bring dishonour upon all. Laziness was scorned; work was respected.

Skilled manual labour was the common experience of the great core group of householding guild members and their families. But the character and significance of work began to change as one moved either up or down the social ladder. Moving up the ladder, work became progressively more skilled and less manual. Even further up were those who did less work or no work at all. Moving down the ladder, work became progressively less skilled and more manual, eventually also giving way to those who performed no visible labour. Both the very top and the very bottom of the social scale, then, were occupied by people who did no work – though the way in which

6. Corfield, *Impact of English Towns*, 86–8.

these different forms of idleness were interpreted remained entirely different.

Certainly the character of the work a man performed was a major component of his own and his family's social rank. 'Refined' craftsmen like goldsmiths and silversmiths were always among the most prestigious guildsmen, not only because of their traditional wealth but also because they worked cleanly with the most noble of metals. Higher still were those who worked only with ink and paper, especially if they had professional training or university degrees. Lawyers were of high status to start with and moved steadily upward in the early modern era. A parallel principle applied to the realm of commerce: the less physical contact a merchant had with the goods he traded, the greater the prestige he enjoyed. Retailers who personally waited on their customers, purveying merchandise item by item, always ranked lower than wholesale merchants who, in the words of a French decree, 'carry out their trade in a warehouse, selling their merchandise by bales, cases, or open lots, and . . . do not have open shops or any display counter and sign at their doors and houses'.[7] In many communities even more respect was accorded to those who could live in a dignified style without engaging in any form of commerce: the rentier who supported himself exclusively by property rents or other forms of investment income normally stood close to the pinnacle of the social ladder. This was regarded as 'living nobly'; in most cities only actual nobles ranked higher on the scale of prestige. To enjoy prosperity without having to work for it normally engendered deep respect, for it freed a man and his family to devote their lives to cultured leisure or public service.

Moving down the ladder from the guild artisans, the character of work also changed: it became less skilled, less autonomous and less regular. The journeyman, the hired hand, the servant, the day-labourer all performed less specialized and less permanent forms of labour, with a corresponding diminution of social prestige. Then there were those who did not work at all. It was understood that many people, due to age or illness, could not work – but others, it was assumed, simply would not. The idleness of the wealthy, seen as freedom from the necessity of having to engage in labour, was ennobling – but the idleness of poor people, interpreted as a refusal to submit to the necessity of working for a living, was demeaning. At the very bottom of the social ladder were those who were perceived

7. From a decree of 1701 issued by Louis XIV: Ranum and Ranum (eds) *Century of Louis XIV*, 349.

– rightly or not – as unwilling to conform to the commandment that man should gain his daily bread by the toil of his arms and the sweat of his brow.

II

These, then, are some of the principles that guided early modern town-dwellers in their attempt to understand and describe the communities in which they lived. Of course no amount of theory could ever adequately reflect the full diversity of social life. We may, however, get a fuller view of urban social structure if we turn from abstract value systems to empirical data about the distribution of occupations and wealth in specific cities. Records that cast some light on the occupational and wealth structure of European cities abound: wills, marriage contracts, guild registers, muster rolls, citizenship lists and more. Historians have used them all. The most useful of these sources tend to be those related to taxation – but only some cities preserved systematic records pertaining to taxes levied on specific inhabitants. And even the fullest such records still provide less than a comprehensive view of the community. Personal taxes were normally levied on property, not income, so those who owned nothing worth taxing were often ignored. It was customary to tax households rather than individuals. The property owned by a husband and wife, though often counted separately for inheritance purposes, would generally be pooled when it came to tax assessments. Women were listed as taxpayers only if they were widowed or lived on their own. Even the best-maintained records had errors and omissions. Yet even so, records of this sort, where they exist, may bring us closer to the reality of urban social structure than any other source.

Of course every city had a distinct social profile derived from its location, economic function, political status and cultural traditions: there was no 'typical' case. But we can still learn much about urban social structure in general if we take a close look at some individual communities. Let us begin, then, by comparing what the tax records reveal about two European cities of comparable size in the late sixteenth century.[8]

Dijon was the administrative and economic capital of the rich winegrowing province of Burgundy in eastern France. It was also one of the few major French cities in which the *taille* was levied:

8. The following comparison is based on the data presented in Farr, 'Consumers, Commerce and the Craftsmen of Dijon', 134–73, and Bothe, *Frankfurts wirtschaftlich-soziale Entwicklung*, 2: 142–56.

Table 6.1 Social and occupational structure of Dijon, 1556

MALE HOUSEHOLDERS			
HIGH OFFICIALS	73	(3.0%)	
GENTLEMEN	6	(0.2%)	
LAWYERS AND OTHER PROFESSIONALS	121	(4.9%)	
LESSER OFFICIALS	23	(0.9%)	
MERCHANTS AND RETAILERS	116	(4.7%)	
INNKEEPERS AND TAVERNERS	34	(1.4%)	
ARTISANS	910	(36.9%)	
GOVERNMENT EMPLOYEES AND SOLDIERS	111	(4.5%)	
CARTERS AND OTHER UNSKILLED WORKERS	48	(1.9%)	
AGRICULTURAL WORKERS	379	(15.3%)	
SERVANTS AND MISCELLANEOUS	25	(1.0%)	
NO OCCUPATION GIVEN	617	(25.1%)	
TOTAL MALE HOUSEHOLDERS	2,463	(100.0%)	(87.3% of total)
FEMALE HOUSEHOLDERS			
WIDOWS	313	(87.7%)	
OTHERS	44	(12.3%)	
TOTAL FEMALE HOUSEHOLDERS	357	(100.0%)	(12.7% of total)
TOTAL HOUSEHOLDERS	2,820		(100.0%)

Source: Adapted from Farr, 'Consumers, Commerce and Craftsmen', 138

though this tax was paid by almost all peasant households in France, many cities had obtained exemption from this burden. Even in Dijon not everyone was covered. Members of the clergy – a large group in this Catholic town – were not listed on the tax roll. Nor were most servants and other dependents. Some of the city's rootless poor also escaped the tax-collectors' notice. But most householders in Dijon appeared on the list of taxpayers, even when they were excused from actual payment.

Dijon had close to 15,000 inhabitants in the mid-sixteenth century.[9] In the year 1556, 2,820 adult heads of households were listed on the tax roll. Table 6.1 shows who they were. The first thing one notices

9. Farr, *Hands of Honor*, 271–4.

is that only one-eighth of the listed households were headed by women. A few of these women were recorded as having specific occupations – seamstresses, laundresses, midwives and the like – but most female taxpayers were simply listed as 'widows'.

Seven-eighths of the taxpayers were men. We do not know what all of them did for a living, for a quarter of these men are listed without an occupation. Most of the men in this group paid only modest taxes, suggesting that many of them may have been labourers or other less skilled workers. For three-quarters of the men, however, we do know about their occupation or station in life. As the seat of a *parlement* and a centre of royal administration, Dijon had a substantial community of officials, lawyers and government employees. Situated at the heart of one of the great winegrowing regions of France, Dijon also had a large number of agricultural workers, many of whom were vinedressers. But over one-third of all the males who headed a household in Dijon were artisans, practising one of the more than eighty crafts recorded in the city.

Table 6.2 Social and occupational structure of Frankfurt am Main, 1587

MALE HOUSEHOLDERS			
PATRICIANS AND RENTIERS	50	(2.2%)	
HIGH MUNICIPAL OFFICIALS	11	(0.5%)	
LAWYERS, CLERGY, TEACHERS AND OTHER PROFESSIONALS	46	(2.1%)	
MERCHANTS AND RETAILERS	219	(9.9%)	
INNKEEPERS AND TAVERNERS	31	(1.4%)	
ARTISANS	1,247	(56.1%)	
MUNICIPAL EMPLOYEES	92	(4.1%)	
CARTERS AND OTHER UNSKILLED LABOURERS	197	(8.9%)	
AGRICULTURAL WORKERS	254	(11.4%)	
NO OCCUPATION GIVEN	76	(3.4%)	
TOTAL MALE HOUSEHOLDERS	2,223	(100.0%)	(79.8% of total)
FEMALE HOUSEHOLDERS			
WIDOWS	524	(92.9%)	
OTHERS	40	(7.1%)	
TOTAL FEMALE HOUSEHOLDERS	564	(100.0%)	(20.2% of total)
TOTAL HOUSEHOLDERS	2,787		(100.0%)

Source: Adapted from Bothe, *Frankfurts wirtschaftlich-soziale Entwicklung*, 2: 142–56

We shall return to Dijon, but first let us look at the distribution of activities and trades in another European city: Frankfurt am Main. In the late sixteenth century Frankfurt was slightly larger than Dijon. In 1587, there were 2,787 Christian households headed by citizens or by 'denizens' who enjoyed secure residence rights in the city. As a Protestant city, Frankfurt had a relatively small clergy, and its members were taxed along with others. But the city's large Jewish population was listed and taxed separately.

Table 6.2 shows who comprised the city's 2,787 Christian taxpayers in 1587. One-fifth of them were women; as in Dijon, most were widows. Among the male taxpayers, the occupations of almost all were recorded. Unlike Dijon, Frankfurt had no administrative functions beyond its own municipal government, so the proportion of officials and lawyers was lower. As the seat of two international trade fairs every year, Frankfurt was a more important commercial centre than Dijon – which was reflected in Frankfurt's higher proportion of merchants and retailers. But as in Dijon, the most important sector was the artisanate: here, in fact, over half of the male taxpayers were craftsmen.

Table 6.3 enables us to compare the craft structure of the two cities.[10] Some crafts were practised by only one or two people: each city, for example, had only one button-maker. But there were some major trades. Dijon, for example, had 70 tailors and 58 masons. Frankfurt had 94 tailors and 74 makers of barrels. Yet one craft was even more prominent: Frankfurt had 192 *passamentiers*, who made silken lace and braid; Dijon, by contrast, had only 4. The importance of this one activity in Frankfurt meant that almost one-fifth of the craftsmen there were engaged in making 'luxury cloths'. This degree of specialization was not echoed in Dijon. But if we broaden our focus to ask how many craftsmen in either town were involved in producing any type of textile, clothing or footwear, we find a striking similarity: in both cities, just over two-fifths of all craftsmen were engaged in these activities. This is not entirely surprising. In countless European towns, in fact, the cloth and clothing sector, broadly defined, accounted for the greatest number of artisans.

But tax rolls do not only reveal the distribution of occupations; in those cities where, as in Dijon and Frankfurt, tax assessments were

10. In order to make it possible to compare the two cities I have not always assigned specific occupational groups to the same broader categories that Farr and Bothe used. For example, whereas Bothe counted carpenters among the woodworking trades, I have followed Farr in putting them among the construction trades.

Table 6.3 Distribution of crafts in Dijon and Frankfurt

	Dijon *1556* 910 men + 40 women	*Frankfurt* *1587* 1,247 men
FOOD AND DRINK	16.2%	10.7%
ORDINARY CLOTHS	11.8%	4.7%
LUXURY CLOTHS	1.4%	19.2%
CLOTHING	12.7%	8.0%
LEATHER AND FURS	15.1%	10.7%
BOOKS, ART AND LUXURY GOODS	4.7%	12.6%
METALWORKING AND WEAPONRY	10.0%	6.4%
CONSTRUCTION	15.3%	11.1%
WOODWORKING	8.9%	12.2%
OTHER CRAFTS	3.9%	4.4%

Source: Adapted from Farr, 'Consumers, Commerce and Craftsmen', 169–73, and Bothe, *Frankfurts wirtschaftlich-soziale Entwicklung*, 2: 142–56

specifically based on total household wealth, we can also study the distribution of wealth. To be sure, the data do not always answer all our questions. In Dijon, for example, the results are compromised by the frequency of tax exemption – a privilege which was ardently pursued and often achieved by wealthy French families throughout the *ancien régime*. Thus, the tax roll for 1556 includes the names of 133 men and women whose families were excused from making tax payment by virtue of noble rank or 'privileged' office. Yet even among those who did have to pay taxes, a huge range of wealth was still apparent. Just among craftsmen there were significant differences. The median tax payment of tanners, for example, was 30 sous, while that of cobblers was 2 sous; thus, those who made new leather from hides were, on average, fifteen times richer than those who repaired old leather goods.

In Frankfurt no citizen was exempt from taxation, though the very richest did have one advantage: while as a rule the tax was a fixed percentage of the household's total wealth, anyone worth more than 15,000 gulden – the top 2 per cent of the taxpayers – could instead pay a flat fee. Thus we cannot know exactly how rich the richest Frankfurters were. Even so, the vast difference in wealth among the city's households is fully apparent from the data summarized in Table 6.4. Over one-third of all male taxpayers and half of all female

Table 6.4 Distribution of wealth in Frankfurt am Main, 1587

	No.	*Under 100 gulden*	*100 –400 gulden*	*400 –1,000 gulden*	*1,000 –5,000 gulden*	*Over 5,000 gulden*
ALL MALE TAXPAYERS	2,223	37%	32%	11%	14%	6%
ALL FEMALE TAXPAYERS	564	51%	24%	7%	12%	5%
Selected groups (male taxpayers)						
PATRICIANS	46	—	—	—	28%	72%
MERCHANTS	43	—	7%	5%	47%	42%
TAVERNERS	31	3%	23%	19%	39%	16%
SHOPKEEPERS	75	9%	32%	21%	28%	9%
COOPERS	74	28%	27%	24%	19%	1%
BUTCHERS	54	24%	44%	20%	11%	—
TAILORS	94	32%	38%	18%	12%	—
SHOEMAKERS	60	35%	30%	18%	17%	—
LACEMAKERS	192	42%	44%	9%	4%	1%
WINEGROWERS	154	64%	29%	6%	1%	—
DAY-LABOURERS	98	86%	13%	1%	—	—

Source: Adapted from Bothe, *Frankfurts wirtschaftlich-soziale Entwicklung*, 2: 142–56

taxpayers had an assessed worth of less than 100 gulden – while men and women in the top 5–6 per cent were worth at least fifty times as much.

Not surprisingly, different social and occupational groups showed highly variant patterns of wealth. All the patricians and almost all merchants were worth at least 1,000 gulden. Shopkeepers and taverners were found in all wealth categories. Coopers, butchers, tailors and shoemakers all illustrate the broad range of wealth levels that could be found among members of a single craft. Members of the city's largest craft – the *Passamentiere* or lacemakers – were clustered in the lower wealth levels, though a handful were anomalously rich. Winegrowers and unskilled day-labourers were all at the bottom of the wealth range. Wealth and poverty, then, were strongly correlated with the occupations of highest and lowest prestige. In the middle ranks the correlation was less pronounced.

What do these cities illustrate about the general distribution of wealth and occupations in the early modern city? Obviously they cannot be taken as 'typical', for the specific proportions always differed from one city to the next. Indeed, even within any given city there was a constant mutation over time – nor were the changes always unidirectional. In Dijon, for example, the proportion of textile workers had been almost twice as high in the 1460s as it was ninety years later. During the sixteenth and seventeenth centuries, textile weaving declined in Dijon, evidently because much of the actual weaving was done by rural villagers. Yet in the eighteenth century the trend was reversed, and the proportion of weavers in Dijon began to rise again. In Frankfurt, the late sixteenth century represented the high-water mark of the lacemaking trade; a century later, this particular craft had sharply declined.[11]

Yet in cities all over Europe during the early modern era, many of the basic patterns we can identify in Dijon and Frankfurt tended to recur. Whenever the distribution of wealth can be studied, it proves to be highly skewed. Every town had an elite group of officeholders, merchants and, in some cities, rentiers who generally held a high proportion of the total wealth. Depending on a city's political functions and economic profile, there would be larger or smaller groupings of professionals, retailers, innkeepers and the like. Artisans always made up a substantial part of the total number of householders – and among them, people engaged in the textile, leather and clothing trades often represented the largest share. But among the householders would also be found a substantial number of less specialized labourers or agricultural workers who were normally clustered at the bottom end of the wealth hierarchy.

Consider one more example: the English town of Norwich. In 1525 the city had 1,414 taxpayers, among whom a mere 29 men owned over 40 per cent of the community's total wealth. The tax levied in 1525 covered a broad spectrum of the city's inhabitants; scarcely half of the taxpayers were freemen of the town with specific trades. Among these 705 men, over 30 per cent were engaged in textile production, while another 11 per cent belonged to the leather crafts and 8 per cent made clothing.[12] In later years, as Norwich became a major supplier of cloth to the rapidly growing capital city of London, weaving assumed an even greater role in the town's economy. By the early eighteenth century, in fact, over half of the freemen of Norwich were engaged in the textile trades.[13] To be sure, Norwich was famous as a cloth-making town and the proportion of weavers

11. Bothe, *Geschichte der Stadt Frankfurt*, 479. The general decline of luxury industries is also evident from the data in Soliday, *Community in Conflict*, 50–1.
12. Pound, 'Social and Trade Structure', 49–52, 55–7.
13. Corfield, 'Provincial Capital', 274–87.

there was unusually high. There were certainly specific European towns in which some other trade – anything from shipbuilding to metalwork or beer-brewing – might represent the dominant industry. But there is little doubt that if we take the cities of early modern Europe as a whole, then textiles, clothing and other items of apparel easily represented the most important branch of urban production.

Norwich also illustrates yet another characteristic of the early modern city: the correlation between the size of a town and the level of occupational differentiation. This has been demonstrated by comparing Norwich to other towns in the same region of eastern England. In the sixteenth century there were over forty towns in East Anglia, ranging from Norwich, with a population of about 8,000, down to tiny communities like Ixworth and Watton with just a few hundred souls each. Documents from Norwich show that over 200 distinct occupations were practised in the regional metropolis, and many were highly specialized: at one point or another in the sixteenth century Norwich had at least one basketweaver, bell-founder, embroiderer, parchmentmaker, spicebread-maker, spindle-maker, upholsterer, chimney-sweep and so on. Towns like King's Lynn or Great Yarmouth, which were roughly half the size of Norwich, had about 100 distinct occupations each. Going down the list of towns by size, the number of occupations progressively contracted; the smallest towns in East Anglia had scarcely half a dozen non-agricultural trades: a few weavers, tailors, shoemakers, butchers, and little else.[14] Elsewhere in Europe the number of occupations may not have been so precisely a function of town size as it proved to be in East Anglia, but the basic pattern was the same. A small town could offer only a limited range of services to its own inhabitants and those of the surrounding region. The bigger a town became, the more likely it was that people could support themselves by offering highly specialized services.

Certainly any attempt to discuss the social and economic structure of the early modern town must take as its starting-point the distribution of occupations and wealth revealed by tax registers, muster rolls, lists of citizens and similar records. Yet at the same time, one must never lose sight of the inevitable limitations of such sources. Data like these reflect the predominant assumption of early modern society that the basic unit of society was the individual household, normally headed by a male householder or his widow. Yet work is ultimately performed not by households but by individuals. To

14. Patten, *English Towns*, 252–70.

be sure, the household often functioned as a unit of production, but not all of its members worked exclusively as members of the household economy. Often household income was supplemented by unrelated work performed outside the home. A man might serve as a watchman or beadle, or a woman might work as a midwife or healer, yet the household might appear in the records under the rubric of weaving or shoemaking.

Even the fullest tax register for any given year can never provide more than an evanescent snapshot of the community's social structure at a given moment. The overall structure was always undergoing changes. Individual careers, of course, were even more mutable. A man who appears in the bottom wealth category near the beginning of his career might well show up on a much higher rung twenty years later. The reverse, of course, was just as likely. Economic failure or an overlarge family could push someone steadily downward.

As a result, though we may know much about a community's social and economic structure, neither an individual's wealth nor that person's occupation in any given year will always provide a definitive key to identifying the social position of that particular householder. Consider the lacemakers of Frankfurt. Most of the *Passamentiere* were religious refugees from northern France or the Netherlands. As Calvinists they were disbarred from full participation in the city's political life. Furthermore, many of them were unable to sustain their economic independence and worked on a putting-out basis for a handful of prosperous silk merchants.[15] As we have seen, most of them belonged to the lowest wealth brackets in 1587. Certainly lacemakers as a group would have been placed on the lower end of the social ladder. But what are we to make of Balduin de Ferret? An immigrant from Waterloo, he was listed as a *Passamentier* in the tax register of 1587. But his wealth amounted to 1,000 gulden, which placed him within the top 20 per cent of the population, and he is listed in some records as a *Krämer*, or shopkeeper.[16] Where exactly would the magistrates of Frankfurt have placed him in their scheme of five orders? Would his foreign origins, Calvinist faith and original craft of lacemaking have confined him to the fourth 'order' of craftsmen and ordinary retailers – or would his wealth, which could have made him a 'distinguished' retailer, have enabled him to move up one rung? We do not know – and perhaps he never knew himself.

15. Bothe, *Geschichte der Stadt Frankfurt*, 359–61, 378–81.
16. Bothe, *Frankfurts wirtschaftlich-soziale Entwicklung*, 2: 71.

III

The social structure of the early modern city, then, was not based on a rigid hierarchy of fixed strata. Instead the city had a system of social relations which were strongly shaped by tradition but always subject to gradual change and adaptation. This was the system into which the man or woman on the brink of adulthood hoped to be integrated, the system through which he or she hoped to achieve success or security or, if nothing else, at least sustenance. The major way by which this could be achieved was, of course, through work.

Lots of work was available in the early modern city – though never, it seemed, quite enough to go around. Depending on one's skills and connections, there were plants to be cultivated, animals to be tended, loads to be carried, clothes to be washed, meals to be served, records to be maintained – but above all, for those who qualified, there were skilled crafts to be practised and their products to be exchanged. Skilled labour, of course, was the province of the guilds. Not all forms of urban work fell under the purview of the guilds – but any discussion of work in the early modern city must still begin by considering the impact of these most fundamental of all urban institutions.

The guild was predominantly a male organization. Women were by no means untouched by the guild and its practices, but their role was always peripheral. For one of the main purposes of the guild was to prepare some people to perform skilled labour and to prevent others from doing so. Most skilled techniques were regarded as specifically male tasks. But this was only the first of many barriers which were imposed in order to limit the number of people qualified to practise particular trades.

Let us begin by taking a close look at how the guilds structured work in one community: the city of Tallinn in Estonia. In the seventeenth century Tallinn, also known as Reval, was a predominantly German-speaking city in a coastal region ruled by Sweden. Its location on the Gulf of Finland placed Tallinn on the very periphery of European civilization – yet in its economic and social organization Tallinn typified norms that prevailed over most of Europe. Centuries of trading contact with the Hanseatic cities of the Baltic region had kept the citizens of Tallinn thoroughly abreast of German customs. Guild norms in Germany, moreover, had much in common with those that prevailed in France and elsewhere.

Almost every craftsman in seventeenth-century Tallinn belonged to a guild. Each major craft had its own guild, while smaller crafts were grouped together in catch-all guilds of related trades.

Increased specialization throughout the seventeenth century led to the formation of new guilds: coppersmiths, locksmiths and clockmakers, for example, broke away from the general guild of metalworkers. Each guild, old or new, had detailed statutes ratified by the city government.[17]

Every guild had detailed provisions for the training of apprentices and journeymen. A potential apprentice had to be approved by the guild council. Once accepted, the apprentice signed up for a term of four to seven years with a master who provided him with room and board in return for his labour service. When his term was up the apprentice normally received a small payment from his master and was accepted by the guild council as a journeyman. Now his compulsory 'wandering' began. Armed with documents that certified his background and apprenticeship, the journeyman headed for Germany or Sweden to spend three or four years working for wages with a series of masters. Meanwhile journeymen from other cities turned up in Tallinn. The guild guaranteed every arriving journeyman at least two weeks of work with some master. If the journeyman's services were really needed, as was often the case, he might be kept on for much longer.[18]

Having completed his wander-years and carefully saved his earnings, the journeyman was free to apply for admission to mastership. In doing so he had to pay a series of application fees and, more importantly, submit a masterpiece according to requirements laid down by each guild: the would-be potter had to make a pot, pitcher and vat of specified dimensions; the mason had to produce detailed drawings along with a scale model of a three-storey house. If the masterpiece was accepted, the successful candidate was expected to host a luxurious banquet for the masters whose craft he hoped to join. While completing his masterpiece, however, the candidate also had to conduct a successful courtship, for before being accepted as a master he was required to submit the name of his proposed bride – whose background and reputation would then be checked by the guild. Personal connections always smoothed the way: if the candidate was the son of a guild member, or the bride was the widow or daughter of one, the application fees or waiting period might be reduced.[19]

Once accepted as a master and enrolled as a citizen, the new guild member was free to open his own shop. Yet his prospects of economic

17. Soom, *Zunfthandwerker in Reval*, 13–14, 33–9.
18. ibid., 95–103.
19. ibid., 103–8.

security were still tenuous, since the market for his wares was never unlimited. Now, however, he could count on the help and support of his fellow-masters. The main strategy adopted by the guilds of Tallinn to bolster the economic security of their members was to minimize competition. To start with, competition within the guild itself was firmly discouraged: it was forbidden, for example, to hire extra journeymen or to lure apprentices or customers away from a fellow-master. A more serious threat was posed by non-guilded craftsmen who worked in the cathedral precincts or operated in the countryside under the protection of noble landowners. Throughout the seventeenth century the guilds of Tallinn struggled persistently against these rivals and interlopers. But despite support from the city's magistrates these efforts were generally fruitless, for the interlopers had powerful patrons. At times the magistrates themselves lost patience with the restrictiveness of the guild mentality. In the early 1660s the city council tried to force the guilds to accept more candidates and reduce the costs of applying for mastership. Resistance by the guilds was broken only after officials in Stockholm intervened to support the council in its determination to loosen the guilds' most monopolistic practices.[20]

All this happened in Tallinn – but it could have been anywhere. Throughout the early seventeenth century, for example, the magistrates of Dijon were engaged in a very similar struggle to force guild masters to open up their ranks and get them to stop demanding the excessive fees, lavish banquets and impossible masterpieces which prevented qualified journeymen from advancing to mastership. The guilds, in turn, banded together to guard their customary practices from municipal intervention.[21]

All over Europe, in fact, guilds wanted to protect their traditional right to restrict and control the admission of new members. Like all institutions in early modern Europe, the guilds demonstrated a passionate determination to preserve their existing privileges. Yet the image of early modern guilds as completely rigid in their structures and policies – an image vigorously promoted by eighteenth-century critics who saw the guilds as obstacles to economic progress – is certainly exaggerated. In fact many guilds responded in flexible ways to new economic and political realities. Often, for example, guild leaders acknowledged the need for new techniques or permitted their members to undertake new types of economic activities.[22]

20. ibid., 111–12, 120–36, 142–72.
21. Farr, *Hands of Honor*, 44–56.
22. cf. Mackenney, *Tradesmen and Traders*, 113–25.

Of course a guild was not always a fellowship of economic equals. Despite the usual efforts to preserve equality of opportunity among the masters, differences in wealth always arose – and almost always it was the richer masters who monopolized the most influential or prestigious guild offices. In larger guilds, richer and poorer masters might find themselves pitted against each other on questions of economic policy. This was certainly the case in a huge organization like the weavers' guild of Augsburg, which had around 2,000 members in the late sixteenth and early seventeenth century.[23] The interests of rich members, who wanted to expand their output by adding more looms and introducing quasi-industrial techniques, would naturally have differed from those of poor masters who lacked the means to hire extra hands. The rich weavers enjoyed obvious advantages in pursuing their goals, but poorer weavers continued to be heard. This is all the more remarkable because after the mid-sixteenth century, in the strict juridical sense, guilds had ceased to exist in Augsburg. In 1548, as a punishment for their involvement in political activities which promoted the rise of Protestantism, the guilds of Augsburg were officially dissolved: they lost their guaranteed seats on the city council and their powers of internal self-administration. Now officially known only as a 'craft', the weavers' guild was placed under the control of six delegates appointed by the magistrates. But masters who feared that only the needs of the richer weavers were being served soon found ways to defend their own interests. In 1575 a group of poorer weavers organized a 'common committee of weavers who produce fustian and linen on two or three looms' to articulate their concerns. Three appointed officials of the craft, the 'inspectors', were often asked to serve as spokemen for the weavers who wanted their views presented to the city council. Yet when the 'inspectors' proved unhelpful, the poorer weavers bypassed them and pressured the delegates instead to voice their concerns to the council. In short, despite its formal loss of political power, the weavers' guild continued to serve as a flexible institution through which specific groups of weavers could pursue their interests.[24]

The guild system was a universal mechanism for organizing and regulating skilled work in cities all over Europe. But part of its strength came from the adaptability of the guild system to particular situations and local needs. One basic premise of the guild system was that each master would manufacture goods in his own shop.

23. Clasen, *Augsburger Weber*, 17–19.
24. ibid., 82–5, 237–60, 286–9.

But this obviously did not apply to the construction trades, where masons, carpenters, roofers and other masters would have to work together on a common building site. The same applied, of course, to shipbuilding. A remarkable adaptation of the guild system to the special needs of this particular industry emerged around what was probably the largest manufacturing enterprise in early modern Europe: the Venetian Arsenal. This great shipyard, operated by the republic of Venice, was served by three large guilds – shipwrights, caulkers and oarmakers. Each guild had masters and apprentices; the intermediate stage of journeyman was skipped. Because the labour requirements of the Arsenal fluctuated, the guild masters were not permanently hired as employees of the state; when work at the Arsenal was slack, they could seek employment at higher wages in private shipyards. But some project was always underway, and to make sure that a basic core of skilled workers would always be available, the Arsenal promised a day's wages to any master on its rolls who turned up for work. This seemingly inefficient system actually produced a stable long-term workforce which met the state's changing labour needs at a relatively low cost.[25]

Even more fundamental than the concept of work in one's own shop was the principle that only masters who had acquired the unique skills of a particular craft should be allowed to practise that trade. Yet the idea that guild members could enjoy a privileged monopoly over their line of work, with the power to discourage rivals and interlopers, inevitably proved attractive to some unskilled workers as well. In seventeenth-century Paris the *vidangeurs*, whose job was to cart off human and animal wastes, were organized along rudimentary guild lines into masters and journeymen – and the journeymen were sternly reprimanded by the authorities when they tried to break away from their masters' authority.[26] By the eighteenth century many of the water carriers, dockworkers and porters in Paris were organized into clearly defined collectives, each with its particular task which nobody else was permitted to perform. Some of these groups had only informal monopoly rights which they had to defend by hand and fist – but many others had been granted a recognized privileged status by the local authorities.[27]

Such organizations of unskilled labourers, however, were never true guilds. For one of the fundamental characteristics of the guild

25. Davis, *Shipbuilders*, 10–46.
26. Bernard, *Emerging City*, 130.
27. Kaplow, *Names of Kings*, 41–4.

mentality was pride in the special skills that the master had acquired over years of training. All work was honourable, but skilled work was always more so. Such work, moreover, was expected to be public, visible, and open to scrutiny. Not only the product but also the process was to be subject to inspection by officials and neighbours alike: in many towns it was expected that the shutters of the shopfront would remain open so that members of the public could watch the master and his journeymen as they worked.[28] Finished products were carefully inspected and certified by guild officers or municipal officials. The collective honour of the guild depended on good work being done by all; if but one master made defective wares, the reputation of the whole guild and its products would suffer. The guild's honour was a source of economic security – and if it was damaged, there could be unfavourable consequences.

Yet the honour of the guild was based on more than work itself. The members of the guild had to be above reproach in their background and their personal conduct. In many parts of Europe only persons of suitable origin were even permitted to apply for mastership. The son of a serf or a member of an ethnic or religious minority would often be rejected. Normally the candidate also had to attest his legitimate birth: if he was of local origin, his background would be common knowledge, but if he came from another town he might have to submit documentation proving that his parents were married at the time of his birth.[29] In the German guilds even a child who had been conceived before his parents' wedding might be ineligible for mastership.

But it was not only the sexual probity of a new master's parents that interested the guild. His own was no less important. A case that erupted in Tallinn in 1660 was entirely typical of the German guild mentality. The cabinet-makers had recently accepted Paul Unsell as a new master – but when his wife gave birth to a healthy child only seven months after the wedding, the guild cancelled Unsell's membership and warned journeymen not to work in his shop lest by doing so their own honour be stained. Only under pressure from the city council did the guild reluctantly reinstate the 'premature father', declaring all the while that they would never regard him as a truly honourable master.[30] To be sure, the German guilds were particularly obsessed with the fear that even one dishonest or impure master could

28. Farr, *Hands of Honor*, 14; Palliser, *Tudor York*, 179–80.
29. Farr, *Hands of Honor*, 22–3.
30. Soom, *Zunfthandwerker in Reval*, 108–9, 155.

undermine the reputation of the guild, rendering its goods and even its members unacceptable in other towns.[31] But the insistence that a prospective craft master had to be of legitimate birth and exemplary character was common to many parts of Europe.

The deep-seated assumption that personal attributes underlay a person's qualifications to do certain kinds of work meant that work roles were also profoundly influenced by the most permanent and personal attribute of all: gender. The organization of labour in the guild system accepted as a fundamental premise that the kind of work performed by men was and should be different from that performed by women. As in most traditional societies, women were primarily responsible for childrearing and managing the kitchen. They also engaged extensively in retailing, both selling wares made in the household and, in some cases, working outside the home as pedlars or operators of market stalls. In addition, women were heavily involved in production of goods for sale – but their participation in productive activity was shaped by a division of labour which excluded women from those processes which were thought to involve a high level of skill or training. Just as there were things no man would do in the kitchen, there were things no woman would do in the shop. In 1541, a weaver in Augsburg complained that his productivity was being undermined because his wife did the cloth-finishing more slowly than he did the weaving. It would not have occurred to him to pitch in and help with her womanly chore, any more than she would have thought to sit down at his loom.[32]

Not only were women excluded from specific forms of labour, but also as a rule they were excluded from participation in the affairs of the guild. Yet this may not have always been so. In medieval times, at least in some cities, women appear to have done more skilled craft labour and to have been accepted more readily as craft masters than was later the case. But if so, this reflected a general pattern of greater overall fluidity in the way guilds accepted members or controlled their work. By the late middle ages guilds had tended to become increasingly rigid and restrictive across the board in their policies concerning the admission and activities of members. Tightening up the rules which defined and limited women's roles was part of a broader pattern by which guilds attempted to sharpen the boundaries between craft masters and all others engaged in similar work – including both rivals outside the guild and the people who

31. cf. Walker, *German Home Towns*, 73–107.
32. Roper, *Holy Household*, 46.

worked as subordinates in their own shops. The limitations placed on women's work roles were part of a larger pattern of restrictiveness.

Yet the gender-based division of labour had to be harmonized with the fact that a master's wife was almost always a part-owner of the shop. Hardly any craft master could have launched his enterprise without his wife's dowry or operated it without her labour. If the husband died, his widow had an obvious claim to continue supporting herself and her family through the shop they had jointly owned. The usual solution was to permit the widow – at least as long as she remained unmarried – to continue to own and operate the shop. But the actual work, or at least that part of the work normally done by men, would be carried out by paid journeymen. And the widow was almost always excluded from participating in the deliberations of the guild masters. The shop run by a widow was, in fact, never quite equal to one run by a man. Evidence from Augsburg suggests that few artisan widows in that city could successfully maintain their shops in the long run. The more prudent or fortunate widows remarried. Many others eventually fell into debt and poverty.[33] In Oxford the number of widows who took apprentices was always small, though it tended to rise a bit when the economy was stagnant; presumably when times were bad apprentices could not be so choosy about where they found work.[34]

Many women supported themselves, their children and sometimes even aged or incapacitated husbands by forms of work that did not challenge the gender-based division of labour. Spinning, sewing, embroidery, nursing, midwifery – all these were almost exclusively female preserves. But whenever the work done autonomously by women became too similar to the skilled labour which male artisans claimed as their exclusive province, the masters or journeymen who felt threatened were liable to protest successfully against female competition.[35] It is true that some work done by women was organized in ways that mimicked or echoed aspects of the guild system. In England young women were occasionally bound as apprentices, with contracts similar to those drawn up for young men. Yet a study of indentures in Bristol shows that the women concerned were almost always apprenticed to be trained in specifically female activities – as seamstresses, spinners, knitters, domestic servants or even 'in the occupation of a housewife'. In the sixteenth century

33. ibid., 49–54.
34. Prior, 'Women and the Urban Economy', 104–10.
35. e.g. Wiesner, *Working Women*, 163–8.

a handful of women were still trained for actual crafts, but by the seventeenth century this option had disappeared.[36] In Cologne in the fifteenth and early sixteenth centuries there were three women's guilds, for yarn-makers, gold-thread spinners and silk-makers. All of these were activities normally undertaken only by females. The guildswomen operated their own enterprises and hired apprentices in accordance with detailed statutes. But they were hardly regarded as equal to men. In fact the three women's guilds were excluded from the political bodies in which all other guilds in Cologne were represented. And many of the most active of these women were married to prosperous merchants, who may have contributed to the capital for their wives' ventures.[37] In short, it was quite possible for the terminology and indeed some of the customs of the guild system to be applied to women's activities – just as it was applied, in some places, to the activities of unskilled male labourers. But this did not make these organizations into true guilds. In fact women in the early modern town never fully shared the social and political status of male craft masters.

For men of the crafts, membership in the guild was a privileged status, one to be protected from every possible intrusion by interlopers, outsiders, foreigners, villagers – and women. The monopoly rights promoted and protected by guild solidarity were, for many men, their best guarantee of economic security. But of course there were also some men whose work was less manual or more refined than that normally done by guild masters. For just this reason, such men often scorned to be linked too closely to the craft guilds. Many cities, for example, had merchant guilds – but such guilds, where they existed, were often sharply differentiated in their customs and practices from those representing the crafts. Young men who were destined for a mercantile career were often sent to learn the business with a merchant in another town – but the arrangements were generally less uniform than those governing the training of apprentices and journeymen in the crafts. The merchant guild itself was apt to be less concerned with closely regulating the economic activities of its members than with providing opportunities for social contact and serving as a pressure group to promote the merchants' interests. Higher up the social ladder, one would not find guilds at all. But where the numbers warranted, there were almost always corporate organizations which grouped together members of

36. Ben-Amos, 'Women Apprentices', 228–38.
37. Wensky, 'Women's Guilds'; Howell, *Women, Production and Patriarchy*, 124–33.

a particular profession, be they lawyers, notaries, physicians or the like. Finally, there were special societies for members of the city's most prominent families. Such organizations might take the form of exclusive confraternities which engaged in charitable activities. They might be corps or companies whose chief function was simply to march in the periodic processions which animated the public life of countless cities, especially in France and southern Europe. Or they might be convivial organizations like the patrician drinking clubs and dance societies which existed in many German cities. The only real purpose of these societies was to make clear who did and did not belong – but this gave them the power to regulate many aspects of group behaviour, such as the choice of careers and marriage partners.

Membership in a corporate organization was normally a lifetime commitment. Upward mobility was expected or even encouraged, so long as it took place within the confines of a single corporate group: a master who prospered could reasonably hope to be named to positions of increasing responsibility within his guild, and having reached the top of his guild hierarchy he might well be eligible for some form of civic office. To leave the guild, however, was another matter. In German cities artisans who had become active in retailing or commerce could petition the authorities for permission to resign from the craft and join the merchants' guild instead. Permission would normally be granted, but the process was not without its dangers. In the 1590s, for example, a group of goldsmiths in Augsburg who had advanced from doing their own work to contracting out work to others were permitted to leave their guild and join the Chamber of Merchants. Some of them, however, could not sustain their putting-out enterprises and requested readmission to the guild as ordinary masters. This was blocked by the officers of the goldsmiths' guild, who clearly took a malicious pleasure in the discomfiture of their former colleagues. Any goldsmith who had become a merchant, they declared, had made clear in doing so that 'the goldsmiths' craft was no longer good enough for him, or at least too lowly, and by obtaining membership in the Chamber had become much higher and greater'. Motivated by 'ambition or avidity for honour', the former goldsmiths had moved up to a 'higher level' – but in doing so, they had permanently progressed beyond working with their hands. Now it was too late to turn back, and the guild would fight any attempt by the former masters 'secretly or openly to do the tiniest bit of work'.[38]

38. Roeck, *Stadt in Krieg und Frieden*, 1: 346.

The overly ambitious goldsmiths of Augsburg had obviously miscalculated their chances of success in a broader sphere of enterprise, and in doing so they had come to grief. But technically what they had done was simply to move from one corporate group to another. In this sense their actions reflected the deep-seated assumption prevalent in many parts of Europe that everyone in a city – or at least every male householder – should belong to some clearly defined collectivity. During the political disturbances that erupted in Frankfurt am Main in 1612, one of the first demands made by the craftsmen who launched the uprising was that 'henceforth no citizen should be permitted in the city who is not enrolled as the member of a guild or society'.[39] The individual householder who worked alone, following his own rules of conduct and pursuing his own self-interest, was a profoundly mistrusted member of urban society. The Frankfurt agitators in 1612 were in the midst of launching a serious challenge to established authority in their community – yet at the same time they echoed a widely shared belief that everyone in the city should be subject to the kind of discipline and control imposed by membership of one of the collective groups that played such a central part in the economic and social life of every European city.

39. Meyn, *Reichsstadt Frankfurt*, 68.

CHAPTER SEVEN
Family and Household

For countless men and women in the early modern city, work not only provided some measure of economic security, but also helped to define their place in the system of social relations. Yet in the struggle to survive and prosper, family relations were equally important. It is the family, after all, that sustains a child before he or she can begin to work – and in many cases for long after that. And even more so than today, in early modern times the family was a major determinant of what kind of work people did and what social status they were perceived to possess.

But what exactly was the family in early modern Europe? Who belonged to it? How did its members interact? And what was the relationship between the family and that other great institution of social and economic life, the household? These questions have deeply perplexed modern historians. We are a long way from any final answers – but the general outlines are clear.[1]

I

In a society in which so much productive work was done in the household, the relationship between work roles and family roles was often very close. The master craftsman, for example, was simultaneously the head of a productive enterprise and of a family unit. Many historians have emphasized the central role of the household in early modern life, seeing its head as a powerful master and father whose authority extended with equal rigour over all its

1. For some fundamental introductions to the subject, see Flandrin, *Families in Former Times*, and Stone, *Family, Sex and Marriage*.

members whether they were related to him or not.[2] It is certainly easy to see household and family as one and the same. But in fact they were far from identical.

Consider a characteristic passage from the diary of Samuel Pepys, written on New Year's Eve in 1664:

> My family is my wife, in good health, and [I am] happy with her; her woman Mercer, a pretty, modest, quiet maid; her chambermaid Bess; her cook-maid Jane; the little girl Susan; and my boy which I have had half a year, Tom Edwards, which I took from the King's chapel – and a pretty and loving quiet family I have as any man in England.[3]

Pepys and his wife had no children of their own, and in the glow of holiday feeling, having just noted how much his physical and financial health had recently improved, Pepys may have enjoyed depicting his ménage of servants as a 'loving quiet family'. But the 'family' was hardly a very stable one: within a few weeks the cook-maid Jane had been fired (though she eventually returned) and the chambermaid Bess had quit, 'she having of all wenches that ever lived with us received the greatest love and kindness and good clothes, besides wages, and gone away with the greatest ingratitude'.[4]

In fact there was no confusing servants with true family. Pepys did form a lasting attachment to one of his servants, Will Hewer, but many of the cooks, maids and servant-boys who populate the voluminous pages of his diary rotated in and out of the household at frequent intervals. This was entirely normal. Journeymen, apprentices and servants came and went. As long as they were in service, the householder might owe them wages, training or supervision *in loco parentis*, but the obligation was time-bound and limited. Servants were expected to be loyal to their masters. Often masters showed their gratitude to servants by helping to arrange marriages for them or remembering them in their wills. But servants could take nothing for granted.

Camilla from Parma learned this the hard way. Camilla was a servant in the household of Gieronimo and Giulia Piccardi, a well-to-do couple in sixteenth-century Rome. The unfortunate situation in this particular household has been reconstructed in some detail from the Roman court records.[5] The Piccardis were unhappily married. Gieronimo was a tyrannical and jealous husband who locked his wife

2. cf. Brunner, 'Das "ganze Haus"', esp. 109–11.
3. Pepys, *Diary*, 31 December 1664. Spelling is modernized.
4. ibid., 2–4 February, 6 March 1665.
5. Cohen and Cohen, 'Camilla the Go-Between'; for the transcript of the trial, see Cohen and Cohen, *Words and Deeds*, 159–80.

in when he left the house; Giulia, in turn, was a far from devoted spouse. Camilla soon became the intimate confidante of her young mistress, so much so that she regularly helped to sneak Giulia's lover into the house. But one day in 1559 Giulia's amours came to a sudden end in a farcical scene which must have made even the grim Roman judges smirk: Gieronimo came home unexpectedly to find his wife's lover stuck with his legs dangling down from a hole in the ceiling through which he had tried to escape. After the initial commotion, what ensued was a complicated legal inquisition – in which, however, attention soon came to be focused as much on Camilla as on Giulia and her lover. For Giulia accused her serving-woman of tempting her into adultery and procuring the admirer who visited her. The exact resolution of the case was not recorded, but Giulia's strategy was clear enough: to beg her husband's forgiveness and put all the blame on her servant. In fact Giulia's only hope of rescuing herself from disgrace lay in abandoning her serving-woman – a person whose loyalty to her mistress had led her to ignore what most contemporaries would have seen as an even higher obligation to her master.

Not every servant, of course, would even have been able to expedite an employer's romances; Camilla's initial intimacy with her mistress obviously reflected her rather high standing among the Piccardis' servants. For in a large household there were always sharp distinctions in status among the servants of various sorts. These gradations were reflected in differing wages. Elizabeth Pepys's waiting-woman, for example, was paid about £10 a year while the lowly cook-maid got only £3 and the footboy earned even less.[6] Sometimes differential wages were set by law: in sixteenth-century Venice the household gondolier could earn up to 10 lire a month, while a wet-nurse received a maximum of 7 lire and an ordinary maidservant got less than that.[7]

But a far more important distinction was the one which existed in many households between all domestic servants, male and female, on the one hand and any apprentices and journeymen on the other. The domestic servants were simply paid for their labour. Apprentices and journeymen, however, were being trained in a craft and socialized – at least in theory – for eventual roles as masters themselves. The distinction was understood by all. In the religiously divided city of Augsburg, for example, it was entirely common for householders of one faith to have domestic servants of the other confession. But apprentices and journeymen were always supposed to have the same

6. Pepys, *Diary*, 10: 193–7. See also Earle, *English Middle Class*, 220–9.
7. Romano, 'Regulation of Domestic Service', 673–4.

religion as their masters. Their bond was just a bit closer than that between masters and mere servants.[8]

Yet ultimately what all servants, apprentices and journeymen had in common was more important than the differences among them. For all of them belonged to the household only as long as the real or implied contract that bound them to their master remained in force. Occasionally a journeyman married his widowed mistress or a maid her widowed master – but unless that happened, no permanent tie ever linked servants to the household or to the master's family.

Ties of blood and kinship, however, were permanent – and often very significant. For most people in the early modern city, membership in a family was not only a matter of identity but also a major determinant of economic status. To be sure, the huge disparities in wealth evident among the different inhabitants of any early modern city arose in part from the fact that some careers were more lucrative than others. But this would hardly explain why, for example, one butcher was ten times as rich as another. In fact differences in wealth also resulted in large measure from accidents of family history. Though most people lived off current income, the property they owned was, in many cases, obtained by inheritance – and such property often accounted for substantial differences in wealth.

Indeed, the preservation and transmission of inherited wealth was invariably considered one of the most important functions of the family. The amounts concerned were not necessarily large – but the transmission of property from one generation to the next was always a matter that demanded scrupulous attention and thorough documentation. The transfer of property was not something that simply happened when somebody died; it was a carefully planned process which began, in a sense, not after death but before birth. A will, if written at all, normally played only a minor role in this progress, for in most cases it simply confirmed arrangements made many years before. A far more significant document was generally the marriage contract. Whenever a couple got married, the bride and groom each provided a specific amount of money or goods, and the size of this marriage portion was carefully recorded. One or both partners might already have children. They might have children together. The children might live or die. The marriage contract had to cover every possible eventuality, specifying what would happen to each marriage portion, and to any property acquired in the future, if either partner died. How much would go to the surviving spouse?

8. François, *Unsichtbare Grenze*, 112–22.

How much to the children from a previous marriage? How much to any children yet unborn?

Every marriage contract had to conform to local laws and customs of inheritance. Such customs differed enormously, not just from country to country but even from region to region. In southern France, for example, a father could single out one child to receive the largest share of the inheritance. In western France, by contrast, a parent had to distribute wealth equally among all children – or, in Normandy, among all sons. Furthermore, any property given over to a child during a parent's lifetime – as a dowry or marriage portion, for example – was regarded as a temporary transfer; when the parent died, everything was returned to the common pool to make possible a rigidly equal distribution. But in north-central France, around Paris, a more flexible system emerged, permitting heirs either to keep property they had been given or return it to the pool for a more equal distribution.[9] In any case, inheritance was never a simple process. Every piece of property given, lent, transferred or promised had to be duly noted. When anybody died, an inventory of everything he or she left might have to be drawn up. Every procedure had to be carefully recorded and explained to the relatives.

In 1593 two professional appraisers needed three days to inventory all the property owned by Guillaume de Courlay, a wealthy Parisian magistrate who had invested heavily in land. Each rural holding was visited and surveyed, and the appraisers even consulted local peasants about the value of specific parcels. Meanwhile, in order to be able to join in the distribution of her father's estate along with her two brothers, de Courlay's daughter had returned her dowry of 8,000 écus. Including this in the total, the appraisers arrived at a value of 42,000 écus for the entire estate, which they carefully divided into equal lots for distribution among the three heirs.[10]

It is hardly surprising, of course, that such meticulous procedures should have governed the transmission of property among the rich. But scarcely less care was taken by people of much more limited means. Let us look, for example, at a marriage contract drawn up in the German town of Nördlingen in 1698. The groom was Hans Georg Wörner, a wool-weaver whose assessed worth of 25 gulden placed him among the city's poorest householders. (His grandfather's first cousin was the richest man in town, worth almost 20,000 gulden, but Hans Georg got no benefit from the relationship.) The bride

9. Le Roy Ladurie, 'System of Customary Law'.
10. Diefendorf, *Paris City Councillors*, 265–7.

was Dorothea Freymüller, daughter of a journeyman carpenter. Hans Georg's previous wife had died, leaving two children. Her actual dowry had apparently been dissipated in the struggle to make ends meet, but to preserve appearances Hans Georg promised his son and daughter 'in lieu of their maternal inheritance' because 'at present his means do not permit more' the pathetic sum of 4 gulden each. As her portion, the bride brought into the marriage 25 gulden in cash plus the customary bedstead with accoutrements which were listed in an attachment. If Hans Georg died first, the bride would reclaim her dowry, the two existing children would get their tiny maternal portion, and after that the rest of Hans Georg's meagre property would be distributed evenly between his existing children, his widow, and any children they might yet have. A corresponding clause covered the eventuality of her death. But if either one died within less than a year the surviving spouse would receive a smaller share than otherwise.[11]

Not every marriage on this modest social level required a formal contract. But every such marriage was still carefully negotiated: exactly how much property each partner brought into the marriage and how it would be disposed of when either partner died was precisely established. Marriage and inheritance were always part of a single continuum. It is hardly surprising, then, that parents were normally deeply involved in helping to arrange their children's first marriages. The fully arranged marriage, in which parents flatly dictated the choice of marriage partners, was rare except among enormously wealthy families in which the property stakes were so high that the children's wishes were simply disregarded. But at all social levels it was expected that first marriages should be made with the parents' consent. Where parents were dead, as was often the case by the time people expected to marry, the approval of the legal guardians was called for instead. Without their parents' or guardians' consent, the married couple might face severe legal penalties – and they could certainly not be sure of getting their share of the parental inheritance.

For just this reason, young people who migrated to the city often tried to remain in touch with their families. If necessary, a parent's consent could always be sent long-distance. Inevitably, however, some migrant servants lost touch with their families. In a case like this, especially for a female servant, the master or mistress might step

11. Stadtarchiv Nördlingen: Heiratsbriefe, 1698; Steuerregister, 1697–9. For more information on the Wörner family, see Friedrichs, *Urban Society*, 239–87.

in to help negotiate the marriage and perhaps even offer a modest dowry.[12] It simply ran against the grain for a first marriage to be made without some expression of approval and support from the older generation.

There were always some couples who insisted on marrying without parental or communal approval, creating situations which raised perplexing issues for jurists and theologians alike. But such situations were rare. Arranging for the present and future transfer of property formed such an essential part of the process of getting married that the close involvement of parents or guardians was normally taken for granted. Far from seeing parental involvement as intrusive, most people would have regarded parents as lax in their duties if they neglected the obligation to assist their offspring in making a suitable marriage.

Yet there were also cases in which parents were simply too poor to provide a marriage portion. Journeymen and servants of modest background were expected to save up their wages for just this reason, to be able to marry on the basis of their own resources. In fact a man might marry without a portion, on the expectation of success in the craft for which he had trained. But a dowerless woman was much less likely to find a match – which explains why the provision of dowries for impoverished girls was one of the most customary forms of charity in late medieval and early modern cities.

II

Not all marriages were first marriages. As is the case today – though for very different reasons – many adults were married more than once in the course of a lifetime. Divorce was virtually unheard of, but death was all too familiar. To remarry after a brief period of mourning was entirely acceptable. But not all widows and widowers did so. Remarriage always depended on just the right mix of inclination and opportunity.

Certainly widows and widowers showed no particular inclination to marry each other. In a sample of over 2,000 marriages contracted in early seventeenth-century London, 45 per cent of the cases involved a remarriage for at least one partner. Of the widowers in the sample, three-fifths married widows. But of the widows, a majority married bachelors – often men younger than themselves. Many of these women were widows of tradesmen or craftsmen, and often they must have wanted someone to take over the shop. For such a woman,

12. Elliott, 'London Marriage Market', 91–2.

a young bachelor with the right training but no establishment of his own may have been more desirable than a widower with his own shop to look after – and his own children to provide for.[13]

In general, the better-off a widow or widower was, the more options he or she enjoyed when it came to deciding whether – and whom – to remarry. But remarriage was never simply a function of wealth. This becomes evident, for example, when we take a close look at the tiny town of Oppenheim on the Rhine – a community whose very smallness has made possible an exceptionally thorough investigation of the patterns of marriage and remarriage.[14]

In three-fifths of all the weddings held in early modern Oppenheim, both the bride and the groom were getting married for the first time. Some of these couples, of course, remained married to each other for the rest of their lives. Yet the average duration of a first marriage in Oppenheim was about thirteen years; in one-fifth of the cases one spouse had died within four years of the wedding. Inevitably many a widow or widower was soon looking for a new partner. By law a man had to wait six months before remarrying; a woman had to wait ten months, presumably to make sure that any child she was carrying would be born before she remarried. Some Oppenheimers petitioned the authorities for permission to remarry even more quickly.

Men had a better chance of remarrying than women. During the eighteenth century only 44 per cent of all widows in Oppenheim remarried, while 76 per cent of widowers did so. Among men the frequency of remarriage varied sharply in accordance with the widower's social status. One might suspect that a wealthy man was more likely to remarry than a poor one, but in fact this was not so. Only 50 per cent of all widowed officials remarried. Among widowers from the prosperous crafts, the rate was 63 per cent. But fully 82 per cent of all widowed masters from the more modest crafts got married again.

The reasons for this relate to the helplessness into which the male householder was plunged when his wife had died. Many aspects of housekeeping were so gender-specific that a man could not conceive of engaging in them himself. A widowed official or wealthy craftsman could afford, if he preferred, to hire a housekeeper or maidservant to undertake these chores. A poorer master, however, could not:

13. Brodsky, 'Widows', 127–32. This sample is based on marriages by licence, which tended to involve people in the middling and higher ranks of London society. Among poor people, who did not marry by licence but by having banns read, the proportions may have been different.
14. Zschunke, *Konfession und Alltag*, 189–93.

his only option was to find a new wife, and to do so quickly. When Stephan Rothenkirch, who made his humble living as a whitewasher, asked in 1739 for permission to remarry before the end of his mourning period, the reason he gave was simple enough: his 'householding was being imperilled by his having to remain in the state of widowhood'.[15] For a woman the loss of a spouse could be even more devastating than for a man, for her opportunities to earn a living were more restricted and her prospects of getting remarried were statistically smaller. But to a man like Stephan Rothenkirch this was of no concern. What he needed in a hurry was a wife, so that he could get on with his whitewashing and she could cook, clean, mind the children and show the neighbours that Rothenkirch's home was, once again, an orderly household.

III

Marriage almost always involved the establishment – or re-establishment – of an autonomous nuclear household. This itself was one of the important ways in which European society differed from other traditional cultures in which it was customary for a young couple to move into the home of a married parent. The nuclear household might be temporarily extended by the addition of a widowed parent or other adult relative. But permanently extended formations – stem families, in which married parents lived together with one or more married children, or joint families, in which two or more pairs of married siblings lived under one roof – were rarities in European society.[16]

Every household had a head – normally the male spouse. His formal powers were extensive. The husband frequently exercised control over his spouse's property, and he was expected to discipline members of the household. But the community imposed limits on the power exercised by the master of a household. If he squandered his wife's portion or used unacceptable force in exercising discipline, he would usually find himself called to account. Certainly there were times when a husband's tyranny was upheld by the authorities. In 1637, for example, a patrician woman in Augsburg flatly refused to continue living with her husband. She was imprisoned for over a year, all the while steadfastly rejecting orders to return to her spouse. Eventually she was permitted to separate from him after returning the valuables he had given her.[17] But the very rarity of a case like this

15. ibid., 192.
16. cf. Wheaton, 'Family and Kinship'.
17. Roeck, *Stadt in Krieg und Frieden*, 1: 318.

made it a sensation in its day. For in fact the authorities in Augsburg, as in every city, devoted a considerable amount of time to trying to patch up marital quarrels and alleviate tensions between spouses – which often meant punishing husbands for acts of violence which clearly exceeded any acceptable form of chastisement.[18]

Outward shows of deference to masters and parents were routinely demanded, and the right to use physical discipline against children, servants and in certain cases wives was always taken for granted. But countervailing pressures moderated the extent of brutality. Neighbours were expected to report cases of domestic violence to the authorities, and often did so. Teachers frequently complained about tender-hearted parents who intervened to protect their children from schoolroom discipline.[19] Pepys occasionally beat his servants, usually for trivial offences, but subsequently felt embarrassment or shame about having done so.[20] Disparities in age, strength and authority always have the potential to lead to abuse, but it would be difficult to argue that early modern society was unique in this respect.

Yet the dominant texture of family life – the normal character of relations between husbands and wives or parents and children – remains one of the most elusive topics in the social history of the early modern city. Certainly it is possible to document every conceivable form of family interaction: we can find devoted spouses and indulgent parents along with brutal husbands, insufferable wives and abusive mothers and fathers. But which types of behaviour were customary and which were aberrant is harder to determine.

One potential source of information is the vast body of prescriptive writings – published sermons, moral treatises, books of advice – produced by clergymen, doctors and others who felt they had something to say about family life.[21] The general thrust of the advice they gave always ran in the same direction: husbands should be firm but loving, wives should be obedient and supportive, parents should be strict but caring, children should be obedient and grateful. The authors were rarely naive about the nature of family life, but the genre itself imposed an optimistic view of the subject: if human behaviour could not be improved, what was the point of giving advice? A different but also distorted perspective on family relations is provided by the records of church, civil and criminal

18. Roper, *Holy Household*, 185–94.
19. Strauss, *Luther's House of Learning*, 180–2.
20. e.g. Pepys, *Diary*, 1 December 1660; 2 November 1661; 20 January 1666.
21. Pertinent examples of this literature are discussed by Perry, *Gender and Disorder*, 53–63; Ozment, *When Fathers Ruled*, 50–72, 132–54; Dugan, 'Funeral Sermon'.

courts which were frequently called upon to sort out family disputes or punish perpetrators of family violence. The testimony is often highly revealing, yet legal and criminal cases can hardly be said to reflect the dominant norms of any society. Countless other documents give tantalizing glimpses of family relations – yet rarely do we see the whole context. Thomas Salmon, an impoverished cutler of Elizabethan London, wrote in his will that 'if he had a thousand pounds more he would give it all to his wife'.[22] Surely we can hear in this the voice of a devoted and loving husband. But how did his wife react when he died – with appreciation for the sentiment he voiced or scorn for the pittance he presumably left her? We shall never know.

A somewhat fuller and more balanced view of family life, however, can sometimes be gleaned from the personal letters and diaries which survive from the early modern era. No one diarist or letter writer, of course, is 'typical' – but each one is an authentic product of his or her age. We may never penetrate to the heart of the early modern family, but we can get a bit closer if we examine in detail what a source like this can tell us.

The greatest diary that survives from early modern times reveals much about what it was like to be a husband, son, brother, cousin and master in the seventeenth-century city – but not what it was like to be a parent, for Samuel Pepys had no offspring. So we shall look instead at the diary of Dr Johann Morhard, the municipal physician of Schwäbisch Hall in the late sixteenth and early seventeenth century.[23] Morhard had many attributes in common with Pepys: both were hard-working men with a lively curiosity and a gift for the apt turn of phrase. But Morhard differed from Pepys in one fundamental respect: in the course of his life he raised eighteen children.

Morhard's diary was much shorter than Pepys's. In fact it was actually a typical house-chronicle, in which the author recorded news events from near and far – the death of a king, the execution of a criminal, the quality of the harvest – along with the major and minor landmarks of family life. Much of the family news was entered in a completely dispassionate way. But from time to time Morhard slipped into a more introspective mode, giving a glimpse of how he actually felt about the members of his family – especially his children.

Morhard was born in Schwäbisch Hall in 1554. His education culminated in a leisurely round of medical studies in Tübingen, Padua

22. Brodsky, 'Widows', 147.
23. The following is based on Morhard, *Haller Haus-Chronik*.

and elsewhere. In 1585 he was awarded his MD and must have started looking for a permanent position. As it happened, just a few months later the municipal physician of Schwäbisch Hall suddenly died, leaving his wife with one 6-month-old child and another on the way. Johann Morhard was promptly appointed to replace the deceased Dr Brenz – and two months after the posthumous child was born he married the young widow as well. It is clear from the diary that Morhard took a fatherly interest in his wife's two children. But he and Anna also had five of their own, not to mention three more children who were stillborn or died at birth. When Anna died in 1603, Morhard married Barbara Koch, who bore him eight children. Soon after Barbara died in 1622, the 68-year-old Morhard married for the third time and proceeded to father three more children before he died in 1631.

Morhard always referred to his wives with affectionate respect, but judging from the diary his most passionate emotions were invested in his children – especially his sons. He recorded with care each son's progress from grade to grade in school and noted with pride their capacity in reading German and Latin. As his sons matured he took pains about their further education. Some were sent to university, though Morhard tended to worry about the corrupting influences of student life. Others were apprenticed to be trained for professions consistent with his own station in life: one was trained as an apothecary, two were to become minor officials.

Some of Morhard's children were obviously gifted and dutiful – none more so, it seems, than his son Hans Georg. In 1610 Morhard noted proudly that 'My Hans Georg, at the age of only 4 years and 9 months, can read German and Latin from having been taught at home by his mother.'[24] (That the child's mother commanded both languages occasioned no comment: literacy, at least in German, was well-nigh universal among women and men alike in seventeenth-century Schwäbisch Hall.[25]) Hans Georg began school when he was 6; two years later Morhard had occasion to glow once again when his son got a prize for outstanding work.

Some of Morhard's other sons, however, were a source of worry to their father. His oldest son, Hans Ulrich, ran away from his first master when he was 14 and from his second two years later. In his father's eyes Hans Ulrich was a 'fugitive Cain' – though his sin lay not in slaying his brother but in upsetting his father's careful plans.

24. ibid., 96.
25. Wunder, *Bürger*, 172.

In 1605 the 12-year-old Hans Jacob ran away 'because he was treated too harshly in school'. Morhard responded to his son's distress in a highly self-centred way: the boy's action was a source of such deep humiliation to him that only religion, he felt, could provide any consolation. 'Lord,' Morhard wrote solemnly, 'it is good that I am humbled, so that my sin will die and I will turn to you as my only true friend. All other creatures in whom we put our trust are idols . . . . Punish me, Lord – but with measure, like a father and not like a judge.'[26] Whether he himself punished Hans Jacob more 'like a father' or more 'like a judge' is not mentioned – but the boy was soon back in school.

Seven of Morhard's children – six sons and a daughter – predeceased him. Judging from the diary, he responded to their deaths in highly variable ways. Sometimes a child's death was recorded briefly and almost dispassionately; at other times he gave way to heartfelt sorrow. Morhard's emotions were deeply touched when Hans Georg died from a protracted infection of the lungs at the age of 18: 'This is indeed a sorrow to me,' the father wrote. 'He was the one of all my sons in whom I placed my greatest hopes. I had prayed long and hard that he might have a longer life'.[27] It is perhaps not surprising that Morhard deeply mourned his brightest son who died on the brink of manhood. But fifteen years earlier he had suffered just as deeply when a sickly infant named Johann Friedrich died after eleven weeks of life: 'I have never prayed as earnestly for a child's life,' he wrote, 'as I did for this one, when it was still in its mother's womb and during and after its birth. May God protect you, beloved child! I would gladly have had you for longer'.[28] Why Morhard – who at that point had seven living children – felt this particular loss so deeply is hard to say. In the course of the next few years two more sons (also christened Johann Friedrich) were born and soon died. The father took their deaths much more calmly.

Of course Morhard's wives and children are not the only members of his family who appear in the pages of his diary. There is also an endless procession of other relatives. In addition to his parents, his sister, his cousins and his step-relations, by the end of his life Morhard had acquired three entire sets of relatives by marriage. As a consequence the diary is full of reports of births, marriages and deaths of people to whom Morhard was or had been related. There were

26. Morhard, *Haller Haus-Chronik*, 61.
27. ibid., 127.
28. ibid., 86.

countless visits to and from kinfolk in neighbouring communities. And there were endless weddings and christenings to be attended. At one celebration in 1624 Morhard heard the aged councilman David Finsterbach mention that this was the 388th wedding he had attended in his lifetime. No doubt Morhard's own total was substantially lower than that, but such festivities still represented an important part of his social life.

Morhard's dealings with his huge network of relatives by blood or marriage were not always entirely harmonious. He was bitter, for example, about cousins who had inherited property which he thought should have come to his father and himself. When his second wife's father died in 1619 he attended the settlement of the estate full of apprehension, expecting the usual trouble. But this time he was pleasantly surprised: 'Although there would have been reason enough,' he wrote, 'to stir up a big stink and divide the estate with a lot of quarrelling.– God be praised, it was all divided in peace and friendship!'[29]

One would like to know more about Morhard's relationship with his daughters. But what he does not say, as much as what he does, makes it clear that his strongest feelings were directed towards his sons. Morhard was, by modern standards, an intrusive and demanding parent. He had high expectations of his sons and suffered acutely when they failed to live up to them. He may have had little or no empathy for his offspring. But he perceived and treated them as individuals. And he was, in his own way, a deeply caring parent.

None of this, of course, should be taken to suggest that Morhard's style of parenting was 'typical'. The only thing we can say for sure about the emotional texture of the early modern family is that almost anything was possible. In fact every additional source of information brings us further away from any stereotyped views of the nature of family life in the early modern city. The recently rediscovered letters exchanged by members of the wealthy Behaim family in sixteenth- and seventeenth-century Nuremberg, for example, illustate nothing so much as the variety of individual temperaments and the range of possible interactions that could emerge within any group of relatives.[30] Michael Behaim, whose letters cover his service as an apprentice merchant in Milan and Breslau in the 1520s and 1530s, was a gloomy and suspicious youth, obsessed with the conviction that while he suffered under an unjust master in Breslau his mother

29. ibid., 118.
30. Ozment, *Magdalena and Balthasar*; Ozment, *Behaim Boys*.

and brothers were cheating him out of his inheritance back home in Nuremberg. Half a century later, Michael's younger cousin Friederich corresponded avidly with his mother in Nuremberg while attending school in the nearby town of Altdorf; he emerges as a cheerful but demanding child with an indulgent but overbearing parent. The letters exchanged by Friederich's sister Magdalena and her husband Balthasar Paumgärtner prove them to have been a deeply affectionate couple whose devotion to each other helped them weather the devastating loss of a beloved only child. Friederich's and Magdalena's nephew Stephan Carl, whose father died when he was about 10, left a large cache of letters which reveal him to have been an appealing and clever but undisciplined youth whose spirit was eventually crushed by the insufferably self-righteous older brother who served as his guardian. In fact family relations in the early modern city exhibited nothing less than the full range of emotional interactions of which human beings are capable.

IV

The family in early modern times stretched far beyond the confines of the household. Yet even so, the relationship between family and household was fundamental – they were never identical, but neither one could exist without the other. The household was the basic economic unit of the early modern city. Most urban production and consumption and much exchange and wage-labour took place within it. At the same time the household served as the basic administrative unit for the guild, the parish, the neighbourhood and the city itself. Most households were relatively small, but to live entirely alone was considered objectionable: single women in particular were discouraged from living by themselves and were urged to attach themselves to some household where they could live under a master's authority.[31]

Every household had its origin in a marriage, yet the household did not necessarily include all of the couple's own children. Parents who could afford to do so might send a newborn infant away to a wet-nurse, bringing the child back home – if it survived – only once it was weaned. Girls and boys might be sent out as servants or bound as apprentices, though not necessarily at quite so young an age as is sometimes imagined: an apprenticeship often began in the boy's mid- to late teens.[32] Yet while the householder's own children might

31. e.g. Roper, *Holy Household*, 225.
32. e.g. Rappaport, *Worlds within Worlds*, 297; Dinges, *Stadtarmut*, 81.

be sent away from home, a household could also expand with the addition of step-children, relatives, journeymen, apprentices, servants or lodgers. As long as they lived there, most of these people had to acknowledge the authority of the head of the household. But the link to one's family of birth and lineage was rarely broken and never forgotten. 'Good parentage' was often the first requirement for being accepted as an apprentice, journeyman or servant. It helped in getting married. And it often provided the dowry, portion or inheritance which cushioned young householders from the impact of economic or family crisis. Altogether it was the family which gave most people the support they needed in their ceaseless struggle to secure a firmer footing on the social ladder or, if possible, to move up the ladder rung by rung.

CHAPTER EIGHT
Power and Pride

The ducal procession in Venice was one of the great spectacles of early modern Europe. Travellers to Venice always hoped to witness a procession, and those who stayed a few weeks were bound to be rewarded: some sixteen processions were held every year to observe the great Christian holidays or commemorate the city's deliverance from various outbreaks of pestilence or episodes of political danger. Though guilds and confraternities sometimes participated, the heart of every such event was always the ducal procession, staged-managed by a small knot of officials who made sure that everything was done according to established tradition. Preceded by standard-bearers, musicians, clerics, and officials of the *cittadini* class, at last the doge himself would appear, to be followed by all the great noble dignitaries of state from the ducal counsellors and procurators of San Marco down to members of the Senate. Through piazzas, down passageways, over canals, sometimes even crossing a great pontoon bridge constructed for the occasion, the procession would advance at its measured pace, permitting visitors and Venetians alike to observe the dignity and splendour of the most famous urban elite in Europe: the nobility of Venice.[1]

Nowhere else in Europe were power, prestige and wealth so completely and so visibly united in the hands of a single group of urban families. For two and a half centuries, from 1381 to 1646, not a single new family was admitted to the exclusive ranks of the Venetian nobility. Members of the nobility dominated the city's economic life and completely monopolized political authority in Venice and its empire. It is hardly surprising that travellers from all over Europe

1. Muir, *Civic Ritual*, 185–230.

relished the opportunity to see this embodiment of urban power on parade.

Nobody ever went out of his way to observe the elite of Zlín. Situated in eastern Moravia, halfway between Vienna and Cracow, Zlín was a town of some 200 houses which accommodated about 1,500 inhabitants in the early seventeenth century. Though heavily dominated by the great feudal estate which surrounded it, the community did have distinct urban attributes: a series of privileges granted by the feudal lords had given Zlín considerable powers of self-government along with the right to hold two annual fairs. And Zlín had an elite. The municipal government consisted of the mayor, aldermen and ordinary councilmen. Most of these magistrates belonged to the town's most prominent guilds: the butchers, clothiers and shoemakers. Particular prestige was enjoyed by the group of families who had been allowed ever since the early sixteenth century to pay a monetary fee to the feudal lord in lieu of performing labour services – a right extended to all other citizens of Zlín only in 1592. These prestigious families lived in the twenty or so big houses clustered around the market square. They were, in the words of a modern historian, the 'patriciate' of Zlín.[2]

An almost incalculable gap separated the *nobeli* of Venice from the 'patricians' of Zlín who stood just a few generations removed from servile status. Yet in functional terms they had much in common. Every town in early modern Europe had an elite, a group of families whose wealth, prestige and privileges placed them at the upper end of the social ladder and invested them with the power to dominate the community's economic and political life. No community could have functioned without a visible elite to serve both as a centre of authority and a focus of emulation and admiration for those who aspired to move up the social ladder. But the actual composition of the urban elite in early modern Europe remains a highly problematic issue in social history. For only rarely were social, political and economic power as perfectly and permanently conjoined as they were – or at least seemed to be – in a place like Venice. In many cities, in fact, political and economic power were only partially linked, creating tensions and generating rivalries that rendered the elite far from cohesive. Exactly who constituted the urban elite and by what criteria they belonged to it were problems that bedevilled contemporaries and continue to baffle historians.[3] Behind the sumptuous clothes and stern

2. Polišenský, *Thirty Years War*, 58–62.
3. Cowan, 'Urban Elites', 122–5.

gazes of the burgomasters and merchants whose portraits can be seen in a thousand local museums lay economic worries and status anxieties that neither the artists nor their patrons ever wanted to admit.

I

In most early modern cities, the most visible demonstration of elite status came from participation in the upper reaches of the political system, which usually meant membership on the city council. Obviously not every member of the urban elite could be politically engaged – indeed, many cities had rules that specifically forbade immediate relatives from holding civic office at the same time. And of course women were totally excluded from municipal politics. But for a man or woman to belong to a group of families whose male members were considered eligible for high political office was often the clearest mark of elite status.

There were cities, in fact, in which the authorities had drawn up an exact list of all those families whose members were eligible for high office. The purpose of any such list, of course, was not to provide a convenient directory of the pool of civic talent, but to demarcate a specific group of families as belonging to a social and political elite from which all others were excluded. Obviously no such list would have had any credibility unless it reflected long-standing social practice; its purpose was simply to clarify which borderline families did or did not make the grade. In the year 1521, for example, the magistrates of Nuremberg drew up a precise list of those families – forty-three in all – whose members would henceforth be summoned to dances at the city hall. Of course the list concerned more than dances, important though they were. For it also confirmed exactly which families could be called upon to fill any of the thirty-four 'patrician' seats on the city council.[4] (Another eight seats were reserved for ordinary citizens, but nobody had any illusions about their importance.) In fact the dance statute was intended to reinforce and perpetuate the link between political and social status.

Nuremberg was not the only city in which members of the elite undertook to limit key political offices to specific families. But this was not the most common practice. In most cities membership on the city council was at least formally open to any male citizen who seemed fitted for such a position. The criteria were often left vague, and purposely so – but the economic standing of the individual or his family was almost always a crucial factor.

4. Hirschmann, 'Nürnberger Patriziat', 265; Strauss, *Nuremberg*, 79.

Of course this could mean different things in different cities. In small towns where commerce was limited – towns like Zlín, in fact – political leadership was often drawn from the guilds; the most prosperous and respected craftsmen usually became members of the municipal council. In larger towns with a more dynamic commercial life, the council was apt to be made up chiefly of merchants. But some even larger cities also had a substantial number of wealthy rentiers – people whose families, though often descended from active merchants, had now forsworn commerce and lived exclusively off the income of rents or other investments. In France rentiers were generally known as *bourgeois*; to support oneself without having to work was connoted by the phrase 'vivant bourgeoisement'. In fifteenth-century Germany rentiers were sometimes known as *Müssiggänger*, or 'idlers',[5] a term which could have either positive or negative connotations, depending on whether the idler was rich or poor. Whatever they were called, rentiers were generally considered particularly well suited for the dignity and responsibility of civic office.

Yet there was always a potential for tension in those cities where a large group of rentiers coexisted with a group of merchants still active in trade – particularly if, as sometimes happened, the merchants were richer than the rentiers. To be able to support oneself without having to work normally conferred greater dignity than having to earn a living. But the rule was by no means absolute, and there was always a point at which sufficiently great wealth cancelled out any scruples about how, or how recently, it had been earned. There were certainly many cities in which the political and social elite accommodated both active merchants and rentiers. But there were also cities where members of a rentier elite tried to exclude merchants from political power and from recognition as their social equals.

Of course the categories 'merchant' and 'rentier' by no means exhausted the range of groups which might be included in the urban elite. One of the classic themes of early modern history is the 'rise of the professions' and certainly one of its most visible manifestations was the growing prominence and political power of professional men among the upper reaches of urban society. For the most part this trend involved only two professions: medicine and, far more importantly, law. The study and practice of medicine increasingly came to be seen as compatible with high social status – though only for university-trained physicians, not for surgeons and other humble

5. cf. Bátori, 'Patriziat', 1.

practitioners. An even larger and far more conspicuous addition to the urban elite, however, consisted of lawyers. Like medicine, the law had practitioners of varying types and credentials. But it was those who had studied at the universities – or, in England, at the Inns of Court – who were most likely to enjoy the wealth and prestige that could help them get accepted as members of the urban elite.

Yet it would be a mistake to regard lawyers and other professionals as belonging to a self-contained group which was clearly differentiated from the mercantile and rentier components of the elite. Many lawyers, after all, were the sons of merchants. In the middle ages, almost the only way a merchant father could prepare his son for an adult career was by apprenticing him to another merchant or by putting him into the church. By the sixteenth century, however, more and more merchants were sending at least some of their sons to university to study for legal or administrative careers. Many of these trained jurists attached themselves to the expanding law courts or bureaucracies of the princely and royal regimes. But others worked for city governments. Often they came from the same social background as the council members whom they advised – and even those who did not might find it easy to act as if they did. Increasingly lawyers and some other professionals, no matter what their origins, found themselves treated as part of the urban elite. It was ever more common for lawyers not only to serve as legal advisors to a city council but also to be offered seats on the council itself. A lawyer's son would not necessarily follow his father's career – he might become a rentier. But it was also not uncommon for a rentier's son to study the law. In many cases, then, the profession of the law was not so much an avenue into elite status as a manifestation of it.[6]

The most cohesive urban elites were those in which economic superiority, political power and social prestige were all united. In theory these three elements should have reinforced each other, but in actual fact they often became dissociated. In many cities, members of the elite retained their political and social primacy while letting others take over economic leadership. Occasionally even elite groups lost or surrendered both economic and political domination, while still retaining or even strengthening their social prestige. The patterns varied enormously from city to city. But we can understand something about the forces at work if we recognize the degree to which wealthy and powerful urban families were influenced by the pursuit

6. cf. Schilling, 'Differenzierungsprozesse', 141–8; Amelang, 'Barristers and Judges', esp. 1271.

of a particular social goal: the acquisition of noble rank. For in the upper reaches of urban society, getting ennobled or being recognized as having noble status could become the most powerful factor in a family's economic or social behaviour. Certainly the concern was far from universal. In smaller towns, where even the mayor was likely to be a mere craftsman or a minor merchant, the acquisition of noble status was remote from the concerns of the urban elite. But in large towns all over the continent one could find members of the urban elite who either were nobles or claimed to be – or desperately wished they were.

In formal theory, nobles were a caste whose status derived from military service to the ruler and the possession of lands held in fief. By early modern times, these strict conditions scarcely applied – if indeed they ever had. Actually the nobility had never been a closed caste, for the power to raise commoners to noble status had always been a major instrument of a ruler's power; and if ennoblement had once been linked chiefly to military service, it had long since come to be awarded for 'services' of a more general kind – including financial. It was also possible to slide into nobility through a strategic marriage or possession of a suitable country estate. Yet if noble status were too widespread, it would lose whatever value it had for its owners. So disputes about the legitimacy of noble status were endemic. Nobles whose families could trace their status back a few generations inevitably challenged the credentials of the more recently ennobled – although they could hardly deny, in the candid words of a sixteenth-century commentator, that 'the families that die out must obviously be replaced by others if the noble estate is to be maintained, for what is now "new" will eventually become "old," and what is now "old" was "new" years ago'.[7]

The possibility of being ennobled or, better still, getting recognized as being inherently noble was an almost irresistible prospect for some members of the urban elite. Noble status did have some practical advantages: it conferred immunity from certain types of judicial proceedings and granted exemptions from particular taxes. But this was hardly the main motivation for the pursuit of noble standing – which, in fact, could also involve substantial financial sacrifice. In many cases the procedure involved in getting ennobled was itself a costly proposition. But in addition, in many parts of Europe, in order to be accepted as noble a family was supposed to give up all involvement in trade and be prepared to live solely off rents

7. Euler, 'Wandlungen des Konnubiums', 63.

and financial investments, which were often safer but usually less lucrative than commercial ventures. What inspired urban families to seek noble status was not, in most cases, any rational pursuit of economic advantage. It reflected the fact that for many early modern people the acquisition of wealth was often only the means by which to obtain something of far greater value: social honour.

Filippo Strozzi was one of the richest men in late fifteenth-century Florence. He spent his younger years laboriously developing his fortune by intense entrepreneurial activity which involved a shrewd mix of mercantile and financial investments. But at some point Filippo lost interest in continuing to maximize his profits: as income poured in from his lands and business enterprises, he simply let the money pile up. When Filippo died in 1491, fully half of his wealth was in the form of cash sitting in moneybags which he kept at home. For by his middle years Filippo had long since acquired what he needed in order to pursue the true aims of his life: to build a stupendous palazzo in the heart of town and be known as one of the great men of Florence.[8]

Florence was dominated by a strongly republican ideology in the late fifteenth century, and it would have been tactless for Filippo Strozzi – who in fact had spent some of his early life in political exile – openly to pursue a noble title. But he well illustrates the fact that for many a merchant or rentier in the early modern city, the pursuit of wealth was only an instrument by which to achieve some form of social recognition. This could take many forms, depending on local circumstances. But in many cities the most valued mark of recognition for which ambitious people strove – and paid – involved the acquisition of a noble title.

Many cities already had an established resident nobility at the start of the early modern era. Some of these nobles belonged to aristocratic clans who had lived in the town for generations. Exactly how these families had initially acquired their noble status was of interest, if at all, only to antiquarians; their rank was so firmly grounded in the past that it was accepted by all. In some cities these urban nobles of medieval origin were still a large and cohesive group with a recognized role in civic affairs. But often their numbers – and sometimes their political influence – had shrivelled to inconsequence by early modern times.

Some cities also had noble inhabitants whose rank and wealth derived chiefly from their established position as landholders in the countryside. Most nobles, after all, had rural estates, but not all chose to live there. Some considered the town their primary seat and

8. Goldthwaite, *Private Wealth*, 62–5.

expected to play a major role in municipal affairs. Others regarded the town as a place to spend an occasional season, and would have held it beneath their dignity to be involved in the details of civic administration.

But the very existence of nobles in urban society merely stimulated the eagerness of other wealthy families to be acknowledged as belonging to their ranks. Just how this could be achieved was a hotly disputed topic. The rigorist position was well formulated by a jurist in fifteenth-century Vicenza: 'Nobility', wrote Daniele Dall'Aqua, 'is a rank conferred by a sovereign, by which a person is accepted above honest plebeians . . . . No one has rank by his own standing. It is necesssary that rank be conferred on him by another.'[9] Yet this was a difficult proposition to enforce in Italy, where sovereigns were in short supply: nobody questioned the sovereign rank of the pope and the king of Naples, but in northern Italy only the Holy Roman Emperor fully counted and his involvement in Italian affairs was sporadic and unpredictable. There were other sources of political authority in Italy, such as bishops, who were widely accepted as having the power to ennoble. But many urban elites tried to circumvent the obstacles to getting individually ennobled by declaring that membership in a particular group automatically conferred noble status to all its members. Some jurists advanced the rather self-serving position that possession of a law degree itself conferred noble rank, but this claim was not universally accepted. Far more successful, at least in some cities, was the argument that members of a city council were collectively members of the noble estate. This was by no means accepted on all sides – but the position was easier to sustain wherever the councillors displayed such 'noble' traits as avoiding trade and making it difficult for newcomers to enter their ranks.[10]

Much the same situation applied north of the Alps. There were always ways by which individual urban families in the Holy Roman Empire could get themselves recognized as nobles. The gradual approach involved buying noble estates in the countryside and trying to merge slowly into the rural aristocracy. Or there was the more direct approach of purchasing a patent of nobility from the imperial court or from one of the officials appointed by the Emperor to sell titles to suitable applicants.[11] But as in Italy, there were many German

9. Grubb, *Firstborn of Venice*, 88.
10. ibid., 86–93.
11. Benecke, 'Ennoblement and Privilege'.

cities in which the council families tried to assert their noble status on a collective basis. There were no absolute criteria to establish the noble quality of such families. The Emperor was generally far less willing to concede noble status to an entire group than to individual families. But in many towns the 'patricians' – to use the Roman term which was resuscitated in the sixteenth century – tried to demonstrate their noble credentials by the customary device of trying to keep out new families, or at least restricting their membership to those families which had given up trade and commerce.

Occasionally these aspirations were formally recognized. In Nuremberg, for example, ceaseless lobbying by the families listed in the dance statute finally secured a patent from the Emperor in 1697 permitting their members who sat on the council to insert the word *Edel* – 'noble' – before their names. But the Emperor would not openly concede that the Nuremberg patricians had collectively been granted noble status; instead his patent endorsed the legal fiction that these families always *had* been noble, that 'before they moved to the city, they had lived as members of the noble and knightly estate'. Most of these families had long since given up their involvement in trade; now some of them celebrated their recognition as nobles by destroying the family archives that contained records of their commercial activities.[12]

In France the aspiration of wealthy urban families to achieve noble status was, if anything, even more intense. But the mechanism was different. Municipal councils never enjoyed the same degree of autonomy and thus the same potential for prestige as they did in many Italian and German cities. Instead, noble status was obtained in larger towns by purchasing royal offices. Beginning in the sixteenth century the supply of such offices grew at an explosive rate, as the crown began to meet its increasingly urgent financial needs by selling more and more positions in the legal and fiscal bureaucracy. A royal office was certainly attractive to the buyer for objective economic reasons: it normally involved a tax exemption while also providing income both from the salary itself and from the fees paid to the officeholder by those who had business to transact with the crown. The value of any such office was further enhanced when it became possible, for a small extra fee, to guarantee its continuation in the family from one generation to the next. Yet these offices were also

12. Hofmann, 'Nobiles Norimbergenses', 83. For a useful general discussion of the German patriciate, see Bátori, 'Patriziat'.

pursued for another, less rational but more fundamental reason: for as a rule, they conferred noble status.

There were negative features. Like all investments, purchase of office involved an element of economic risk: an office could lose value if the crown created too many similar positions in the same town, thus thinning out income by spreading the fees around more broadly. And no matter how much had been paid, the new officeholder still became only a noble of the robe, far inferior in status to the exalted nobles of the sword. But none of this deterred merchants and rentiers from snapping up offices for themselves or their sons whenever a fresh offering was announced. By the seventeenth century, any town in France large enough to accommodate a sovereign court or similar royal institution was bound to have any number of *trésoriers, receveurs, contrôleurs* or *conseilleurs* who had made a substantial financial investment in order to enjoy the proceeds of officeholding – and to be able to claim noble status.

It would be misleading to think that the lust for noble status among members of the urban elite was an equally powerful force all over Europe. In England, for example, it played scarcely any role. The English peerage – the nobility narrowly defined – encompassed such a small segment of the population that even the most prosperous merchant would have been wasting his time to fantasize about joining it. In a broader sense, of course, the entire English gentry corresponded to the continental nobility. But membership in the gentry was never strictly defined and access was never difficult for those of sufficient wealth. Social relations and intermarriage between urban elites and members of the rural gentry were entirely routine. English urban elites were not without status obsessions of their own, but a hankering for recognition as nobles was not one of them.

Even on the continent, where the desire for noble rank was far more widespread, it never directly affected every sector of what, broadly, can be called the urban elite. After all, only members of the highest fringes of urban society could even begin to envision entry into the ranks of the nobility. Yet the pull of noble rank was in many ways the *primum mobile* of the urban status system, for it indirectly shaped the ambitions and aspirations of people much further down the ladder. The desire for noble status formed the apex of a much broader pattern of social aspiration. For the very same 'ambition or avidity for honour' that made goldsmiths aspire to become merchants, or merchants to become rentiers, also inspired rentiers and others at the top of the urban hierarchy with the hope of acquiring – for themselves or, failing that, for their sons and grandsons – the honour and prestige of a noble rank and title.

II

The desire to move up the social ladder was a constant of European urban life in the early modern city. The degree of success people had in doing so, however, was highly variable – particularly towards the upper end of the ladder. In some cities membership in the elite was readily accessible to newcomers; in other cities, upward mobility was diminished or blocked by social or political barriers. Indeed, the degree to which the elite was 'open' or 'closed' was one of the most telling ways in which the social system of one European city could differ from that of another. To be sure, there is no rigorous method to compare how open or closed the elites of different cities were, because it is not always clear exactly who counted as members of the elite. And even individual cities could change over time – over the course of generations, the elite could get more open or more closed. Almost any attempt to identify a general pattern is bound to founder. But a detailed look at some individual cities can at least illustrate the range of possibilities.

The classic case of a closed elite was – or for centuries seemed to be – the nobility of Venice. The famous *serrata* or 'closing' of 1297 had established a list of about 200 noble clans whose adult male members were the only people entitled to sit in the Great Council and to be named to higher offices of state. Another thirty families were added in 1381 – but after that the ranks of the Venetian nobility were almost completely sealed off.[13] For over two centuries, the Venetian elite was large enough and rich enough to maintain its domination of the community without any strain. At any given time during the sixteenth century, for example, a pool of over 2,000 adult male noblemen stood available to fill the various civil and military offices through which the nobility controlled the city and its overseas empire.[14] Members of the nobility also had effective strategies for maintaining their collective wealth. The concept that commerce was incompatible with noble status was unknown in Venice. Overseas trade was in fact the main source of wealth for many of these families. An unusual dynastic custom prevented the dissipation of

13. Some foreign families were granted 'honorary' membership in the Venetian nobility and a handful of local families were quietly added to the 1297 list as if they had always been on it: Cowan, *Urban Patriciate*, 64–5, 65n.
14. Davis, *Decline of the Venetian Nobility*, 54–7.

wealth among too many heirs: in many families only one brother would marry and produce legitimate offspring while the remaining brothers would remain unmarried.[15] The bachelor brothers might also have children – but only illegitimate ones, who had no claim on the family property.

There were certainly wealthy merchants within the two lower social groups in Venice, the *cittadini* and the *popolani*. There is no hint that members of these lower groups ever seriously questioned or challenged the social and political domination of the *nobeli*. Yet eventually the nobility itself could not quite maintain its position. By the sixteenth century, not a few noble families had fallen into genteel poverty, dependent for survival on their salaries from political offices or even, in a few cases, on outright charity.[16] Many other noble families, while still prosperous, had withdrawn from active commerce into a rentier lifestyle which diminished the likelihood of any fresh infusions of wealth. The total size of the nobility began to drop as well – a few too many brothers, it seemed, had remained unmarried. When the city faced a wartime financial crisis in 1645, patrician pride gave way before practical needs and newcomers were permitted to join the nobility – upon payment of the stupendous sum of 100,000 ducats. A few wealthy *cittadini* who could have bought their way into the nobility haughtily refused to do so. But many *cittadini, popolani* and nobles from the Venetian territories welcomed the opportunity to join the Venetian elite: between 1646 and 1718, a total of 127 families did so.[17] Even the most celebrated urban caste in Europe, then, eventually had to open its ranks to those whose wealth matched or, in some cases, exceeded that of its own members.

Many of the largest German cities also had socio-political elites which tried to maintain themselves as closed patriciates – though, as in Venice, over the long run none of them remained entirely exclusive. The most successful was the patriciate of Nuremberg – though even there an additional family was admitted after the dance statute had been promulgated.[18] More characteristic was the case of Frankfurt. In the late middle ages the patrician families organized themselves into the Alt-Limpurg Society, whose members held their gatherings in the Limpurg building right next to the city hall. By the sixteenth century the members of this society had successfully

15. ibid., 62–5.
16. Pullan, 'Occupations and Investments'.
17. Cowan, *Urban Patriciate*, 66–74.
18. Hirschmann, 'Nürnberger Patriziat', 265.

asserted their claim to occupy a permanent majority of the seats on the city council. Their ancestors had mostly been merchants, but the Limpurger increasingly tried to distance themselves from trade and firm up their noble credentials. New families continued to be admitted, but only – according to a rule adopted in 1584 – if the applicant could prove that neither his father nor either of his grandfathers had practised a craft or engaged in retail trade. Even wholesale commerce was strongly discouraged: the ideal Limpurger lived off rents, investments and the salaries, fees and gifts that always flowed to holders of high political office.[19] The Limpurger never loosened their socially exclusive standards, but they did pay a political price for their tenacity: their grip on city council seats was slightly reduced after political disturbances in the early seventeenth century and further reduced after more upheavals a hundred years later. Yet they continued to play an influential role in city government until the end of the *ancien régime*.

Sometimes outside pressure was needed to crack open the ranks of the patriciate. The Augsburg patriciate had declared itself closed in 1383, but by the early sixteenth century the original group of about fifty families had shrunk to scarcely ten. For decades the patricians resisted suggestions from the Holy Roman Emperor that they add more members, but they finally gave way in 1538 and invited thirty-nine families to join their number.[20] Included among these were the richest merchants in Europe, the Fuggers – whom the Emperor himself had already ennobled as imperial counts a few years before they were admitted to the patriciate of their own home town. Once their initial resistance collapsed, however, the Augsburg patricians continued to admit other families.[21]

Yet even when they consented to accept newcomers, patricians continued to bar potential members who didn't quite make the grade. A number of German cities had a clearly demarcated group of sub-patricians who were superior in rank to the ordinary citizens but did not count as true patricians. In Augsburg they were known as the 'augmenters', and in Frankfurt they belonged to the Frauenstein society: in both towns they were allotted a small number of guaranteed seats on the city council. In Braunschweig the patricians had lost much of their economic and political power by the sixteenth century – but they were all the more determined to differentiate

19. Soliday, *Community in Conflict*, 72–84.
20. Sieh-Burens, *Oligarchie, Konfession und Politik*, 24–5.
21. Bátori, *Reichsstadt Augsburg*, 18–21.

themselves sharply from those of lower rank by keeping the list of their members rigidly closed. Barred from patrician gatherings, the sub-patricians had to form their own association of the 'white ring' – so named because on formal occasions the women of this group could wear only silver jewel-clasps on their bosoms, as opposed to the gold ones worn by the wives of true patricians.[22]

Yet try as they might, even the most exclusive urban patriciates had trouble getting themselves accepted as authentic nobles. Perhaps no group of German patricians tried harder than the *Erbmänner* of Münster. In the mid-fifteenth century these 'hereditary men' had been forced to concede some seats on the city council to members of the guilds, but this, if anything, only reinforced their determination to mark themselves off clearly as a social elite. They married almost exclusively among themselves, and by the sixteenth century they had completely withdrawn from commerce. Most of them lived in country houses and some even tried to avoid serving in the city government. Actual control of municipal affairs passed largely to a second-tier elite, which consisted chiefly of merchants but included some people who themselves were moving into rentier status. In 1557 the *Erbmänner* were gravely humiliated when one of their members, though specifically recommended by the papal curia, was denied appointment as a canon of the Münster cathedral. Only true Westphalian knights were named to the chapter – and for all their efforts to distance themselves from the civic milieu, the *Erbmänner* still did not qualify. They objected furiously to this rebuff, and launched a series of protests and lawsuits which ultimately dragged on for 150 years. Only in 1715, long after they could demonstrate that they no longer took the oath as citizens and no longer served in civic office, were the *Erbmänner* begrudgingly granted general recognition as Westphalian knights.[23]

Now it was entirely customary for individual members of an urban elite to leave the city behind and move to country seats in hopes of being accepted as nobles. What made the *Erbmänner* unusual was that in order to achieve their status goals they had to do so not as individuals but on a collective basis. Yet, ironically, when the members of this most 'closed' of urban elites finally dissociated themselves entirely from their home town, they left the city to be dominated by a heterogeneous mixture of rentiers, merchants and professionals – and Münster came to have something much closer to an open elite.

22. Spiess, *Braunschweig im Nachmittelalter*, 2: 466–7, 475–6.
23. Lahrkamp, 'Patriziat in Münster'; Hsia, *Society and Religion*, 19–21.

In fact most European cities had an open elite. Demographic and economic pressures made this almost inevitable. Urban leaders generally shared the view that a city's affairs were best managed by old families of established standing. But neither the number nor the wealth of these families remained stable. When elite families died out or lost their wealth, wealthy newcomers were eager to move into their places.

Sixteenth-century Seville well exemplifies the character of cities with a highly open elite.[24] At first glance this may seem surprising, because in Seville, as in most of the great cities of Spain, members of the nobility enjoyed a constitutional monopoly on all important positions in the municipal government. Almost a hundred offices – mayors, judges, aldermen, councilmen – had to be filled by men of noble rank. Many Sevillian nobles, moreover, were among the greatest magnates in Spain, with extensive rural landholdings from which they drew large and secure incomes. Yet even so, wealthy commoners – mostly merchants – were constantly moving into the political elite. Usually this involved a payment to the royal treasury: either the newcomers purchased noble titles which made them eligible for council seats, or they purchased council seats which made them eligible for noble status.

Some of the new nobles were even *conversos* – descendants of Jews who had been pressured or forced to become Christians. In later generations, this 'impure' background led to severe social disabilities for *converso* families, but little was said about this in the sixteenth century. Marriages between members of old and new noble families – including some *conversos* – were common. None of this precluded continued involvement in commerce. In Spain as elsewhere noble status was theoretically incompatible with trade. But nobody in sixteenth-century Seville had a vested interest in enforcing this doctrine. Seville was the economic capital of Spain's new overseas empire, and opportunities for getting rich were so spectacular that old nobles and newly ennobled alike were deeply involved in commercial enterprises. Few people in Seville enjoyed so dramatic a rise in status as Antón Bernal, a *converso* who began as a gold-beater, got rich by investing in trade with the New World, got even richer by lending money, and ended up on the city council – having moved from artisan to noble status in scarcely ten years.[25] But while his case was extreme, during most of the sixteenth century the opportunities for upward

24. Pike, *Aristocrats and Traders*, 21–52; see also Perry, *Crime and Society*, 13–18.
25. Pike, *Aristocrats and Traders*, 100–1.

advancement in Seville were certainly widespread, and membership in the social and political elite was open to anyone who could pay.

Of course the Seville city councillors followed the usual practice of the newly ennobled. Having reached the lowest rung of noble status, the council members tried to diminish the social distance between themselves and those higher up – while at the same time trying to prevent those below them from joining their ranks. In 1573 the city council blocked a proposal by some of the most venerable noble families to form a highly exclusive confraternity which 'new' nobles would be unable to join. The real purpose of such a brotherhood, the council argued, would not be to perform pious deeds but to accentuate social differences within the nobility by accepting some applicants and blackballing others. Yet at the same time the council persuaded the king – by means of the usual financial gift – not to sell any more patents conferring simple noble status in Seville.[26] This, however, was a futile measure – for it was still possible to secure noble rank by purchasing a council seat. And higher titles were available as well. The sale of noble titles remained a major source of revenue for the crown in the following century: in 1679, for example, two countships and twelve marquisates were sold to gentlemen of Seville.[27]

The Sevillian elite, in short, was a highly 'open' one. The high degree of social mobility available in Seville was no doubt related to the city's explosive economic growth, especially in the sixteenth century. But the situation in Seville was reflected at least to some degree in other Spanish cities. In the far less dynamic town of Ciudad Real, for example, members of old noble families tended to monopolize the highest municipal offices, but newcomers could buy their way into lower positions and purchase noble titles.[28]

Wherever membership in the urban elite was linked to claims of noble status, it was generally easier for a family to get into the elite than to be pushed out of it. A wealthy family could buy social status and political power, but when such a family began to lose its wealth, the noble status it had acquired could support a continuing claim to social recognition and to membership on the city council. An even more open urban elite, by contrast, was one into which new families were absorbed at roughly the same rate at which old families were

26. ibid., 23–5.
27. Domínguez Ortiz and Aguilar Piñal, *El Barroco*, 28–9.
28. Phillips, *Ciudad Real*, 100–12.

discarded. In such a community, wealth was needed not only to secure status in the first place but also to sustain it.

Exactly this situation prevailed in most English towns during the early modern era. In sixteenth-century Worcester, for example, the list of men who belonged to the top civic council – the 'Twenty-Four' – corresponded very closely to the list of the town's richest inhabitants. Many of these men had become rich as cloth merchants. Family background counted for nothing – for as a recent historian writes, 'in Worcester everyone was *nouveau riche*'. The families which belonged to this instant oligarchy were closely linked: they socialized with each other and their sons and daughters intermarried. Yet the group was far from permanent. Only a small number of sons ever followed their fathers on to the council. Membership in the oligarchy was in constant rotation.[29]

Much the same applied to York. Throughout the sixteenth century, members of the two crucial municipal councils – the Aldermen and the Twenty-Four – were chosen ovewhelmingly on the basis of their wealth. At the time of their appointment, most of these men were merchants or retailers, though some – especially among the Twenty-Four – belonged to the victualling trades or the more refined crafts. The social and geographical origins of the York councillors were diverse. Some, of course, belonged to local mercantile families; some were sons of local craftsmen; some belonged to gentry families from the surrounding countryside; a few came from more distant parts of England and one even came from Spain. What they all had in common was adequate wealth. There were councillors whose fathers had also been on the council, but no families were represented for three generations in a row. Some council families moved up and out to become members of the country gentry. Others sank back into the ranks of ordinary tradesmen. But there were no dynasties among the York elite in the sixteenth century.[30]

This was the normal pattern in English towns of the early modern era. There were, of course, minor variations. Sometimes a family remained active in the civic elite for three or four generations.[31] But everywhere in England membership in the urban elite remained wide open, for political power and social recognition were readily available to any family of sufficient wealth. If a merchant or other

29. Dyer, *Worcester*, 224–6.
30. Palliser, *Tudor York*, 92–110.
31. e.g. in Exeter: MacCaffrey, *Exeter*, 253–4.

citizen was rich enough to seem suited for civic office, nobody was likely to enquire about his social origins. Members of the English urban elite were by no means immune to the continental mania for titles of honour: aldermen and mayors welcomed the chance to be known as gentlemen or even, though it happened more rarely, to be knighted. But the widespread continental supposition that high social status was incompatible with commercial activity carried no weight in England. In fact there was an easy movement back and forth between the urban elite and the rural gentry: younger sons of landowners were sent to town to become merchants, while successful merchants purchased rural estates and became country gentlemen.

There is no doubt that all over Europe wealth was the most important factor in determining membership in the urban elite. But this does not mean that even the most 'open' elite was nothing more than an amorphous grouping of rich families. To be recognized as members of the elite, families needed some visible mark of social or political integration. The newcomer might know that his family had arrived when he was invited to stand as a godparent or give his son or daughter in marriage to another elite family. Even better was to be given some conspicuous title or to be admitted to some organization – a drinking club, say, or a confraternity – whose membership was known to be highly exclusive. But in many communities the simplest and surest sign that one had been accepted into the communal elite was to be elected to membership in the highest ranks of municipal government.

To become a member of the urban magistracy, however, could confer no personal dignity unless the magistracy as a whole was perceived to be of exalted status. Thus it was crucial that the collective standing of the urban elite be constantly affirmed in a visible and public manner. This is what lay behind the persistent efforts by urban magistrates in the early modern era to devise ways of demonstrating the degree to which they stood above and apart from their fellow-citizens.

One way, of course, was through public ceremonies to celebrate their election or installation into office. Most of these ceremonies were of medieval origin, but in early modern times they often became increasingly elaborate. In London, for example, by the end of the eighteenth century the annual procession and banquet associated with the inauguration of the Lord Mayor had become so imposing that an eyewitness could compare these events only to the grandest of all Venetian ceremonies – the *sensa*, in which the doge dropped a ring into the Adriatic to symbolize the city's dominion over the sea.[32] Few cities could offer spectacles quite so impressive, but everywhere attention was lavished on ceremonies designed to give public expression to the magistrates' authority. The symbolic importance of such rituals was understood by all – sometimes almost too much so. In 1714, when the new Bourbon rulers of Spain conquered Catalonia and took direct control of the city of Barcelona, they swiftly suppressed the traditional ceremony for installing the city's magistrates and replaced it with entirely new rituals designed to honour the king.[33] But such changes were rare. In most cities, ceremonies designed to focus attention on the authority of the local elite continued to flourish throughout the early modern era.

Many urban magistrates were also determined to upgrade the physical manifestations of their collective importance. Of course this could be done on a piecemeal basis by commissioning more imposing regalia to be carried in processions or by installing more impressive furnishings and works of art in the council chamber.[34] But the most effective way to achieve this end was to construct a grand new town hall that could give visual expression to the magistrates' perception of their role. Almost every city already had a town hall dating from the middle ages – but having been constructed at a time when more civic energy was directed to religious structures, many such buildings were relatively modest in size. Some magistrates were content with their old town halls, or lacked the means or vision to replace them. But in other cities during the early modern era, magistrates took the initiative to construct a new town hall which more impressively reflected the sense of authority they wanted to convey. Even the rulers of a small town like Rothenburg ob der Tauber could find the means in the late sixteenth century to build an imposing city hall in the latest German Renaissance style.[35] Larger cities, of course, could do even more. In Augsburg a massive new city hall, rivalling even the cathedral in its visual impact, was built in the early seventeenth century. Building materials of the highest quality were ordered: marble from Salzburg, copper from Hungary, glass from Venice. From outside, the sheer mass of the new structure towering over the marketplace could not fail to inspire awe among the city's inhabitants. And inside, decorative motifs throughout the building – especially in the enormous Golden

32. Marshall, *Dr. Johnson's London*, 81–3; on the Venetian *sensa*, see Muir, *Civic Ritual*, 119–34.
33. Amelang, *Honored Citizens*, 196–7.
34. cf. Tittler, *Architecture and Power*, 102–22.
35. cf. Hitchcock, *German Renaissance Architecture*, 193–4.

Hall – trumpeted the wisdom and beneficence of good government such as the magistrates of Augsburg were sure they provided.[36]

Even more grandiose than the Augsburg *Rathaus* was the palatial town hall constructed by the magistrates of Amsterdam in the mid-seventeenth century. Virtually every function of municipal government was to be carried out in this vast building, and every room was embellished with sculptures or paintings alluding in direct or allegorical terms to the specific service being provided there. Even the torture chamber on the ground floor, where criminal suspects were interrogated, had sculptured reliefs of the instruments of torture delicately carved in the vaulted ceiling. The whole building, in fact, was designed as a monument both to the importance of the city and to the power of its magistrates. Nobody who entered the town hall, willingly or otherwise, would be allowed to forget that every aspect of municipal affairs in Amsterdam fell under the unified authority of the city's small, cohesive and powerful ruling elite.[37]

III

Not every town, however, had a single, recognizable and integrated socio-political elite. For some cities had parallel elites – separate clusters of families of equally high rank who were committed to distinct forms of economic activity or political aspiration. Even more cities had what might be called overlapping elites.

Lyon was one of the great boom towns of sixteenth-century Europe – so much so that it could support two entirely distinct mercantile elites. One group consisted of wealthy French merchants. Many of them were relative newcomers to the city, but by the early sixteenth century they had come to dominate the institutions of municipal government and had sharply reduced the traditional political influence of the archbishop of Lyon. The other group consisted of foreigners, chiefly Italians. These were the merchants and bankers who really made Lyon one of the great centres of international finance and commerce in the sixteenth century. Many belonged to families which stayed in Lyon for generation after generation – the immensely wealthy Bonvisi, for example, had arrived from Lucca by 1504 and remained active in Lyon until the 1620s. The Bonvisi and other Italian merchants were recognized as indispensable participants in the city's economic life – but, largely by their own choice, they were never fully absorbed into the city's social life. They declined to be naturalized,

36. Roeck, *Elias Holl*, 186–221.
37. Fremantle, *Baroque Town Hall*, 77 and passim.

stayed clear of municipal politics, married among themselves. They formed a distinct, parallel elite.[38]

Parallel elites also emerged for religious reasons. Hostility between Protestants and Catholics, or between members of different Protestant denominations, could create sharply differentiated clusters of families: while contacts across religious lines would be reduced, patterns of intermarriage, social interaction and economic cooperation within the group were likely to increase. Usually when a city had two religiously defined elites, the groups were not equal in status – for no matter how well matched they might be in economic terms one religious group was likely to be shut out of the municipal government while the other would enjoy a monopoly of political power. There were some cities, however, where religious conflicts had resulted in a stalemate or compromise under which two denominations were both entitled to participate in the municipal government. Where that happened – as in those German cities where religious 'parity' was guaranteed by the Peace of Westphalia which ended the Thirty Years War in 1648 – two sharply differentiated but politically equal elites would coexist within a single community.

Parallel or overlapping elites were especially likely to emerge in cities which harboured more than one locus of political power. Some cities, for example, had a bishop or other ecclesiastical authority whose officials formed an administrative elite quite distinct from that of the municipality. Other cities had organs of royal or territorial government whose membership was distinct from that of the municipal regime. And there were capital cities, with an array of civil and military officials whose origins and outlook were often quite distinct from that of the local elite.

In most of these cities, however, there was some interpenetration between the different elites. This was certainly the case, for example, in the French cities which had *parlements* or other important fiscal or judicial agencies whose authority was derived from the crown. In cities like these, one could almost always distinguish between a 'municipal' elite which dominated the city council and a 'robe' group whose members sat on the sovereign courts. Yet the relations between them often changed over time.

In Toulouse two elite groups were sharply differentiated in the early sixteenth century. Membership on the highest municipal council, or *capitoulat*, was dominated by local merchants – especially wealthy entrepreneurs engaged in the sale of woad, which was then a prized

38. Gascon, *Grand Commerce*, 1: 357–81, 407–8, 432–3.

ingredient for the manufacture of dyes. Many of these merchants were of foreign origin, but unlike their contemporaries in Lyon they welcomed a chance to join the municipal government – chiefly because a royal privilege had granted noble status to any member of the *capitoulat*. A second, clearly differentiated elite was made up of officers of the Parlement of Toulouse, drawn largely from nobles and officials who came from outside the city. (To be a member of the parlement, of course, also conferred noble status if one did not already have it.) Despite some intermarriages, in the early sixteenth century the two groups remained clearly distinct – and roughly equal in status. Later things changed. After the trade in woad collapsed and the city's economic vitality declined, merchants lacked the prestige to get named to the *capitoulat* – so its composition increasingly came to resemble that of the parlement, consisting largely of lawyers and nobles. The actual members of the parlement did not join the *capitoulat*, but lawyers associated with it gladly did so. Politically the parlement and *capitoulat* retained their distinct identities, but their members were now strongly linked by shared social values and the lines between the 'municipal' and 'robe' elites became increasingly blurred.[39]

A comparable pattern was evident in Montpellier, where the crown had established a *cour des aides* and several other prestigious tribunals. In the sixteenth century, it was easy for members of merchant families to buy their way into positions in these royal courts, but in the seventeenth century direct progress from commerce to royal office became increasingly difficult. This was partly because the merchants' wealth and prestige had ebbed by 1600. But in any case the number of 'robe' families in Montpellier was by then so great that vacancies could be filled largely from within their own ranks. Even the city council, which had traditionally been dominated by local merchants and rentiers, came to include more and more lawyers and 'robe' officials in the course of the sixteenth century.[40]

The composition of the elite in provincial cities could thus be profoundly shaped by the political and financial concerns of the monarchy. But Europe also had scores of capital cities, ranging from the great national centres like London or Paris down to the modest princely residence-towns of central Europe. As a rule in such towns the gulf between the municipal and the court elites was

39. Schneider, *Public Life*, 16–21, 34–6, 40–2, 59–70, 181–3; Schneider, 'Crown and Capitoulat'.
40. Irvine, 'Renaissance City'.

bound to be substantial, since the court always included nobles and military men whose power base or place of origin lay elsewhere in the realm. Yet some links between the two elites always emerged. Impoverished courtiers might look to the town elite for marriage partners with substantial dowries. Young townsmen, trained as lawyers, might look to the court for more promising appointments than the municipal regime could offer. Of course the stakes were higher wherever the capital was also a major commercial centre, with merchants or financiers whose wealth the prince needed to tap and whose assistance had to be rewarded by high political office or noble titles. This was certainly the case in Paris. In the fifteenth and sixteenth centuries many a Parisian merchant moved smoothly into royal officeholding while remaining active in the city's affairs. In the seventeenth century, however, as the court became increasingly isolated from Parisian life, this became more rare.[41] By the time of Louis XIV, when the centre of royal administration was transferred to Versailles, the elites of 'court' and 'city' had little in common.

A somewhat different pattern prevailed in London. Of course there had always been some members of the gentry who got involved in City commerce and some rich merchants who became members of the gentry. Consider Sir Geoffrey Boleyn, a merchant and Lord Mayor of London in the fifteenth century: his son married an earl's daughter, his grandson became an earl and his great-granddaughter married King Henry VIII. Yet as a whole the London elite remained sharply differentiated from the royal court and national administration. During the seventeenth century it became increasingly apparent that the English crown could not function without the financial cooperation of the London financiers, but the loyalty of the City elite was more effectively secured by guarantees of sound fiscal policy than by titles and royal offices. Even residential patterns reflected the relative separation of the municipal and court elites. During most of the seventeenth century, when the open areas west of London were being developed as elegant housing tracts for the rich, the new districts chiefly attracted aristocrats, professionals and officials connected to the institutions of national government. Members of London's mercantile elite continued to live inside the traditional boundaries of the City. Only in the early eighteenth century did the richest London merchants start moving to the fashionable squares in the 'polite end of the town' – and only then did the level of

41. cf. Diefendorf, *Paris City Councillors*, 109–11.

social interaction between aristocrats and great merchants significantly increase.[42]

IV

Clearly the structure of the urban elite followed no single pattern all over Europe. But its composition normally remained flexible. Even in those few cities where the elite tried rigidly to limit its membership, the attempt generally failed: either the elite eventually had to bow to economic pressures and admit some newcomers, as in Venice, or the elite preserved its caste-like purity at the price of becoming irrelevant to the community, as in Münster. In most cases the elite remained open enough to absorb newcomers. Normally, in fact, this process was a source of social stability. If the established patricians posed too many obstacles to the admission of new members, it was far more likely that the ensuing resentment from rich but excluded citizens could contribute to political tensions.

It may sound from all this as if the elite was composed entirely of men. Of course this was not so: the urban elite was always a collection of families, not individuals. But it was masculine activity that normally accounted for a family's elite status. One of the most standard ways, after all, by which a family entered the elite was by the acquisition of specific political offices – and such offices were always held exclusively by men. The wealth that made this possible, however, often came from women: in many cases it was the inheritance from his mother or the dowry provided by his wife that gave a man the economic standing he needed to be recognized as a member of the elite.

Once a man had reached this point, his elite status was shared by his wife and children. It was difficult, however, to guarantee that the family would maintain sufficient wealth to sustain this status for generation after generation. This was exactly why so many members of the urban elite, at least on the continent, were obsessed with achieving noble rank. For in most of Europe a noble father transmitted his status to all his legitimate descendants. To be sure, a daughter kept her father's status only until she married, at which point she assumed her husband's rank. But a nobleman's son normally kept his status for life and transmitted it on to the next generation. A hereditary rank certainly made it harder to dislodge someone from his standing as a member of the urban elite. But even a noble title could not protect a family from eventual extinction – for

42. Stone, 'Residential Development', 186–9; Rudé, *Hanoverian London*, 52–6.

if a family lost its wealth, it became increasingly difficult for parents to arrange marriages for their children and eventually the line would die out.

Obviously no urban patrician could definitively arrange his family's future. He could, however, try to add to his family's lustre by rearranging its past. In sixteenth- and seventeenth-century Spain the growing obsession with 'purity of blood' made it indispensable for some families to obliterate any record of Jewish antecedents. In the rest of Europe, concern with ancestry was less urgent – but even so, members of the urban elite often showed a passionate interest in their own genealogy. Family honour, not accuracy, was the main concern. Happily, family records were rarely so complete or well-organised that a history-minded patrician or his paid genealogist could not embellish the facts by producing some more illustrious ancestors.

Ultimately, of course, most members of the urban elite were absorbed less by thoughts of the past or distant future than by concern with the present. Membership in the elite imposed significant obligations, above all to one's family and to one's community. Urban patricians may have had more freedom to shape their own way of life than other members of society, but even so their activities were profoundly shaped by existing assumptions and expectations. Obviously there were local differences, shaped by religious and cultural norms and, perhaps even more importantly, by the size and economic vitality of specific towns. Yet even so, urban elites shared a common set of concerns and engaged in a common set of activities. Some of these activities involved men and women alike. Others were rigidly gender-specific.

All over Europe male members of the urban elite were heavily engaged in the political management of their communities. This was, of course, a source of enormous power. In many cases political authority provided patricians with the means to sustain or extend their wealth – either indirectly, by pursuing economic policies for the community that would favour their interests, or quite directly from salaries, fees, gifts and occasionally even crass expropriation from the public treasury. But members of the urban elite were apt to stress not the advantages of office but its burdens. Certainly municipal offices could be highly time-consuming. Meetings of the city council or its committees occurred once or more a week and lasted for hours. Many municipal offices required extensive hands-on activity; mayors, sheriffs, aldermen spent hours in the city hall or the marketplace hearing complaints, adjudicating disputes and making sure that regulations were enforced. Indeed, one of the reasons why rich men were generally considered better suited for political positions was that they were thought to have more free time available for public service. Appointment to public office was often an ardently pursued goal of those who wanted recognition of their elite status – but there were also men who had to be coerced into accepting a position or fined for refusing to do so.

Membership in the urban elite depended on wealth, and this wealth had to be maintained. Many members of the elite were still directly engaged in commercial activities which required extensive planning, negotiation, supervision and, in many cases, travel. But even living off rents and interest required a considerable amount of effort: the rentier had to maintain records, visit his country estates, decide on loans, make investments and collect payments. Litigation over disputed inheritances or failed enterprises could absorb hours of preparation and consultation. Many of these activities involved men and women alike. It is true that when the household was headed by a man he would often act on behalf of his wife. But a woman was expected to understand and approve any transactions involving her own property. Many men routinely entrusted their wives with significant business responsibilities. When their husbands were travelling or, even more likely, when they were widowed, women might buy and sell property, sign contracts or make investments. Certain of these transactions required the consent of a male relative or guardian, but this was often a mere formality: the more property a woman had in her own right, the more able she was to assert some control over its disposition.[43]

Men and women of the urban elite were always concerned to sustain and extend their wealth, but there were constant pressures to spend as well. Urban patricians were expected to dress, dine and dwell in a manner befitting their family's rank and honour. The most ambitious members of the urban elite sometimes poured their family's wealth into the construction of elegant town houses or the purchase and development of grandiose country estates. Obviously some indulged in extravagances that exceeded their means. But they were the exceptions. A far more normal pattern was a persistent obsession with money, a careful reckoning of assets and liabilities, and a constant attempt to maximize incomes while controlling expenditures.

We can get a vivid glimpse of patrician household management from the account books of the Weinsberg family of Cologne. The Weinsbergs in the sixteenth century were well-established members of the Cologne elite, who were represented on the city council

43. cf. Perry, *Gender and Disorder*, 14–16; Diefendorf, *Paris City Councillors*, 285–8.

though they did not belong to the uppermost fringe of families that monopolized the mayoralty. Hermann von Weinsberg, whose voluminous diary is a treasured source of information about life in sixteenth-century Cologne, studied law and served on the city council for a number of years before settling down to life as a rentier. It was a full and comfortable existence, as he himself recorded: 'I don't have to perform rough manual labour, neither riding nor travelling, nevertheless I am always busy with reading, writing, advocating, soliciting and negotiating'. Weinsberg had a secure income in money rents, to which were added grain and wine from his landholdings and fees from some minor civic offices. In 1573, Hermann was widowed for the second time; his only child, an illegitimate daughter, had long since been placed in a convent, but he was raising two orphaned nephews and helping his sisters to manage their income. In the autumn of 1575 Hermann, his sisters and his married brother Gottschalk decided to cut their expenses by living in adjacent houses and eating all their meals in common. These meals – lunch at 11 a.m. and supper at 7 p.m. – would be cooked and consumed in Gottschalk's house, but the cost of the food and the cook-maid's wages would be apportioned among the siblings. A thorough inventory of all food supplies was maintained along with a painstakingly exact expense account, from which we can see that the family consumed chiefly meat, bread, butter and cheese, with some cabbage or carrots. The men drank modest amounts of wine and beer, the women even less. Hermann and his brother were invited to some thirty festive meals a year – chiefly civic banquets, marriage feasts or the like – and they reciprocated by holding about one feast a year. Aside from that, their consumption remained modest and consistent.[44]

The Weinsbergs may have been a particularly frugal family and Hermann was certainly an unusually meticulous record-keeper. But the values evoked by their careful husbandry were certainly echoed by members of the urban elite all over Europe. Thorough inventories of a family's wealth were undertaken from time to time, notably after a death or in connection with marriage negotiations. It would have been unwise or even dangerous for a patrician householder to be too extravagant or spendthrift when he was bound to be held accountable, sooner or later, for any mysterious losses – especially since a good bit of the property concerned was not his own to

44. Jütte, 'Household and Family Life'; see also Ozment, *When Fathers Ruled*, 72–80, 154–61.

dispose of. Much of what he administered, after all, was property actually belonging to his wife or his children.

To make adequate provision for the next generation was a solemn obligation for almost all adult members of the urban elite. Even those who had no children of their own were often entrusted with the guardianship of orphans, nieces, nephews, step-children or other relatives. The task of providing for one's own children was always complicated by the fact that one never knew just how many would survive. Daughters in particular posed a grave challenge for parents. The higher one moved up the ladder of wealth and status, the bigger the dowry one would have to provide for each daughter if she was to marry someone of her own rank.

We can see this clearly from the well-documented circumstances of parlementaire families in seventeenth-century Aix-en-Provence. An average member of the Parlement could count on an annual income of 5,000–10,000 livres from salaries, fees and the rents from his and his wife's landholdings. This was certainly a substantial amount at a time when a craftsman or minor official would be lucky to pull in 200 or 300 livres a year. Most parlementaires lived in great comfort, certainly more lavishly than the frugal Weinsbergs of Cologne. But a typical dowry among parlementaire families in the seventeenth century could run to 20,000 livres. With a little careful planning, one daughter might be easy to place. But if a father had two or three, he could run into serious difficulties. Many women simply remained unmarried.[45]

Children were a blessing, but too many of them were a problem. Don Antonio de la Cueva of Ciudad Real and his wife María Bermúdez, who married in 1668, had a total of twenty-four children. Fifteen died before reaching adulthood. But even the surviving nine were more than the parents could really provide for. All five surviving daughters were placed in convents. Two sons remained bachelors. One was sent to the Indies and never heard from again. Only one son married and he inherited the bulk of his parents' fortune.[46]

Providing for one's offspring, however, involved more than securing their financial future. It also meant getting them educated. By the sixteenth century it was taken for granted that all members of the urban elite, male and female alike, would be literate. For daughters, basic instruction in reading and writing would be supplemented by training in the conventional feminine accomplishments: embroidery,

45. Kettering, *Judicial Politics*, 231–6; for wage levels in Aix, see Fairchilds, *Poverty and Charity*, 49–51.
46. Phillips, *Ciudad Real*, 102.

music and the like. Sons would be prepared more rigorously for their adult responsibilities. Once he was literate in his own vernacular, a boy would normally be sent to a local grammar school to learn Latin and possibly some Greek. If his family was still active in commerce, the next step might be apprenticeship to a merchant. In families that had moved beyond trade – or hoped to – a son might instead be sent to university. The most common course of study for such sons was law. But attitudes towards education were never strictly utilitarian: higher learning was prized for its own sake. Members of the urban elite, male and female alike, were expected to know enough about art, music and culture in general to function as intelligent patrons. But many of the men were intellectuals in their own right. They maintained diaries, wrote chronicles, authored books, composed music, collected curiosities, and organized academies to sponsor lectures or debates about everything from natural philosophy to affairs of state.

Much of this higher intellectual activity was almost as gender-specific as urban political life. Much intellectual discourse took place only in Latin, and many of the most vital topics of discussion, especially political, were framed with reference to legal concepts and precedents. Yet Latin and law were normally inaccessible to women, since they required levels of schooling from which women were barred. Some women ventured into these territories, but their efforts were rarely taken seriously, even by other women. In seventeenth-century Paris a woman of high social rank might host a salon, but it was her male guests who were expected to dominate the discussions. An accomplished woman was admired; a learned one was not. By and large a female scholar was regarded as a puzzling if not threatening aberration. When the erudite traveller Johann Georg Keysler came to Nuremberg in 1730, he was eager to visit the 'celebrated Dr. Thomasius', whose library and cabinet of curiosities included 800 volumes of letters by noted scholars and an impressive collection of ancient and modern coins. Yet the most remarkable curiosity on display was the learned lady of the house – a young woman who preferred knowledge to marriage:

> Dr. Thomasius has an only daughter [Keysler reported] who has made such a progress in foreign languages, natural philosophy, morality, history, and other sciences, that she may justly be ranked among the most learned of her sex. She has had several advantageous matches proposed to her; but philosophy has so far engaged her affections, that for the sake of it she has hitherto declined all overtures of that kind.[47]

47. Keysler, *Travels*, 4: 191.

Exceptions like these merely illustrate the point that scholarship was an overwhelmingly male preserve. But there were spheres of activity in which men and women of the urban elite both participated, though the women's undertakings might be segregated from the men's or subordinated to male control. This was apparent above all in the closely related spheres of religion and charity.

By the late middle ages it was customary for families of the urban elite to take a strong interest in the affairs of a particular monastery, convent, hospital, or parish church. Gifts and bequests from wealthy families were often indispensable for the functioning of such institutions. Self-interest and charity were deeply intertwined. The rich patrician who provided money for inmates of an almshouse was simultaneously doing a good deed and guaranteeing a stream of prayers for himself and his family. The person whose will ordered masses to be said for his soul at a special altar in the parish church hoped thereby to speed his way into heaven, but he also provided a welcome source of income for the altar-priest. Collective religious action directed towards charitable purposes had a strong attraction for members of the urban elite. This urge was most commonly expressed through elite confraternities. To be sure, confraternities could be found on many social levels; often they were closely linked to specific craft guilds. But members of the urban elite, with their greater wealth and influence, could turn their confraternities into powerful instruments of local philanthropy.

For women of the urban elite, excluded from other forms of participation in civic affairs, religious and charitable activity often became a powerful form of self-expression. It had long been customary, of course, for elite women to join convents, but this was usually at their fathers' command. Some women became nuns on their own initiative, but for many other women of deep religious devotion this was not an option, for example if they were already married. Such women were instead attracted to unofficial forms of religious association. In the late middle ages, women of the urban elite in the Netherlands and the Rhineland had organized *beguinages*, houses in which they could live together under unofficial, self-imposed vows while carrying out works of charity. In fifteenth- and sixteenth-century Spain women of the urban elite found numerous ways to channel their religious devotion into concrete undertakings: they founded new convents, they established small hospitals, or they lived as *beatas*, latter-day beguines who took vows of chastity and maintained their homes as centres of prayer and good works. Such autonomous expressions of lay piety among females made the male ecclesiastical authorities intensely nervous. But the women concerned were widely admired for their piety and were, in many cases, socially prominent, so the churchmen tried to control their activities without overtly disbanding them.[48]

The Protestant Reformation, wherever it was successful, terminated many of the institutional vehicles through which urban elites had expressed their religious commitment: monasteries, convents, confraternities, and chapels or altars devoted to masses for the dead. All these institutions, however, were maintained and strengthened in Catholic countries. The Counter-Reformation reaffirmed traditional practices while emphasizing the need for more rigorous discipline and deeper spiritual commitment – and in many cities it was precisely members of the urban elite who most fully absorbed and implemented these values. This was apparent, for example, in seventeenth-century Grenoble. Though members of the local elite often asked for simple, unostentatious funerals, it was still entirely normal for a judge of the Parlement to bequeath funds for a thousand or more masses to be said for his soul – preferably within three days of his death, when the impact was thought to be greatest. But religiosity was also outer-directed: separate male and female confraternities whose members belonged to the city's elite strove to transmute their devotion into concrete measures to alleviate social distress. Elite women founded two confraternities in Grenoble to operate charitable asylums – one for orphans, one for former prostitutes – and members were expected to promote both the well-being of their charges and the state of their own souls by frequent visits and direct participation in the work of these establishments. Males of the local elite belonged to the Grenoble chapter of the secretive but influential Company of the Holy Sacrament, whose members personally visited pauper households to determine what forms of social assistance were needed. Intense spirituality was combined with a direct, hands-on approach to charity.[49]

Social activism among the elite in Protestant cities took a different form. Reformation doctrine rejected the notion that works of charity contributed to salvation, and Protestantism lent no support to the Counter-Reformation notion that intimate personal contact with the needy was a sanctifying experience. But Protestant thinkers certainly encouraged charity as a manifestation of individual faith and communal godliness: good works were not a means of achieving

48. Bilinkoff, *Avila*, 39–52; Perry, *Gender and Disorder*, 97–117, 153–5.
49. Norberg, *Rich and Poor in Grenoble*, 20–39, 126–8.

salvation but a demonstration of divine grace already granted. To a greater extent than in Catholic cities, however, elite philanthropy in Protestant towns was likely to take an institutional form. There was certainly no shortage of potential beneficiaries. Protestant and Catholic towns alike abounded in schools, hospitals, orphanages, old-age homes and other worthy organizations that required support and direction. In Protestant towns these institutions became the primary focus of the elite's philanthropic thrust. Education was a high priority for the Protestant patricians, who supported local schools and endowed scholarships to send promising youths to university. But mechanisms to deal with poverty and alleviate distress were no less important. Some of these institutions were municipal and some were privately endowed, but the difference hardly mattered, since it was normally the same group of wealthy citizens who ran them. Even if philanthropy would not save their souls, it would still help save their cities. For in Protestant and Catholic towns alike, purely practical considerations required members of the urban elite to devote a large part of their time and energy to the problem of poverty. The expectant beggar standing at the door, the fitful patient lying in the hospital, the destitute widow awaiting help in her home, the furtive vagabond slipping through the city gate – all were a constant threat to the communal order, a reproach to the municipal government and a perpetual, nagging challenge to the patrician conscience. They could never be ignored or overlooked.

CHAPTER NINE
Poverty and Marginality

Christina Bobingerin was desperate. She was 19 years old in the summer of 1601, a peasant girl from the village of Göggingen just outside the walls of Augsburg. One day in June she sneaked into the city, trying to locate the soldier with whom she had been living some months earlier. He had long since abandoned her, but she had heard that he was in Augsburg and she thought if she found him he would have to take her back. As soon as she got into the city, however, Christina was arrested and jailed. Two days later she was interrogated.

This was not the first time Christina had been detained as an unwelcome visitor to Augsburg. At least half a dozen times before she had been arrested, whipped, led to the city gate and warned never to return. Knowing that she was unwanted, why did she insist on coming back? 'Do you really think', the authorities asked her gravely, 'that we should have to suffer such defiance from you?'

Christina's answer was simple. Sheer need had driven her to sneak into the city. No, she was not a prostitute, nor was she a thief. She had simply come to find her soldier or, failing that, to beg. But she was allowed to do neither. Once again she was banished from the city.[1]

Christina's story was repeated not hundreds but thousands of times in European cities of the early modern era. Every city had its share of male and female beggars and vagrants who were desperately trying to make a living while eluding the authorities. Almost every city also had its beadles and beggar-wardens whose job was to apprehend vagrants and lock them up, kick them out, or – occasionally – permit

1. Roeck, *Bäcker*, 68–9.

them to carry on with their activities. Yet public begging was, in turn, only part of a vastly greater structural problem of urban poverty in early modern Europe. For countless people in the early modern city, life was not a struggle for power or prestige nor even for economic security: it was simply a struggle to survive from day to day.

'Countless' is said advisedly, for the numerical dimensions of urban poverty in early modern Europe can never be determined. Many of the poor, after all, belonged to the least systematically documented members of urban society. We may know how many households a city had, how many families paid taxes, how many people took communion, how many were born or died. Sometimes we even know how many families received welfare payments or how many beds were occupied in civic institutions. But we can never know for sure how many vagrants were living furtively in cellars or sleeping in sheds or huddled outside the city walls hoping to slip inside when the gates were opened. Nor did the size of this floating population remain constant. In times of distress - especially during wars or famine – the number of vagrants ballooned as outsiders flooded into the city in search of food or money.

Nor could the permanent residents of the city be divided with certainty into those who were poor and those who were not. Poverty itself is always difficult to define. Certainly a family which could not support its members without sustained recourse to private or public assistance would always be included among the poor.[2] To some analysts, however, this group – the truly indigent – represented only the most extreme form of poverty; the urban poor can also be said to have included many householding families who, in normal times, seemed to be economically independent. For often these people were able to support themselves and their families only so long as they – and the local economy – remained in good health; they were liable to slip over the edge into destitution as soon as they faced some unmasterable catastrophe – a sudden collapse in the market for the goods they made, a sudden rise in the price of bread, the onset of a disabling illness, the death of a provider, or the birth of yet another dependant.[3] In late fifteenth-century Nuremberg a city ordinance required that labourers in the building industry be given their daily wages in the morning, so that they could bring the money

2. cf. Jütte, *Armenfürsorge*, 18.
3. Dinges, *Stadtarmut in Bordeaux*, 67, stresses the distinction between the bare capacity to support oneself (*Armut*, or poverty) and direct dependence on assistance (*Bedürftigkeit*, or indigence).

to their wives when they went home for a midday snack.[4] People like this obviously lived perilously close to the margins of poverty; even when they were able to support themselves, they were bound to be conscious of indigence as a constant, looming threat.

Yet members of even the most modest householding families in the early modern city did have some resources with which to cope with the fear or fact of poverty. Every such family belonged to a network of institutions and relations which could be drawn upon for assistance. The best strategy, of course, was to anticipate and minimize economic distress in advance. Here the guilds played a central role, by protecting the right of each member to earn a living and fighting to preserve traditional markets and monopolies. In addition to this, guilds often provided short-term assistance to distressed members or their widows. Sometimes confraternities played this role, for often the strongest charitable impulses within the brotherhood were directed towards its own members. There were certainly cases in which poor citizens joined confraternities chiefly as a form of social insurance, knowing that in cases of illness or unemployment they would have the first claim on assistance from the richer brethren.[5] Family relations provided another resource: in times of need, people borrowed from their relatives, or moved in with them. Only social custom could reinforce a sense of obligation between siblings or cousins, but the law often imposed an obligation among closer relatives. In some communities, for example, adult children were required to support indigent parents.[6]

On top of all this, cities had long-established systems of private, church and municipal charity to which poor people could turn in times of need. Both the organization and the philosophy of urban charity underwent significant changes during the early modern period, but certain principles remained unchanged. Charity could take different forms, involving the distribution of food, clothing, firewood or money. But whenever possible, established residents were to be supported in their own homes. If householders were ashamed to let their neighbours know that they had become dependent on charity, discreet means of providing assistance were often arranged. Only in extreme cases would a person be removed from his or her own home to be looked after in a hospital or other institution.

In every city it was understood that recognized members of the

4. Maschke, 'Unterschichten', 59.
5. e.g. in Venice: Pullan, *Rich and Poor*, 63–83.
6. Jütte, *Armenfürsorge*, 332–3.

community had a legitimate claim on the community's resources. This view of things owed much to the teachings of the church, but it was reinforced by the communal philosophy that lay behind the organization of the guilds and the very concept of citizenship. In fact the various forms of organized charity which had developed in European cities by the end of the middle ages would almost certainly have been sufficient to alleviate poverty without undue strain on local resources if cities had maintained a closed, stable population. But this was never the case. Urban poverty was always a serious social problem, and there is every indication that it became steadily more acute in the course of the early modern era. In city after city, the number of poor people and the desperation of their circumstances seemed to be growing. New measures to deal with poverty were constantly being devised and some of them were actually implemented. But they were never adequate, for the problem always ran far ahead of the solution.

The reason for this was simple: immigration. Not all of the poor were immigrants, and not all immigrants were poor. But immigration and poverty were always linked. Every community recognized that some immigration was inevitable and immigrants were often a valuable resource. Many male immigrants did well in the city, arriving as apprentices or journeymen and moving successfully into the ranks of householding artisans. Some even ascended into the urban elite. Many female immigrants also prospered: arriving in most cases as servants, they acquired husbands and founded stable households. Even immigrants with less promising prospects could still fill important niches in the urban economy as long-term servants or unskilled labourers. But the supply of immigrants always exceeded the city's capacity to absorb them effectively into the urban economy.

Immigration flows were never constant. The overall volume of migration to cities probably increased substantially in the sixteenth century, when the population of Europe as a whole was rapidly growing. It may have dropped somewhat during parts of the seventeenth century when the rate of demographic growth declined. But municipal authorities were little aware of any long-term trends. They were far more conscious of seasonal shifts or sudden increases in the migration rate during times of crisis. And they always felt, year after year, that far too many immigrants were turning up.

In theory only immigrants with the requisite wealth or skills would be allowed to stay in the community and settle down as permanent residents. In practice this was impossible to enforce, for the distinction between temporary and permanent residents was often blurred. This was especially the case in the rapidly expanding metropolitan centres with their sprawling outer districts – the suburbs and *faubourgs* outside the walls where work and residence patterns were particularly hard to control. Unlicensed artisans and unskilled workers abounded in these outer neighbourhoods, where overlarge parishes and underdeveloped institutions made it difficult to keep track of exactly who lived there. But even within the city walls, municipal governments found it hard to keep a close grip on the number of inhabitants. Every market-day, every seasonal fair brought a host of travellers. Not all of them left again. Innkeepers and citizens were constantly warned not to provide accommodation to visitors without notifying the authorities. It never helped. There always seemed to be more and more people in the city – and many of them, far from contributing to the urban economy, were in desperate need of help.

I

When all else fails, people beg. There had always been beggars in the European city, and what they did was powerfully sanctioned by medieval theology and social practice. To give alms to a beggar was the classic good work, as beneficial to the soul of the giver as it was to the body of the recipient. But the beggar did something good too: not only did his prayers aid the donor, but also his very existence gave donors the opportunity to do good by giving alms. In addition, the presence of mendicant religious orders, whose members were supposed to support themselves by seeking alms, powerfully legitimized begging as a social activity. Nobody really imagined that all beggars were tinged with holiness and every act of giving sanctified the donor; people of the late middle ages were robust realists who knew that not every intimidating beggar who demanded a handout would ever remember the benefactor in his prayers. Occasional legislation condemning the idleness of vagrants and beggars can be traced back to the fourteenth century.[7] Until the sixteenth century, however, such laws were largely ignored. For even when the recipient was not worthy, the act of giving was. And begging itself was still a legitimate enterprise in many communities. Beggars were listed as citizens in a number of German cities in the fifteenth century and sometimes they even paid taxes; in Cologne an unofficial guild of beggars was organized in the 1450s.[8]

7. Pullan, *Rich and Poor*, 200.
8. Jütte, *Armenfürsorge*, 27–8; cf. Maschke, 'Unterschichten', 68–9.

As long as begging remained socially and spiritually acceptable, every random act of almsgiving was regarded as commendable. But much charity was also given in the form of bequests after death, for this too, could help speed the donor's soul heavenward. Clothing, food or cash could be distributed at the deceased's funeral. Yet other, more lasting forms of posthumous charity were also common. Testaments often included bequests to support existing institutions in their work of charity or to establish new ones. Many of these institutions were of course religious, but it was by no means uncommon to bypass the church and establish a private charity to be administered by the secular authorities. By the start of the sixteenth century, every sizeable European city had a hodgepodge of hospitals, leper-houses, pilgrim hospices and other philanthropic institutions, supported largely by rents or other forms of income bequeathed by the faithful in their wills. Nobody had to restrict his or her bequest to existing institutions; any sincere gift would be equally commendable. In the early sixteenth century, for example, the Frankfurt merchant Jacob Heller bequeathed funds for the establishment of a public warming-house in the city. Every year from November to February this house was to be open from dawn to dusk, with a two-hour closure at midday, as a place where beggars and other poor people could find relief from the chills of a German winter.[9] Where the visitors would spend the night was not considered; this was a day-time facility, not an attempt to deal with poverty on a structural level. But it was a classic act of traditional Christian charity.

Poverty, then, was a religious challenge. But it was also a social problem. Its dimensions could be masked by almsgiving and charity, but whenever a sudden crisis occurred the full extent of human need became glaringly apparent. In the late 1520s, for example, all over northern Italy a cycle of severe famines compounded by the disruptions of warfare drove huge masses of peasants into the cities in search of succour. A patrician of Vicenza described the situation in 1528:

> Give alms to two hundred people, and as many again will appear; you cannot walk down the street or stop in a square or church without multitudes surrounding you to beg for charity: you see hunger written on their faces, their eyes like gemless rings, the wretchedness of their bodies with the skins shaped by bones. . . . Certainly all the citizens are doing their duty with charity – but it cannot suffice.[10]

9. Jütte, *Armenfürsorge*, 88–9.
10. Pullan, *Rich and Poor*, 243.

Indeed it could not. Yet it was in exactly these years, beginning in the 1520s, that all over Europe a sudden burst of interest in the reform of poor relief became apparent. This movement began in cities, but it engendered widespread discussion among thinkers and policymakers and in some countries contributed to the enactment of new legislation on the national level.[11] The details differed from one community to the next, but municipal leaders avidly followed what was happening in other cities, and the reforms had much in common. The most fundamental principle, reiterated in almost every community that drafted new poverty legislation, was the prohibition of indiscriminate public begging. The scattered complaints about dishonest beggars and occasional laws against public begging were consolidated into a universal condemnation of the practice. Everyone understood, of course, that some people were driven by desperate need to engage in begging. But the beggar would no longer be regarded as a universal category. Instead, each case would be assessed on an individual basis. Those who were entitled to assistance would receive it. Those who were not would not.

To implement this principle required new administrative arrangements. Commissions were appointed to distinguish between those who deserved aid and those who did not. The deserving poor were identified and listed; in many communities they were required to wear badges so that all could know who they were. They would no longer have to beg, for they and their needs were now clearly recognized, and they could wait at home for food or money to be delivered. The undeserving were also identified. Once they were, they might also be marked – generally with a whipping – before they were sent back to their home towns or simply led to the city gates with a warning never to return.

The commitment to support all the deserving poor called for a higher level of coordination than had formerly been the case. The money previously handed to individual beggars was now to be deposited in poor-boxes and offering plates or collected by officials who went from house to house. The money thus gathered would then be distributed to the deserving poor according to their needs. This often required the establishment of a new municipal agency. In addition, many city governments set up systems of inspection and supervision to ensure that existing charitable institutions were

11. For some important treatments of poor-law reform in the sixteenth century, see Pound, *Poverty and Vagrancy*, 39–68; Slack, *Poverty and Policy*, 113–37; Pullan, *Rich and Poor*, 216–371; Davis, *Society and Culture*, 17–64; Martz, *Poverty and Welfare*; Jütte, *Armenfürsorge*; Wandel, *Always Among Us*.

fulfilling their responsibilities in a fiscally sound manner. Sometimes the municipal government went even further, taking over existing charities to consolidate them into larger, more efficient units under the direct control of the city council.

In many cities of central Europe, the reform of poor-relief systems went hand in hand with the introduction of the Protestant Reformation. Certainly Protestant theology, with its rejection of salvation by works, saw no spiritual benefit in the act of giving alms to a beggar – and a rationally organized welfare system corresponded closely to the Protestant vision of the godly community whose members obeyed God's commands not in hopes of grace to come but in gratitude for blessings already received. There were practical reasons, too, why so many Protestant communities reorganized their welfare systems: when monasteries, convents and other church institutions were disbanded, it was only natural for municipal governments to take over some of their functions along with all of their revenues. But there was nothing inherently 'Protestant' about the wave of welfare reforms which swept across Europe beginning in the 1520s. In Protestant cities they were often part of a larger package of ambitious social, political and educational reforms associated with the optimistic mood of the early Reformation. But in Catholic cities very similar welfare reforms were often enacted in response to a specific social or economic crisis – typically a severe famine which drove up food prices for the inhabitants while simultaneously flooding the city with refugees. One of the most characteristic manifestations of the new approach, for example, was the famous *Aumône-Générale* established by the predominantly Catholic leaders of Lyon in the 1530s. This municipal agency was set up to receive charitable donations in lieu of the alms formerly given directly to beggars. Once a week, the *Aumône-Générale* distributed bread and money to the city's deserving poor, who were listed on the basis of careful house-to-house surveys.[12]

Unlike Protestants, Catholic theologians were deeply divided over the issue of begging: some insisted that the spontaneous relationship between almsgiver and recipient must be retained, while others held that a less personal but more effective gift was equally meritorious. Virtually all Catholic theologians would have agreed, however, that alms must be given voluntarily. The idea of a compulsory poor-rate imposed on all prosperous householders – as was implemented in England by the end of the sixteenth century – would not have

12. Davis, *Society and Culture*, 39–40.

appealed to Catholic thinkers. But heavy moral suasion to pressure donors to give something was acceptable. In any case there were certainly enough Catholic theologians who favoured the thrust of the new approach to inspire or at least endorse the efforts of municipal leaders intent on welfare reform in cities like Lyon.

At times urban leaders, especially in Catholic cities, fell back on a more spontaneous approach to the problem. This happened in Toledo in 1546, when severe winter floods in the surrounding region left thousands of peasants destitute and desperate for aid. As refugees poured into the city, church leaders insisted that in accordance with Christian charity the newcomers should be not only fed but also housed: many of these beggars were placed in the city's various hospitals and some were housed in the archbishop's palace, but hundreds more were put up in private homes of well-to-do citizens. A half-hearted attempt was made to isolate the 'healthy' beggars and put them in jail, but the main concern was to respond to a sudden crisis with a dramatic display of Christian charity. Most of the refugees apparently stayed for months, until the good harvest of 1546 began to relieve the pressure.[13] But such a large-scale programme of personalized poor relief, orchestrated by a coalition of lay and clerical leaders, was a rare undertaking. The enthusiasm of a single year could never be sustained in the long term – not in Toledo, and certainly not in most other cities. In Catholic and Protestant towns alike, the notion that poverty needed to be addressed in a more systematic manner had firmly taken hold.

To be sure, no city ever succeeded in consolidating all its welfare services. Some institutions were protected from absorption by traditional privileges or powerful patrons. In every city, an assortment of public and private institutions continued to address the needs of the poor. But the reforming impulse never died out. Throughout the early modern era, European cities continued to experiment with new mechanisms to deal with the ever-present problem of poverty. Much attention was focused on hospitals: old ones were reformed and new ones founded. Traditionally hospitals had served a variety of different purposes, in most cases reflecting the wishes of their original founders or subsequent benefactors. Some hospitals took in the sick of every description, others accepted only victims of a specific disease. Some were primarily rest-houses for travellers, some functioned as homes for aged paupers, some took in well-to-do widows or widowers who paid for their room and board. But before

13. Martz, *Poverty and Welfare*, 123–30.

the sixteenth century, nobody expected hospitals to do more than relieve distress on an incidental basis. Now some reformers saw in hospitals a potential solution to broad social problems. If banishing beggars did not work, perhaps confining them to hospitals would. In 1581 a beggars' hospital was founded in Toledo. Public begging was forbidden and beggars were ordered to check into the new institution where all their needs would be met. Many chose to leave the city instead – and wisely so. Funding for the new hospital never lived up to expectations, and within a few years the project collapsed.[14]

But the idea of confining the unstable elements of society survived. In the course of the seventeenth century, increasingly many institutional solutions to the problem of poverty were advanced. Workhouses were introduced. A hospital merely succoured the beggar; in the workhouse he or she would be taught some skill and, it was hoped, be habituated to a more industrious way of life. Closely linked in spirit to the workhouse was the orphanage, where the child who lacked parents would be introduced to good work habits before being put out as a servant or apprentice. Some workhouses even accommodated children whose parents were still living but could not afford to raise them. In the English town of Salisbury the tiny workhouse established to confine twelve adults in 1602 was expanded two decades later to include lodgings for poor children who would be taught the rudiments of a trade before being bound over as apprentices. At the same time, the city financed a programme under which masters in the textile trades would put poor people to work in their own shops, keeping them occupied with relatively unskilled tasks like spinning and knitting. But it soon became apparent that both funds and employment opportunities were too limited to make the programme a success; the workhouse survived, but the training programmes collapsed.[15]

All such schemes turned out to be inadequate to the need. Yet in city after city, a new generation of municipal leaders would tackle the problem with a fresh burst of optimism. The vision of a comprehensive institution to combine confinement and training was particularly powerful in French towns of the seventeenth century. This normally took the form of an *hôpital-général* which would enclose the ill, the aged, the orphaned, the insane and the idle all at once, providing palliative care or disciplined training as appropriate to each category. Many such institutions were proposed and quite a

14. ibid., 141–51.
15. Slack, 'Poverty and Politics', 178–92.

few were actually founded in the course of the seventeenth century. The *Hôpital-Général* of Paris, which was launched in 1657 with a spectacular round-up of beggars from the streets of the city, may have housed close to 10,000 inmates at a time.[16] Smaller but similar institutions were founded in many provincial cities, often in the hope that systematic confinement would finally eliminate social disorder and wipe out habits of idleness among the poor.[17] But even so it was never more than a small fraction of the rootless poor who were effectively confined. The costs were too high and the potential clients, in many cases, preferred the risk of remaining free to the punitive security of institutional confinement.

Begging could not be eliminated. No matter how many vagrants were banished or confined, desperate people still found their way on to the streets of the city, determined to collect whatever they could while staying out of the beadle's sight. Catholic town-dwellers continued to believe that handing alms directly to a beggar was a work of mercy; even in Protestant cities it was hard for inhabitants to resist the insistent appeal of the outstretched palm. Completely consistent policies were impossible to enforce. Even communities which tried to maintain a general policy of expelling or confining beggars often made exceptions for special cases, for example by granting crippled or blind vagrants permission to beg in the streets.[18] But the real problem was that no amount of charity, private or public, would ever be sufficient to cope with the dimensions of poverty.

Everyone agreed that scarce resources should be directed primarily to the deserving poor. But establishing exactly who was 'deserving' was not a simple matter. Three intersecting systems of categorization were involved.[19] One category was geographical: the local person – especially someone actually born in the community – was always more deserving of support than the outsider. A second category was physical: the person unable to work due to illness, youth or age was more deserving of aid than the person who had the physical capacity to earn a living. The third category was moral: the person who was willing to work was more deserving than the shirker. The 'sturdy beggar' – the healthy person who was able to work but unwilling to do so – was a popular target of fierce moralizing and repressive legislation. In fact everyone knew, or could have known, that many

16. Bernard, *Emerging City*, 145–55.
17. Fairchilds, *Poverty and Charity*, 29–37; Schneider, *Public Life in Toulouse*, 197–203.
18. e.g. Seville: Perry, *Crime and Society*, 180–2.
19. Dinges, *Stadtarmut*, 248–53.

such people were idle not by choice but by circumstance. But this was often ignored. For there was little that could be done even for paupers who were willing and able to work. Occasionally the physically able beggars were commandeered for public works projects such as rebuilding or reinforcing the city fortifications. But such undertakings and the funds to support them were usually short-lived. Nor was it easy to arrange private employment for the poor. Even when the law provided that local orphans were to be put out as apprentices, the guilds sometimes raised objections.[20] The likelihood that outside beggars could be converted to productive workers with an accepted niche in the local economy was always slight. It was altogether easier to act on the premise that beggars were deliberate shirkers, constitutionally unwilling to submit to the discipline of labour. Vagrants were depersonalized, seen not as distressed individuals but as a collective threat to the city's well-being. The city had to protect itself against the 'plague of beggars' by quarantine measures not unlike those which were applied in the case of contagious illnesses.[21] In actual fact, beggars were as hard to stop as infectious diseases. Many a gate-keeper or beadle found it convenient or even lucrative to let a beggar elude his notice. But whenever the authorities found the beggars too bothersome, it was easy to solve the problem: with a little effort, the current crop of beggars could always be apprehended, whipped, banished and forgotten.

The local poor, by contrast, could be neither removed nor ignored. The social obligation to meet their needs was conceded by all. But cities did everything they could to restrict their number. In many German towns, anyone who applied for citizenship or even just for local residence rights had to give evidence of an adequate degree of wealth before being accepted. Sometimes the applicant also had to promise to make no claim on the city's welfare institutions for a specific number of years.[22] In England, where poor-rates were collected and distributed on the parish level, there were even obstacles to moving from one parish to another within the same city. Newcomers were often asked to post a bond to cover the initial costs of any poor-relief they might incur; if they failed to do so, they could be sent back to their original parish. In seventeenth-century Southwark, just south of London Bridge, a parish 'searcher' promptly visited every new arrival who took up residence in the district.

20. e.g. in Venice: Pullan, *Rich and Poor*, 305–6.
21. cf. Dinges, *Stadtarmut*, 258–85.
22. Jütte, *Armenfürsorge*, 214–17.

Anyone who lacked obvious means of support or refused to post a bond was quickly evicted by the constable.[23]

Even in the face of such measures, however, every European city had an irreducible core of impoverished inhabitants – the 'house poor' or 'parish poor' who enjoyed an undisputed right to live in the community yet could not support themselves without assistance. How many people belonged to this category? Naturally the proportion varied enormously from town to town, and it could rise or fall drastically within a given community as economic conditions changed. A few examples can, however, give some evidence of the extent of poverty.

Start with the well-recorded case of Augsburg. For the year 1558 the tax register recorded a total of 8,770 citizen households. Of these, a total of 4,161 households – about 47 per cent – were listed as 'have-nots'. This was a tax category, not an indication of total destitution – but it does show that almost half the householders in Augsburg lacked any property worth taxing and lived almost entirely off their income. Many of them could not break even: in the same year exactly 404 households, containing a total of 1,038 men, women and children, received regular support in the form of bread, lard, firewood and other supplies from the city alms office. Thus, in 1558 about one out of every twenty citizen households were living in definite poverty. But the exact numbers receiving support fluctuated from year to year, due both to economic conditions and changes in policy. In 1563, for example, the magistrates ordered that more stringent eligibility criteria be imposed, and for a few years there was a drastic reduction in the number of recipients. At other times, however, the numbers rose sharply. In the famine year 1571, almost 900 households – over 10 per cent of the citizen families – needed sustained assistance.[24]

In every town, in fact, there would have been a similar difference between the number of 'structural' poor who were permanently dependent on relief and those who needed assistance only in times of famine or other crisis. This was vividly apparent, for example, in the English town of Warwick. In 1582 St Mary's parish, which encompassed most of the town, had a total of 373 families. Of these, only 42 families, or 11 per cent, actually received poor-relief. But another 68 families were said to be at risk of decaying into poverty.

23. Boulton, *Neighbourhood and Society*, 272–3.
24. Clasen, 'Armenfürsorge in Augsburg', esp. 75, 86–9; for the 1558 tax figures, Blendinger, 'Bestimmung der Mittelschicht', 71; Roeck, *Stadt in Krieg und Frieden*, 1:154.

Precisely this happened to many of them five years later when a drastic famine hit the town, for in 1587 a total of 93 families in St Mary's parish – close to a quarter of the total – stood in urgent need of assistance.[25] A number of London neighbourhoods in the same era showed a similar pattern, with 5–10 per cent of the parish families regularly receiving relief and a second group, perhaps twice as large, needing assistance in times of crisis.[26] Much the same applies to late sixteenth-century Lyon: it has been estimated that in normal years 6–8 per cent of the city's population needed poor relief, but in times of famine 15–20 per cent of the inhabitants required support.[27] Not all cities, of course, maintained records of relief distributions – and if they did, the figures were sometimes kept only during years of crisis. In Toledo, for example, over 11,000 people – about one-fifth of the city's total population – needed assistance during the famine of 1558. The number of parish poor who received aid in normal years would certainly have been much lower. But the fact that 20 per cent of the established, householding inhabitants of Toledo needed help to survive a few months of higher bread prices gives us a powerful indication of the extent of urban poverty in the early modern era.[28]

II

Early in the year 1635, the authorities in Salisbury undertook – not for the first time – a survey of the poor in each parish of the city. In one parish, St Martin's, the enumerators even distinguished between two levels of poverty. Thirty-three households were listed as regularly receiving alms. One was headed by a man, three were headed by married couples, and fully twenty-nine were headed by women – widows, spinsters or wives whose husbands had abandoned them. Among the much larger group of 174 parish households which, though poor, did not need regular alms, 105 were headed by married couples. Among the rest, 48 were headed by women and only 21 by bachelors and widowers.[29]

Figures like these were entirely typical of early modern cities. Among the much larger group of 174 parish households which, unmarried or widowed women were always more common than those headed by unmarried or widowed men. Women were, by and large, less mobile than men – and more economically vulnerable.

25. Beier, 'Social Problems', 58–60.
26. Archer, *Pursuit of Stability*, 153–4.
27. Gascon, *Grand Commerce*, 1:403–4.
28. Martz, *Poverty and Welfare*, 113–19.
29. Slack, 'Poverty and Politics', 166, 173–6.

An unmarried man was more likely than an unmarried woman to leave his home town, whether as a journeyman, a soldier, a sailor or even a vagabond. Among married couples, husbands abandoned their families far more often than wives. But above all, the poor widow was a much more common phenomenon than the poor widower. A man's chances of remarrying were normally greater, and even if he did not remarry his economic resources were normally larger. It is true that among the social elite, widowhood could open up opportunities for a woman to deploy her property independently and find a new marriage partner of her own choosing. Among the poor, however, widowhood was always a disaster. The paltry dowry a poor woman had brought into her marriage – if it was even intact – offered no economic security, and her opportunities to continue to earn a living were always circumscribed. Even if the law guaranteed a widow the right to continue operating her husband's shop, in practice most poor women lacked the capital and the contacts to do so effectively.

Yet the 'house poor' widow may still have been regarded with envy by some other women in the community. She at least had a recognized claim on a modest degree of social assistance. Women who had never established a household in the first place were often even more vulnerable. Among these were servants. To be sure, not all servants, male or female, were ill-treated. Some worked for patriarchal masters who recognized an obligation to care for those who had loyally served them. But mistreatment of servants was no less common, and female servants ran the additional risk of being subjected to sexual exploitation. In early modern Bordeaux many a last will included bequests for servants, often with a specific reference to the recipients' faithful service.[30] But evidence from the same city also illustrates the risks that female servants faced. In the 1620s about thirty babies were abandoned by their mothers every year, to be taken in by the Jesuit foundling hospital. Generally, of course, babies were abandoned in secret, but occasionally the hospital staff was able to identify the parents. Looking after foundlings was an expensive proposition – in each case a willing wet-nurse had to be found and paid – and whenever possible the authorities hoped to pin the expenses on the responsible party. The fathers who were traced came from every social level – but ten of the eleven mothers whose circumstances were recorded were listed as domestic servants. In most such cases, a master had made his servant pregnant and then fobbed her off with a promise of regular child support – and when

30. Dinges, *Stadtarmut*, 120, 498–9.

the payments eventually tapered off, the mother could see no other recourse than giving up the baby.[31] Occasionally even more callous treatment of female servants was recorded in Bordeaux: in 1664 a servant who was staying, between jobs, in a rented room in one of the city's finer neighbourhoods was terrorized and gang-raped by three armed men of high social station. The perpetrators were tried but acquitted on the basis that they had accidentally mistaken the house for a bordello – in which, it was implied, such behaviour was fully acceptable.[32]

Such a defence, transparent as it was, could not even have been put forward if bordellos had not been so commonplace in Bordeaux. But in fact prostitution was firmly established in every European city. As in most societies, prostitution was above all an expression of the social and economic vulnerability of women. Homosexual prostitution was not unknown, but it was rare.[33] Most prostitutes were women – and while the way in which sexual commerce was organized underwent some significant changes in the early modern era, these changes did nothing to ameliorate the plight of the prostitutes themselves.

Prostitution had been endorsed by the medieval church as a necessary evil, a practice which would confine and channel sexual impulses which might otherwise spread more widely. Taking their cue from such teachings, many European cities had authorized the establishment of licensed brothels, subject to regulation and inspection by municipal officials.[34] Yet the legitimization of prostitution did not render the prostitute herself respectable. Prostitutes were expected to be sharply demarcated from the rest of the population; in many cities they were commanded to wear specific articles of clothing to distinguish them clearly from respectable townspeople. It was always hoped that the prostitutes would primarily come from outside the community, but some of them were actually local women, driven into the brothel by economic necessity. Indeed, women were occasionally placed in the brothel by their own male relatives. A statute of 1470 in Nuremberg attempted to forbid the customary practice by which men who owed money would lend or pawn female family members to the brothel-keeper until the debt was paid.[35] A century later the same practice had to be prohibited in Seville.[36]

31. ibid., 149–52.
32. ibid., 152–3.
33. e.g. Perry, *Gender and Disorder*, 125–6.
34. For a full treatment of these institutions in Germany, see Schuster, *Frauenhaus*.
35. Irsigler and Lassotta, *Bettler and Gaukler*, 193.
36. Perry, *Gender and Disorder*, 139.

In theory these brothels were established solely to be frequented by unmarried men. Of course brothels were also visited by married men and by members of the generally far from celibate clergy. But such clients ran some risks if they were recognized. In Cologne a licensed prostitute who discovered that her client was a married man or priest was permitted to plunder his clothing and valuables before handing him over to the authorities for a humiliating punishment.[37] By contrast, journeymen or other bachelors were permitted and even expected to visit the brothels; this, it was generally felt, would diminish the risk of their sexual energies being directed towards the daughters or wives of the town's respectable inhabitants.[38]

All this, however, had begun to change by the sixteenth century.[39] The sudden spread of syphilis, beginning in the 1490s, cast some doubts on the suitability of sexual commerce. Far more important, however, were changes in moral outlook. Already in the fifteenth century some cities had imposed measures to reduce the amount of casual contact between prostitutes and other inhabitants. Licensed prostitution was increasingly seen as an affront to notions of communal order and discipline – ideas which initially contributed to and were in turn reinforced by the religious changes of the sixteenth century. Protestant reformers and, more gradually, Catholic ones as well demanded a higher standard of sexual morality which made the existence of officially licensed brothels seem increasingly inappropriate. In some Protestant towns, the official brothels were closed soon after the Reformation was introduced. Elsewhere the closures came more gradually. In Catholic Cologne the official brothel – a full-service establishment with its own alehouse for luring customers and private cemetery for the prostitutes – lasted until the 1590s.[40] In Seville, the municipal brothel, far from being closed, was reorganized and placed under tighter municipal control in 1570. Half a century later the authorities were still wavering as to whether to shut down or reorganize the establishment, until the king himself settled the matter by ordering the closure of all brothels in Spain.[41]

None of this eliminated prostitution. It simply meant that all prostitutes now operated illegally, usually under the control of pimps

37. Irsigler and Lassotta, *Bettler und Gaukler*, 190.
38. cf. Rossiaud, 'Prostitution', 22–3.
39. This process has been studied with particular thoroughness for Germany: see Schuster, *Frauenhaus*, 155–202; Wiesner, *Working Women*, 97–109; Roper, *Holy Household*, 89–131. For a brief European overview, see Orme, 'Reformation'.
40. Irsigler and Lassotta, *Bettler und Gaukler*, 184, 192.
41. Perry, *Gender and Disorder*, 137–9, 148–50.

or procuresses. In sixteenth-century London there were repeated crackdowns on commercial sex, which sometimes involved the prosecution of brothel-keepers and clients alike. Yet in the 1570s the city still had at least a hundred bawdy-houses – either actual brothels or inns where prostitutes rented rooms to practise their trade.[42] In late sixteenth-century Vienna there were about fifty private bordellos, and a lot of sexual commerce also took place in the shadow of the city walls.[43] As in most societies, teenage prostitutes were heavily in demand and a virgin available for deflowering commanded a high price for her handlers.[44] Prostitutes past their prime had few options. Some slipped into unskilled work as washerwomen or alehouse servants. Some became procuresses themselves, often offering their own daughters to clients.[45] Many others died of neglect or venereal disease.

Most authorities eventually recognized that prostitution could never be eliminated. Many devout members of the social elite, however, poured their energy into attempts to rescue prostitutes, getting them to renounce their lives of sin and enter a house of rescue where they would be taught Christian virtue along with some honest trade. Though such institutions – often named in honour of Mary Magdalene, the patron saint of repentant sinners – had existed since the middle ages, they became particularly popular among the moral reformers of the Catholic Reformation. Yet similar projects were also undertaken by Protestants. In the 1750s a Magdalen House was founded in London, and within a few years its proud governors could report that over a hundred former prostitutes had been sent home to their parents or placed as servants in respectable households.[46] Like all such projects, however, this one scarcely dented the surface of the problem. Many prostitutes were never reached by the reformers, and of those who were, many could not stomach the stifling discipline of a Magdalen house. Anyway a single establishment could normally accommodate only a few dozen inmates at a time. For every one prostitute who was successfully rescued by the moral reformers, there were hundreds of others who were unwilling or unable to turn away from the life to which they had

42. Archer, *Pursuit of Stability*, 211–15.
43. Schuster, *Frauenhaus*, 204.
44. Norberg, *Rich and Poor*, 48; Roper, *Holy Household*, 129; Archer, *Pursuit of Stability*, 232.
45. Norberg, *Rich and Poor*, 49–50.
46. Marshall, *Dr. Johnson's London*, 278–80.

become accustomed. Reintegration into mainstream society was an option for very few indeed.

III

Prostitutes in most larger cities were only part of a broader but amorphous social group of socially marginal inhabitants. Some historians have argued that, at least in large cities, some members of this marginal population formed a clearly defined criminal underworld.[47] There is certainly no question that many people earned their living entirely through activities which the authorities labelled as crimes. Begging itself, after all, was increasingly identified as a criminal act, and for desperate people the step from begging to petty theft was often a short one. Nor is there any doubt that many of a town's inhabitants belonged to social networks in which small-scale crime and evasion of the authorities played a major part. The concept of an urban underworld is useful in helping to conceptualize how such people organized their struggle for survival. But it must not be assumed that all its members were sharply and permanently separated from the mainstream of urban society.[48]

Certainly every large city did have a small core of professional criminals, organized into bands whose members preyed systematically on the rich or unwary.[49] Theft of property was certainly the most common and most lucrative activity of such groups: housebreaking was common enough, but much theft was focused on more readily accessible locations like docks or public markets. Organized theft, of course, required a network of collaborators: taverners or innkeepers to provide safe-houses and pedlars or petty retailers to fence the goods. All this implied some degree of structure, but the extent or permanence of criminal organization must not be exaggerated. Even in early eighteenth-century London, where organized crime had reached a highly sophisticated level, criminal bands rarely included more than a dozen members.[50]

Theft of property was the most common activity of the professional criminal, but some groups specialized in exploiting human gullibility. By the late fifteenth or early sixteenth century gangs of professional gamblers, tricksters and con artists were well established in France, Germany, England and elsewhere.[51] Gambling with dice or cards

47. Notably Perry, *Crime and Society*, 8–10, 19–32; McMullan, *Canting Crew*, 49–51.
48. cf. the discussion in Archer, *Pursuit of Stability*, 204–10.
49. McMullan, *Canting Crew*, 100–13.
50. McLynn, *Crime and Punishment*, 9–10.
51. Jütte, 'Anfänge des organisierten Verbrechens'; Jütte, 'Nepper'.

was a widespread passion in early modern Europe, and it was easy enough to victimize inexperienced players, especially the peasants and traders who flocked to every city during fairs and markets. Many of these small gangs moved from city to city, managing with considerable success to stay one step ahead of the urban authorities, though occasionally a notorious rogue was arrested and punished. Taken together, these groups of swindlers formed an elite stratum of vagabonds who passed tips and information to each other in their own well-developed argot. They were a source of endless fascination to contemporaries, forming the subject of numerous books which both warned and titillated readers by exposing the rogues' tricks and decoding their secret language. These publications may have saved a few people from the embarrassment of losing their money to a dishonest dice-thrower, but they also fostered the false impression that townspeople were being victimized by a vast flood of itinerant rogues. Much of the deep-seated hostility towards all beggars, in fact, was nourished by the illusion that criminal vagabonds were far more numerous, organized and dangerous than really was the case.

There certainly was much crime in the early modern city, but little of it was committed by professional criminals. As in any society, members of every social group were punished for criminal acts. But it seems likely that most crimes were committed by men and women whose social situation placed them somewhere between the great mass of well-established householding families on the one hand and the tiny core of professional criminals on the other.

Evidence from early modern Cologne supports this impression. The evidence comes from a sample group of almost 2,000 persons arrested on criminal charges between 1568 and 1612.[52] Not all of these people were criminals – indeed, many were released without being convicted – but they were individuals whom the authorities of Cologne seriously suspected of criminal behaviour. Five-sixths of the suspects were men. In about two-thirds of all cases, something is known of the suspect's social or occupational status. Of these two-thirds, over 40 per cent belonged to social groups whose members generally fell beneath the level of established householders: vagrants, day-labourers, servants, soldiers, porters, carters, agricultural workers and the like. Another 40 per cent were identified as craftsmen – but they were not necessarily householding masters. In fact, for almost half of the craftsmen, the individual's status within the craft is specified, and four out of every five turn out to have been

52. Schwerhoff, *Köln im Kreuzverhör*, 178–94.

journeymen or apprentices. The great majority of suspects, then, were people with a smaller, less permanent stake in society than that of the established householders. No doubt some of these suspects were, in effect, professional criminals. But most were simply members of the working poor.

Every city, in fact, had a substantial group of inhabitants who were only partially integrated into the social order: journeymen, apprentices, domestic servants, hired hands and day-labourers. Many of these people were immigrants. Most were unmarried. Some lived in the households of their masters, others lived in cellars, garrets or other rented accommodations. Many of them aspired to marry and become established householders once they had saved sufficient wages to make this possible – and many of them succeeded in doing so. Others spent their lives in dutiful dependency. But some inevitably succumbed to the more lucrative prospects of casual criminal activity.

Buried in the Cologne criminal records is the report of a conversation that took place, sometime around 1590, between a carpenter named Gerd Kogler and a 19-year-old journeyman listed only as Leonhard. The trade for which Leonhard was training was a particularly unpromising one – he was learning to be a *Schinder*, or disposer of carrion – but evidently he was trying his best. 'So why do you work so hard?' taunted the carpenter. 'One can go one's own way and have just as good a life as anyone.'[53] The 'good life' to which he referred, of course, was the life of crime. Everyone knew that for some, this way of life would eventually end with their arrest, conviction and execution or – if the judges were lenient – banishment from the community. Yet even so, thousands of Leonhards must have sat in the taverns of early modern Europe, hearing just such talk. Some, inevitably, were tempted.

One of the most famous of William Hogarth's 'progresses' was the set of twelve engravings issued in 1747 under the title 'Industry and Idleness'. This series compares the careers of two imaginary apprentices of London: the industrious Francis Goodchild, whose hard work and good conduct result in economic success and political eminence, and Tom Idle, whose laziness and irreligion lead via petty crime and underworld activity to the scaffold at Tyburn.[54] The whole series, like most of Hogarth's work, is didactic, moralistic and ironic all at once. The contrast between the careers is unrealistically extreme.

53. ibid., 357.
54. Reproduced in Shesgreen, *Engravings by Hogarth*, plates 60–71.

Yet the point Hogarth made was a valid one: that for any young person arriving in London, or indeed in any city of early modern Europe, many options were still open. Whether the newcomer would eventually rise into the more secure world of the established householders or would sink into permanent marginalization was, in many cases, determined by economic factors far beyond his or her control. But personal conduct could make a difference. Parents, church, school and guilds all promoted values of hard work, deference and sexual morality which are easy to interpret as instruments of social control. But these were also values which helped the young adult to maximize his or her chances of securing a foothold on the social ladder – and by doing so to climb into the circle of established householders who formed the core of every urban community.

IV

Most people who were marginalized in the early modern city were victims of economic circumstances: either their own resources were too limited or the city's economic capacity was too narrow to make it possible for them to be absorbed into the mainstream of the community. But some people were condemned to marginalization by an accident of birth or a personal attribute which made it virtually impossible for them even to aspire to be fully integrated into the ranks of urban society.

In central Europe one of the strongest barriers to social integration was derived from the standards of 'honour' enforced by the guilds. Honour is often thought of as a special concern of the aristocracy, but in fact people of every social level were equally obsessed by the need to uphold their individual and group reputations. In France an artisan's honour was a highly vulnerable attribute that needed constant defending: every insulting word or gesture had to be avenged. But honour, though easily lost, could also be regained – by winning a fight, by humiliating one's rival or even, in some cases, by securing a court order to restore one's reputation.[55] By contrast, in the Germanic lands of central Europe the loss of honour was generally a permanent condition – and it often carried over into the next generation or beyond. In most cities those who were held to be lacking in honour were barred from membership in the guilds, which in turn meant they were excluded from citizenship and sharply limited in the ways they and their families could earn a living. Lack of honour invariably meant permanent marginalization.

55. Farr, *Hands of Honor*, 177–95.

There were many ways by which honour was lost.[56] Illegitimate birth was one; indeed, in many German towns even having been conceived before the parents' wedding could render a person ineligible for admission to guilds and citizenship. Racial purity was also a factor: in the eastern parts of Germany, Slavic blood was often dishonouring. So was a criminal record, particularly if one had ever been publicly punished by being whipped or mutilated. Anyone who wanted to join a guild and thus become a citizen could be required to swear that he had no such disqualification; in the town of Kyritz, northwest of Berlin, the oath prescribed in the late sixteenth century began as follows: 'I swear that I was begotten by my mother and father as good pious parents in a proper marital bed and that I was baptised as a Christian, that I am not of Slavic but of good German blood, and of good honest background and behaviour'.[57] Of course an applicant could try to conceal his origins, but if there were any doubts then the officials were likely to write back to his home town before accepting his word.

Numerous occupations were also dishonouring. The exact list varied from town to town in the Germanic world; in some cities, for example, linen-weavers were considered dishonourable, presumably because so many were of peasant background, while in other cities the linen-weavers formed an entirely respectable guild with its own rigid membership rules. But certain occupations were on every list – notably gravediggers, executioners and the *Abdecker* who disposed of carrion and performed other degrading chores. Not only were the practitioners of these trades barred from normal social contact with other town-dwellers, but their taboo status extended to all their relatives too. The executioner, for example, was well paid for his work, but his son could never hope to practise a normal trade and his daughter could never marry into an 'honourable' family. It was unthinkable for an ordinary citizen even to sit down for a drink or take a meal with the executioner: to socialize with him posed the risk of being thrown out of one's own guild. To actually help the hangman do his job was even more risky. No carpenter, for example, ever wanted to help build a new gallows, for this might be regarded as assisting the executioner in his work: normally municipal governments could get around such a boycott only by insisting that

56. The fullest treatment of the subject is by Wissell, *Recht und Gewohnheit*, 1: 145–273.
57. ibid., 1: 159.

all the carpenters in town must jointly construct the new scaffold after one of the city officials hammered in the first nail.[58]

Most of the time the authorities readily accommodated the guild taboos: the guilds' obsessive concern with the honour of their members, after all, helped to discourage many forms of aberrant or disruptive behaviour. Occasionally, however, when the authorities felt the guildsmen had gone too far, they would step in and force the guilds to modify the rules. Sometimes even private individuals overturned the most rigid taboos. In 1614, for example, the impoverished widow of a pastor in Schwäbisch Hall permitted her daughter to marry the local executioner. But the marriage was made over the stringent objections of most of the bride's relatives and the status of the couple remained ambiguous.[59] Marriages of this sort, rare as they were, were always bound to make trouble. In 1696 the butchers' guild in Bergstadt reprimanded and fined one member for permitting his wife to receive visits from her own mother – who, after being widowed, had married a hangman. The guild maintained that social contact with his mother-in-law might render the butcher, his apprentices, his journeymen, and perhaps even other members of the guild liable to dishonour. Eventually the ban was lifted, but only after a lengthy wrangle.[60] The disputes and publicity generated by cases like these obviously discouraged all but the most determined members of guild families from contemplating marriage or social contacts with anyone connected with the dishonoured trades. For the most part, all over central Europe and in the Baltic lands where German customs prevailed the 'dishonoured' and their families remained firmly and permanently marginalized.

Of course an even more rigid form of social exclusion was practised wherever people were held as slaves. In the mid-sixteenth century, white and black slaves made up about 7 per cent of the population of Seville; the proportion of slaves in Lisbon was about 10 per cent.[61] To be sure, within Europe the institution of slavery was largely confined to the Iberian peninsula. But social marginalization as a more general phenomenon was not limited to specific regions. All over Europe there were people who were partially or wholly excluded from the mainstream of urban society on some basis or other – typically ethnicity or religion.

58. Dülmen, *Theatre of Horror*, 71–3.
59. Wunder, *Bürger*, 150–1.
60. Wissell, *Recht und Gewohnheit*, 1: 192.
61. Pike, *Aristocrats and Traders*, 172.

It is important to remember that numerous cities, especially larger ones, had substantial ethnic subgroups. For early sixteenth-century Rome, to cite but one example, the ethnic identity of 40 per cent of all householders can be established – and among these one out of every five was of non-Italian origin, being instead Spanish, French, German, Slavic or Jewish.[62] In fact every major centre of political or economic activity had its colony of foreigners. Originally the main factor that attracted foreign settlers was economic. Beginning with the Reformation, however, religious refugees were added to the pool. In the late sixteenth century, for example, Protestant émigrés from the Spanish-controlled sections of the Netherlands started arriving in cities all over northern Europe; a century later it was Protestants from France who followed in their path.

Few places in Europe boasted quite as rich a variety of ethnic groups as the cities of early modern Poland. Though municipal policies were far from uniform, most Polish cities welcomed foreigners and readily granted many of them rights of citizenship. In the sixteenth century, when Polish religious policies were particularly tolerant, the cities attracted religious refugees from all over western Europe in addition to the usual flow of immigrants in search of economic opportunity. By 1600 Polish cities had German, Italian, Scottish, English, Flemish, French, Scandinavian, Armenian, Persian, Greek and Jewish inhabitants in addition to ethnic Poles. Though immigration policies became somewhat stricter in the seventeenth century and minorities faced increasing pressure to assimilate to local norms, Polish cities retained their multi-ethnic character throughout the early modern era.[63]

In many other European cities foreigners were granted citizenship less readily. But this did not mean all of them were socially marginalized. Great merchants were often welcomed as an economic asset: even if they did not participate in the city's political life they could enjoy close economic and social relationships with the local patriciate. Colonies of foreign artisans also throve in many cities, especially if they organized their own institutions of social welfare so as to assure the authorities that their sick and aged members would not become a burden on the city's resources. A very different experience, however, faced the impoverished foreigners who drifted into distant cities in hopes of casual employment or charitable handouts. Not only did they confront all the usual obstacles faced by unwelcome visitors, but

62. Partner, *Renaissance Rome*, 75–7.
63. Bogucka, 'Nationale Strukturen'.

also their isolation was often compounded by hostility due to their foreign origins, language or customs. Such people were completely marginalized.

Perpetual marginalization was also the norm for non-Christians. They, in fact, were isolated from the mainstream of urban society in a way that even adherents of the most extreme Christian denominations never were. Bitter as the religious conflicts of the sixteenth and seventeenth century often became, the denominational barriers within Christianity were never impermeable. Intermarriages and conversions were common occurrences, and in some cities members of different denominations managed to live in relative harmony as members of a common political community. Non-Christians, however, were always outsiders.

There were some Muslims in European cities, especially in the Mediterranean region. Venice, for example, had a large contingent of merchants from the Ottoman Empire, most of whom by the seventeenth century were lodged in a special establishment designed in part to minimize non-economic contacts between them and the Christian population. The Iberian peninsula had traditionally housed a large Muslim population, but by the sixteenth century the open practice of Islam was no longer possible. Around 1500, shortly after conquering the last Muslim kingdom on the peninsula, the Spanish monarchs required all Muslims who wanted to remain in Spain to convert to Christianity. As a result many Spanish cities soon acquired a substantial population of Moriscos, nominal Christians who retained traditional Arab customs along with a shadowy allegiance to the religion of their ancestors. Most were distrusted by the authorities and were confined to menial jobs; certainly they were never integrated into the host society. In 1609 even this marginal status became politically unacceptable to the crown and the Moriscos were banished, mostly to North Africa.

Taking Europe as a whole, however, the most openly and conspicuously marginalized town-dwellers were certainly the Jews. In fact Jews were not dispersed across the entire continent, and even where they could be found their numbers were not particularly high. Yet the distinctness of the Jewish way of life and the historically embittered relationship between Judaism and Christianity made the Jews into objects of intense curiosity and powerful emotions even in places where none of them actually lived.

Jews could live only in countries and cities where their presence was specifically permitted by the authorities. Since the ground rules were constantly being changed, much of the Jewish experience in the early modern era consisted of migratory movements from one part of Europe to another.[64] In 1450 there were major Jewish populations in Spain, Portugal, Italy, Germany and various parts of eastern Europe, but no Jews in England or France. Within fifty years, however, the Jews of Spain and Portugal had been forced to convert to Christianity or leave the Iberian peninsula. This not only produced a large number of conversions in Spain itself, but also unleashed an immediate dispersion of Jews throughout the Mediterranean world and a more gradual dispersion towards northern Europe of converts whose descendants reverted to the Jewish faith when conditions permitted. In central Europe Jews were also on the move. The decentralization of political power in the Holy Roman Empire meant that Jewish residence patterns underwent constant changes: while many cities expelled their Jewish populations in the fifteenth and sixteenth centuries, other cities, such as Frankfurt am Main, accepted growing Jewish communities. Meanwhile migration from the west contributed to the steady growth of Jewish populations in Poland. In the seventeenth century Jews were readmitted to England; by the eighteenth they were again a presence in France.

The Jews were useful adjuncts to the dominant society. Prohibited from owning real estate or engaging in most trades, the Jews often specialized in moneylending, moneychanging and long-distance trade in jewels and other portable objects of value. But the positive role played by the Jews in the perpetually cash-poor economic system of early modern Europe was often appreciated more readily by political and social elites than by the poorer Christians who perceived Jews only as usurers. Religious hostility and economic resentment among the Christian population often reinforced each other so as to make the Jews into objects of venomous hatred.

Except for economic contacts, the Jews were often totally isolated from their Christian neighbours. Up to a point this reflected the Jews' own preferences; certainly Jewish leaders discouraged intermingling and condemned intermarriage with members of another religious community. But it was Christian leaders who insisted on measures to accentuate and perpetuate the Jews' physical separation, often in highly humiliating ways. It was entirely customary, for example, to insist that Jews wear a distinctive mark on their clothing so that none could mistake them for Christians. In almost every city with a substantial population, the Jews lived in their own streets or

64. For a useful overview of the Jewish experience in early modern Europe, see Israel, *European Jewry*.

neighbourhoods. In some cities residential segregation was enforced by the establishment of a formal ghetto. The concept of the ghetto was pioneered in Venice but it reached its fullest development in Frankfurt am Main, where the Jews were rigidly confined to a single long street surrounded by its own walls and accessible only through its own gates. In fact the city's policy towards the Jews echoed and amplified the fear of physical contact that governed German attitudes towards other taboo-laden groups which were condemned to formal marginalization. According to the famous code which regulated Jewish life in seventeenth-century Frankfurt, the Jews were forbidden to leave the ghetto on Sundays and Christian holidays; on other days they could appear in the streets of the city but only if they had business to do and never in groups of more than two. When they came to Christian markets they were not allowed to touch any fruits or vegetables unless they had already paid for the produce. There were numerous other regulations in a similar vein.[65]

To Christian city-dwellers the Jews appeared as a unitary social group, utterly marginalized and sharply differentiated from the host community by their dress, dialect and social conduct. Within every Jewish community, however, there were substantial differences in wealth and social prestige. The extremes of Jewish poverty and Jewish wealth were usually little evident to the outside world: the poor were looked after by Jewish communal institutions, while the rich had few opportunities to flaunt their wealth in the manner of Christian patricians. Yet within the Jewish community itself the range of wealth levels was often enormous.

It was, moreover, at the two ends of the scale that the barriers to contact between Christians and Jews sometimes began to break down. Impecunious Jewish pedlars occasionally had close links to the vagrants or criminals of the urban underworld whose own marginal status meant they had little to lose from intimate contact with the Jews. Among wealthy Jews the incentives for social contact were obviously very different. But by the late seventeenth century, especially among wealthy Jews of Iberian background who lived in tolerant cities like Amsterdam or Hamburg, there was some tendency to adopt styles of dress and deportment that reflected the manners of the Christian elites with whom they conducted business. This in turn made possible a modest degree of social interaction. When the eccentric ex-Queen Christina of Sweden visited Hamburg in 1667, she rejected a house offered by the city's magistrates in order to stay

65. Bothe, *Frankfurts wirtschaftlich-soziale Entwicklung*, 2: 247–319, esp. 2: 261–6.

with the wealthy Jewish financier who served as her own agent in the city.[66]

Such an episode, of course, was extremely rare. A queen who visited a Jew was as anomalous as a pastor's daughter who married a hangman. But cases like these illustrate that even the most deep-seated taboos were never inviolate. Social marginalization was a profoundly determinative experience for many groups and individuals in the early modern city. But unlike some traditional societies, Europe never had a rigid caste system and no barrier was ever absolute.

66. Whaley, *Religious Toleration*, 77.

PART THREE

The City in Calm and Crisis

CHAPTER TEN

Urban Routine

Disorder was the eternal enemy of urban life. Violence, of course, was the most visible and dangerous form of disorder, and municipal authorities were constantly concerned to prevent arguments from turning into fights, fights into brawls, brawls into riots – or riots, as occasionally happened, into revolts. But violence was only the most extreme manifestation of disorder. In fact all forms of disorder were held to be virtually synonymous with sin. And any behaviour that seemed to violate the divinely ordered pattern of human existence also threatened to upset the harmony of urban life. When women acted like men, or children disobeyed parents, or servants defied masters, or the poor aped the rich, then the world was in a state of disorder which cried out for correction.

The obsession with order was almost universal. It would be misleading to think of order only as something that the social and religious elites attempted to impose on the unruly masses. People of every social level were equally convinced of the dangers of disorder and shared a common sense of obligation to root it out. Some forms of correction obviously involved the imposition of authority by the more powerful over the weak: masters disciplined their servants, parents their children, teachers their pupils, husbands – within limits – their wives. But much discipline was also imposed by social equals against those whose behaviour was felt to undermine the status or solidarity of the group to which they belonged. And sometimes discipline was even imposed on social superiors. Journeymen, for example, normally stood under the authority of their masters. But the journeymen's association could punish members whose bad behaviour – in or out of the workshop – brought dishonour to the whole group. And occasionally the journeymen would even boycott or harass a master who had mistreated or underpaid one of their members. Social discipline, then, was a multidirectional process.

It was also a last resort. Punishment and correction, after all, were required only when there was a breakdown in the system. Most of the time the system worked. In every European city by the beginning of the early modern period the inhabitants' lives were shaped and structured by a firmly established set of customs, expectations and institutions. Obviously customs and institutions – and, to a lesser extent, expectations – varied from town to town, and of course they changed over time. But the fundamental elements of the urban routine remained constant – and they proved highly effective in structuring urban life. Life in the early modern city was as peaceful and predictable as it was because so many people knew exactly what they were expected to do – and were willing to do it.

I

The routines of urban life were structured by the clock and the calendar. For most people, however, the clocks that mattered most were not mechanical timepieces. Such devices did exist: by the beginning of the fifteenth century, many cities had installed a complex mechanical clock in some prominent place, generally the tower of the city hall.[1] By the eighteenth century, smaller clocks for domestic use were relatively widespread luxury items. Most inhabitants of the early modern town, however, had no need of mechanical clocks. They knew what time it was from the bell in the tower of the town hall or the nearest church, which would chime every hour and sometimes every quarter hour as well. It is no happenstance that the English word 'clock' is derived from *clocca*, the medieval Latin term for 'bell'.

It may be, as some have suggested, that rural peasants lived and worked in accordance with a 'natural' rhythm based on the weather and the change of seasons. But town-dwellers did not. Subordination to the discipline of hourly time had originated in the early medieval church with the rigid sequence of monastic services, but by the end of the middle ages it had spread to other spheres of organized activity. Numerous aspects of urban life were regulated by the ringing of the hours. In the late fourteenth century, special bells were introduced in Flemish and northern French cities to mark off the hours of work in the textile trade.[2] Countless urban ordinances of the early modern

1. Cipolla, *Clocks and Culture*, 40–3.
2. Le Goff, *Time, Work and Culture*, 35–6, 45–6; see also Landes, *Revolution in Time*, 67–82.

era specified when city gates would be locked and unlocked, when markets would be open for business, when councils and courts would commence their sessions, or when city officials would hold their office hours. School by-laws listed the hours when pupils were to arrive and depart, the times allocated for recess, and the specific hours to be devoted to particular subjects. Festive occasions were regulated by the clock as well: in Germany, at least, municipal ordinances routinely specified how many guests could attend a wedding and when the partying was to begin and end.

Above all, the times of work were regulated. In 1620 the municipal ordinances of Godalming in Surrey authorized a tax on each householder for maintenance of the town clock, because 'the use of a clock in the said town is very necessary for the inhabitants thereof for the keeping of fit hours for their apprentices, servants and workmen'.[3] This was an entirely typical attitude. Even though most labour was carried out in private homes, the ordinances governing particular trades often specified when journeymen were to begin their work and when they could quit for the day. Natural time was not totally neglected. Some regulations specified that activities would begin at dawn and continue until dusk. But it was just as common to stipulate distinct winter and summer hours. The Hamburg hatmakers' ordinance of 1583 was typical: in the summer journeymen should 'be at work at five bell-strokes and in the evening for as long as they can still see, but in winter they should be at work at six bell-strokes and in the evening until ten bell-strokes'.[4] Of course there would be breaks during the day – but often their exact timing was specified as well.

For townspeople's lives were constantly being regulated by the bells. The old monastic stress on punctuality had long since been carried over into urban life: many ordinances imposed a fine on those who failed to turn up for work or appear at meetings within a few minutes of the last chime. In the north German town of Schleswig, journeymen in some trades were routinely expected to begin work at 5 a.m. The tailors' ordinance of 1655, recognizing that some journeymen would need extra time to sleep off their weekend revels, made one modest concession: on Mondays a journeyman had to appear in his master's workshop only by 9 a.m. But if he was late he would forfeit half a week's pay – and if he missed the whole Monday, he would lose a full week's income. Despite this loss of income 'thereafter for the rest of the week he should be in the shop at

3. Tittler, *Architecture and Power*, 137.
4. Wissell, *Recht und Gewohnheit*, 2: 408.

five o'clock in the morning, and keep hard at work until the evening when the bell strikes ten'. If he stinted any of these unpaid hours, he would owe a fine of 2 marks – not to his master, however, but to the journeymen's own common fund.[5]

The hours of the day, then, represented the first time-cycle that structured urban life. The second one was the week. Six days of work, one day of rest and worship – this fundamental pattern of the Judaeo-Christian tradition was deeply ingrained in every European community. Work was extremely rare on Sundays, though the taboo was not absolute – the rule among the Schleswig tailors was that if a master required his journeyman to work on the sabbath, for that day's labour he had to pay a whole week's wages.[6] Yet Sundays could be problematic, as there was often some tension between those who wanted to emphasize religious observance and those for whom Sunday represented virtually the only opportunity for relaxation. Municipal authorities might be vigilant in making sure that drinking establishments remained closed during the actual hours of divine services, but after that nothing could prevent the heavy consumption of liquor. Sunday-night drinking often spilled over into the following day, making 'Saint Monday' into a time of missed work or absenteeism which was often tolerated more generously than it was by the strait-laced burghers of Schleswig.

The third great time-cycle was annual: the yearly recurrence of political, economic or religious events, some universally observed, some of only local importance. Almost all of these events were scheduled according to the calendar of religious feasts and saints' days with which all Christians were familiar, both before and after the Reformation. There were fixed and movable feasts: saints' days recurred on the same date every year, while holidays in the great Easter cycle, from the weeks before Lent down to Pentecost and Corpus Christi, shifted every year. All over Europe, the annual cycles of municipal governance were based on the religious calendar. In London chamberlains and sheriffs were elected on the feast of St John the Baptist ('Midsummer Day'), 24 June, while the Lord Mayor was chosen on Michaelmas, 29 September.[7] In Toulouse the annual election cycle began on St Clement's day, 23 November, and new officials were sworn in on the feast of St Lucie, 13 December.[8] In

5. Schütz, *Handwerksämter*, 55, 159.
6. ibid., 159.
7. Pearl, *London*, 51–2.
8. Schneider, *Public Life*, 62.

Nuremberg the political year varied in length, since elections took place during the week after Easter no matter when it fell.[9] Each city had its own dates and customs, but the pattern was universal. In many cities the annual political procedures would have had only a limited public impact – in Nuremberg, for example, the elections involved a small group of patricians who met in secret. But some events in the annual political cycle were major public occasions: in Ulm, for example, the great collective *Schwörfest*, when magistrates and citizens alike took a public oath to uphold the city's laws, took place every year on St George's day, 23 April.[10]

Economic life was also shaped by the calendar of religious holidays. Many of the major feasts and saints' days were routinely taken as days off from work – so much so that in some cities the working period actually averaged out to five days a week. Countless economic events were dated by the religious calendar. These ranged from great public gatherings, such as annual or seasonal markets and fairs, to less public but equally familiar dates for the payment of rents or the settlement of accounts.

Markets and fairs normally had more than strictly economic functions, as they provided ancillary opportunities for entertainment and socializing. But for people in every town until the Reformation – and in Catholic communities after it as well – the most emotion-laden events in the annual cycle were generally the religious holidays derived from the ecclesiastical calendar. The major festivals of the Christian tradition were observed in every community. But other annual holidays were strongly local in character: a saint who was neglected in one city might be the object of major veneration in another. In Lincoln, for example, until the Reformation the great religious event of the year was the feast of St Anne on 26 July. A special confraternity, closely supervised by the city council, spent weeks organizing the costumed procession, making sure that each of the city's corporate groups fulfilled its traditional responsibilities: the tilers' guild, for example, had to provide men to march as 'kings', while each alderman had to provide a silk gown for one of the 'kings' to wear.[11] There were only some towns in which the cult of St Anne had achieved such prominence. But other towns had other saints. The character of the event was entirely typical.

Some phases of the religious year imposed specific limits on

9. Strauss, *Nuremberg*, 60–1.
10. Specker, *Ulm*, 56.
11. Hill, *Tudor and Stuart Lincoln*, 33–4.

personal behaviour. This was above all the case during Lent, the forty-day period of heightened devotion, dietary restrictions and, at least in principle, sexual abstinence which preceded Easter. But the religious calendar also provided occasions for a temporary loosening of customary social restraints. Christmas had some of this character, but even more important was the carnival season which immediately preceded the onset of Lent. Carnival was more than just a period of revelry and feasting to counterbalance the coming rigours of Lent; it was also a time when the normal distribution of political and social power was subjected to ritual challenge. In plays, pageants and parades the weak either mimicked or mocked the strong. Things that would be punished at another time of year were said or done with impunity: scurrilous theatricals ridiculed the elite, women masqueraded as men, adolescents hectored their elders. The revellers often wore masks and costumes, but they were protected less by their disguises than by the temporary suspension of social norms.

Such events were not absolutely confined to the weeks before Lent. In some communities there were other recognized times when ritual challenges to authority could take place. In England many such practices are recorded: at Christmas masters sometimes waited on servants; on Hock Tuesday, shortly after Easter, women staged mock battles against men; at May Day and Midsummer, young people invaded private property to gather branches and blossoms.[12] The festive inversion of social norms – the 'carnivalesque' – could not be rigidly confined to the week before Lent, but its manifestations were always time limited and its rules were clearly understood.[13]

Carnival behaviour provided a means for inferiors to attack their betters without displaying the customary respect or using the deferential language in which criticism from below normally had to be couched. Carnival also offered a temporary release from the tedium of everyday life. Yet in order to be effectively cathartic, carnival behaviour had to be extreme. Occasionally it went over the edge, spilling into bloodshed or revolt. Yet what is most striking about the carnival season is not that in some cases it went too far, but that in most cases it did not. Political challenges to authority were a recurrent theme in early modern cities, but carnival was not the occasion that most often triggered them. For all of its apparent disorder, carnival with its universally acknowledged time limitation was in fact part of the urban routine.

12. Phythian-Adams, 'Ceremony and the Citizen', 66–9.
13. cf. Burke, *Popular Culture*, 191–6.

Beginning in the sixteenth century, however, some aspects of the annual cycle, with its irregular pattern of alternation between solemn and festive occasions, increasingly came to be challenged by members of the religious and social elite. The main assault came from leaders of the Protestant Reformation. There certainly was a theological basis for their attack on the ritual cycle. By rejecting the veneration of saints, Protestants undermined the religious basis for almost all the processions and pageants of the traditional year. Denying the concept of salvation by works, they questioned both the exaggerated spiritual rigours of Lent and, by extension, the counterbalancing revelry that preceded it. Among the more extreme Protestant leaders, these theological objections to aspects of the ritual year were reinforced by a deep-seated, visceral rejection of festive ritual itself. Christmas, carnival, Corpus Christi – all were seen as equally abhorrent manifestations of papal if not pagan superstition. The rich varieties of temporal experience were to be flattened out into a simple alternation between sabbath and weekdays and a restrained and respectful observation of Easter and other festivals known to the ancient church.

Not all Protestant leaders, however, were equally committed to the extirpation of traditional rituals. Processions and pageants directly related to the cult of saints or the veneration of the Host disappeared quickly in all Protestant cities, but other customs derived from the religious calendar lingered on. Protestant cities continued to organize the calendar around the sequence of saints' days long after the veneration of saints had totally disappeared. Some popular holidays stubbornly resisted all attempts to stamp them out, and Protestant craftsmen sometimes insisted on taking the traditional numbers of days off from work. But the basic trend could not be resisted. In London the traditional Midsummer festival, which had combined militia displays and popular amusements with religious pageants, was steadily stripped of its importance in the course of the sixteenth century and ended up as a colourless military exercise. Meanwhile the purely secular festivities associated with the annual inauguration of a new Lord Mayor became ever more grandiose.[14] A non-religious celebration designed to enhance the prestige of the governing elite was always acceptable. But in Protestant cities the traditional alternation of exuberant and solemn religious holidays which had once structured the whole annual cycle had lost most of its energy by the seventeenth century.

14. Berlin, 'Civic Ceremony'.

Even in Catholic communities, the character of traditional festivals slowly changed. The uncontrolled exuberance of carnival and other festive holidays was also distasteful to many leaders of the Catholic Reformation who favoured a more reflective tone in religious life. What Protestant leaders tried to abolish Catholic leaders tried to reshape, stripping religious festivals of their unpredictable elements and encouraging a greater focus on their devotional content.[15] But the formal calendar of religious observances remained untouched. In fact new objects of devotion were put forward and new, ever more earnest processional rituals were introduced. In every Catholic city, the annual cycle of religious observances continued to remain a central element of the urban routine.

II

Efforts to curtail the exuberance of festive life were not confined to members of the clergy. Urban patricians, Protestant and Catholic alike, were equally concerned to curb the latent potential for disorder in traditional holidays. Some were motivated by a concern to raise the tone of urban culture – a goal not unrelated to the patricians' insistent striving for recognition as nobles at a time when noble culture itself was affected by the call for more dignity and civility. In Venice, for example, the effort to raise the tone of public festivities was already apparent in the 1520s, when Doge Andrea Gritti tried to eliminate the more vulgar aspects of the Venetian carnival, especially the bloodthirsty pig-baiting which normally took place right in front of the ducal palace, and replace such events with dignified ballets and theatrical entertainments.[16] Such goals were rarely achieved in full – but even when the tone of popular festivities could not be effectively upgraded, members of the social elite might make a point of distancing themselves from the festivities. Carnival remained popular all over Catholic Europe, but in some places patricians eventually took to watching the celebrations from their windows and balconies rather than plunging right into the street scene as their predecessors had.[17]

In any case the issue concerned only the character of public festivities, not their inherent value. Everywhere civic elites recognized the importance of public rituals as a fundamental part of urban life. To be sure, the patricians no longer appreciated the role that the

15. cf. Burke, *Popular Culture*, 207–16.
16. Muir, *Civic Ritual*, 161–4.
17. Amelang, *Honored Citizens*, 195–210; cf. Schneider, *Public Life*, 344.

'carnivalesque' could play in reconciling the lower orders to the hierarchical system by giving them a structured opportunity to criticize it. But members of the urban elite were only too glad to uphold or institute less subtle ways of asserting the legitimacy of the social system though public events that celebrated aspects of the political order.

Some of these events could be scheduled long in advance, especially if they were linked to the city's annual political cycle. Other such occasions were triggered by unpredictable events: military victories, peace treaties, dynastic happenings and the like. Many of these ceremonies involved some expression of loyalty to the broader political regime under whose authority almost every city ultimately stood. A royal or princely visit always called for a grand ceremony, orchestrated by magistrates whose conspicuous display of deference emphasized not only their obligations to the ruling house but also their own power as indispensable mediators between the prince and the town-dwellers. Royal births, deaths, marriages or coronations might also be occasions for carefully organized displays of loyalty. The exact character of such demonstrations, however, often reflected shrewd political calculations. In almost all cities, for example, the death of an old ruler or coronation of a new one routinely called for appropriate public ceremonies of mourning or celebration. But in Hamburg in the late seventeenth and early eighteenth century the celebrations in honour of the Holy Roman Emperor and his family became ever more lavish: the birth of an imperial prince or election of a new emperor would be marked with an entire cycle of public orations, pageants, fireworks and operas, the details of which were faithfully reported to Vienna. The reason for all this was not so much to manipulate local opinion as to impress the imperial authorities with Hamburg's allegiance at a time when the king of Denmark was continuing to claim sovereignty over the city. By the 1760s the Danish claims had been extinguished and Hamburg's status as an imperial city was secure. Subsequent celebrations were far more modest in scope.[18]

Even more dramatic rituals that represented and reinforced the relationship between governors and governed were the ceremonies associated with the punishment of wrongdoers. In most of Europe – England was the important exception – trials were held in secret. But everywhere in Europe punishments normally took place in public.

18. Whaley, *Religious Toleration*, 179–85.

For it was important not only that justice be done but also that justice be seen to have been done.

Suspected wrongdoers were normally imprisoned while their offences were investigated, but once they had been tried they were rarely kept in jail. Some were released, some were fined, some were commanded to leave the city, but most were subjected to a public punishment. This could take the form of a public humiliation, such as an hour or two in the stocks. It might involve a branding or mutilation, such as the removal of a hand or ear. But it was far more common for the convicted wrongdoer to be whipped, after which he or she might be escorted to the city gates and formally banished from the community.

It was always expected that a crowd would gather to watch the sentence being administered. But even the most protracted whipping was a less than sensational event, for it was merely an extreme form of the sanctioned beatings that took place every day in the households, schools and workshops of the early modern city. A vastly more impressive ritual of punishment was the actual execution of a criminal. The right formally to terminate a human life was one of the most exalted attributes of government in early modern Europe. Generally it was not the municipal council but the representative of some higher level of government that enjoyed the power to pass the actual sentence of death. Nor were executions very common; even many of those who were initially condemned to death were subsequently pardoned to suffer lesser sentences. The city of Nuremberg, which had a reputation for harsh treatment of criminals, conducted an average of four executions a year between 1500 and 1750. In Amsterdam, which became much larger than Nuremberg in the seventeenth century, the annual rate between 1650 and 1750 was exactly the same.[19] Public executions were infrequent enough to make a considerable impression when they happened – but they were common enough to form a predictable part of the urban routine.

Various methods were used to end the wrongdoer's life. Traditionally different forms of execution were considered appropriate for specific crimes: drowning for infanticide, burning for heresy or sodomy, crushing of the limbs for robbery with murder. But the most common methods by far were hanging and beheading, and over the course of time the more exotic methods became increasingly rare.[20] As late as 1750 two young men were burnt at the stake in

19. Schwerhoff, *Köln im Kreuzverhör*, 468; see also 154–6.
20. Dülmen, *Theatre of Horror*, 88–106.

Paris for having engaged in homosexual intercourse, but by then this method of execution had become highly unusual.[21]

What did remain constant throughout the early modern period was the presence of the public as an essential part of the execution ritual. Obviously one reason for this was deterrence. But public executions were not simply a technique by which the authorities attempted to intimidate the lower orders by demonstrating the consequences of crime. In fact onlookers were required to be present as participants in a great moral drama through which the wrongdoer made visible amends to the community for the harm that he or she had done.[22] The ritual of execution always proved most effective if both the prisoner and the public were persuaded of its legitimacy. Either the prisoner would make a penitent speech from the scaffold or the authorities would read the sentence and assure the crowd that the prisoner had duly confessed. Members of the public were also supposed to help the criminal face the rigours of execution. This did not always work: sometimes the crowd was too hostile to the criminal to show any sympathy. But generally the prisoner was given moral support. In Catholic cities, especially in Italy, members of a special confraternity would offer comfort to prisoners in their final hours, often accompanying them right on to the scaffold to offer assurance of salvation for those who felt remorse for their sins.[23] A good death – brave but not defiant – would win the crowd's approval.

A public execution was always conceived as a ritual of justice, not an act of vengeance. But just as the authorities passed judgement on the criminal, so the public passed judgement on the execution. At this point it no longer mattered that confessions were often extracted by force or that sentences were arbitrary and inconsistent: by now the sentence itself became the embodiment of justice and the crowd was conditioned to demand its precise application. If the executioner bungled the job, keeping the victim in agony longer than called for by the sentence, a riot might ensue. In a few instances, the executioner himself was attacked and killed by the mob.[24] Normally, however, the authorities made elaborate preparations to ensure that things would go according to plan. As in any society, only a small number of criminals were ever apprehended and punished. But for just this reason, public executions were an important part of the

21. Kaplow, *Names of Kings*, 142.
22. cf. Bée, 'Le Spectacle de l'exécution'.
23. Terpstra, 'Piety and Punishment'.
24. Dülmen, *Theatre of Horror*, 113–18.

urban routine. For members of the community were supposed to leave the site of an execution duly impressed that crime did not pay, that justice was firm but fair, and that in the eternal cycle of urban life wrongdoing would surely be followed by due retribution.

III

Public punishment was a predictable part of the urban routine. But it was also a mark of partial failure, an indication that ordinary means of maintaining order had not sufficed. Hangings and whippings, after all, were only the dramatic outcroppings of a much larger structure of correction and control to which every inhabitant of the early modern city was routinely subjected. In fact what really maintained order in the early modern town was the constant pattern of supervision, regulation, inspection and admonition by which members of the community were reminded of their obligations – and penalized for their transgressions.

The English port of Liverpool in the 1630s had 300–400 freemen, suggesting a total population of at least 2,000. As in every town in Europe, large or small, the officials kept a close watch on the behaviour of all the inhabitants. Every few months the mayor of Liverpool summoned a group of citizens to sit as jurors of the portmoot court and deal with the accumulated list of transgressions. Serious crimes were dealt with elsewhere; but a look at the portmoot court proceedings shows how the entire range of routine misdemeanours would be handled.

When the court met in January 1638, six people were charged with having committed acts of violence. Five of them were fined three shillings and fourpence each – four for engaging in 'tussles' and one, Cuthberte Culcheth, 'for punching a child of Richard Blevines upon his belly to his great hurt'. Thomas Man was fined double for having bloodied his victim. Four inhabitants were fined for letting visitors gamble in their houses at improper times of the night or simply entertaining guests at unseemly hours. Nine men and women, including one alderman, were fined sixpence each for failing to keep their pigs fenced in, two others for letting rubbish lie in the street to the annoyance of their neighbours. One person was fined for bringing suspect meat to market, and fourteen others for 'using the faculty of a freeman, not being free' – presumably this meant they had claimed customs exemptions or other advantages to which they were not entitled. One man from a nearby village was cited for gathering gorse from the Liverpool town common. City officials were not exempt from punishment: two market supervisors were fined for letting streets near the butchers' stand get dirty, two others for 'not keeping the fish boards clean'. Yet the dignity of civic office was upheld by the heavy fine of ten shillings levied on John Wainewright for abusing one of the town's former bailiffs 'in most undecent and unseemly words'.[25]

Three months later the mayor convened the portmoot court again. The list of transgressions was much the same: people were fined for 'tussles', for not keeping the streets clean, for letting their pigs run loose, or for misusing the town common. Thomas Kewckroicke was fined ten shillings for abusing the new bailiff, 'saying, if he came near him he would stab him' – but the bailiff himself was fined two shillings 'for keeping unlawful company in his house at unlawful times in the night'.[26]

The procedures differed from town to town, but the basic thrust of urban administration was everywhere the same. To protect the city's rights and uphold the dignity of civic officials were always matters of high priority. But maintaining order was no less important. Officials and inhabitants alike were bound by strict rules of conduct. Fighting in the streets, cheating in the marketplace, offending your neighbours, neglecting your duty – all these were transgressions that had to be reported, recorded, remembered and reprimanded when the time was ripe. Nothing was overlooked, nothing forgotten.

All this in turn required detailed written records. For the urban routine was not only maintained by custom, but also sustained by an extensive system of documentation. Some records were maintained by government officials, some by the church, some by guilds, hospitals and other quasi-public institutions, some by private notaries whose files bulged with legally binding wills and contracts. One cannot begin to grasp the way the early modern city functioned until one appreciates the thoroughness with which every piece of correspondence was preserved and every administrative act was documented. Every decision, great or small – whether to surrender the city to an approaching army or whether to grant firewood to an impoverished widow – had to be noted in the appropriate protocol or minute book. Every branch of the municipal government and every charitable institution kept detailed financial accounts. Budgets were rarely drawn up, and it was generally impossible to estimate total assets or liabilities – but each penny received, each penny spent had to be noted in the correct column under the appropriate heading of a

25. Chandler, *Liverpool*, 241–2; spelling modernized.
26. ibid., 242–3; spelling modernized.

great ledger book. Perhaps the most thorough records of all, however, were those relating to criminal investigations. In England, where trial by jury was the norm, court records might be relatively brief. But on the continent criminal cases were decided by a judge or magistrate on the basis of investigation and interrogation, and each scrap of evidence had to be preserved in writing. Every question put to a suspect or witness – and every answer elicited – had to be taken down verbatim. Nor was there any let-up in the flow of documentation when the trial moved from the magistrate's chamber to the dungeon. Even as the suspect was being tortured, a scribe sat quietly behind a grille faithfully recording every question the authorities posed and every intelligible word the prisoner managed to utter between each anguished gasp of pain. A single trial could generate hundreds of pages of testimony. If outside jurists were consulted on the finer points of the case, the dossier would grow even thicker.

We are accustomed to think of the early modern period in connection with the development of printing. Certainly the printed word had an incalculable impact on the spread of information and ideas. Nor was printing irrelevant to urban administration: every now and then an important ordinance would be printed or a published collection of codified statutes would be issued. But the records which sustained the urban routine consisted overwhelmingly of handwritten documents. Most of these records were maintained according to patterns and formulas which had been developed by the end of the middle ages; the most important administrative innovation in the early modern city was probably the introduction of parish registers in the course of the sixteenth century. Once any record series was firmly established, it might well be maintained without any change in format until the end of the eighteenth century. Year after year fresh bundles of documents would be neatly tied up and consigned to the archives or new volumes would be added to the shelves with their long rows of council minutes, account books, parish registers and the like.

Most documents were maintained by and for governments or institutions. But some crucial papers were issued to individuals, especially people on the move who might not be known in the next community they visited. Every journeyman, for example, travelled from town to town with a packet of certificates attesting to his honest birth and honourable service in previous positions. A merchant might need passes or letters of introduction. People who had lost all their goods due to fire or theft were given certificates entitling them to beg in towns where this might otherwise be forbidden. Former soldiers needed documentation to show that they were not deserters but had been properly discharged. Every Venetian sailor carried a set of *fedi* – testimonials signed by each captain under whom he had served. Without such documents the sailor would find it hard to get a new position on land or at sea. When Iseppo di Antonio Tesser was captured and enslaved in Tunis in the early 1620s he lost not only his liberty but also his papers; when he finally managed to escape and return to Venice after sixteen years he had to search his old neighbourhood with a notary, looking for former companions who could vouch for him and provide new statements about his personal history.[27]

Municipal governments received more and more written communications from the inhabitants. If you wanted to save a relative from the gallows, or gain admission to the almshouse, or be considered for the next vacancy as underclerk of the river tolls, you submitted a petition. Of course people frequently appeared before the authorities in person, hotly demanding their rights, or, more often, deferentially requesting some grant or favour. But they were normally told to put it in writing – and if this gave the petitioner any trouble, an experienced notary was always near at hand to draft a suitable document. Verbal exchanges were unpredictable and hard to verify. Written petitions could be considered, compared, copied and acted upon at the measured pace which the authorities preferred. It was ink that greased the wheels of government in the early modern city.

All this took place in the broader context of ever-growing literacy.[28] Not many aspects of urban life underwent radical change during the early modern era, but this one did. The spread of literacy is generally illustrated by the increasing proportion of people who could sign their names instead of simply making a mark on official documents. Obviously this is an indirect form of evidence which raises significant methodological questions. But the general trend is unmistakable. Literacy was increasing everywhere – though it certainly grew more rapidly in some parts of Europe, notably Britain and Germany, than in others. Literacy was always higher in towns than in the countryside. The literacy rate was almost always linked to gender and wealth: at any given time, in any community, literacy was higher among men than among women and higher among the rich than among the poor. But sooner or later the rates for all groups, except the very poorest, showed an increase. At the beginning of the

27. Davis, *Shipbuilders*, 192–3.
28. For a useful overview, see Houston, *Literacy*, esp. 130–54.

early modern era, only a small stratum of urban men and women were literate. Three centuries later the capacity to read and write was, though not universal, at least entirely normal among the vast group of householding families who made up the core of urban society.

Printing, of course, was a major factor. Printed matter was of little importance in the administrative and commercial routines of urban life, but it was an indispensable tool in teaching people to read and in sustaining literacy once acquired. Equally important, however, was the growth of schools. Almost all towns had grammar schools where young males, mostly from the upper social levels, were taught Latin and exposed to Greek. Some towns also had universities where a selection of these young men were trained for careers in religion, law or medicine. But the fundamental ability to read and write in their own language was imparted to boys and girls in the small vernacular schools which spread rapidly from the sixteenth century onward. Protestant towns got a head start, since vernacular education for children of both sexes was strongly promoted by the earliest leaders of the Reformation. Within a few generations, however, Catholic reformers had become equally ardent proponents. Religious and secular authorities agreed that the ability to read, write and reckon, along with some knowledge of Christian fundamentals, would help to turn children into disciplined, devout and productive adults.

Implementation often ran behind aspiration. Many of the vernacular schools were private enterprises, operated by teachers with no obvious aptitude for the task. The municipal authorities were likely to be more generous with curricular guidelines than financial support. If, as was often the case, the teachers' only source of income consisted of payments by parents, there was an obvious incentive to maximize the number of children in the classroom. The main teaching method was ceaseless repetition. But over time it worked. In 1450 in most European cities a literate craftsman would still have been an anomaly. Three centuries later the reverse would have been the case. To be effective in the workshop and perform one's duties as a Christian and a citizen, one had to be able to read and write. Certainly this was taken for granted by the cabinet-makers of Berlin in the early eighteenth century. According to the guild statutes of 1734, no master of the craft was to accept a new apprentice without checking if the boy could read, write and recite the main passages from the Lutheran catechism – and if the child could not, the master had to send him to school for four hours a week until he could.[29]

29. Stürmer, *Herbst des alten Handwerks*, 84–5, 155–6.

IV

All urban authorities, whether they represented government, church, guilds or other institutions, normally worked closely together. All were moved by a common concern to sustain the urban routine and maintain stability against all the forces that seemed to threaten it. Yet each source of power in the city operated in a different way and responded to a different set of expectations.

Certainly the dominant role in maintaining the urban routine was played by secular governments. The structure of municipal government, as we have seen, could differ substantially from one town to the next: sometimes a city council was virtually autonomous, elsewhere the municipal council shared power with institutions representing another level of government. But what remained constant was the broad range of responsibilities assumed by the governmental authorities. People in early modern Europe had many of the same expectations of local government that people have today: it was taken for granted that urban authorities would try to regulate the use of public spaces, enforce rules regarding the exchange of goods, promote public health, relieve destitution and prevent crime. But in addition, people expected local authorities to do many of the things that today are seen as the province of national governments, especially to intervene in economic life in order to assure a basic supply of food and fuel, maintain prosperity and reduce the impact of economic inequality. Then as now, governments could never satisfy all the expectations laid upon them. But it was not for want of trying.

Urban authorities always recognized an obligation to maintain the city's infrastructure. Major projects normally required the involvement or intervention of higher levels of government. Princely funds and influence lay behind many of the greatest construction undertakings in the early modern city: new boulevards cutting through old neighbourhoods, new parks and squares, new citadels and new residential districts. Some public works projects were launched on the initiative of the city governments: new town halls, paved streets, improved wharves, upgraded canals and the like. But on the whole municipal governments devoted more time and energy to maintaining the existing physical fabric of the community and making sure that the most elemental needs of safety and sanitation were being met.

In every city inhabitants had to be reminded or forced not to place their private advantage ahead of the common good. Sometimes, of course, the issues were simple enough. If shopfronts were extended or upper stories cantilevered out too far, traffic might be impeded and fire hazards increased: stern reprimands were clearly in order. When animals were let loose to root in neighbouring gardens, common fairness required that their owners be fined or warned. But some problems were harder to adjudicate. This was especially the case when it came to regulating the disposal of animal and human wastes. Excrement was clearly offensive to the nose and eye – but it also had a high recycling value. Urine, for example, was used in certain industrial processes, notably dyeing: to maintain their supply, some dyers in France put barrels in front of their shop-doors so that passers-by could obligingly relieve themselves.[30] Faecal wastes were useful as fertilizer, so householders were often permitted to maintain manure piles next to their homes for eventual sale to dung-collectors. But inevitably there would be problems when the heaps were left for too long or got too large and obstructed the streets.[31] In many communities a popular site for the disposal of wastes was right outside the city walls. But in Bordeaux the garbage heaps near the town gates grew so high that they could have been used to scale the city wall – an obvious source of concern at times when a military siege was anticipated.[32] All these situations required vigilance and intervention. To be sure, no amount of decrees and ordinances could ever guarantee uncluttered streets or orderly waste disposal. But individual offenders could be punished and others thus discouraged from following their example.

The use of water was particularly difficult to organize and regulate, chiefly because water served so many contradictory purposes. Most cities were on or near a river, and many cities had a supplementary network of canals, moats and tributary streams. These waterways often played an important part in urban transportation; small boats and barges could bring supplies from the main docks up to individual houses along the canals. Many trades, such as dyeing and tanning, depended on a convenient supply of water. At the same time, canals and rivers were an inevitable repository for human, animal and industrial wastes. Yet rivers and urban waterways were also a major source of drinking water.

Most cities had wells, but they never seemed sufficient to meet the demand – and in any case, well-water was often considered undesirable for drinking purposes. It was widely known that wells were more likely to become polluted than rivers and streams. In 1513 the citizens' assembly in the Hungarian town of Sopron, faced with

30. Guillerme, *Age of Water*, 150–1, 160.
31. King, 'How High is Too High?'
32. Dinges, *Stadtarmut*, 181–2.

rising prices that affected the community's normal drinking habits, requested in a petition that 'since wine is getting more expensive, the wells both inside and outside the city should be improved, cleared and kept clean, so that the poor people do not get sick from drinking water'.[33] The poor of Sopron, it seems, had to drink water only in bad years; in most European cities, however, it was consumed all the time.

The case of Hamburg clearly illustrates the complexity of water regulation. There was no shortage of water in Hamburg: the city lay on the great river Elbe and was intersected by a network of canals. The problem was that water served too many ends. The canals received much of the city's wastes. Streets had drainage gutters which emptied into the network of waterways and some houses boasted latrines with pipes that led into the canals as well. But the canals also provided some of the city's drinking water. The tidal action of the Elbe was relied upon to flush out the wastes, but activities that would increase the pollution were discouraged. From the fifteenth century onward, the municipal authorities issued one decree after another ordering inhabitants not to dump garbage, faeces or other wastes into the city's waterways. City inspectors were appointed to cruise the canals and arrest violators. Grates were installed at the mouths of street gutters to block large items from getting into the canals. Yet Hamburg's inhabitants had few illusions about the effectiveness of these measures. The pail-bearing women who trudged about the city selling bucketfuls of water charged the lowest prices for canal water. They got more for water taken from the swift-flowing Elbe. The most expensive product was spring water from privately owned fountains.[34]

For in Hamburg, as in many other cities where the terrain permitted, some water was brought in from freshwater springs in the countryside. Such water was normally transported through a pipeline made of lead, clay or bored logs. No city could afford to become completely dependent on piped water, as this would make the community more vulnerable in a siege. And in any case to pipe water in was always an expensive proposition. So in many towns the piped water was initially reserved for privileged sectors of the population and only gradually become more widely accessible.[35] In

33. Kubinyi, 'Wasserversorgungsprobleme', 185n.
34. Hilger, 'Umweltprobleme', 123–4, 129–31; Lange, '"Policey" und Umwelt', 14–20, 26–8.
35. Dirlmeier, 'Die kommunalpolitischen Zuständigkeiten', 131–9; cf. Bernard, *Emerging City*, 192–3.

the fifteenth century, for example, the cathedral priory of Worcester got its water from the hills west of the city through a pipe that crossed the Severn bridge and led to the cathedral enclave. In the seventeenth century the municipal government arranged to tap into the pipeline and distribute water through additional lines to cisterns in the city.[36] Much the same happened in Stuttgart. The first pipeline was installed in 1490 by the count of Württemberg so as to bring spring water from the nearby hills down to fountains in his palace precincts. Half a century later the municipal authorities installed a second pipeline to distribute water to fountains in the city centre. Such a system worked best, however, in a hill-ringed city like Stuttgart. And even in Stuttgart the system had its flaws. In 1645 the prince complained that his horses were getting sick because they drank from cisterns in which housemaids had been washing dishes. And later on the prince's lines ran dry when winegrowers in the nearby hills tapped into the pipes to water their vines.[37]

Good water was, in most towns, a luxury. But bread was a necessity. Indeed, one of the most fundamental duties of any urban government was always to guarantee an adequate supply of bread for the population. Every government recognized this obligation, yet to fulfil it was never entirely simple. Some cities owned or controlled rural lands which yielded dues or rents in the form of grain – but there was never enough to supply the wants of an entire community. Every city therefore depended on market forces to feed the community: typically the grain was purchased by merchants who sold it – chiefly to bakers – at open markets in the city itself. Ideally grain would be purchased from landholders in the city's own hinterland. If this did not suffice, grain would have to be brought in from afar – normally by ship, since it was always cheaper to transport bulk goods by sea than by land.

When harvests were abundant, grain prices dropped; when harvests were poor, prices rose. Of course city officials could try to impose limits on the price of grain, but this was a risky proposition, for in times of scarcity the sellers could always take their produce to other markets. Grain prices therefore tended to fluctuate according to market conditions. But changing prices could never simply be passed on to the consumer. To many of the city's poor, even a small rise in the cost of bread could prove catastrophic. Unlike the price of grain, therefore, the price of bread was always closely regulated.

36. Dyer, *Worcester*, 206–7.
37. Hagel, 'Mensch und Wasser', 127–31.

Strictly speaking, what the government determined in most cities was not the price but the weight of a standard loaf of bread. The reason was simple: some consumers were so poor that if the price of bread rose too much they could not have afforded even a single loaf. So instead, the price of a loaf was kept constant – but its weight was permitted to fluctuate in response to market conditions.

Setting the official bread-weight or price, however, was never a simple matter. Relations between municipal officials and bakers were invariably strained. Nobody could deny that when grain prices rose, bakers had to cover their costs by charging more for bread. But bakers were always suspected of exaggerating their expenses and pressuring the magistrates into setting higher prices than necessary. Yet if their wishes were not granted, the bakers could hold the community hostage by going on strike. In 1640, for example, the bakers of Dijon refused – and not for the first time – to go on producing bread until their complaints were addressed. The magistrates first reacted by threatening to impose massive fines or even demolish the bakers' ovens – but eventually they had to concede a new bread-tariff which would provide a more satisfactory profit.[38]

Some cities tried to develop sophisticated methods to balance the competing claims of the bakers and their customers. In Augsburg, for example, the price of coarse rye bread was kept artificially low and the price of wheaten bread was kept correspondingly high. Thus wealthy customers who preferred white bread partially subsidized the lower cost of coarse loaves for the poor.[39] But nothing could eliminate the authorities' persistent suspicions that bakers were hoarding their products, cheating customers or entering into collusion with the millers who ground their grain. In 1609 the millers of Augsburg were forbidden by law to invite any bakers to eat or drink with them, so as to reduce the opportunity for making dishonest deals.[40]

High bread prices were bad enough – an even graver prospect was the possibility that in years of harvest failure there might be no grain at all. To forestall this, some cities routinely purchased grain to be stockpiled for emergencies. Augsburg's municipal granaries had enough grain stored up in 1595 to feed the city's inhabitants for about a year; the vast granaries of Rome in the mid-eighteenth century could have sustained the city for even longer.[41] Yet stockpiling grain was

38. Farr, *Hands of Honor*, 40–1.
39. Roeck, *Bäcker*, 149.
40. ibid., 171.
41. ibid., 96; Gross, *Rome in the Age of Enlightenment*, 179.

by no means a universal practice. Bordeaux, for example, had no municipal granaries; spoilage due to the city's moist climate made long-term storage inefficient. Nor was grain from the Bordeaux hinterland adequate to the city's needs, since most of the nearby country was given over to winegrowing. In fact Bordeaux was almost entirely dependent on the importation of grain from elsewhere in France. Magistrates closely monitored the sale of grain and production of bread, and normally the system functioned well – so much so that even poor people in Bordeaux consumed mostly white bread. But a city like this remained acutely vulnerable to the consequences of harvest failure.[42]

An adequate supply of grain and bread always stood at the centre of urban provisioning policy. But in fact all of the victualling trades were subjected to close scrutiny. Food and drink were always liable to spoilage or adulteration. The activities of butchers, fishmongers and brewers were strictly monitored and weekly markets were tightly supervised. But this in turn was only part of a broader pattern of control and that affected every form of economic activity in the early modern town. Manufactured goods had to conform to precise standards of size, weight or appearance before they would receive the inspection seal without which, in many cases, they could not be sold. The service sector was no less tightly regulated. Innkeepers in sixteenth-century York knew exactly what to serve each visitor for dinner: pottage, boiled meat, roast meat, bread, and ale or beer. All this was specified by law; mine host and his guest would have expected nothing less.[43]

V

Every city, of course, required both a mechanism for formulating policies and an administrative framework for carrying them out. City councils were constantly engaged in reviewing and revising the rules and regulations by which the town was governed. Tradition had its place, of course, and some administrative practices remained unchanged for centuries on end. But the inertia of custom was constantly challenged by pressures for policy revision. Sometimes the pressure came from above, in the form of directives from the prince or his counsellors. Often it came from below, as guilds or other pressure groups demanded more effective means to protect their rights or interests. Yet not infrequently the council members

42. Dinges, *Stadtarmut*, 290–4.
43. Palliser, *Tudor York*, 166.

themselves identified a social need that called for rectification. Experts would be consulted or other cities canvassed. In 1505 the council of Nuremberg became troubled by irregularities in the administration of orphans' property, and wrote to the Senate of Venice for copies of the Venetian laws on wardship.[44] Guided by the information provided, the council appointed three of its members to serve as Guardians of Widows and Orphans, and in 1516 the city's chief legal advisor could write with satisfaction, 'The office of Guardians was established twelve years ago on the Venetian model, and since then we have had no trouble with suppressed or fraudulent testaments.'[45] This was an entirely typical development. Every city was constantly engaged in tinkering both with its policies and with the mechanisms for enforcing them.

The new office of Guardians in Nuremberg also illustrates another characteristic of urban administration. Members of the city council not only made policy, but also were deeply involved in carrying it out. Some if not all members of the council were likely to have specific portfolios which placed them in charge of particular aspects of municipal administration. In smaller towns mayors or aldermen might play a highly visible role, appearing in the streets and marketplaces to give directions and settle disputes on the spot. In larger towns the council members were more likely to operate out of sight as the heads of various government departments. But everywhere membership on a city council could mean more than meeting once or twice a week to vote on policy. At least some members of the council elite were deeply engaged in poring over accounts, hearing testimony, settling disputes and deciding the merits of individual petitions.

Of course every city also had a large number of subordinate officials. Even a small town like Liverpool in the seventeenth century had dozens of officials. The recorder gave legal advice. The town clerk maintained all the records. Two bailiffs, a sergeant-at-mace and two stewards of the hall assisted the mayor in the administration of justice. Two merchant praisors assessed taxes and determined the value of goods in commercial disputes. Two market superintendents, or leve-lookers, ensured that food for sale was fit for consumption. Two registers of leather inspected and sealed the tanners' products. Two ale-founders checked the quality and price of ale and beer. Board-setters and booth-setters – two of each – supervised the

44. Pullan, *Rich and Poor*, 256.
45. Strauss, *Nuremberg*, 65.

physical premises of the weekly markets. The water bailiff supervised the mooring of ships and maintained order in the port. The customs collector and his assistant gathered tolls and dues payable to the town. The hall-keeper maintained the warehouse where goods were weighed or consigned for storage. Scavengers cleaned the streets. The hayward and moss reeves maintained fences and made sure public spaces were not infringed upon. A bellman toured the town twice every night, calling out the hours and informing citizens of the wind and weather conditions.[46]

In Liverpool almost all of these offices were part-time positions, undertaken by citizens as a public service in return for a small wage from the town or fees paid by those who benefited from their services. In a larger town, many or most of these functions would have been undertaken by full-time officials. Their income came from wages or from a share of the fines and fees they collected, or perhaps some combination of both. The municipal bureaucracy might include dozens if not hundreds of positions. Yet except for the very highest town officials, such as the university-trained legal advisors, most municipal officeholders were nothing more than citizens who had managed to land a city job by petition or patronage. To be a scribe or collector or a watchman or inspector rarely involved any special qualifications beyond, at most, basic literacy and numeracy. The ordinary citizens of every early modern town were certainly subject to a vast system of supervision and inspection, but much of it was carried out by people very much like themselves.

In fact no city could be governed without the involvement and cooperation of the citizens. No matter how exclusive a grip on political authority the council maintained and no matter how loftily its members might assert their noble status, no urban government commanded the means to rule by coercion alone. Effective governance always required a substantial measure of consent – if not from all inhabitants, at least from the adult male citizens or freemen. In some cities there were formal organs through which this consent could be registered: there might be a large council or even an assembly of all adult male citizens. But what really mattered was that citizens willingly participated in the routines of urban governance. Citizens had to cooperate in paying taxes. They had to perform watch duty on the walls or streets. They had to report crimes and be willing to testify against the perpetrators. They had to participate in the processions and ceremonies by which the community represented itself to itself and to

46. Chandler, *Liverpool*, 47–91.

visitors. And they had to assume minor civic offices when asked, even if no pay was involved at all.

In larger cities much of the administrative routine was handled on the neighbourhood level. But 'neighbourhoods' were not always clearly defined. Almost every city was divided into a number of parishes, but many were also split into administrative units – wards, quarters or districts – whose boundaries only rarely coincided with those of the parish. The division of functions between the parish and other units was by no means sharp or obvious. Members of the parish council or vestry were obviously concerned with the maintenance of the church and its outbuildings, but often they were invested with many other responsibilities as well – notably the administration of poor relief. The functions of the ward, quarter or district varied enormously from town to town.[47] In many towns these districts had originally been established for defensive purposes, to organize the inhabitants to perform their duties as members of the city watch or militia, but often they acquired other chores as well, such as the apportionment of taxes or regulation of economic activity. Sometimes the quarter officials were appointed by the magistrates and remained strictly under their authority. In other cities leaders of the quarter were elected by the inhabitants. Either way, as a rule the magistrates were only too glad to have some administrative chores handled on the neighbourhood level. But occasionally the city's rulers would be distressed by the degree of autonomy which neighbourhoods had obtained and suddenly there would be an effort to impose tighter control.

Government on the neighbourhood level, then, was always susceptible to change. In Florence, for example, sixteen *gonfaloni* were established in the mid-fourteenth century. Initially these were neighbourhood associations comprised of all adult males who undertook to protect each other from unfair exactions by the city's powerful magnates. In time, however, the defensive character of these associations gave way to administrative functions: by the mid-fifteenth century the *gonfaloni* were primarily concerned with the allocation of taxes among the neighbourhood's residents. Typically an assembly of some thirty taxpayers might meet once or twice a year merely to elect the syndics who were burdened with the unpleasant chore of collecting taxes and sequestering the assets of those who would not pay. Yet the *gonfaloni* retained the potential to interpret their powers more broadly, as became apparent when they plunged into political

47. Jütte, 'Das Stadtviertel', 245–9.

agitation during the heady days of the Savonarolan regime. When the Medici family finally imposed a more autocratic system of municipal rule in the sixteenth century, the *gonfaloni* disappeared.[48]

The larger a city was, of course, the more indispensable was administration at the neighbourhood level. This was certainly the case in London, which grew into the biggest city in Europe during the early modern era.[49] The city of London was divided into two sets of administrative units: about twenty-five wards and over a hundred parishes. In formal terms the wards were the fundamental unit of local government. At meetings of the adult male propertyholders in each ward members of the city's common council were elected, neighbourhood offices were filled and grievances were voiced. Yet the parishes were equally important as agencies of neighbourhood administration. Outside the formal boundaries of the city of London, where there were no wards and the authority of the city government was limited or non-existent, the parish even emerged as the main instrument of local government. In some London parishes an assembly of all inhabitants played the dominant role; in others a 'select vestry' of richer parishioners made the crucial decisions. But either way it was parish officials who often played the central role in deciding who could live in the neighbourhood, who was entitled to assistance and who should be punished for misbehaviour or a disorderly way of life.

Historians of London have found it difficult to identify any long-term trends in the structure of the city's government. Did power gradually devolve from the centre to the neighbourhood level, or was it increasingly concentrated in the hands of the city's elite? Did parish government become more open or more exclusive? In fact it is almost impossible to recognize any clear patterns, partly because London itself changed from a compact, walled city of under 50,000 in the late fifteenth century to a sprawling metropolis of 750,000 three hundred years later. Some of the new districts came under the control of the city of London, others did not. The city government tried to keep a grip on things with a ceaseless stream of ordinances and directives covering every aspect of urban activity. But the actual collection of taxes, maintenance of infrastructure, enforcement of regulations and apprehension of wrongdoers could take place only

48. Kent and Kent, *Neighbours and Neighbourhood*, 13–37, 75–86, 173–8.
49. Recent treatments of neighbourhood government in London include Pearl, 'Change and Stability'; Boulton, *Neighbourhood and Society*, 262–75; Rappaport, *Worlds within Worlds*, 173–83; and Archer, *Pursuit of Stability*, 58–99; see also Rudé, *Hanoverian London*, 118–42.

on the neighbourhood level. All this, in turn, required that each neighbourhood have a small group of paid constables, beadles or watchmen – and a much larger number of volunteer officeholders. It was entirely normal for one out of every ten householders in a parish to hold some form of major or minor office. To the women, children, tenants, parish poor and vagrants who played no part in government at all, the power vested in the Lord Mayor and Aldermen of London would have meant very little. But the power vested in the male householders of their own parish would have meant very much.

VI

Certainly government, broadly defined, played the major role in any community when it came to maintaining order and organizing the provision of public services. But other institutions played an important auxiliary role. Chief among them were the guilds. Most guilds used either an assembly of masters or a special guild court to discipline errant members – and since a disorderly life could bring as much discredit on the guild as dishonest practices, such a court could exercise a broad jurisdiction indeed. This was certainly the case in sixteenth-century London, where the courts operated by the city's livery companies not only dealt with every manner of economic infraction, but also intervened in personal disputes within the families of their members.[50] Similar guild courts were familiar on the continent. In France and Germany the journeymen's associations were scarcely less active, often taking the initiative in disciplining members before the issue even came to the masters' attention.

Municipal governments generally reacted with mixed feelings to the quasi-judicial activity of the guilds. On the one hand, they could only appreciate the extent to which the system of internal guild discipline was indispensable for the smooth functioning of urban life. In London the aldermen, loath to spend their time judging 'suits in law for words which are but wind', insisted that whenever a freeman was accused of offensive or slanderous behaviour the case first had to be submitted to the court of his own company.[51] On the other hand, municipal governments jealously preserved their ultimate jurisdiction. A master or journeyman who felt he had been mistreated by the guild court normally had the right to appeal any judgment to the magistrates. In Cologne, a miscreant could even be imprisoned in the guild headquarters pending his trial by the court of guild masters

50. Rappaport, *Worlds within Worlds*, 201–14.
51. ibid., 212–13.

– but the city's magistrates had to be informed of the circumstances forthwith and they always had the option to transfer the case to their own jurisdiction.[52] In other towns the guild courts might be given final authority – but only for less important cases. In Schleswig, for example, most routine disputes between members of a craft could be judged by the guild without any appeal. But if a dispute had led to bloodshed, it would be referred to the municipal authorities.[53]

All these rules worked well enough when the ultimate political authority of the city council was accepted by all. This was not always the case, however. Sometimes a guild which resented a ruling by the municipal authorities would appeal over their heads to the king or prince. Throughout central and northern Europe, moreover, the authority of magistrates could be undermined by the widespread system of blacklisting. Any journeyman who had stolen from his master or committed some other form of dishonesty could be blacklisted; his name would be communicated to the guild in other cities by letter or would be posted in hostels by other journeymen as they moved from place to place. A master who hired a blacklisted journeyman ran the risk of being blacklisted himself, which in turn made it impossible for any other journeyman to work in his shop. Up to a point this was an entirely useful system by which communities could be protected from dishonest or dishonourable workers. But at times the system of blacklisting could spin out of control. In 1722, for example, the tanners of Nuremberg declared the entire tanning industry of Augsburg off-limits: no journeyman from any place in Germany was to accept employment there. With their productivity crippled by the lack of workers, the tanners of Augsburg appealed to the high court of the Holy Roman Empire in Vienna for a cancellation of the ban. Over the course of the next few years a series of increasingly sharp injunctions arrived from Vienna addressed to the tanners and the council of Nuremberg. But the Nuremberg tanners held their ground for five years until the ban was apparently lifted.[54]

In almost every city, secular institutions – the various levels of government along with the guilds – played the dominant role in regulating urban life and organizing the urban routine. But the church also played a significant part. The church potentially represented

52. Schwerhoff, *Köln im Kreuzverhör*, 71–2.
53. Schütz, *Handwerksämter*, 72–8.
54. Wissell, *Recht und Gewohnheit*, 2: 241. For an example of the blacklisting system in Scandinavia, see Österberg and Lindström, *Crime and Social Control*, 98–9.

an alternative locus of power, and sometimes tensions emerged between lay and clerical leaders. Mostly, however, they worked in cooperation. Their social goals were largely the same.

There were cities in which a prince of the church was also the secular ruler and the political power of the church was paramount. Rome was the most important such case; by the early modern era the traditional municipal institutions of the city had largely atrophied, as papal officials came to control more and more aspects of the city's affairs.[55] There were also little Romes in central Europe, cities in which a bishop or archbishop maintained his residence and exercised his power as secular ruler to the full. But such cases were rare. In most cities secular authorities had the upper hand.

This was accentuated, of course, in many of the cities which underwent the Protestant Reformation. Protestant practice routinely placed religious affairs under secular control, and to many Protestant thinkers it seemed entirely right that the clergy should be a branch of the municipal administration. To be sure, relations between Protestant pastors and the city officials who appointed and paid them were not always entirely smooth. Protestant ministers often relished their role as the conscience of the community and gladly used the pulpit to scold the magistrates for lacking doctrinal rigour or showing a dangerous tendency to extend religious toleration. But things hardly ever came to an open breach.

The church had always played a major role in encouraging orderly personal behaviour. Traditionally the moral teachings of the church were translated into personal terms by the discipline of confession and penance. In Catholic cities this continued to be the case. Protestants, however, had to develop new mechanisms, detached from all sacramental implications, to achieve many of the same ends. In Calvinist communities the characteristic device was the consistory, the mixed board of laymen and pastors whose chief function was to investigate and punish impious, disrespectful or disorderly behaviour. Pioneered in Calvin's own Geneva, the consistory soon became a characteristic institution in Calvinist cities all over Europe.[56] Of course there were occasional disputes about the exact extent of its power, but the ultimate subordination of the consistory to the authority of the secular magistrates was never in doubt.

Throughout the early modern era, in Catholic and Protestant towns

55. Gross, *Rome in the Age of Enlightenment*, 51–4.
56. For examples of the consistories' organization and policies, see Monter, 'Consistory'; Mentzer, 'Calvinist Reform'; Schilling, *Civic Calvinism*, 40–68.

alike, one role of the church was to function as an arm of urban administration. Political announcements were read from the pulpit. With the introduction of parish registers, the church took over the job of registering vital events. Poor relief and other forms of charity, even when orchestrated by the municipal authorities, were often channelled through the ecclesiastical structure. All this seemed perfectly natural to secular and religious leaders alike, for despite their occasional differences they almost always upheld a consistent set of values. Civic leaders – magistrates, preachers and guild elders alike – shared a common vision: the belief that an orderly, honest, hard-working and God-fearing community might just be able to protect itself from the shocks and strains of crisis and conflict that seemed to beset so many other cities. In fact few cities, if any, were ever successfully insulated from crisis or conflict. But it was not for lack of effort.

CHAPTER ELEVEN

Urban Crisis

The early modern city was, even at the best of times, a highly fragile community. The concept of a united body of inhabitants working together to achieve the goals of peace, justice and the promotion of the common good was readily voiced, especially by members of the urban elite.[1] Yet in actual fact nobody could fail to recognize that any community was a collection of groups and individuals whose competing interests and inclinations were difficult to harmonize. Hard as this was in times of relative stability, it was all the more difficult to sustain the solidarity of the community in times of crisis.

'Crisis' is an ambiguous concept. Historians have long debated the exact meaning of the term and its applicability to various situations in the history of early modern Europe.[2] But there is no question that a local crisis occurred whenever the customary routines and practices of a community were threatened or disrupted in a serious and sudden way. No matter how carefully members of the community could try to forestall and prevent any threats to the urban routine, no city in early modern Europe ever remained entirely immune to crisis. The causes of crisis took many different forms. In the long run, the most serious threats to urban stability often came from a breakdown of customary social relations within the community itself. But some of the gravest crises were caused by real or imagined threats from without. War, famine, pestilence, death, natural disaster and the machinations of Satan himself – such a list of dangers may look very eclectic indeed. But to the men and women of the early modern city,

1 cf. Rublack, 'Political and Social Norms'.
2 cf. Starn, 'Historians'; Rabb, *Struggle for Stability*, 7–34.

all of these ancient scourges were equally liable to assault the city and undermine its painfully acquired stability.

I

Nature itself seemed at times to conspire against the city. To the early modern mind, the world beneath the heavens was made up of four elements: earth, air, water and fire. All were indispensable for life, yet all could also destroy. The earth sometimes trembled ominously. Small earthquakes were common in many parts of Europe, and of course not all were destructive. The minor quake that shook Venice in 1592 merely demonstrated the stability of the new Rialto bridge.[3] But the great Portuguese earthquake of 1755 claimed thousands of lives and destroyed the centre of Lisbon: the damage done by the quake itself was compounded by a huge tidal wave and by fires which continued to burn for almost a week.[4] Water was always a potential threat. Floods were especially common in low-lying regions like the Netherlands, but in cities all over Europe rivers might overflow their banks in the spring, inundating neighbourhoods and impeding ship traffic. In sixteenth-century Rome, for example, flooding of the Tiber turned riverside districts into virtual marshland every ten years or so.[5] Even the air could be destructive. Windstorms toppled chimneys or even, at times, church steeples. In August 1674 a sudden tornado ripped through the centre of Utrecht, shearing the city's great cathedral in two: the destroyed nave was never rebuilt, leaving an open square with a huge free-standing tower on one side and what remained of the sanctuary – the choir and transept – with one makeshift wall on the other.[6] Yet of all the elements, it was not earth, water or air that most persistently threatened the well-being of the early modern city. The most dangerous element was fire.

Life without fire was unthinkable. Every dwelling had a hearth whose open flame was indispensable for cooking and light and, during part of the year, for heat as well. In rooms that had no hearth, at least on winter nights, candles were routinely used. Many industries depended on fire: baking, brewing, glassmaking and of course every form of metalwork required an oven or an open flame. Yet fire was a constant hazard. A few stray sparks from an untended hearth or guttering candle could easily start a blaze. Many fires were started

3 Lane, *Venice*, 448.
4 Kendrick, *Lisbon Earthquake*, 24–42.
5 Partner, *Renaissance Rome*, 81.
6 Müller, *Dom van Utrecht*, 24.

by inevitable acts of momentary carelessness, when somebody left a hearth unattended or fell asleep before blowing out the candle. No city was safe from fire. Even Venice – where water, after all, was always conveniently at hand – suffered numerous serious fires in the early modern era, including repeated blazes in the doge's palace and the basilica of St Mark's.[7] Between 1500 and 1750 in England alone there were over three hundred urban fire disasters in which ten or more – often many more – houses were destroyed.[8]

Yet the number of fires which got out of hand was dwarfed by the number of cases in which fires were effectively confined to a single site. Fires were constantly breaking out in the early modern city – but most of them were quickly doused. Many cities had detailed ordinances specifying how fires were to be dealt with. Often each street was required to have a cistern full of water and a pile of buckets for fighting fires. Some cities had well-organized fire-fighting units. In Nuremberg, for example, most male citizens belonged either to the civic guard or a unit of the fire brigade; when the fire bell sounded, members of the brigade were required to rush to the scene or stand by in reserve.[9] In other cities all the inhabitants of a neighbourhood were expected to help quench any fire that broke out. If passing buckets of water did not suffice, hooks were used to tear down burning roofs. If necessary, neighbouring houses were demolished to prevent fires from spreading.

Even so, every now and then a fire did get out of control – either due to a disastrous shift in the wind or an error of judgement about how to engage the blaze. When that happened, the greater part of a city could be destroyed. It was then, during the fire itself or in its aftermath, that communal solidarity was truly tested.

One night in December 1583 a kitchen fire broke out in the small town of Nantwich in Cheshire. Unlike most fires, it was not quickly extinguished: a strong westerly wind soon spread the fire to adjacent houses. As the fire raced towards the Bear Inn, four large bears which were kept in stables behind the inn for bear-baiting on market days were released from their confinement. This humanitarian deed loosed four terrified beasts among the inhabitants and considerably impeded the fire-fighting efforts. By the next morning, though few lives had been lost, well over a hundred buildings had burned to the ground. The town was largely destroyed,

7 Lane, *Venice*, 439–40, 446–7.
8 Jones *et al.*, *Gazetteer*.
9 Willax, 'Bürgerausschuss und Feuergehorsam', 111–20.

but communal solidarity was not. Members of the local elite quickly launched a nation-wide fund-raising campaign to make possible the reconstruction of their community. The campaign was endorsed by the queen's privy council and bolstered by a donation from the queen's own revenues, yet even so it took years of travelling and lobbying by members of the Nantwich elite before the undertaking yielded significant returns. Carefully maintained accounts showed that some early revenues were used for bribes, gifts and rewards to people who could influence towns or institutions to make substantial donations. But the campaign eventually raised over £3,000, most of which was distributed to various inhabitants to help them to rebuild their burnt-out houses.[10]

The most devastating urban fire in early modern Europe also took place in England. This was the Great Fire of London in September 1666.[11] It began long before dawn one Sunday in a baker's house in Pudding Lane. When neighbouring houses started to catch fire, the Lord Mayor was summoned; his reaction is reliably recorded: 'Pish,' the mayor said, 'a woman might piss it out.'[12] This was in fact a standard method for extinguishing small indoor fires; forty years earlier when Nehemiah Wallington's apprentice and servant awoke one night to discover a blaze in their garret room they had quickly 'pissed out the fire', much to their master's relief and satisfaction.[13] But the fire in Pudding Lane had long since passed this point. Even so, the mayor was reluctant to order houses pulled down: he was uncertain who would be willing to compensate the owners. Within hours the fire was completely out of control. The royal government assumed control of the situation and large-scale pulling-down of buildings began. The king himself arrived at the scene and dismounted to join in the operations. But nothing availed. The fire continued to spread for four days until a sharp shift in the wind caused it to sputter out. Few lives were lost; the flames spread slowly enough for people to escape. But most of the inner city of London – some 13,000 houses in all – had been destroyed.

A devastating fire like this seriously tested communal solidarity. Many fought the flames, but many others desperately tried to carry their belongings to safety. Gougers charged vastly inflated prices for

10 Lake, *Great Fire of Nantwich*, 67–90.

11 The following draws largely on the standard treatment by Bell, *Great Fire*, and the more recent account by Bedford, *London's Burning*.

12 Bell, *Great Fire*, 24n, 347.

13 Seaver, *Wallington's World*, 54–5.

the use of carts and wagons. Pillagers broke into abandoned houses. A contemporary moralist – the pastor of a church destroyed by the fire – put the issue squarely: 'Had the care and diligence both of magistrates and people', said Thomas Brooks,

> been more for the securing of the public good than it was for securing their own private interest, much of London, by a good hand of Providence upon their endeavours, might have been standing, that is now turned into a ruinous heap . . . much of London was lost by the sloth and carelessness of some, and by the fears, frights and amazements of others, and by others endeavouring more to secure their own packs and patrimonies than the safety of the whole.[14]

The aftermath of the fire continued to reveal the tension between private and communal interest. Plans to redesign the City along bold new axes were dropped in favour of re-erecting buildings on the established sites. But the law was ambiguous as to whether landlords or tenants were financially responsible for rebuilding destroyed houses and some landlords tenaciously defended their legal rights – few more so than the bishop of London, who refused to let booksellers re-establish their stalls on church property until they had paid backdated rents for the entire period since the fire broke out. Eventually an *ad hoc* court was established to settle each case on an individual basis. Within five years, most of the city was rebuilt.

A disaster like this had to be blamed on something more than wind or human error. Two very different frameworks of explanation were favoured: the great fire was attributed either to human conspiracy or to divine intervention. The conspiracy theory emerged during the fire itself. England was then at war with the Netherlands, and it was easy to suggest that foreign agents had started the fire. Foreigners of every nationality were assaulted during the fire itself and some barely escaped being lynched. Yet theological explanations were equally common, especially since the fire conveniently illustrated divine retribution and divine mercy all at once: God had justly punished London for its sins, yet had shown his compassion by sparing almost every life.

The fear that secret enemies were conspiring to burn down cities was by no means confined to London. But even more common was the inclination to seek transcendent explanations for a disastrous conflagration. How else could one account for the sheer unpredictability of city fires? A town could remain unscathed for centuries and then experience repeated disasters in just a matter of years.

14 Bedford, *London's Burning*, 133, 147–8.

Frankfurt am Main, for example, was beset by three major fires between 1711 and 1721. The first fire was largely confined to the walled Jewish ghetto inside the city. It began in the rabbi's own house and the initial spread was furthered by the rabbi's ineffectual response: though Jewish law places any action to save lives before every formal religious obligation, the hapless householder bethought himself of nothing other than prayer. As the fire started to spread, the Jews refused to let Christians into the ghetto to fight the fire for fear that Jewish homes would be plundered. By the next day, the ghetto was in ashes – but the fire had not spread beyond its walls. Jews and Christians alike explained the fire in theological terms: Jews saw the disaster in the customary moralistic framework as a punishment for their sins, while Christians saw a message in the fact that the ghetto had been destroyed while Christian neighbourhoods were spared. One assertive group of citizens took the fire as a divine hint that the Jews should be banished from the city, but Jewish rights were firmly grounded in law and the ghetto was slowly rebuilt.[15]

Eight years after the 'Jewish fire' of 1711, a devastating 'Christian fire' in the heart of Frankfurt destroyed 400 houses. New building ordinances mandated that the lower storey of each rebuilt house had to be made of stone.[16] Comparable rules had been issued for the reconstructed Jewish ghetto, but they proved of little avail when another fire erupted there in 1721. This time Christians did make their way into the burning ghetto and, exactly as had been feared eight years earlier, many proceeded to plunder Jewish houses instead of protecting them. A timely turn in the wind saved part of the ghetto, but 100 houses lay in ashes. Once again theological explanations were sought. But mindful of the 'Christian fire' two years earlier, the city council could see no denominational message in God's handiwork: clearly, as the magistrates wrote in a message to Vienna, God was angry at the whole city.[17]

Yet the very fact that fire could be interpreted as a sign of divine retribution could have a positive impact on the community. This was certainly the case in the English town of Dorchester, where the devastating fire of August 1613 was seized upon by the city's preachers as a sign that the community had been summoned to mend its ways and follow a more godly path. In the ensuing decades, Dorchester's inhabitants were inspired to perform good

15 Kracauer, *Geschichte der Juden*, 2: 121–40.
16 Duchhardt, 'Frankfurt', 281.
17 Kracauer, *Geschichte der Juden*, 2: 143–4.

works which, measured concretely in terms of charitable donations per capita, have made it possible to describe their community as the 'most philanthropically generous town in western England'. None of this, in fact, sufficed to spare Dorchester from experiencing a second fire disaster in 1623 – but that one was at least smaller than the fire ten years earlier. Certainly the more high-minded sector of the town's inhabitants continued to believe that the 'fire from heaven' which afflicted their city had helped to guide the community on to a far more righteous path.[18]

II

In fact a different kind of disaster could prove far more threatening to the social fabric of an early modern city. This was a major outbreak of epidemic disease – especially the bubonic plague. A fire's duration was always limited; no matter how many problems emerged in the aftermath, the immediate danger was over in a matter of days. An outbreak of the plague, however, could last all summer and recur the following year. A serious epidemic not only shattered individual lives but also undermined the hard-won routines of urban society.

Of course there were many diseases which could occasion mortality of epidemic proportions. But the bubonic plague was feared more than any other, and rightly so. A major outbreak of the plague was almost always interpreted as a manifestation of God's anger. This did not mean, however, that communities were expected passively to accept the divine punishment. In moral terms it was just as permissible to combat the plague as it was to fight a fire. But the methods employed were rarely effective, for the causes of plague were not understood. One major school of thought attributed the plague to something in the air – 'miasma' was the usual term. Another approach emphasized contagion, blaming the spread of plague on direct contact with infected persons or transmission via infected clothing, bedding or goods.[19] In fact human agency was not entirely irrelevant, especially in the early stages of an outbreak. Infected rats or fleas were introduced to some previously plague-free environments by ships, land transport, armies or even individual travellers. But once the plague was established in a new site, most victims were infected not by other people or their belongings but by fleas which carried the bacillus from an infected rodent to a human host. This part of the process was never recognized, so measures to prevent the introduction

18 Underdown, *Fire from Heaven*, 90–129, esp. 128.
19 Slack, *Impact of Plague*, 23–36.

or spread of the bubonic plague could focus only on the presumed dangers of human contact.[20]

In the course of the early modern era, European town-dwellers developed highly standardized patterns of reacting to the plague.[21] To some extent this was because municipal governments consciously instituted measures which were thought to have worked elsewhere – but it also reflected the fact that parallel conditions repeatedly generated similar responses. At the first news of the incidence of plague elsewhere, municipal officials would impose a strict ban on all travel from the infected regions. Ships were forbidden to berth and travellers were halted at the city gate until it was established that they came from a safe area. Occasionally such measures may have had an impact. Usually they did not. All too often news of the plague in a neighbouring region or even a foreign port was the prelude to a local outbreak shortly thereafter.

Everyone agreed on the best thing to do in case of plague. In a treatise issued in 1564 the municipal physician of Strasbourg put it bluntly enough: 'the best medication consists of going away as fast and as far as possible, and returning only slowly'.[22] But this was an option only for some – especially the rich who had homes in the countryside or, lacking that, friends or relatives elsewhere to whom they could repair. For certain members of the urban elite this posed a problem of conscience: municipal officials, clergymen and physicians were often torn between the impulse to leave and the disgrace they knew they would encounter for abandoning their duties. For most inhabitants, however, leaving was not even an option. Lacking any means of earning a living elsewhere, they normally stayed in town even as the epidemic reached its peak – and if at that point they finally tried to leave, they were generally barred from entering other cities and ended up wandering helplessly on the open road.

The municipal officials – those who stayed – immediately put the standard plague regulations in effect. But many of the customary instructions inevitably generated resistance. It was easy enough to order that bonfires be lit to clear the air or streets be cleaned to remove suspected sources of infection. But what about public gatherings? To

20 Slack, 'Response to Plague', 174–8.

21 Important treatments include Amelang, *Journal of the Plague Year*; Calvi, *Histories of a Plague Year*, esp. 1–196; Cipolla, *Cristofano and the Plague*; Kintz, *Société strasbourgeoise*, 149–60; Lottin, *Chavatte*, 144–55; Pullan, *Rich and Poor*, 249–52, 314–26; Slack, 'Metropolitan Government'; Slack, *Impact of Plague*, esp. 255–310.

22 Kintz, *Société strasbourgeoise*, 149.

minimize the risk of contagion the magistrates routinely ordered that large assemblies be kept to a minimum – but in doing so they might face objections from members of the clergy who wanted to stage penitential processions or public prayers to appease God's wrath and implore his mercy.

Even more difficult to enforce were the rules for segregating the victims. Whenever possible, plague victims were removed to pest-houses on the outskirts of the city. Even where such facilities existed, however, in most epidemics their capacity was quickly overwhelmed by the rising number of victims. As a next resort most cities ordered that as soon as anyone came down with the plague, his or her household was to be placed under quarantine. Sometimes the non-infected members of the household were allowed out of the house, so long as they wore a badge or carried a rod to warn others of the potential danger. More often the quarantine applied to all members of the household – most of whom, it was assumed, were already sick or would be soon enough. The house was padlocked, typically for a period of forty days; only special plague-officers could enter the quarantined houses, to deliver food and to carry off the bodies of the dead. When everyone in the house had died, the officers were often required to burn all bedding and clothing.

Such regulations could scarcely be enforced without resistance. There were many attempts to conceal plague cases or, once a house had been quarantined, to escape the premises. Relatives or robbers broke into empty houses to retrieve household goods before they were burnt. Some plague-officers were suspected of taking bribes to help families evade the rules; others were accused of abusing their power to rob or cheat the house-bound victims. The quarantine system inspired some instances of heroic self-sacrifice – and many cases of desperate self-preservation. In Lille any house struck by the plague was initially locked up for three weeks – but once a death occurred the sequestration was extended to six weeks. Desperate inmates pushed their dying relatives out into the street moments before death occurred in order to avoid a doubling of the quarantine period.[23]

Economic life was crippled. Simply provisioning the city became difficult. During the Barcelona epidemic of 1651, peasants were terrified to enter or approach the stricken town. A system of make-shift turntables was set up outside the gates to make possible the

23 Lottin, *Chavatte*, 148–9.

sale of produce with a minimum of physical contact. An eyewitness described the mechanism:

> When the farmer brought his goods, chickens or eggs or fruit or anything else, he put them on the end of the plank and spun it around to the other side. If the buyer liked it they agreed on a price, and then the person from the city put the money on the plank and spun it again.

After rinsing the coins in a pot of vinegar, the peasant took the cash and quickly left.[24]

Inside the city, mandatory quarantine was compounded by voluntary sequestration: even healthy people stayed in their homes to avoid any contact with the sick. But they needed food. In the plague at Uelzen in 1597 there were numerous households in which every member survived – except for the maidservant. The scenario is easy to reconstruct. A family huddled indoors, fortunately in a house with no rats. But eventually the maid was sent out to buy bread. Bakeries tended to attract rats – so it may have been there that the maid was infected. She brought the bread home, got sick and died.[25]

Wherever it struck, the plague undermined traditional social values. The quarantine system, though generally endorsed by the church, was at odds with the traditional Christian commandment to visit and comfort the sick. The swift removal of corpses and rapid burials ordered by the authorities deprived the dead of a proper funeral and denied their families the comfort of the usual mourning rituals. Nor could the overworked plague-officers always be trusted to do their job properly. Ghastly rumours circulated about people being buried alive. In Strasbourg plague-officers were specifically warned not to declare any victims dead before they really were.[26]

Strictly theological explanations for a visitation of the plague, accompanied as it was by horrors like these, did not always satisfy – and the medical explanations of the day, voluminous as they were, never seemed to cover all the observed phenomena. Inevitably conspiracy theories emerged: it was easy to imagine that the city was beset by secret enemies intent on starting or spreading the plague. During the Florentine plague of 1630, a doctor at the Bonifazio hospital was specifically charged with using poison to induce cases of plague. The fact that he was an outsider, from Naples, who had

24 Amelang, *Journal of the Plague Year*, 51.
25 Woehlkens, *Pest und Ruhr*, 71–5.
26 Kintz, *Société strasbourgeoise*, 154; cf. Calvi, *Histories of a Plague Year*, 105–6; Slack, *Impact of Plague*, 274–5.

heatedly criticized members of the hospital staff certainly worked against him. He was arrested, tried, and eventually acquitted.[27] The evidence in this case was too flimsy to permit a conviction. And in any case it was more customary to attribute an onslaught of the plague either to the inscrutable will of God or the unfathomable mysteries of nature. But the temptation to seek a cause in human malice could never be entirely suppressed.

III

The fear of secret enemies runs as a hidden thread through the history of the early modern city. People were reluctant to attribute all the bad things that happened either to the will of God or to sheer accident. Sometimes it made more sense to blame misfortune on a malicious person or group whose alleged misdeeds were all the more frightening because they were carried out in secrecy. The Jews, for example, had long been suspected of everything from poisoning wells to kidnapping and murdering children for ritual purposes.[28] Rumours of political enemies who sneaked into towns to open city gates or set off fires were scarcely less prevalent. In the course of the sixteenth century, however, much of the fear of secret enemies came to be focused on a single target: the witch. The pursuit of witches was, of course, by no means confined to cities: taking Europe as a whole, in fact, a majority of those accused of witchcraft were certainly villagers. But cities were also exposed to the explosive combination of universal beliefs and local tensions which could give rise to an episode of witch-hunting.[29]

People of any age and either gender could be suspected of witchcraft. But by and large witches were assumed to be women. The reason for this was simple: females were regarded as the weaker sex, and it was precisely their weakness that was thought to make them resort to secretive methods of doing harm rather than employing such manly forms of conflict as duelling, street brawls and physical ambush. Occasionally witches were accused of malicious acts directed against an entire community – causing hailstorms, for example, which could ruin a year's crop in moments. But most of the deeds attributed to witches were minor acts of malice directed against individual

27 Calvi, *Histories of a Plague Year*, 181–92.

28 Hsia, *Myth of Ritual Murder*.

29 The literature on the European witch-craze is vast. For useful overviews, see Klaits, *Servants of Satan*, and Levack, *Witch-Hunt*. Exemplary regional studies with some emphasis on urban cases include Midelfort, *Witch Hunting in Southwestern Germany*, and Monter, *Witchcraft in France and Switzerland*.

targets: rendering men impotent, making children sick, causing cows to give bad milk, casting spells that resulted in death. These were small-scale actions, yet in carrying them out the witches were part of a large-scale enterprise: for they acted as servants of the Devil himself.

The belief in witches was old but the satanic element was not. It was only in the fifteenth century that the church fully endorsed the doctrine that the real evil done by a witch lay not so much in her malicious deeds as in the pact with the Devil to which she had subscribed. The first step on the road to witchcraft was normally a highly intimate act, during which Satan seduced his victim and thus secured her allegiance. But witchcraft as a whole was seen as a collective conspiracy, for once the witches' loyalty was secured they were commanded to gather at a huge witches' sabbath where, together with others who had taken the same vow, they worshipped the Devil before being sent home to wreak secret havoc on their families and neighbours. In some parts of Europe, notably in England, this collective concept of witchcraft never took strong root. But in most parts of the continent it was widely accepted. After the Reformation, Protestant and Catholic theologians vied with each other in affirming the orthodoxy of belief in witches.

So furtive were witches that much of the harm they allegedly did was not readily recognized as such. Children got sick, animals died, milk went sour – these things all might have happened anyway. Occasionally, however, people would detect what they considered a pattern of malicious harm, and then a woman would be denounced as a witch. Such accusations were always taken seriously by the authorities. Sometimes after an initial investigation the charges were dismissed. Often they were not. If the suspect denied the charges, wherever the law permitted torture – which was the case almost everywhere but England – then torture was soon applied. In most continental courts a confession was necessary for conviction in a criminal case; often torture was used when the magistrates already had sufficient evidence but the criminal refused to confess. In cases of witchcraft it was sometimes applied even where the evidence was thin, in order to counteract the help that Satan supposedly provided his minions. It was generally assumed that God would protect the innocent by giving them the strength to withstand the pain and refuse to confess. Some did so, and were released. But most suspects inevitably broke down under relentless questioning and not only confessed to being witches but also named those they had supposedly seen at the witches' sabbath. Some, of course, named their own accusers; more often, however, the tormented victims mentioned people whose social profile conformed to the existing image of likely witches. Occasionally the names generated by this method were discounted by the authorities; most, however, were carefully noted and a new round of arrests and interrogations would be undertaken.

Almost all of those who were convicted were executed. Most of them were women. In England, where the emphasis was on the suspect's criminal acts rather than her spiritual state, the customary sentence was hanging. On the continent, where the fundamental crime was the suspect's heretical allegiance to the Devil, most convicted witches were burnt alive at the stake. Sometimes dozens, occasionally even hundreds of convicted witches were executed in a single community until the exhausted magistrates were sure that they had ferreted out all local adherents of the satanic conspiracy. Most of what had transpired in the courtroom and the torture chamber was never known to the public. Communication between the accused and their families was tightly controlled or simply forbidden. Often it was only after months of incarceration that the suspect would be seen again, emaciated and broken in spirit, as she was led to the scaffold. The confession would be read, the faggots lit. One more secret enemy had been detected and destroyed.

Witch-hunting tended to follow certain general patterns. But the way in which the witch trials exposed the tensions of urban society can only be comprehended by looking closely at individual communities. We may take as a particularly revealing example the witch-hunt which took place between 1628 and 1630 in the small German town of Rhens, just south of Koblenz on the Rhine.[30] In October 1628, the bailiff, councillors, mayor and citizens of Rhens submitted a petition to their overlord, the landgrave of Hessen, asking for permission to launch a witch-hunt in the community. The landgrave's officials were hesitant, chiefly for financial reasons, but once the community promised to pay for all expenses by levying a special tax the magistrates were allowed to proceed.

The initial target was, as in most such episodes, somebody with a long-standing local reputation as a witch. Appolonia Lehmel, aged about 80, had long been shunned by her neighbours: though she was routinely invited to weddings and christenings, nobody ever sat with her. She had a reputation for poisoning people or casting spells which injured children and killed cows. Once a witch-trial

30 The following is based on Bátori, 'Rhenser Hexenprozesse'.

had been authorized, Appolonia Lehmel was arrested along with two other women of comparable reputation. Appolonia Lehmel was harshly interrogated but suddenly died in prison. The other two were subjected to further interrogation and started to give names. Both were executed. Meanwhile other women were arrested on the basis of their testimony.

The town was undoubtedly awash with rumours and gossip about witchcraft. Children got caught up in the excitement. The 8-year-old Philipp Nuhngesser announced that his grandmother had taken him with her to a witches' sabbath. The magistrates were dubious about the validity of such testimony, especially since there were no other accusations against his grandmother, but nothing could be ignored. They wrote for guidance to the theological faculty of the University of Marburg; the reply urged that the case be dropped, and it was. Another woman was arrested when her son bragged that his mother had conjured up animals for his amusement. She escaped interrogation only because she suffered a mental breakdown which required the family to chain her to her bed.

No doubt some of the arrested women had reputations as people who were hostile or at least disrespectful to the town elite. Certainly the testimony of Anna Schorges reflected animosity towards the 'rich' so deep-seated that it shaped her rack-induced description of the witches' doings. When asked if she had consumed anything at the witches' sabbath, she said she

> did not eat much there; the rich ones had a lot of good things, but the poor ones did not get to enjoy any of it; over there it was just the way it always is with people, the rich are respected and have good times and the poor are never taken seriously.[31]

A single case could reveal the intensity of hatred and devotion within one family. Christine Mey's name first emerged in another suspect's testimony, but further evidence was provided by her sister-in-law, a bitter enemy ever since the two had quarrelled over an inheritance many years before. Yet Christine's husband stood loyally by her, submitting a petition which not only affirmed his wife's piety but also dared to criticize the use of 'unchristian torture' and pointed out that testimony by convicted witches was not to be trusted, 'since also in the case of thefts, murder and arson, the real criminals often falsely accuse other people'.[32] His petition was ignored. Despite being

31 ibid., 142.
32 ibid., 143.

tortured, Christine Mey resisted confessing. At one point she even managed to escape from jail, but was soon recaptured. Unable to face another torture session, she provided a confession. Because of some doubts about the reliability of evidence in their cases, the death sentences for Christine Mey and Anna Schorges were commuted from burning to beheading.

All the remaining suspects, who by now included one man, were apparently released, either for lack of sufficient evidence or because they withstood torture and refused to confess. One such suspect, however, was arrested fifteen years later and executed along with nine other victims when Rhens experienced a second serious witch-panic.

The witch-hunt in Rhens was, like many others, a self-inflicted crisis. It began in a great burst of communal solidarity: the town's elite thought they knew who the main witches were – a handful of highly marginalized women – and simply asked for permission to root them and others like them out. Once the process got underway, there were unanticipated twists which posed unexpected legal and moral problems. This was an entirely typical pattern. The initial burst of confidence that a community could finally get rid of its secret foes was often undermined by the ambiguities and uncertainties which inevitably arose as unconvincing suspects were named or doubts were voiced about the validity of particular evidence. None of this weakened the basic belief in witchcraft. But it helps explain why, sooner or later, every local witch-hunt fizzled out.

It took much longer before the European witch-craze as a whole came to an end. But by the end of the seventeenth century, more and more magistrates were unwilling to prosecute witchcraft cases, or to do so with great vigour. This did not represent a dramatic turning-point or a resounding rejection of past beliefs. Magistrates had always investigated witchcraft cases carefully, weeding out what they considered false accusations based on malice or misinformation. By 1700, however, more and more cases were handled that way. Eventually prosecutions for witchcraft became so infrequent that few people bothered to propose them. During the middle of the early modern era the pursuit of witches had been a major obsession all over Europe, in villages and cities alike. But by 1750 witchcraft was once again what it had been in 1450: a minor side-issue in European life and thought.

IV

The machinations of Satan involved a secret attack on the well-being of the city, carried out through a series of seemingly unrelated misfortunes which only gradually came to be exposed as part of a dark pattern of organized maleficence. A food shortage, by contrast, was an entirely public misfortune, and one which could often be anticipated months in advance. The ultimate origins of a food shortage always lay in an act of God: the excessive or inadequate amount of rain that led to a bad harvest. The impact of harvest failure, however, was never felt right away – it built up only slowly, normally reaching its peak the following spring when food ran out weeks or months before the next harvest was due. There was, or should have been, time enough to anticipate the difficulties and make provision for the coming season of low stocks and high prices. Public resentment emerged only if it became apparent that adequate provision had not been made. If bread grew scarce, people got tense. If, worse yet, grain was seen to leave the city at a time when local supplies were low, anger could erupt into violence.

This is what happened, for example, in Amiens in 1630. The harvest of 1629 had been poor, in some regions much worse than in the region around Amiens itself. As demand for grain grew, the merchants of Amiens continued to sell it to the highest bidder. The amount of grain shipped out of Amiens vastly exceeded the normal levels – yet in the city itself grain prices began to rise. By the late spring of 1630 it was apparent that the coming harvest would be a poor one as well. Growing resentment was voiced against merchants who profited by sending grain out of Amiens even as the city itself faced certain deprivation.

On 23 July, a mob of inhabitants stormed the houses of merchants and commercial agents who were implicated in the export of grain. Two homes were completely plundered. When city officials arrived at the scene, they were mocked and stoned. The civic militia was summoned: firing their muskets at the mob, the guardsmen killed five or six rioters and wounded others. Three people accused of looting were arrested and instantly sentenced to be whipped and banished for nine years as galley slaves. But the city remained in turmoil until the governor of the province arrived with a troop of armed men who marched through the streets in a grand show of force. The governor ordered all artisans to stay in their shops and threatened to execute anyone caught gathering in a group of more than six persons. Order was restored.[33]

Grain riots were often instigated by women who were desperate to feed their families. During a food shortage in 1643 a cattle merchant

33 Deyon, *Amiens*, 437.

was transporting seven carts of feed-grain through the French town of Albi when a large number of women armed with clubs and pitchforks blocked his carts, cut open the sacks – and attacked the town officials who tried to prevent them from taking the grain.[34] This form of social action was considered typically French, but it was certainly familiar elsewhere. During a famine in 1630 a widow in Dorchester began hurling abuse at a countryman at the market who would not sell her any wheat: such people, she screamed, should be 'served as they were in France, to cut holes in their bags'. A few months later women in Dorchester were doing exactly that: they seized a sack of grain in the market and slit it open to pour out the grain.[35]

What happened in Amiens, Albi and Dorchester happened elsewhere as well. Yet in fact, looking at Europe as a whole, what is striking about food riots is not how often they occurred but how infrequently, especially in cities. For an open food riot was a sign of civic failure on many levels. To maintain an adequate supply of bread was, after all, one of the fundamental obligations of municipal government. To fail in this regard not only exposed municipal rulers to the contempt of their fellow-citizens but also, as in Amiens, perilously revealed the limited capacity of the government to maintain order. Just enough food riots took place to remind municipal governments of the urgency of avoiding them. This is why civic authorities invested as much effort as they did in assuring a steady supply of grain or maintaining stockpiles for emergencies.

Whenever poor harvests occurred and grain prices began to rise, one could anticipate not only hardships among the city's existing inhabitants but also the arrival of refugees from the countryside. Generally municipal governments could foresee the crisis and swung into action long before it reached its peak. Bread prices were kept under control, even at the risk of antagonizing bakers. Hoarding or speculating in grain was strictly forbidden. Grain exports were prohibited. As prices rose, stockpiled grain was released in appropriate doses to maintain an adequate supply. In cities without public granaries, civic officials or trusted merchants might be sent on distant missions to negotiate emergency grain purchases.

But a food shortage was always too grave a matter to be left to government officials alone. To be sure, some merchants always saw the chance to maximize their profits during a food shortage, but most members of the urban elite were likely to recognize both the moral

34 Beik, 'Urban Factions', 47–9.
35 Underdown, *Fire from Heaven*, 87.

obligation and the practical necessity of responding to the looming crisis in ways that would diminish popular distress.[36] Church leaders encouraged an increase in charitable giving. Customary strictures against giving alms directly to beggars might be overlooked. Dealers in grain were encouraged to sell some of their product at reduced prices to the poor. In early modern England, it has been argued, 'it was of crucial importance for the maintenance of the social order that dearth was not only met, but was *seen* to be met by action on the part of the authorities'.[37] This was no less true of the continent. People did not riot just because they were hungry. They rioted when they detected indifference or callousness on the part of the government or members of the civic elite. It was this that the urban officials strove to avoid – and for the most part they succeeded.

V

Many and grim indeed were the troubles that beset the early modern city. The worst disasters were always seen as acts of God, and the more people suffered the more clearly the divine punishment seemed to be manifested: as late as 1755, the Lisbon earthquake unleashed a torrent of theological and popular discussion, in Portugal and elsewhere, about the reasons for God's wrath.[38] The Devil worked on a smaller palette. Only God could destroy London or Lisbon; Satan's minions could get little further than curdling milk or causing individuals to sicken and die. And in strict theological terms even their evil deeds were ultimately made possible only by God's own sanction.

Yet none of this bred resignation. When a city was destroyed, one was supposed to repent – and rebuild. Better yet, precautions should be taken to avoid potential disasters. As Joseph had stockpiled grain in Egypt against the inevitable coming of famine, so did the elders of many a European city. Actions to prevent fires, ferret out witches, or block the spread of plague were not always successful, but it was always right to try.

But what about war? For many cities, war was the greatest disaster of all. The impact of military operations in or about a city could be devastating. Yet there was nothing cities could do to prevent warfare and little they could do to diminish its impact. The urban role in war during the early modern era was generally reactive. Warfare often

36 cf. Walter, 'Social Economy of Dearth', 113–20.
37 Walter and Wrightson, 'Dearth and the Social Order', 41.
38 Kendrick, *Lisbon Earthquake*, 72–111.

presented the city with a variety of options – all of them bad, but some worse than others. Invariably the city's rulers strove to make the least harmful choice. They did not always succeed.

During the middle ages, cities or leagues of cities had occasionally initiated wars, but by the early modern era this rarely happened any more. In the fifteenth and early sixteenth centuries some German, Swiss and Italian city-states were still in a position to wage war against other cities, or indeed against princes. But after the mid-sixteenth century such situations became increasingly uncommon. This does not mean that henceforth wars were waged only by princes or national states. Many of the most violent conflicts of the early modern era were civil wars in which one or more parties consisted of a league or association united by some common political or religious purpose. Cities were often invited or pressured to join such leagues, but the initiative and leadership generally came from elsewhere, typically from the ranks of the great aristocracy. By the end of the seventeenth century even this type of conflict had become archaic. Warfare increasingly pitted one prince or national state against another.

Cities, then, had less and less to do with the making of wars. But during most of the early modern era their role in warfare was still pivotal. An army wandering through the countryside was always vulnerable; scavenging for food in one small village after another was hopelessly debilitating. Only control of cities provided the physical security and access to resources – especially money – which every army needed to wage war effectively. Occasionally a decisive pitched battle was fought. But to a large extent the outcome of warfare in early modern Europe depended on which side had control of more cities.

All this generated situations which became deadeningly familiar to European town-dwellers in the sixteenth and seventeenth centuries. When hostilities began or a military commander decided that a particular town was strategically important, officers would be sent to ask that a garrison be admitted. Of course if the army represented a political or religious movement which the municipal leaders supported, the request would be received more warmly, but ultimately the town had little choice in the matter. Only details about how the garrison would be maintained were really open to negotiations, and the exact terms were liable to be neglected once the soldiers were safely installed. The presence of a garrison was always a burden for the community. Soldiers were normally quartered in citizens' homes. On top of this the inhabitants were generally subjected to special taxes, not only to maintain the garrison itself but also to underwrite whatever cause or prince the soldiers represented.

Yet cities were fortunate if this was all that happened. Often the opposing army was also active in the region, and if the city were rich or its location seemed vital, it could soon find itself under siege. Traditional military etiquette normally shaped the opening stages of a siege as heralds brought messages back and forth between the enemy encampment and the city gates. The occupying garrison was normally given the option to leave the city peacefully. If it did so, the city merely exchanged one master for another. But this rarely happened. Unless a city's provisions were low or its fortifications were weak, it might take weeks or months before the city could be starved into submission or taken by a direct attack. Ideological commitments or the expectation that a relief army would arrive to break the siege would encourage the defenders to hold out. But this was risky. Sooner or later supplies would run out. Meanwhile the city would be subjected to bombardments which were intended to break open some part of the fortifications. The defenders could always change their mind and offer to negotiate the terms of surrender, but as time went on the terms were likely to become increasingly harsh. Tensions often arose between the commandant and the magistrates, or between the magistrates and other inhabitants, as to whether the city should give up or hold out. Yet all knew that even the most supine surrender would still be better than letting the city be taken by storm. Under the conventions of early modern warfare, if a defiant city was conquered by force no mercy had to be shown: the soldiers could plunder the city at will.

This was a fearsome prospect. Just what it could entail was vividly demonstrated in 1527 when Rome was sacked – an event that seemed all the more sensational to contemporaries because it involved the pope's own city being plundered by largely Catholic troops.[39] The attacking army was a collection of mercenary troops which nominally owed allegiance to the Emperor Charles V. By the time it reached Rome, however, the army's commanders were less concerned with any broad political commitments than with unrest among their own troops: the soldiers' wages were long in arrears and provisions were almost gone. The Imperialist commanders sent an offer to spare the city and march elsewhere if they were paid a ransom of 300,000 ducats. Unwilling or unable to raise such a sum

39 For detailed descriptions, see Chamberlin, *Sack of Rome*, 119–208; Hook, *Sack of Rome*, 156–240.

and confident that a relief army was on the way, the pope ignored the message. This was a mistake. Within hours the attacking army had discovered a weak spot in Rome's long and uneven system of walls and easily broke into the city. The pillage that followed was relentless; atrocities of every sort were reported and most such stories were probably well-founded, for under the prevailing codes of war, since the town had declined to surrender no quarter had to be offered to civilians. Yet there was a method to the soldiers' meanness: their main objective was to get hold of money or plate, so civilians were held captive until ransoms were paid or tortured until they revealed where their treasures were hidden. The pope barricaded himself in the city's one defensible fortress and thus escaped immediate molestation, but his control of the city collapsed. Indeed, for a while there was no authority in Rome at all; a contemporary recorded the ultimate manifestation of municipal helplessness: 'The gates of Rome are wide open and whoever wishes to may go in and out.'[40] Eventually the sated troops moved on, but it was well over a year before the city of Rome, drastically diminished in wealth and population, could begin to function normally again.

A century later an equally spectacular sack took place during the Thirty Years War. In the summer of 1630 King Gustavus Adolphus of Sweden landed in northern Germany to advance the Protestant cause. Within weeks he sent a commissioner to ask the staunchly Lutheran town of Magdeburg to accept a Swedish garrison. After scrupulous promises were made – most of the soldiers would stay in a camp outside the town, and the citizens would not have to pay for their upkeep – the magistrates consented. But the Catholic army of the Holy Roman Emperor, commanded by the celebrated general Johann Tserclaes von Tilly, was also active in the region. By the spring of 1631 the imperial army had begun the siege of Magdeburg, laying waste to its outer defences and bombarding the city wall. Ignoring the promises made earlier, the Swedish commandant pressed the citizens to provide more funds and supplement his own soldiers by performing watch duty. Messages from General Tilly warned, predictably enough, that the city could still hope for clemency if it surrendered – but faced certain ruin if it did not. By May the magistrates, after consulting delegations of citizens, voted to open negotiations. The Swedish commandant, certain that the full Swedish army was on the way, gave a passionate address to the magistrates urging them to hold out longer. But his timing was poor: even as

40 Chamberlin, *Sack of Rome*, 179.

he spoke, a party of imperial soldiers smashed through one of the city gates and began to enter houses looking for money and booty. The magistrates desperately sent heralds to offer the city's surrender, but of course the moment had passed. Imperial troops stormed into Magdeburg and began to plunder the city, remorselessly killing any civilians who got in their way. Their efforts were impeded only by a fire which, after burning unnoticed for some time near the wall, suddenly swept across the entire city. The combined impact of pillage and fire destroyed 90 per cent of the city's buildings, killed thousands of inhabitants and rendered the city uninhabitable for months to come.[41]

There were other such events as well. The sack of Antwerp by Spanish troops in 1576 took thousands of lives and permanently crippled the city's economic vitality. When Leicester was taken by troops under the direct command of King Charles I during the English civil war the city was cruelly plundered; even the ardently royalist earl of Clarendon had to admit that 'the conquerors pursued their advantage with the usual license of rapine and plunder, and miserably sacked the whole town without any distinction of persons or places'.[42]

Yet in the history of early modern warfare, episodes like this were relatively rare. For one thing, even when cities were taken by storm the soldiers did not always pillage as brutally as they did in Rome or Magdeburg. Killing unarmed civilians is, in its own way, a strenuous activity, and many soldiers were satisfied to make off with money and goods while ignoring the dazed inhabitants whose houses they stripped. But even more importantly, few sieges ever reached the point at which a city was taken by storm. Too many people knew only too well what might happen if it was.

The most spectacular cases of pillage were widely reported and discussed. Almost 300 pamphlets, broadsides and newssheets, appearing in various languages all over Europe, described the sack of Magdeburg in harrowing detail.[43] Most of them were issued as Protestant propaganda in order to blacken the Catholic and imperial cause. But the salaciously recorded particulars of rape, murder and pillage in Magdeburg were a useful reminder, if one was even needed, of just how dangerous it could be to let a siege run its full course. Not

41 Hoffmann, *Geschichte der Stadt Magdeburg*, 2: 123–92.
42 Clarendon, *History of the Rebellion*, 451; spelling and punctuation modernized.
43 Parker, *Thirty Years' War*, 125.

only townspeople but also garrison commanders knew that a timely surrender was often the wisest choice.

Thus the real impact of warfare on an early modern town is better illustrated by a city like Bristol, which changed hands repeatedly during four crucial years of the English civil war but was never fully sacked.[44] As in many cities, war did not come to Bristol only as an external force; the citizens themselves were deeply caught up in the issues that divided King and Parliament in the early 1640s. Ardent Puritans, predictably enough, all favoured the parliamentary cause. But religion was not the only factor that determined partisan loyalties. Most of the city's great merchants, whose monopoly privileges had been granted by the crown, tended to favour the king; more modest retailers and artisans, some of whom resented the advantages long enjoyed by the richest merchants, generally leaned towards the parliamentary side.[45] By the time hostilities had opened on the national level in 1642, the magistrates of Bristol fully recognized the existence of two parties within the community. But it went against the grain to accept that the city should be divided in this manner. In November 1642 they tried to gloss over the differences in a grand show of unity: 'This day', the council minutes recorded, 'the Mayor, Aldermen, Sheriffs and Common Council have declared themselves to be in love and amity one with another, and do desire a friendly association together in all mutual accommodation.'[46]

Mutual amity was soon put to the test. A few weeks later parliamentary troops arrived and the city had to accept a garrison of 2,000 soldiers. Control over anything remotely related to defence of the city – including the levying of special weekly taxes – quickly passed from the city council to the parliamentary commandant and his advisors. When in the spring of 1643 a plot by some citizens to open the city gates to a royalist army was exposed, the commandant, Colonel Fiennes, himself presided over the trial which resulted in the execution of two principal conspirators. By the summer, however, the city was subjected to a full siege by royalist troops, and the commandant's resolve weakened. Though strongly pressed by a delegation of Puritan women to hold out, he and his advisors chose instead to follow the advice given by male leaders of the municipal oligarchy. As he explained later in defending his decision,

44 The following is based chiefly on Latimer, *Annals of Bristol*, 154–217; but see also McGrath, *Bristol and the Civil War*, which emphasizes more strongly the neutralist sentiments of most inhabitants.

45 Sacks, *The Widening Gate*, 237–48.

46 Latimer, *Annals of Bristol*, 161.

> Mr Mayor and the Sheriffs did earnestly entreat us, that seeing we could not keep the place, we would not ruin so famous a city to no purpose, nor expose so many men's persons and estates to violence and plundering. Upon all these considerations, it was unanimously resolved that we should entertain a treaty with the enemy.[47]

This was done. The parliamentary troops marched out and the royalist troops marched in. The terms of the treaty were not strictly upheld, however: royalist soldiers did engage in a brief round of plundering. The royalist occupation, moreover, proved even more expensive than the parliamentary one. The day after the new garrison was installed, the city council voted to offer the king a grant of £10,000. The weekly assessments rose substantially. The city had to take out substantial loans, from its own citizens and others, in order to meet the heightened financial demands. In the summer of 1643 the city was also afflicted with a severe outbreak of typhus which drastically increased mortality in the city. A hostile contemporary blamed the epidemic on lice-infested royalist soldiers who spread the infection in the houses where they were quartered.[48] The accusation probably had considerable foundation, for typhus was always strongly associated with military activity.

The royalist occupation lasted for two years. Beginning in the spring of 1645 the city experienced a major outbreak of bubonic plague. Then, in the late summer, the city was besieged by parliamentary forces. High reputations were at stake: the parliamentary commanders included Oliver Cromwell, while the Bristol commandant was the king's own nephew, Prince Rupert. Initially determined to hold the city at all costs, Prince Rupert had ordered the inhabitants to stock up on six months' worth of food. To this end all the cattle from surrounding districts were confiscated and driven into the city. But a few weeks later, after the enemy succeeded in breaking past some of the fortifications, Prince Rupert changed his mind. Though the city's great castle and some neighbourhoods were still under his control, the king's nephew negotiated a surrender. Once again one garrison marched out as another marched in. With Bristol back under parliamentary control some changes in the composition of the city council were undertaken, but there was no need for a wholesale purge: many councillors had managed to avoid being labelled as outright partisans of either side. In any case the war was almost over. As the king's opponents moved towards total

47 Fiennes, *Letter*, 3; spelling modernized.
48 Slack, *Impact of Plague*, 121.

victory, the Bristol garrison was gradually phased out and things slowly returned to normal.

In Bristol the acute phase of the war lasted less than four years. Many European cities had to deal with the direct impact of warfare over a much longer stretch. In cities which were caught up in the French civil wars of the late sixteenth century or the Thirty Years War of the seventeenth, an entire generation could grow up knowing nothing other than the continuous cycle of military occupations. With the rise of standing armies in the course of the seventeenth century it also became common even after hostilities ended to leave a garrison permanently in the city. Soldiers were an unwelcome but increasingly common part of the urban scene.

The speed with which the two sieges of Bristol were terminated meant that the city never faced the agonizing food shortages that invariably accompanied longer blockades. Yet many other aspects of Bristol's experience would have been familiar to town-dwellers in almost every part of early modern Europe. Epidemic diseases were strongly associated with siege conditions or other circumstances in which a town was crowded with soldiers and refugees. Wartime conditions also created social tensions or heightened the divisions which already existed among the city's inhabitants. Often a small core of town-dwellers was passionately committed to one side or the other in the ideological, religious or political conflict which had triggered the war in the first place: these were the people who put their cause before their community. But invariably a large group of inhabitants put the community first, hoping to preserve as much as possible of the town's physical fabric, institutional structure and customary routines. Above all, of course, they wanted to protect the community from pillage and plunder – and they were willing to pay almost any price to do so.

Military commanders were only too aware of this fact, and they exploited it to the full. Most commanders were as hostile to random pillage as the town-dwellers themselves. Under certain circumstances it had to be tolerated, but normally military discipline was strict and soldiers were firmly punished for mistreating civilians. But every commandant wanted a reliable and steady source of income. The town-dwellers would have to pay for their physical security.

Yet these financial demands were made on cities at just the time when their economic base was sharply reduced. Trading patterns were inevitably disrupted by warfare. Fairs and markets were cancelled. Worse yet, even when cities themselves remained relatively protected from physical destruction the surrounding countryside usually did not. Unwalled estates and villages had no protection against casual plunder, and often they suffered depredations far worse than those imposed on cities. Yet it was often from these very estates and villages that members of the urban elite normally drew a substantial rental income. Thus their financial resources often shrank at the very time that the authorities were imposing unprecedented levels of emergency taxation.

It is hardly surprising, then, that warfare could have a devastating effect on the urban economy. German cities, for example, reeled under the financial impact of the Thirty Years War. Special assessments, no matter how often they were levied, never seemed sufficient to satisfy the military commandants. So city governments also had to borrow huge amounts – from their own citizens, from wealthy nobles, from abbeys and convents, from anyone they could – in order to meet their obligations. The municipal debt of Nuremberg, for example, quadrupled in the course of the Thirty Years War.[49] Such figures were by no means uncommon. Some of the tribute money handed over to the military did get recirculated back into the local economy as soldiers paid for provisions and services. But much of the tribute was sent off to sustain the war effort elsewhere. In fact a long period of military occupation almost always meant a net loss for the local economy.

These were the long-term effects of war. But often the day-to-day impact of warfare was far more devastating. It was war's unpredictability that made it so harrowing for the early modern city. The timing of other disasters – fire, famine, flood or disease – could never be foreseen, yet once they had occurred there were well-established means of diminishing their impact or dealing with their consequences. But war had many more variables. Every choice was risky. A day's delay in surrendering could bring about rescue and the end of a siege – or it could result in a storming of the town and a round of merciless pillage. Today's enemy was tomorrow's overlord. The veil of social cohesion which but thinly masked the competing interests of different groups in every community was all too quickly shredded as ultimate loyalties were tested by the demands of military occupation.

No city was ever completely destroyed by warfare. Even Magdeburg was repopulated by a straggling remnant of its former inhabitants and eventually became a substantial city again. For some town-dwellers, war represented an opportunity for economic advancement

49 Schwemmer, *Schulden der Reichsstadt Nürnberg*, 8.

or social recognition. When Matthias Scheffer, a merchant in the Austrian city of Graz, died in 1679, he perpetuated his memory by leaving 100,000 gulden to the orphanage of his home town. Scheffer's fortune was born of war: as an official supplier of cloth to the imperial armies which were waging war against the Turks, he had exploited his privileged access to the market to sell cloth and clothing to soldiers at grossly inflated prices.[50] Individuals could always profit from warfare in early modern Europe. So could whole cities which provided provisions and supplies to armies in some distant theatre of conflict. Once the soldiers actually hove into sight, however, no city could ever hope to benefit from war and its demands.

VI

Every type of crisis which afflicted the early modern city could threaten the social fabric. Long-suppressed conflicts between specific segments of the community might suddenly be exposed, and the ever-latent tension between the well-being of individual groups and the good of the community as a whole could abruptly come to the surface. The outbreak of fire normally brought forth an immediate mutual effort by the community as a whole – but the aftermath could engender differences between those who were determined to restore things just as they had been and those who wanted to redesign the levelled district. An outbreak of the plague could force municipal leaders, in the interests of the common good, to condemn individuals to certain death by locking them up with their infected relatives – a policy whose social impact was highly uneven, as it affected chiefly families too poor to have fled the city. An acute food shortage was equally likely to reveal the difference in means between those who remained well-provisioned and those who faced starvation. Each of these crises, moreover, could give rise to dark suspicions that the community was infested with internal enemies: secret arsonists or poisoners or profiteers. But an even more frightening form of secret enmity seemed to emerge in the form of witchcraft – for the witch, it was believed, betrayed not just her community but her very family. Nobody – or so it seemed in such times – could be fully trusted.

Yet warfare was potentially the most catastrophic crisis of all – for wars had a way of magnifying both the threat to a city's well-being and the harrowing mood of mutual distrust that every crisis engendered. Cities in the war zone routinely faced food shortages and epidemics. Destruction by bombardment or fire was an ever-

50 Valentinitsch, 'Die innerösterreichischen Städte', 190.

constant danger. Tensions between the inhabitants and the occupying garrison were often complicated by conflicts among the townspeople themselves, especially when the city was directly under siege. Anguished debates about whether to surrender or hold out were rendered all the more bitter because they were often argued on two irreconcilable planes: some people were chiefly concerned with the city's own survival, while others were guided by specific ideological or religious allegiances. Even when cities were spared the horrors of a full-scale sack – and most were – a war with all its uncertainties and financial demands could drag on for decades. Some cities never quite recovered, in economic or demographic terms, from a protracted cycle of warfare. Of all the catastrophes which could disturb the treasured tranquillity of the early modern city, warfare was the one which many town-dwellers had good reason to dread the most.

CHAPTER TWELVE
Urban Conflict

The stability and security of urban life were constantly being challenged by forces which emerged or seemed to emerge from outside the normal nexus of human relations in the city – natural disasters, fire, disease, warfare or the assumed machinations of the community's secret enemies. But the breakdown of harmonious relations among the city's inhabitants could not always be attributed to such external forces. Despite all efforts by the urban elite to maintain order and ensure a minimum level of material and social satisfaction among the inhabitants, it was inevitable that conflicts would occasionally break out among different groups within the community. Many of these conflicts were relatively benign: some, in fact, were little more than particularly animated manifestations of the normal give-and-take that characterized everyday politics in the early modern city. But sometimes the intensity of conflict would escalate, triggering violence and bringing about, at least temporarily, radical changes in the way a community was governed.

Not all potential sources of social tension actually led to conflict. Organized gender-based conflict, for example, was virtually unknown in the early modern city. Inequalities due to gender were often acute, and such differences could lead to sharp disputes within specific families or households. Women were also active in many of the broader forms of social conflict which disrupted urban life: there is ample evidence of women organizing with each other or with men to promote the causes they regarded as urgent. But women almost always articulated their goals in terms of the interests of their family or some broader social group which encompassed both genders. They petitioned, marched and occasionally rioted to demand bread for their children, work for their families, protection for their religion or economic security for their communities. Yet there is no evidence of women in the early modern city collectively organizing, as women, to protect the specific interests of their gender.

Nor did all conflict, even when it was clearly articulated, necessarily become violent. Conflicts between two or more subordinate groups within the community, for example, were common enough. But they rarely erupted into destabilizing violence. Many of these inter-group conflicts were economic in nature, reflecting the ceaseless efforts by guilds or similar groups to protect their market rights or monopoly privileges. Two guilds might find themselves in a dispute over the exclusive right to produce or sell particular goods or provide specific services. Craft masters might find themselves struggling against producers who operated outside the guild system. Sometimes a guild itself was riven with conflict, as when poorer members protested against policies formulated by an elite of rich masters, or when journeymen engaged in work stoppages to protest against mistreatment or low wages. Disputes of this sort were often bitter and acts of violence were not unknown, but the hostilities could often be channelled into socially acceptable mechanisms of conflict resolution such as petitions, boycotts and lawsuits. For even the most intense economic conflicts could normally be debated in rational terms with reference to long-standing precedents and practices, and the right and capacity of higher political authorities to adjudicate such disputes was generally accepted by the parties concerned.

Occasionally, however, the political legitimacy or effectiveness of the urban authorities would be called into question. It was precisely when this happened that urban conflict could become so destabilizing: just because there were so few politically acceptable means for social inferiors to challenge or even criticize their superiors, dissatisfaction among the lower orders, if not quickly stifled, could easily give way to violence. Thus many of the most disruptive episodes of conflict took place along the vertical axes of urban society, pitting members of subordinate social groups against the authority and prerogatives of the urban elite. Movements of protest directed by the poor against the rich or the weak against the strong were a constant theme of early modern history.

This is not to say, however, that all urban conflict took place along vertical lines. Many cities, for example, were riven by ideological disputes which divided members of the community in ways that bore little or no relation to social status. During most of the early modern era, the lines of division in such disputes were usually religious in character. Historians sometimes assume that confessional disputes simply masked a deeper level of conflict based on economic dichotomies, but this can be quite misleading. It is true that confessional differences sometimes paralleled or matched economic divisions within a community – but it more often happened that religious subcommunities encompassed people of very disparate social or economic standing who had nothing in common beyond the compelling conviction that they alone understood God's plan for humanity.

Nor was religion the only factor that could override social differences in determining the line-up of parties in urban conflicts. Some disputes developed along factional lines that reflected networks of influence or patronage. Often these networks extended far beyond the city itself. Indeed, conflict in the early modern city was rarely encapsulated within a single community. Every city, after all, was part of a larger political and economic order. Political or religious conflict on the national level always found its echo in urban politics. But the reverse was also true: when the urban routine was disrupted by conflict, the interests of regional nobles or national rulers were often deeply affected.

The consequences of urban conflict were highly unpredictable. A market riot could end with a few swift reprimands and some exemplary lashings – or, as happened in Naples in 1647, it could shake an entire kingdom. It was for just this reason that the authorities were so likely to take seriously any manifestation of discontent. The latent power of the urban populace could never be lightly dismissed.

I

'Vertical' conflicts encompassed a broad range of situations which pitted socially inferior groups against the communal leaders or other holders of authority. Such conflicts occasionally became intensely bitter – yet they never began and they rarely ended with any fundamental critique of inequities in the social order. Inequality was too widely accepted as a universal constant of the human condition to inspire many people to try to overthrow it. Instead, what generated conflict was more often the perceived failure of members of the higher social orders to fulfil their traditional political or moral obligations to the rest of society. The principal targets of resentment could vary from city to city – the objects of popular hostility could include the city's richest citizens, or members of the municipal council, or local representatives of some higher level of government. Hardly anybody doubted that such people could or should enjoy wealth or exercise power – but it was expected that they would use at least some of their wealth and power for the common weal. It was when they neglected or scorned to do so that they were most liable to face the wrath of the lower orders.

Popular opposition could originate at any level of the social spectrum. The most dangerous threats to the power of the elite, however, rarely came from the very bottom of the social ladder. Riots instigated by the poorest of a city's inhabitants could prove highly unsettling, but they rarely undermined the authority of the urban elite; in such situations, most town-dwellers joined in looking to the civic authorities to restore order and impose obedience. It was when members of the householding families turned against the authorities that the power of the urban elite was much more dangerously threatened. For, as a rule, members of the householding citizenry enjoyed both the strongest moral claim to have their wishes heeded and the greatest ability to organize an effective opposition.

Urban conflict along vertical lines took many different forms.[1] Often the contending parties limited themselves to using peaceful instruments of conflict: petitions, pamphlets, lawsuits and the like. But the potential for violence was always latent. Sometimes an outburst of violence followed months or even years of verbal and written exchanges. In other cases the violence came first, to be followed by a protracted cycle of investigations and litigation. Some conflicts revolved around a single issue. Others involved a confused array of unrelated or even mutually contradictory concerns. Some conflicts came to a clear conclusion – especially when an outburst of violence was suppressed by the exercise of greater force. But many simply petered out when the parties concerned lost the energy or the capacity to pursue their interests further.

Countless disputes revolved around money – especially taxes. Nobody challenged the right of the authorities to levy taxes as such. But when taxes were raised to unprecedented levels, when they were assessed in what seemed to be an unjust manner, or when they were accompanied by extravagance or waste, discontent was bound to surface. Yet the specific targets of popular opposition might depend on the way in which taxes were levied or power was distributed in the community. If the municipal authorities were responsible for tax increases, they inevitably became the main focus of hostility. But often the local authorities were reduced to a passive role while agents acting on behalf of some other power – an invading army, perhaps, or the crown itself – took the initiative in imposing taxes. In such

1 For an important attempt to categorize different forms of urban protest, see Beik, 'Culture of Protest'.

cases those who actually collected the taxes became the main targets of popular protest – though municipal officials could scarcely avoid being drawn into the conflict.

This happened repeatedly in France, especially between the late sixteenth and the late seventeenth century, as the fiscal demands of the French crown spiralled dramatically upward. The actual collection of royal revenues was generally entrusted on the local level to tax-farmers or agents whose incentive to maximize their intake was based on the fact that they kept a share of whatever they collected. The resentment occasioned by their activities was heightened by the fact that in most cities almost everyone with a noble title – which often encompassed the entire urban elite – was exempt from royal taxation. The burden fell overwhelmingly on the ordinary inhabitants. Sometimes it was more than they could take.

What took place in Lyon in 1632 is typical of a scenario that was echoed, with endless local variations, in many French towns of the early modern era. Anti-tax sentiments had been bubbling in Lyon for years. In 1630 hundreds of journeymen had attacked the house of a hated tax-collector. Then in 1632 a new surtax on all imports to or exports from the city was announced – and in December a royal agent arrived to start collecting the new tax. The day after his arrival, a crowd of 2,000 Lyonnais – mostly wage-workers – gathered at the agent's house, smashed their way in, destroyed his belongings and torched all his records and papers. Hoping to restore order, the municipal authorities announced that a delegation had been sent to Paris to negotiate a tax reduction – but this could no longer appease the rioters, who proceeded to attack the houses of the municipal officials themselves. The handful of professional soldiers employed by the city remained completely outnumbered, and the volunteer militia could not be called out to suppress the disturbance since too many members clearly sympathized with the rioters. Once the hated tax-agent fled the city, however, emotions began to cool down, and by the time the provincial governor finally arrived in Lyon with his soldiers, the riots were over. Even so, dozens of participants were arrested. They lingered in jail for months until a special official was sent from Paris to mete out punishments and impose fines designed to discourage any future uprisings.[2]

It was widely recognized in early modern France that the impetus behind tax increases lay primarily with the crown. Although the king himself was not directly criticized, those who levied or collected taxes

2 Porchnev, *Soulèvements*, 151–4.

in his name were. Royal agents and tax-farmers were generally the prime targets of attack, though municipal leaders might be resented for having failed to protect the community adequately from the heightened burdens. Yet there were also times when the city's own leaders were the principal targets. When this happened it was often because anger about taxes merged with a broader perception that civic officials were ruling in a self-interested way.

The celebrated uprising which erupted in the city of Romans during the carnival season of 1580 reflected this pattern.[3] The general background to the uprising was the steadily rising burden of taxation in the province of Dauphiné and the emergence of organized anti-tax movements in the rural areas of the province. But specific grievances were also directed against the political clique which dominated the city of Romans. The dominant figure in this clique was the town judge, Antoine Guérin, a royal appointee who for over a decade had governed the city in collaboration with its four consuls, or mayors. By the late 1570s a large number of householding craftsmen were convinced that the judge and consuls were manipulating the town's finances to favour a small stratum of rentiers and merchants. In 1579 a clearly defined opposition movement emerged under the leadership of Jean Serve or Paumier, a draper of middling wealth. For a year, members of the opposition agitated against the ruling clique, demanding above all that the city's financial records be opened up to public inspection. But things only came to head in the carnival season of 1580, when the normally festive parades, footraces and banquets were turned into political demonstrations with unmistakably belligerent overtones. The mounting tension reached a bloody climax just before the end of the carnival season, when Guérin orchestrated a massacre of Paumier and his supporters and totally crushed the opposition movement.

The events in Romans were unusual in that the carnival season, which in most cities served to relieve social tensions, in this case sharply intensified them. But the substantive issues which animated the political opposition in Romans would have seemed familiar enough to the inhabitants of many European cities. Increased taxation was bad enough. It was even worse when the ruling group was suspected of financial mismanagement or outright corruption – and the mood of distrust was accentuated when magistrates insisted, as they often did, on keeping the financial records or other government documents secret.

3 For a full treatment, see Le Roy Ladurie, *Carnival in Romans*.

Throughout the sixteenth and seventeenth centuries English towns were beset by recurrent conflicts, often triggered when members of the ruling oligarchy were accused of practices which blurred the distinction between public trust and private advantage: magistrates were accused of leasing civic property to themselves on favourable terms, or using their regulatory powers to promote their own businesses, or simply dipping into the city treasury.[4] The English magistrates, like their fellows in towns all over Europe, tended to defend such practices as justifiable compensation for their arduous labours on the community's behalf – but ordinary citizens were rarely persuaded by such arguments. They could smell the corruption in such doings and they did not hesitate to denounce it. In fact the deference which civic officials demanded was never as deep-seated or solid as the magistrates themselves felt it should be. Even the great Lord Mayor of London – the most august of all civic officials in England – was not always immune from personal criticism. Robert Finrutter, a clothworker in late sixteenth-century London, got into trouble with one such mayor when he shouted that 'he himself was as good a man as my Lord Mayor was, setting his office aside. And that when my lord mayor was out of his place, he would care no more for him than for the worst beadle in this town'.[5] An isolated incident like this would lead to swift punishment – but when enough people felt that way, the potential for public protest and organized conflict was great indeed.

Throughout the early modern era, German cities repeatedly experienced episodes of political upheaval in which magistrates were accused of secrecy, incompetence or corruption, especially in the way they levied taxes or managed the municipal finances. The conflict that erupted in the Baltic coastal town of Stettin during the early seventeenth century provides a typical example.[6] Like most German cities, Stettin owed allegiance to a princely overlord, in this case the duke of Pomerania. The powers of the city council were also limited by the fact that in crucial matters a larger council of merchants and guild leaders had to be consulted. Yet even so, by the early seventeenth century many citizens were convinced that the city's magistrates were totally unresponsive to their interests. Mounting civic debts, largely occasioned by the tribute money owed to the duke of Pomerania, brought matters to a crisis. The council was determined

4 Clark and Slack, *English Towns in Transition*, 132–4.
5 Archer, *Pursuit of Stability*, 56, spelling modernized.
6 Wehrmann, *Geschichte der Stadt Stettin*, 247–57.

to cover the debts by imposing a new excise tax on beer and other goods. But the citizens blamed the city's precarious financial situation less on inadequate revenues than on sloppy administrative procedures and the generous payments which the magistrates awarded themselves from the city treasury. Protests were made over the magistrates' heads to the duke himself, who welcomed an opportunity to increase his own control over the town by intervening in the dispute. In 1613, at the duke's insistence, a new commission of sixty citizens was appointed to consult with the council and inspect the city's financial records. But when this commission finally agreed to approve both the tax on beer and a corresponding increase in the price of drink, angry members of the citizenry soon began to riot. The disturbances reached a climax when the city hall itself was stormed: a prominent municipal bureaucrat was murdered and his remains were tossed out of the window. This gave the duke a welcome excuse to intervene again in the dispute and grandly order a rollback of the beer price. Next came a thorough investigation of the city's financial affairs, which revealed countless cases of irregular book-keeping and not a few instances of outright dishonesty. Its moral authority shattered, the council could raise no objection when the duke reordered the civic constitution, installing permanent deputations of citizens to observe and inspect the city's financial management.

The way events unfolded in Stettin would have sounded familiar to the inhabitants of many a German town in the sixteenth and seventeenth centuries. When dissatisfaction with the magistrates went beyond the usual level of alehouse or guildhall grousing, angry citizens would look for ways to formulate their grievances in a more effective manner. Often they formed a citizens' committee, or *Ausschuss*, whose legitimacy was derived solely from the large number of householders who gave it their support. In huge petitions the citizens would enumerate their complaints about fiscal policy, administrative mismanagement or government secrecy. The magistrates would respond with threats of punishment or half-hearted offers of reform. Often months of wrangling would be punctuated by a sudden outburst of violence in which citizens might besiege the city hall or take magistrates hostage until their demands were granted. But ultimately most conflicts were settled only by intervention from outside the community itself. Every German city had an overlord – either the Holy Roman Emperor or the local prince – to whom the citizens might appeal for intervention in their favour. Often the overlord proved sympathetic – but not if the citizens' actions had become so violent as to suggest a challenge to law and authority in general. In such a case the overlord would be more concerned simply to restore order and reimpose the status quo.[7]

Sometimes corruption or maladministration formed only part of a broader range of issues which pitted citizens against their magistrates. In some German cities, for example, the magistrates were also criticized for making unwise political decisions or tolerating unpopular groups within the city. In the early seventeenth century, for example, the presence of large Jewish communities emerged as a major grievance among citizens in the imperial cities of Frankfurt and Worms. In both cities the Jews' residential rights were guaranteed by the Holy Roman Emperor and upheld by the magistrates, who tended to see the ghetto as an economic asset. By contrast, many ordinary householders – especially those who had borrowed money from Jewish moneylenders and now hoped to avoid repaying their debts – responded with growing enthusiasm to anti-Jewish agitation. Between 1612 and 1616 Frankfurt and Worms experienced tumultuous disturbances in which the Jews and the magistrates simultaneously figured as targets. In both cities the Jews were brutally attacked and then driven into exile; in Frankfurt the patrician magistrates were banished as well and the city was ruled for months by the leaders of the citizens' uprising. Such actions, however, were exactly what the existing authorities could not tolerate. In both cases territorial princes acting in collaboration with the Emperor intervened to punish the opposition leaders, readmit the Jews, and restore the power of the old magistrates.[8]

An even more protracted uprising kept the city of Cologne in constant uproar for six years in the 1680s. Here the central issue was plain and simple: the city's mayors were thoroughly corrupt. Led by an obscure ribbon-retailer named Nikolaus Gülich, outraged citizens successfully demanded a formal investigation of the mayors' conduct, which soon confirmed the long-standing rumours that the mayors had practised nepotism, fixed elections, accepted bribes and put municipal employees to work on their own properties. The evidence was clear, but the city was plunged into ceaseless wrangling about how to clean things up until Gülich and his supporters finally occupied the city hall and took control of the government. For two years they hung on to power until, as in Frankfurt seventy years earlier, higher powers

7 For a systematic overview of German urban uprisings, see Friedrichs, 'German Town Revolts'.

8 On Frankfurt, see Meyn, *Reichsstadt Frankfurt*, and Friedrichs, 'Politics or Pogrom?'; on Worms, see Friedrichs, 'Anti-Jewish Politics'.

intervened to arrest and punish the movement's leaders and restore the traditional forms of government.[9]

The uprisings in Frankfurt and Cologne were led by hitherto obscure citizens and supported by ordinary craftsmen and other householders of modest means. But hovering on the fringes of each movement were lawyers and other men of higher social status who detected in all the turbulence an opportunity to become more powerful themselves. In some other German urban uprisings, men from this social group were in fact the actual leaders of the civic opposition.[10] For inevitably there were people who resented their exclusion from actual political authority and welcomed the opportunity to discredit the civic elite. But few vertical conflicts can be explained simply as an attempt by members of one social group to supplant members of another in civic office: almost always the opposition was fuelled by a perception that the existing elite had failed in its obligations to lesser members of the community.

Civic conflicts often involved a coalition of social groups whose members, though sharing a common antipathy towards the existing elite, had little else in common. Inevitably such coalitions were brittle and movements of this sort were bound to collapse when tensions within the opposition became increasingly evident. Distrust of the elite could rapidly give way to fear of the mob.

We can follow this pattern, for example, by looking at what happened in the Spanish town of Avila in the early sixteenth century.[11] Political power in sixteenth-century Avila was strongly concentrated in the hands of noble families who monopolized membership on the city council. The city also had a growing number of prominent non-noble families whose wealth came from trade, moneylending and tax-farming. Wealthy as they were, these *personas ricas* were completely excluded from political power. Suddenly in 1520 traditional political relations were temporarily transformed, as cities all over Castile were caught up in the revolt of the *comuneros*, a massive rebellion against the fiscal policies of the new sovereign, the king and emperor Charles V. In Avila as in many other cities, the original impetus for political opposition lay with members of the municipal elite who felt that the crown's fiscal demands violated customary urban privileges. Their position was supported by representatives of the wealthy but politically excluded merchants and

9 Dreher, *Vor 300 Jahren*.
10 cf. Hildebrandt, 'Rat contra Bürgerschaft', 227–9.
11 Bilinkoff, *Avila*, 62–77.

professionals, some of whom may have hoped thereby to get some access to political power for themselves. But members of the city's lower orders also got involved – and initially, it seems, their support was welcomed: at a meeting of Castilian cities held in the cathedral of Avila in July 1520, an unknown cloth-shearer from one of the city's poorest districts was permitted to chair the sessions. Soon, however, members of the populace moved from attacking the crown to criticizing the tax exemptions and fiscal privileges of the city's own elite. Hostile crowds stormed and plundered the homes of city councillors. Alarming demands were voiced: commoners should be granted political rights, magistrates should pay taxes. Elsewhere things went even further: in Segovia, a prominent member of the urban elite was murdered. By now concerned only to crush the local uprising, members of Avila's elite withdrew their support from the *comunero* movement and piously declared a rediscovered allegiance to the crown. Eleven artisans who had prominently defied the magistrates' authority at the height of the upheaval were executed in the autumn of 1521.

An even more striking example of the mutability of alignments in an urban conflict is provided by the tumultuous cycle of events which unfolded in Bordeaux in the mid-seventeenth century. The upheaval in Bordeaux began as little more than a local manifestation of the Fronde – the factional struggles within the French elite which disrupted the entire French kingdom between 1648 and 1653. It ended with a bold – but unsuccessful – attempt to establish a municipal republic based on principles of social justice.[12]

The Fronde erupted in 1648 when the Parlement of Paris launched its attack on the unpopular policies of the royal government headed by Cardinal Jules Mazarin. The Parlement of Bordeaux quickly followed suit, stirring up popular support for its opposition to the crown. By 1650 Cardinal Mazarin and the Parlement of Bordeaux had apparently patched up their difficulties, but tensions persisted between parlementaires who were now loyal to the crown and supporters of the great princes who had taken over leadership of the struggle against Mazarin. All this political activity stimulated a level of popular excitement that soon acquired a momentum of its own. Ordinary inhabitants of the city gathered daily at an open area surrounded by elms – the *ormiére* – to debate and discuss the latest developments. These informal meetings gradually assumed the character of a popular assembly – the Ormée – whose members

12 The following draws largely on Westrich, *Ormée*.

increasingly refused to accept the authority of either the municipal government or the Parlement. For a while the Ormée supported the princes who were struggling against Cardinal Mazarin. But within months the Ormée had become an entirely independent movement, hostile to all existing authorities. After a short, bloody struggle in June 1652, the Ormists seized control of the city and members of the traditional elites were progressively rotated out of office to be replaced by the Ormée's own supporters.

Most of the Ormists were ordinary householders who were motivated above all by a deep strain of anti-elitism. Convinced by their own success of the political legitimacy of their movement, they soon began to implement their vision of a morally regenerated community in which economic exploitation would be punished, exorbitant rents would be reduced and justice would be dispensed without the interference of venal attorneys and judges. Some leaders even dreamt of making Bordeaux an autonomous republic with support from the newly established English commonwealth of Oliver Cromwell. It was all an illusion, however. No useful help came from England, and a royal army, ardently supported by wealthy Bordelais who had fled the city, eventually gained control of the city and restored the traditional regime. The Ormée of Bordeaux, like most attempts to recast society in accordance with an idealized vision of social perfection, ended in total failure. But while it lasted it had given a taste of power to people who in normal times were fully excluded from any meaningful role in urban politics.

It was by no means uncommon for hitherto obscure town-dwellers to achieve sudden prominence in the course of an urban conflict. The more spectacular their rise, however, the more likely their ultimate fall. Vincenz Fettmilch, the pastry-cook who led the Frankfurt uprising of 1612–16, was eventually condemned to be executed before the entire male population of the city he had virtually governed. This scenario was echoed in other German cities in the seventeenth century. The leaders of citizens' movements in Braunschweig, Erfurt, Hamburg and Cologne all ended up on the scaffold.[13]

The most dramatic career trajectory experienced by an urban rebel of the seventeenth century, however, took place not in Germany but in Naples. There, in 1647, an illiterate but eloquent fisherman named Tommaso Aniello, or Masaniello, emerged from obscurity to lead a major revolt against the government of the Spanish viceroy.[14] The

13 Friedrichs, 'German Town Revolts'.

14 For recent overviews, see Zagorin, *Rebels and Rulers*, 1: 245–53 and Burke, 'Virgin of the Carmine'.

revolt began as a marketplace riot over a new fruit tax; Masaniello suddenly emerged as the spokesman for a crowd of protestors who rampaged through the city, attacking palaces and forcing the viceroy to flee to safety. This initial success seems to have legitimized the revolt among a broader group of the urban population, and Masaniello was soon acclaimed as 'captain-general' with the support of large segments of the city's population. The homes of nobles and financiers were plundered with impunity: neither the viceroy nor the urban elite could muster any force to stem the violence or resist the popular demands for tax reductions and political reforms. Masaniello's sudden acquisition of power, however, appears to have gone to his head, for he soon began to alienate his supporters by presenting himself grandiosely in public as an uncrowned king. The fisherman's public career ended ten days after it began when he was assassinated at the church he had made into his headquarters.

Masaniello's death by no means ended the Neapolitan revolt of 1647. It continued for almost a year, spreading from Naples into the surrounding countryside, until the Spanish crown was able to muster sufficient military force to re-establish its control over the city and its hinterland. Yet it was Masaniello's brief ascendancy that captured the imagination of educated people all over Europe.[15] The story of the uneducated fisherman who had successfully challenged the local authority of the Spanish crown vividly illustrated the mutability of fortune in human affairs and the latent threat to public order which confronted every regime. Put another way, the events in Naples served as an unavoidable reminder of what could happen when urban authorities neglected their obligation to govern with an eye to the needs and expectations of those over whom they ruled.

II

Of course uprisings that pitted the poor against the rich or the weak against the strong were by no means the only form of urban conflict. Indeed, it was often recognized that disturbances which appeared to have such a character really masked conflicts of a very different kind. Jacques Gaufridy, a member of the Parlement of Aix-en-Provence in the mid-seventeenth century, put the matter bluntly when he came to write the history of his native province. 'Revolts', he wrote, 'do not always come from a gathering of the people; they are more often fomented by men of power, and mutinous multitudes usually

15 cf. Villari, 'Masaniello', 125–32.

follow the movements of two or three.'[16] Gaufridy was anything but an impartial observer; in fact he was one of the most unpopular men in Aix, whose house was attacked during the carnival of 1648 and completely sacked in 1649. Yet his comment aptly reflected the causes of the conflicts that repeatedly shook the town of Aix in the seventeenth century, most notably in 1648 and 1649. Acts of violence were largely carried out by anonymous members of the lower orders, but their passions were clearly stirred by factional conflict within the local elite. The ultimate cause of all the hostility in Aix lay in the fiscal policies of the French crown, which was determined to increase its revenues by expanding the size of the Parlement and selling the newly created offices to ambitious jurists. This practice was bitterly opposed by the existing parlementaires, who saw only too clearly that their income from fees, bribes and the resale of their own offices would decline if the total number of positions were expanded. Gaufridy – who had gone to Paris in 1640 to protest against the creation of new offices but returned as president of a newly established *chambre des requêtes* – had long been hated by his fellow-parlementaires as a turncoat. When hostility to the crown reached a fever pitch in 1649, the parlementaires easily won popular support by promising to reduce the cost of grain and banish royal troops – and by distributing gifts of cash to win over waverers. Gaufridy's house was attacked and one of his servants was killed. He himself escaped, but the governor of Provence and other dignitaries linked to the royal cause were placed under arrest, where they lingered for months until a compromise settlement was negotiated.[17]

Factional struggles between different sectors of the municipal elite were in fact an old tradition in some European cities. It was hardly a universal pattern, for the principle of political consensus and the practice of political co-optation often muted the tensions that might have arisen within the urban elite. But open conflict could not always be avoided or obscured. The ultimate model for conflict of this sort went back to the thirteenth century, when the Guelfs and the Ghibellines had struggled for power in the cities of northern Italy. Comparable factions re-emerged over and over in European cities for centuries thereafter – especially at times when royal authority was weak or divided and rival groupings were struggling for political power on the national level. For factions within the urban elite were hardly ever purely 'urban' in their composition and outlook; almost

16 Kettering, *Judicial Politics*, 266–7.
17 ibid., 209–10, 251–77.

always they were linked in some way to broader regional or national networks of allegiance or clientage. Few members of the urban elite would have risked an open struggle with other leading members of the community unless they were confident of support from nobles of the surrounding countryside or influential personages at the court.[18]

It was never entirely politic, of course, to struggle too nakedly for power or revenue. It was far more seemly to justify a factional conflict by appealing to some great issue of principle. The case of Aix exemplifies what was surely the most common issue: the defence of established custom or privilege. Many of the parlementaires who struggled against the crown's attempt to add to their numbers were sincerely convinced that they were fighting to protect the inviolable privileges of their province from illegal encroachment. Yet the legal issues were far from clear – and the number of men who changed sides at strategic moments during the struggle makes it hard to regard such a conflict strictly in terms of high principle.

In fact only one form of principled commitment in the early modern era was sufficiently powerful to override all of the pragmatic considerations which normally coloured the way in which members of urban society acted in conflict situations. This, of course, was religion. To be sure, it was never more than a small minority of men and women whose conduct was guided entirely by religious beliefs. Though almost all Europeans were committed Christians, most people readily adapted their religious practices and indeed their beliefs to the prevailing norms. Yet there were always some people whose religious convictions overrode all other considerations. Beginning in the 1520s, when the ideas of the Protestant Reformation began to spread, religious differences led to grave conflicts in countless European cities. Sometimes these conflicts were resolved peacefully through the political process. But there were also cities in which irreconcilable religious differences led to violence and got resolved, if at all, only by the application of force.

The Protestant Reformation began in central Europe, so the first cities to be riven by confessional conflict were, not surprisingly, in Germany and Switzerland. In many of these cities, as we have seen, the most intense pressure for religious reform came not from members of the social elite but from ordinary householding citizens. Many of them had long harboured a mild but persistent sense of resentment both against clerical leaders whose wealth and laxity defied Christian ideals and against political leaders whose manner

18 cf. Beik, 'Urban Factions'.

of ruling ignored communal traditions. Protestant ideas gave shape to these resentments and justified the agitation for religious reform. In many cities the magistrates firmly repressed the growth of Protestant ideas and reaffirmed the community's allegiance to the old church. But in other cities the magistrates bowed to the popular pressure for religious changes.

It would have been hard enough for most communities just to have to choose between loyalty to the old faith or adoption of the new one. But Protestantism itself soon splintered into competing sects. In many south German cities the decision to adopt the Reformation simply set the stage for a new round of conflicts between adherents of the Lutheran and Reformed outlooks. These groups, in turn, were challenged by radical Protestants who questioned the authority of any political leaders to impose religious norms. The attempts by Anabaptists and other religious radicals to separate themselves completely from the rest of the community were judged very harshly by almost all rulers. Many religious radicals found that their attempt to ignore the state's authority subjected them instead to the ultimate imposition of the state's power – death on the scaffold.

The issues generated by these religious differences disrupted the communal life of countless Swiss and German cities in the early years of the Protestant Reformation. There was no place, however, where events took a more dramatic turn than in the Westphalian town of Münster.[19] The Anabaptist 'Kingdom of Münster' astonished and frightened contemporaries throughout Europe – all the more so because of the abruptness with which it emerged. Until the 1530s there was nothing to set Münster apart from dozens of other German towns. Despite a brief flurry of anti-clerical activity in 1525, the magistrates kept the city loyal to the community's political and spiritual overlord, the bishop of Münster. Beginning in 1531, however, a sudden burst of Protestant agitation stimulated acute hostility towards the bishop's regime, and the new magistrates elected to the city council in 1533 were firmly committed to Lutheran ideas. Protestantism was quickly introduced – but tensions persisted. Emboldened by the defeat of the bishop's authority, some citizens pushed for ever more radical changes in the city's religious complexion and political structure. Yet until early 1534 the sequence of events in Münster conformed broadly to the pattern of conflict found in many German cities of the Reformation era.[20]

19 The best overall treatment is provided by Rammstedt, *Sekte und soziale Bewegung*. For an overview in English, see Hsia, 'Münster and the Anabaptists'.
20 cf. Schilling, 'Aufstandsbewegungen'.

Suddenly, however, the mood in Münster changed. Many conservative citizens, alarmed by the newest developments, slipped out of the city – but at the same time Münster became a magnet for Anabaptist enthusiasts from the Netherlands and elsewhere. Nor were these immigrants ordinary Anabaptists. Most of them belonged to a splinter group of radical millenarians determined to prepare actively for the imminent coming of the messianic age. Their charismatic leaders persuaded hundreds of local citizens that Münster was the place where a new epoch of human history would begin. Members of the city council who came to power in 1534 fully supported the Anabaptist cause. By this time the bishop of Münster had decided to reassert his authority and had gathered an army to lay siege to the city. Yet this only bolstered the conviction of the Anabaptist leaders in Münster that they were engaged in a final struggle against the forces of evil. It was not long before the authority of the city council completely collapsed and one of the Anabaptist leaders, Jan of Leyden, declared himself king of the endangered New Jerusalem. As the bishop's blockade slowly reduced the city to starvation, the self-proclaimed king proceeded to reorganize Münster's social order: private ownership of property was replaced by the community of goods and polygamy was introduced so that men could help themselves to additional wives. The new regime lasted for almost a year until the bishop's army reconquered the city in June 1535 and brutally punished the survivors.

The Kingdom of Münster has sometimes been described as an uprising of the urban poor, driven by deprivation or despair to vest their hopes in an apocalyptic movement. Modern research, however, shows that the Anabaptist regime attracted support from members of every social group in Münster.[21] Hundreds of men and women who belonged to well-established householding families willingly joined a movement which undermined the most fundamental assumptions about power and property. It was perhaps this very fact – the apparent ease with which religious zealotry could undermine allegiance to the traditional social order – which made the Münster uprising so alarming to Catholic and Protestant leaders alike. Certainly the widely publicized events in that city reinforced the determination of urban authorities all over central Europe to deal harshly with any manifestations of religious extremism which they thought might threaten the public peace.

The Münster experiment remained unique, but the antagonism

21 Kirchhoff, *Täufer in Münster*, 78–89.

between mainstream Protestants and adherents of the old church continued to disturb many German cities. The tensions were hardly resolved by the religious peace of 1555, by which every German prince could determine whether the inhabitants of his territory would be Catholic or Lutheran. Although the same power was extended to the magistrates in most of Germany's self-governing cities, the rule was hard to apply in towns where the elite itself was religiously divided or religious minorities enjoyed influential support. And some confessionally mixed cities were specifically exempted from the rule.

The largest city in which a religious division was formally recognized was Augsburg. Its population was predominantly Protestant, but about one-fifth of the inhabitants – including many of the city's wealthiest citizens – remained Catholic. Though members of both confessions sat on the city council, Catholics always dominated the highest civic offices. After decades of grudging compromises, in 1584 a major conflict erupted. It was triggered by a dispute over the reform of the calendar.[22]

In 1582 Pope Gregory XIII had decreed a great revision of the Christian calendar: ten days would be skipped over in order to bring the observed dates back into correspondence with the astronomical facts. The scientific thinking behind the reform was entirely sound, yet all over Europe the Gregorian calendar was adopted or rejected on strictly confessional lines: Catholics dutifully dropped ten days from their calendar while Protestants did not. As a result, Protestants observed various religious festivals ten days later than Catholics. It was confusing enough when neighbouring territories observed different dates: there was even more chaos when two calendars were used in the same city. Yet when the Catholic-dominated council of Augsburg ordered all of the city's inhabitants to adopt the new calendar, the Protestants adamantly refused. The chief Protestant pastor, Georg Müller, not only preached ardently against submission to the new calendar, but also let slip his belief that if magistrates became too oppressive then citizens were entitled to choose new ones. When the council ordered Müller to be banished from Augsburg, thousands of his admirers looted the city armoury for weapons and gathered threateningly at the city hall. Nervous Catholics began to flee the town. Ultimately neither side wanted to push things to extremes, and violence was narrowly averted. Protestant ministers agreed to follow the new calendar – but only after formally protesting from the pulpit. Relations between the confessions remained tense for

22 For an overview, see Warmbrunn, *Zwei Konfessionen*, 360–75.

years. When the city council banished Protestant pastors and installed new ones to take their places, Protestant parishioners boycotted the churches. Only in 1591 was a compromise worked out. The calendar issue was not reopened, but Protestant leaders were guaranteed a greater role in selecting their own pastors.

The conflict in Augsburg was not lacking in social overtones. Nobody could ignore the fact that the city's wealthiest merchants were predominantly Catholic, while most of the poor tended to be Protestant. Resentments about the political and social privileges of the city's Catholic elite certainly contributed to the tensions surrounding the events of 1584 and thereafter. But confessional divisions did not follow rigid social lines: there were also rich Protestants and poor Catholics. The central issues were, in fact, religious. Members of each confession blamed the other side for fracturing the wholeness of the community by celebrating their faith in different ways and on different days. In Augsburg, as in many other towns, citizens eventually learned to live with religious diversity – but the process was a painful one.

Probably there was no place in Europe where religious diversity within individual cities led to more excruciating confrontations than in late sixteenth-century France. Religious conflicts took many different forms in French cities, ranging from violent street brawls to formal political manoeuvring. But wherever such conflicts occurred, they reflected not only the intensity of religious feeling but also the collapse of political authority.

Protestant ideas had reached France already in the 1520s, but for almost a generation Protestants remained a tiny and disorganized sect whose teachings were firmly suppressed as heretical. During the 1550s, stimulated and supported by the powerful Calvinist church of Geneva, French Protestantism began to take much firmer root. But it was a change in the national political climate that first emboldened urban Protestants to dream of seizing power in their communities. The death of King Henri II in 1559 and his replacement by the first of three hapless successors led to a weakening of royal authority which inspired Protestants all over France to profess their views more openly than before. Their confidence in turn attracted masses of new adherents. In many cities a clearly defined Protestant faction emerged for the first time. At the same time, however, political uncertainty at the national level led to the emergence of powerful noble parties whose rivalry helped plunge France into armed conflict. The emergence of religious factions on the local level and formation of new political alliances on the national level were mutually reinforcing processes.[23] The result was a cycle of civil wars which lasted for over a generation.

Until the early 1560s, urban Protestants in France had normally been desperate to escape detection, and much of their activity had been shrouded in secrecy. Now they went boldly public. In some cities Protestants even succeeded, at least briefly, in gaining control of the machinery of municipal government. More often Catholic magistrates maintained their authority. But in many cities, whoever held formal power found it increasingly difficult to prevent violent confrontations between members of the two confessions. Almost any conspicuous religious event – a baptism, a wedding, a funeral or a procession – could trigger a bloodthirsty round of riots or lynchings. The ambiguous role of politically indecisive authorities always loomed behind such episodes. The magistrates themselves were often prevented from following a clear policy by uncertain guidance from above or by religious divisions within their own ranks. Yet rioters frequently felt that they were simply carrying out policies which the authorities had sanctioned or encouraged.[24]

The Massacre of St Bartholomew's Eve in 1572, which was launched in Paris and imitated in cities all over France, represented a major setback for the Protestant cause. After 1572 Protestants in most French towns were reduced to what they had been before 1559: a dissident sect. In some communities, however, they remained sufficiently numerous that their rights had to be acknowledged when the French civil wars ended in the 1590s. It would take almost a century before the corporate and individual rights of French Protestants were completely eliminated by the French crown.

The ferocity of religious conflicts in French towns of the late sixteenth century could reach striking extremes. But some towns, even if they had a significant Protestant minority, were spared confessional conflict.[25] And even when it occurred, the full intensity of religious conflict was often relatively short-lived. After an initial period of searing hostility, it usually became clear which confession would be dominant – and soon the different religious groups might settle into a grudging acceptance of each other's existence. Eventually it would be recognized that the community's survival did not, in fact, depend on vigilant defence of religious purity. Once this was

23 Benedict, *Rouen*, 233–50, esp. 239.
24 Davis, *Society and Culture*, 152–87; cf. Richet, 'Aspects socio-culturels', 770–2.
25 cf. Konnert, 'Urban Values'.

acknowledged, at least tacitly, other aspects of the community's well-being could receive more attention.

This was by no means the case only in France. Countless English towns also underwent phases of intense but temporary religious conflict during the early modern era. Few English towns were untouched by the fundamental antagonism which emerged in the late sixteenth century between the main body of Anglicans and those who espoused the dissenting outlook generally classified as Puritanism. But only occasionally did sharply defined religious factions emerge as major determinants of urban politics. This was most obviously the case in the 1640s when – as in France eighty years earlier – conflict on the national level helped to crystallize informal clusterings of like-minded town-dwellers into identifiable religious factions. For a few years, 'Anglican' and 'Puritan' factions contended for power in many English towns. But their success or failure was often determined chiefly by the arrival and departure of royalist or parliamentarian armies. And even at the height of the conflict, most cities still had a large middle group of citizens who valued the community's physical survival and economic viability more highly than the attainment of religious uniformity.[26] Religious passions never gripped all members of a community with equal intensity. It was this that made it possible, when the acute stimuli to religious conflict had passed, for more cool-headed members of the urban elite to resume governing the community in accordance with the fundamental values that had always guided decision-making among municipal leaders: order, predictability, security and stability.

III

Conflict of one sort or another was endemic in the early modern city, but most of it was contained before it turned violent or tumultuous. Much of early modern urban government, after all, was devoted precisely to making sure that conflict did not get out of hand. Brawls and arguments were normally nipped in the bud and their perpetrators were swiftly reprimanded, fined or even imprisoned until tempers cooled. At the same time, legitimate grievances could always be aired – either directly to the authorities or indirectly through guilds and other associations. Municipal rulers all knew how risky it was to let substantial grievances fester. Incidental disturbers of the peace could always be punished and neutralized: every city had enough watchmen or beadles to deal with individual malefactors. But

26 Howell, 'Structure of Urban Politics'.

collective discontent was far more dangerous to the social order. Few if any cities commanded the military means to repress large-scale disturbances. Often the citizens themselves were armed. To preserve stability the inhabitants had to know, or at least believe, that their city was being well-governed on their behalf.

Reflecting on the lessons of the Frankfurt Fettmilch uprising two generations after the event, a German historian arrived at this conclusion:

> In order to prevent such disorders in free cities and republics (which, as the old Roman and Greek histories show, tend to suffer the worst attacks), there is no better policy – in addition to providing good government – than to be careful and sparing with the introduction of whatever innovations are needed, so that troublemakers are not given any excuse for insubordination, and so that if they do nevertheless act up they can be firmly and boldly put down; however, when there is actual danger of an uprising, then one must, without any delay, while one still has means and power, make sure to have enough soldiers and officers who are dependent exclusively on the authorities, so that without any hesitation the ringleaders can be seized and punished to make sure worse consequences do not ensue.[27]

Behind Hiob Ludolf's ornate phraseology lay a few simple doctrines which many of his contemporaries would have endorsed. In order to prevent urban uprisings, the authorities must provide good government and demonstrate their respect for the customs and traditions to which inhabitants had become attached. But if, despite all this, any disturbances should erupt, they should be firmly and swiftly repressed before things reached a level which the authorities could no longer control.

To a large extent the authorities succeeded. Violent upheaval was not the norm in European cities of the early modern era. Sometimes, to be sure, it seemed as if it was. Riots and rebellions always make news, and the details of every urban disturbance were carefully recorded and, beginning in the sixteenth century, widely disseminated in newsletters and pamphlets. At times – as during the French Wars of Religion – it must have seemed that the entire fabric of urban society was falling apart. But this was an illusion. The riots and disturbances which, understandably enough, made such an impression on contemporaries were in fact occasional episodes, signs that the normal mechanisms of social control and conflict resolution had temporarily broken down.

27 Ludolf, *Allgemeine Schau-Bühne*, 1: 447–50.

Even rarer were the true cases of urban revolt, in which the normal institutions of municipal government were actually displaced or rendered powerless by a civic opposition – episodes like the reign of Savonarola in Florence, the Anabaptist Kingdom of Münster, the Fettmilch Uprising in Frankfurt, the Ormée of Bordeaux or the Gülich Uprising in Cologne. These upheavals never began as a frontal assault on the existing conceptions of government. They started instead as ordinary conflicts in which citizens demanded redress of grievances or insisted on an expanded role in decision-making. Then, however, charismatic leaders would begin to project the vision of a transformed society against which the corruption or irresolution of traditional elites could offer no effective rejoinder. The old authorities would flee or submit to the popular movement, while municipal institutions came to be controlled, supplemented or even replaced by new organs of government representing the freshly empowered elements of the community.

Yet these new regimes were always doomed to collapse. Exiled members of the traditional elite were quick to round up support from nobles or princes alarmed by the implications of the revolt. Meanwhile inhabitants of the community itself always became increasingly disillusioned as the original vision of social justice or dreams of the New Jerusalem gave way to the realities of military siege, food shortages and economic chaos. In the end it scarcely mattered whether the popular regime was betrayed from within or defeated from without. The results were always the same: a stern round of punishments for the rebel leaders and the reimposition of the traditional authority structure. For while there was in fact a recognized role for conflict in the early modern city, this applied only so long as it took place within a traditional framework of power relations. Forms of conflict that challenged or threatened the basic structure of urban society were always bound to fail.

Conclusion
A Way of Looking

CONCLUSION

A Way of Looking

We began this book by accompanying a real person on an imagined walk through the streets of Munich in 1574. We can end this book by accompanying another real person on a walk which actually occurred in the streets of London in 1631.[1]

One late afternoon in August of that year, Sarah Wallington, aged about 4, was idly playing in front of her father's shop on Philpot Lane just north of London Bridge. Suddenly she wandered down to the end of the lane and turned into Eastcheap, one of London's great thoroughfares. Heading east, the child walked further into Tower Street and eventually arrived at the huge bulwark of the Tower of London. Circling around the Tower, Sarah found herself on the road to the suburb of East Smithfield. Here she fell and hurt herself.

A kindly woman passing by found the child and tried to comfort her. But Sarah was unable to explain where she lived. Supposing that the child came from the heavily settled district of Wapping a bit further south, the stranger began to carry Sarah there. Sarah was now a mile from home, and nobody in Wapping would have known who she was. By chance, however, a passing servant recognized the child and explained that she came from Eastcheap, quite in the opposite direction. Sarah was soon delivered safely home.

Her father was not there. As soon as the child went missing, he had started a desperate search all over the neighbourhood. Only when he gave up and returned home many hours later did he discover that his daughter had been found. His relief was tinged with anguished thoughts of what had almost happened. Sarah was her parents' only surviving child; four others had already died. Now she too might have

1. The following is based on Seaver, *Wallington's World*, 90–1.

been lost for good. Only the sheer accident of her being recognized by a passing servant a mile away from home had made possible her return.

In many ways this story has a modern resonance. Children get lost today, and parents are equally distraught. But an unidentified child found by a concerned adult on the streets of modern London would soon be in the hands of the Metropolitan Police, and her anxious parents would quickly be able to locate her. By contrast, if Sarah Wallington had been deposited with the parish authorities in Wapping, she might never have been reunited with her parents. It certainly would have been difficult for either side to establish contact. London was an intensely administered city in the seventeenth century, but the units of administration were overwhelmingly neighbourhood-based. Parish and ward officials knew everything imaginable about the inhabitants of their own neighbourhood. But the flow of information from one district to another was limited and incidental.

In some ways this circumstance reflects the dilemma of the modern historian of the early modern city. We know or can know incredibly much about some aspects of life in particular cities or particular urban districts. But systematic comparisons are often impossible to undertake. The quality of record-keeping differed not only from one city to the next but also within individual cities. Of course every town maintained some records on a community-wide basis, but much record-keeping was decentralized: each parish, district, guild, court or other institution kept its own registers. Some such records were maintained with exemplary care and have survived intact to delight the modern historian; others were kept so carelessly that they can hardly be read today – or else they have simply disappeared. We know exactly how many grocers lived just south of the London Bridge in 1622, for example – for superb local records have made possible the detailed reconstruction of social conditions in that particular neighbourhood. But we do not know how many grocers lived just north of the London Bridge, for the records of that district, if they survived at all, have yet to be examined. We know exactly how many householders paid their taxes in Frankfurt am Main in 1587, since the tax register for that one year was transcribed and published just after the First World War. We will never know as much about social conditions at any other point in Frankfurt's early modern history – for in March 1944 the entire set of tax registers was destroyed in a midnight bombing raid.

Anomalies like this explain why our knowledge of social conditions in the cities of early modern Europe will never rest on the type of standardized statistical data which modern censuses routinely produce for every modern city. Much as we may know about one parish or district or even one whole city during a particular period, the systematic comparisons over space and time which modern social analysis takes for granted can never underlie discussions of the early modern city. Even the most sophisticated comparative analyses of European urbanization in the early modern era ultimately depend on a patchwork of estimates and data of highly variant quality.

Yet this is not to say that we will never know what we most want to know about the early modern city. It all depends on what we are looking for. If we step back from the relentless search for more data about particular cases and ask instead about the character of early modern cities as a whole, we will soon discover not how little we know but how much. For one of the fundamental premises of this book is that whatever we know about any one early modern city can teach us something about all early modern cities. Despite their many differences in size and character, the towns of early modern Europe all belonged to a common urban civilization. Obviously the texture of urban life was not uniform – Edinburgh did not look like Naples, Seville was hardly the same as Danzig. Climate imposed and culture reinforced differences in the design, appearance and use of individual buildings and urban space in general. There were countless variations in the way people acted and interacted. In Italy members of the urban elite gathered to gossip and share the news in public squares; in northern Germany they met indoors in cosy drinking chambers. But the issues that concerned them and their fellow citizens were much the same everywhere. Every city had its own local customs and its own special rules for achieving public office or setting up a household. Yet the underlying institutional structures of urban society were remarkably similar all over Europe – and they remained highly constant in character throughout the early modern era.

Of course there were changes between 1450 and 1750. Trading networks grew in depth and breadth. New techniques of finance and investment were pioneered. Printing transformed communications. The state intruded more directly and persistently in urban life. The religious differences which in 1450 were still obscured by common allegiance to the church of Rome came out into the open and gave rise to rival Christian denominations.

Yet in many fundamental ways, the early modern city remained remarkably stable. How cities were governed, trades were regulated and incomes were earned remained highly constant for centuries. Many towns grew, and physical layouts changed as fortifications were added or new districts were laid out. Yet the basic character of the urban streetscape underwent no dramatic transformations. We can see this if we return to the Sendlinger Gasse in Munich.[2] In 1750 the house once owned by Georg and Margareta Toll belonged to Magdalena Fux, a blacksmith's wife who had inherited the building from her parents. If Magdalena had walked down the street in 1750, she would have found every house from 1574 still in place. The houses which had belonged in Margareta Toll's day to a baker, a brewer and a flour-dealer were still occupied by practitioners of those trades. Of course the occupational makeup of this row of houses had changed: there were no more weavers in 1750, but there were two tailors, two artists, a potter, a gardener, a salt merchant and so on. Stepping indoors into one of these houses, a visitor in 1750 would have found some subtle differences from the way things had looked in 1574. There might have been more furniture, for example, and some of it would have been more refined in construction. More books might have been visible, and more members of the household were likely to have been literate. But the fundamental activities of shop or kitchen and the basic routines of daily life would have remained almost unchanged. Cloth was still woven and bread was still baked as had been done for hundreds of years.

Nor was there any fundamental shift in power relations. Throughout the early modern era, almost everywhere membership in the urban elite remained accessible to those who, by industry or inheritance, had acquired enough wealth to function plausibly as the city's rulers. To be sure, relations between magistrates and inhabitants never remained static. As cities grew larger – and many did – municipal governments were bound to become more aloof and remote. But the tendency for urban rulers to govern in an ever more autocratic manner was always held in check by the recognized right of the ruled to be well-governed – and by their latent power to express their resentments by violence when all else failed. The power of the state to intervene in urban affairs was, as a whole, greater in 1750 than it had been three centuries earlier. But the decline in urban autonomy was more keenly felt by members of the local elite than by the large body of ordinary town-dwellers. The inhabitants' participation in governance had always been limited anyway. At the same time, their moral claims on the authorities remained intact no matter who pulled the strings.

2. *Häuserbuch der Stadt München*, 4: 392–419.

Power relations within the smaller spheres of urban life also remained essentially constant. Guilds were always controlled by the wealthiest masters. Parish affairs were always dominated by the most prosperous residents. And the patriarchal structure of the household remained unchanged. The master's power over his wife, his children and his servants remained strong. But it was never absolute. The economic rights of women and children were always recognized and almost always enforced. From time to time women were able to exploit their rights in ways that enabled them to dominate their families or run independent enterprises. But they were rigorously excluded from political power. The basic parameters of gender relations remained constant throughout the early modern era.

To emphasize these elements of continuity in urban life is not to suggest that life in the early modern city was lacking in drama or tension. It is simply another way of looking – a way of focusing less on those developments which look important to later generations and more on the way life was lived for 300 years in a particular kind of human community. The rise of the modern state, the spread of capitalism, the transformation of science, the growth of cities themselves – all these developments certainly affected many aspects of urban life. But early modern town-dwellers were only dimly conscious of what we can now recognize as unidirectional changes in these and other aspects of life. They were far more aware of how their lives and hopes were shaped within the framework of associations and institutions which had structured urban life for as long as anyone could remember: guilds, parishes, families and households. And they were only too aware that every hard-won gain in terms of wealth, contentment or security could be undermined by the eternal enemies of urban life: fire, famine, disease, disorder and war.

We cannot understand the social history of the early modern city unless we understand both the institutions that provided stability and the forces that threatened it. But ultimately what really matters is the way in which men, women and children coped with circumstances and seized opportunities in the endless human struggle to make individual lives more prosperous or more meaningful. The city with all its institutions was still only a framework for living. The true story of the early modern city is the story of how a dozen generations of human beings, severely constrained by the technological limitations of a preindustrial society and struggling against a broad unyielding background of institutional and economic stability, managed to make the most of their lives.

Suggestions for Further Reading
Bibliography of Works Cited
Map
Index

Suggestions for Further Reading

A vast treasury of historical literature in dozens of languages covers the history of the early modern European city. Almost every town in Europe has a historical society of some kind, and many of these organizations publish their own journals or sponsor the publication of historical works. These local studies often provide an invaluable grounding for the more systematic work of professional historians interested in the social history of specific towns. Even the output of case studies by professional historians is huge.

This brief survey of suggested readings on the social history of early modern cities is essentially limited to a selection of particularly useful or stimulating works available in English, though a handful of outstanding titles in French and German will also be mentioned for the benefit of readers familiar with those languages. For reasons of space this survey is confined to books as opposed to articles. But almost all of these works have bibliographies which can direct the reader to any number of articles and more specialized books concerning the city or the topic concerned.

Only the author and title of each work will be given here. The full publication data for each work cited can be found in the bibliography.

1. GENERAL TREATMENTS

There is no general treatment of the social history of the early modern city as such. But some important general studies of the European city include useful material on the early modern era. The greatest book in this genre, though its author was a theorist of urban planning rather than a historian, is Lewis Mumford, *The City in History*.

Marc Girouard, *Cities and People: A Social and Architectural History* is a more recent work in this tradition. A broad approach to European urbanization, stressing economic and geographic factors, is provided by Paul M. Hohenberg and Lynn Hollen Lees, *The Making of Urban Europe, 1000–1950.* The relationship between urban growth, economics and architecture over the same period is explored by Josef W. Konvitz, *The Urban Millennium: The City-Building Process from the Early Middle Ages to the Present.*

Demographic aspects of urban growth during the early modern era are treated in the rather demanding work by Jan de Vries, *European Urbanization, 1500–1800.* Richard Mackenney, *The City-State, 1500–1700: Republican Liberty in an Age of Princely Power* provides a brief but useful treatment of the political role of the early modern city. Important aspects of urban planning, especially in the seventeenth century, are treated by Josef W. Konvitz, *Cities and the Sea: Port City Planning in Early Modern Europe.*

Systematic comparative treatments of early modern cities are surprisingly rare. But three important works, all of which take Venice as one pole of the comparison, illustrate the rich potential of this approach: Peter Burke, *Venice and Amsterdam: A Study of Seventeenth-Century Elites*; Alexander Francis Cowan, *The Urban Patriciate: Lübeck and Venice, 1580–1700*; and Richard Mackenney, *Tradesmen and Traders: The World of the Guilds in Venice and Europe, c.1250–c.1650.*

The overwhelming majority of works in urban history deal with a single city. Some of these works, including many of the very best ones, focus on a single aspect of the city's history. But most works in urban history cross topical lines to deal with many aspects of a city's history. For this reason the remaining works listed here are organized not according to topics but on a regional or national basis.

2. FRANCE

Like any tourist in modern France, the student of French urban history will probably want to begin with Paris. The impact of religious tensions on Parisian life in the sixteenth century is vividly demonstrated by Barbara B. Diefendorf, *Beneath the Cross: Catholics and Huguenots in Sixteenth-Century Paris.* The same author provides a searching treatment of the capital's political elite in her *Parisian City Councillors in the Sixteenth Century.* Two broad treatments of Paris in the seventeenth century cover the 'grand siècle' in refreshingly different ways: Leon Bernard, *The Emerging City: Paris in the Age of Louis XIV* emphasizes the capital's institutions and infrastructure while Orest Ranum, *Paris in the Age of Absolutism* puts more stress on cultural and religious developments. The lives of labouring men and women are analysed by Jeffry Kaplow, *The Names of Kings: The Parisian Laboring Poor in the Eighteenth Century*.

Many provincial cities have also been well served by works written in (or translated into) English. Robert A. Schneider covers the entire early modern era in *Public Life in Toulouse, 1463–1789: From Municipal Republic to Cosmopolitan City*. Another exemplary work, more sharply focused in time and topic, is James R. Farr, *Hands of Honor: Artisans and their World in Dijon, 1550–1650*. Many works deal with the social background to religious or political conflict in French cities. Philip Benedict, *Rouen in the Wars of Religion* skilfully integrates social and political history. Many of the deservedly influential essays published by Natalie Zemon Davis in her *Society and Culture in Early Modern France* deal with Lyon and other cities during the sixteenth century. In *Carnival in Romans*, the eminent French historian Emmanuel Le Roy Ladurie demonstrates the power of ritual and symbolism in an urban conflict of the late sixteenth century. The complexity of seventeenth-century urban conflicts is well brought out by Sharon Kettering, *Judicial Politics and Urban Revolt in Seventeenth-Century France: The Parlement of Aix, 1629–1659* and Sal Alexander Westrich, *The Ormée of Bordeaux: A Revolution during the Fronde*. The problem of poverty in French cities during the seventeenth century is examined in two important works: Cissie S. Fairchilds, *Poverty and Charity in Aix-en-Provence, 1640–1789* and Kathryn Norberg, *Rich and Poor in Grenoble, 1600–1814*. A number of useful essays can be found in the collection edited by Philip Benedict, *Cities and Social Change in Early Modern France*; the book also includes a helpful bibliography of major books and articles in English and French.

For those who read French, an outstanding example of the 'histoire totale' approach pioneered by the 'Annales school' of French historians is provided by Pierre Deyon, *Amiens, capital provinciale: étude sur la société urbaine au 17e siècle*. For the exact opposite approach – using a single source as the starting-point for a rich analysis of urban life – see Alain Lottin, *Chavatte, ouvrier lillois: un contemporain de Louis XIV*.

3. ITALY

The history of Italian cities has long attracted the interest of historians writing in English, but much of their work pertains to the medieval or early Renaissance periods. There are, however, a number of significant works on cities from the late fifteenth to the eighteenth century.

For background information on Florence at the outset of the early modern era, see Gene A. Brucker, *Renaissance Florence.* A detailed examination of political and social dynamics in one district during the fifteenth century is provided by D. V. Kent and F. W. Kent, *Neighbours and Neighbourhood in Renaissance Florence.* Richard A. Goldthwaite, *Private Wealth in Renaissance Florence* explores the economic history of four families in the fifteenth and sixteenth centuries. The political crisis of the late fifteenth century is treated in depth by Donald Weinstein, *Savonarola and Florence: Prophecy and Patriotism in the Renaissance.* The cultural history of the city following its 'golden age' is explored by Eric Cochrane, *Florence in the Forgotten Centuries, 1527–1800.* The impact of the plague of 1630 on social relations is examined by Giulia Calvi, *Histories of a Plague Year: The Social and the Imaginary in Baroque Florence.*

The history of Venice during the period after 1450 is well covered in English. A good starting-point is Edward Muir, *Civic Ritual in Renaissance Venice*, which places the city's ceremonial life in its broader political and social context. James Cushman Davis, *The Decline of the Venetian Nobility as a Ruling Class* is a useful introduction to the patriciate of Venice; on this topic the works by Peter Burke and Alexander Cowan cited above under 'General Treatments' should also be consulted. Brian Pullan, *Rich and Poor in Renaissance Venice* is an indispensable treatment of the city's charitable institutions. A highly distinctive sector of the city's social and economic life is described by Robert C. Davis, *Shipbuilders of the Venetian Arsenal.* A useful selection of primary sources, with a large emphasis on social history, is provided in translation by David Chambers and Brian Pullan (eds) *Venice: A Documentary History, 1450–1630.* For the city's overall history see Frederic C. Lane, *Venice: A Maritime Republic.*

The social history of Rome in the sixteenth century is vividly recounted by Peter Partner, *Renaissance Rome, 1500–1559.* The texture of everyday life in the city is effectively recaptured by Thomas V. Cohen and Elizabeth S. Cohen (eds) *Words and Deeds in Renaissance Rome: Trials before the Papal Magistrates.* Laurie Nussdorfer, *Civic Politics in the Rome of Urban VIII* examines the nature of Roman politics and the role and composition of the Roman elite in the seventeenth century. For the eighteenth century, see the broad treatment by Hanns Gross, *Rome in the Age of Enlightenment.*

The history of an important urban institution in early modern Italy is treated by Christopher F. Black, *Italian Confraternities in the Sixteenth Century*.

4. SPAIN

In recent years the urban history of early modern Spain has attracted increasing interest among historians writing in English. Seville is a good starting-point. Ruth Pike, *Aristocrats and Traders: Sevillian Society in the Sixteenth Century* provides an excellent introduction to the city's social history. The rather broadly defined 'underworld' of Seville is described by Mary Elizabeth Perry, *Crime and Society in Early Modern Seville*; the same author offers a lucid and tightly argued analysis of the role of women in *Gender and Disorder in Early Modern Seville*. The economic basis of urban society is treated by Carla Rahn Phillips, *Ciudad Real, 1500–1750: Growth, Crisis and Readjustment in the Spanish Economy*. Urban charitable institutions are described by Linda Martz, *Poverty and Welfare in Habsburg Spain: The Example of Toledo*, and by Maureen Flynn, *Sacred Charity: Confraternities and Social Welfare in Spain, 1400–1700*. The social background of religious change is illuminated by Jodi Bilinkoff, *The Avila of Saint Teresa: Religious Reform in a Sixteenth-Century City*. For the social and cultural character of the urban elite in the capital of Catalonia, see James S. Amelang, *Honored Citizens of Barcelona: Patrician Culture and Class Relations, 1490–1714*. A valuable source of information about the same city's response to crisis has been translated by James Amelang as *A Journal of the Plague Year: The Diary of the Barcelona Tanner Miquel Parets, 1651*.

5. GERMANY, AUSTRIA AND SWITZERLAND

Due to the long-standing interest in the history of the German Reformation, the sixteenth century is particularly well represented in works on German cities. An excellent introduction is provided by Gerald Strauss, *Nuremberg in the Sixteenth Century*. Some useful essays on Nuremberg are included in Lawrence P. Buck and Jonathan W. Zophy (eds) *The Social History of the Reformation*. The history of Strasbourg in the sixteenth century is fully covered in English. Miriam Usher Chrisman, *Strasbourg and the Reform* offers the best introduction, while Lorna Jane Abray, *The People's Reformation: Magistrates, Clergy, and Commons in Strasbourg, 1500–1598* can be strongly recommended for its lucid discussion of the different groups involved in the religious reform. A thorough analysis of the city's elite is provided by Thomas A. Brady, jr, *Ruling Class, Regime and Reformation at Strasbourg, 1520–1555.* Tom Scott, *Freiburg and Breisgau: Town–Country Relations in the Age of Reformation and Peasants' War* emphasizes the social and economic background to the upheaval of the early Reformation years. Susan C. Karant-Nunn, *Zwickau in Transition, 1500–1547: The Reformation as an Agent of Change* examines the effects of the Reformation on one Saxon town. Bernd Moeller, *Imperial Cities and the Reformation* is a brief but influential study of the relationship between urban political traditions and the adoption of the Reformation. For a general overview of the impact of Protestantism on German and Swiss cities, see Steven Ozment, *The Reformation in the Cities.* R. Po-chia Hsia, *Society and Religion in Münster, 1535–1618* analyses the tensions surrounding the establishment of the Counter-Reformation in a city which underwent exceptionally dramatic religious changes in the course of the sixteenth century.

The history of women in German cities of the late fifteenth and sixteenth centuries is treated by three important books. Merry E. Wiesner, *Working Women in Renaissance Germany* provides a comprehensive overview of the varieties of work performed by urban women. Martha C. Howell, *Women, Production and Patriarchy in Late Medieval Cities* uses material from Germany and the Netherlands to discuss women's work from a more theoretical perspective. Lyndal Roper, *The Holy Household: Women and Morals in Reformation Augsburg* describes in detail the often negative effects of the Protestant Reformation on the situation of women in one German city.

A number of works in English discuss German towns during the later phases of the early modern era. Joachim Whaley, *Religious Toleration and Social Change in Hamburg, 1529–1819* shows how significant conflicts between ministers and magistrates persisted throughout the early modern period. The social history of one German town in the seventeenth century is examined in detail by Christopher R. Friedrichs, *Urban Society in an Age of War: Nördlingen, 1580–1720.* Gerald L. Soliday, *A Community in Conflict: Frankfurt Society in the Seventeenth and Early Eighteenth Centuries* describes the social background to political conflict in one of Germany's major cities. Mack Walker, *German Home Towns: Community, State and General Estate, 1648–1871* is an original and imaginative analysis of the character of German towns which shows how patterns of communal life established in the early modern era continued to influence German politics and thought long into the nineteenth century.

The special problems of political and social transformation experienced by German towns which were absorbed into the French monarchy are explored in two works: Franklin L. Ford, *Strasbourg in Transition, 1648–1789*, and Peter G. Wallace, *Communities and Conflict in Early Modern Colmar, 1600–1730.*

For those who can read German, a good introduction to the early modern city in Germany is provided by Klaus Gerteis, *Die deutschen Städte in der frühen Neuzeit: Zur Vorgeschichte der 'bürgerlichen Welt'.* Among the countless important works on individual German cities, two can be mentioned as particularly readable examples of urban social history: Gerd Wunder, *Die Bürger von Hall: Sozialgeschichte einer Reichsstadt, 1216–1802*, which describes the various social and occupational groups of Schwäbisch Hall in medieval and early modern times, and Etienne François, *Koblenz im 18. Jahrhundert: Zur Sozial- und Bevölkerungsstruktur einer deutschen Residenzstadt*, a crisp and informative analysis of one town in the eighteenth century.

For Austria one can consult two important works on Vienna. John Stoye, *The Siege of Vienna* shows how the city responded to an acute crisis in 1683. John P. Spielman, *The City and the Crown: Vienna and the Imperial Court, 1600–1740* provides a broad overview while also demonstrating how the growth of the Habsburg bureaucracy helped to shape and transform the city.

The social history of towns in Switzerland is not well covered in English. But E. William Monter, *Calvin's Geneva* offers a well-rounded description of an important city which was politically linked to the Swiss confederation. Some useful material on poverty and charity in Zurich can be found in Lee Palmer Wandel, *Always Among Us: Images of the Poor in Zwingli's Zurich.*

6. THE NETHERLANDS

Despite the importance of urban life in the Netherlands, the social history of towns in the Low Countries in early modern times is not well covered in English. There is, however, an exemplary work which integrates the social, economic and political history of one town in the sixteenth century: Robert S. DuPlessis, *Lille and the Dutch Revolt: Urban Stability in an Era of Revolution, 1500–1582.* C. C. Hibben, *Gouda in Revolt: Particularism and Pacifism in the Revolt of the Netherlands, 1572–1588* emphasizes the political outlook of the town's elite. A highly detailed treatment of one segment of urban society is provided by John Michael Montias, *Artists and Artisans in Delft: A Socio-Economic Study of the Seventeenth Century*. For economic history the older work by Violet Barbour, *Capitalism in Amsterdam in the Seventeenth Century* is still useful. For a broader approach to the social history of Dutch towns, however, the best places to look are often the more general social histories of the Netherlands, in which urban affairs inevitably play a major role. Notable works in this genre are A. T. Van Deursen, *Plain Lives in a Golden Age: Popular Culture, Religion and Society in Seventeenth-Century Holland*, and Simon Schama, *The Embarrassment of Riches: An Interpretation of Dutch Culture in the Golden Age*.

7. BRITAIN AND IRELAND

For obvious reasons, the number of books in English on the history of British towns is vast. Only a limited selection of particularly useful books can be mentioned here.

London has inevitably received the greatest share of attention. Two recent works – Steve Rappaport, *Worlds within Worlds: Structures of Life in Sixteenth-Century London*, and Ian W. Archer, *The Pursuit of Stability: Social Relations in Elizabethan London* – use strikingly different approaches to explain the same phenomenon: the relative stability of London life in the sixteenth century. An absorbingly detailed analysis of social relations on the neighbourhood level is provided by Jeremy Boulton, *Neighbourhood and Society: A London Suburb in the Seventeenth Century*. A sociologist's view of crime in early modern London is offered by John L. McMullan, *The Canting Crew: London's Criminal Underworld, 1550–1700*. Valerie Pearl, *London and the Outbreak of the Puritan Revolution* is the classic account of the period leading up to the English Revolution. The same period is viewed from the perspective of a single individual by Paul S. Seaver, *Wallington's World: A Puritan Artisan in Seventeenth-Century London*. Every student of London's history should be familiar with the *Diary of Samuel Pepys*; those who do not wish to tackle the full text should at least read one of the many available condensed versions. An exceptionally broad and stimulating treatment of London's social history during the late seventeenth and early eighteenth centuries is provided by Peter Earle, *The Making of the English Middle Class:*

Business, Society and Family Life in London, 1660–1730. For eighteenth-century London the old treatment by M. Dorothy George, *London Life in the Eighteenth Century* is still valuable; more recent surveys are provided by Dorothy Marshall, *Dr. Johnson's London* and George Rudé, *Hanoverian London, 1714–1808*. A variety of approaches to the history of early modern London can be sampled in the collection edited by A. L. Beier and Roger Finlay, *London 1500–1700: The Making of the Metropolis*.

Of the vast literature on provincial cities, only a few examples can be cited here. The high quality often attained by work done in the local-history tradition is exemplified by J. W. F. Hill, *Tudor and Stuart Lincoln*. Charles Phythian-Adams, *Desolation of a City: Coventry and the Urban Crisis of the Late Middle Ages* deals with one town's problems at the outset of the early modern era. A number of fine works offer broad surveys of individual cities in the sixteenth century; among these are Alan D. Dyer, *The City of Worcester in the Sixteenth Century*; D. M. Palliser, *Tudor York*; and Wallace T. MacCaffrey, *Exeter, 1540–1640: The Growth of an English County Town*. Much has been written about the experiences of particular cities in the upheavals of the mid-seventeenth century. A classic work in this tradition is Roger Howell, jr, *Newcastle-upon-Tyne and the Puritan Revolution*; an important new contribution is David Underdown's richly detailed examination of the impact of Puritanism on the small town of Dorchester: *Fire from Heaven: Life in an English Town in the Seventeenth Century*. An ambitious treatment of long-term social and economic change in one town is provided by David Harris Sacks, *The Widening Gate: Bristol and the Atlantic Economy, 1450–1700*. The growing cultural richness and refinement of English provincial towns after the mid-seventeenth century is traced by Peter Borsay, *The English Urban Renaissance: Culture and Society in the Provincial Town, 1660–1770*.

Two useful surveys which complement each other chronologically are Peter Clark and Paul Slack, *English Towns in Transition, 1500–1700*, and Penelope J. Corfield, *The Impact of English Towns, 1700–1800*. A number of important and informative articles can be found in the volumes edited or co-edited by Peter Clark: *Crisis and Order in English Towns, 1500–1700* (with Paul Slack), *Country Towns in Pre-Industrial England* and *The Transformation of English Provincial Towns, 1600–1800*.

For Scotland the best starting-point is the collection edited by Michael Lynch, *The Early Modern Town in Scotland*. A detailed social history of a northern Scottish town in the seventeenth century will be found in Gordon R. DesBrisay, *Authority and Discipline in Aberdeen, 1650–1700*. For Irish towns, one should consult the first half of Maurice Craig, *Dublin, 1660–1860: A Social and Architectural History* and the relevant essays in R. A. Butlin (ed.) *The Development of the Irish Town*.

8. NORTHERN AND EASTERN EUROPE

Material in English on the towns of early modern Scandinavia is very scarce. Steen Eiler Rasmussen, *Towns and Buildings* incorporates useful material on Copenhagen and Stockholm into a broader study of European city planning. An informative treatment of crime and its social context in Stockholm and other Swedish towns from the late fifteenth to the early seventeenth centuries is provided by Eva Österberg and Dag Lindström, *Crime and Social Control in Medieval and Early Modern Swedish Towns*.

The urban history of eastern Europe in the early modern era is virtually untouched in English. The obscure survey by Wojciech Kalinowski, *City Development in Poland up to Mid-19th Century* is hard to locate but worth the effort, especially for its superb maps. Vera Zimányi, *Economy and Society in Sixteenth and Seventeenth Century Hungary (1525–1650)* has some useful information on towns. For more information in a western language, however, one must generally turn to works in German; many pertinent essays can be found in the works edited by Wilhelm Rausch, *Die Stadt an der Schwelle zur Neuzeit* and *Die Städte Mitteleuropas im 17. und 18. Jahrhundert*. The essays in Bariša Krekić (ed.) *Urban Society of Eastern Europe in Premodern Times* emphasize medieval rather than early modern conditions. (Early modern Russian urban history, which is a bit more fully treated in English, falls outside the scope of this book.) Recent changes in the political atmosphere of eastern Europe will make it easier for English-speaking historians to undertake research in urban history there; in five or ten years it should be possible to list a substantial number of works in English on the urban history of Poland, Bohemia, Hungary and the Balkans in the early modern era.

Bibliography of Works Cited

Abray, Lorna Jane. *The People's Reformation: Magistrates, Clergy, and Commons in Strasbourg, 1500–1598* (Ithaca, NY, 1985).

Ambronn, Karl-Otto and Fuchs, Achim. *Die Oberpfalz wird bayerisch: Die Jahre 1621 bis 1628 in Amberg und der Oberpfalz* (Amberg, 1978).

Amelang, James S. 'Barristers and Judges in Early Modern Barcelona: The Rise of a Legal Elite', *American Historical Review*, 89 (1984), 1264–84.

Amelang, James S. *Honored Citizens of Barcelona: Patrician Culture and Class Relations, 1490–1714* (Princeton, NJ, 1986).

Amelang, James S. (ed.) *A Journal of the Plague Year: The Diary of the Barcelona Tanner Miquel Parets, 1651* (New York, 1991).

Appleby, Andrew. 'Nutrition and Disease: The Case of London, 1550–1750', *Journal of Interdisciplinary History*, 6 (1973), 1–22.

Archer, Ian. *The Pursuit of Stability: Social Relations in Elizabethan London* (Cambridge, 1991).

Atkinson, Tom. *Elizabethan Winchester* (London, 1963).

Aubin, Hermann. 'Formen und Verbreitung des Verlagswesens in der Altnürnberger Wirtschaft', in Stadtarchiv Nürnberg (ed.) *Beiträge zur Wirtschaftsgeschichte Nürnbergs*, 2 vols (1967), 2: 620–68.

Bainton, Roland. *Here I Stand: A Life of Martin Luther* (Nashville, Tenn., 1950).

Bairoch, Paul, Batou, Jean and Chèvre, Pierre. *La Population des villes européennes de 800 à 1850: Banque de données et analyse sommaire des résultats/The Population of European Cities from 800 to 1850: Data Bank and Short Summary of Results from 800 to 1850* (Geneva, 1988).

Ballon, Hilary. *The Paris of Henry IV: Architecture and Urbanism* (Cambridge, Mass., 1991).

Barbour, Violet. *Capitalism in Amsterdam in the Seventeenth Century* (Baltimore, Md., 1950).

Bátori, Ingrid. 'Das Patriziat der deutschen Städte: Zu den Forschungsergebnissen über das Patriziat besonders der süddeutschen Städte', *Zeitschrift für Stadtgeschichte, Stadtsoziologie und Denkmalpflege*, 2 (1975), 1–30.

Bátori, Ingrid. *Die Reichsstadt Augsburg im 18. Jahrhundert: Verfassung, Finanzen und Reformversuche* (Göttingen, 1969).

Bátori, Ingrid. 'Die Rhenser Hexenprozesse der Jahre 1628 bis 1630', *Landeskundliche Vierteljahrsblätter*, 33 (1987), 135–55.

Bedford, John. *London's Burning* (London, 1966).

Bée, Michel, 'Le Spectacle de l'exécution dans la France d'ancien régime', *Annales, E.S.C.*, 38 (1983), 843–62.

Beier, A. L. 'The Social Problems of an Elizabethan Country Town: Warwick, 1580–90', in Peter Clark (ed.) *Country Towns in Pre-Industrial England* (Leicester, 1981), 45–85.

Beier, A. L. and Finlay, Roger (eds) *London 1500–1700: The Making of the Metropolis* (London, 1986).

Beik, William H. 'The Culture of Protest in Seventeenth-Century French Towns', *Social History*, 15 (1990), 1–23.

Beik, William H. 'Two Intendants Face a Popular Revolt: Social Unrest and the Structure of Absolutism in 1645', *Canadian Journal of History*, 9 (1974), 243–62.

Beik, William H. 'Urban Factions and the Social Order during the Minority of Louis XIV', *French Historical Studies*, 15 (1987), 36–67.

Bell, Walter George. *The Great Fire of London in 1666*, rev. edn (London, 1951).

Ben-Amos, Ilana Krausman. 'Women Apprentices in the Trades and Crafts of Early Modern Bristol', *Continuity and Change*, 6 (1991), 227–52.

Benecke, Gerhard. 'Ennoblement and Privilege in Early Modern Germany', *History*, 56 (1971), 360–70.

Benedict, Philip. 'French Cities from the Sixteenth Century to the Revolution: An Overview', in Philip Benedict (ed.) *Cities and Social Change in Early Modern France* (London, 1989), 7–68.

Benedict, Philip. *Rouen during the Wars of Religion* (Cambridge, 1981).

Benedict, Philip (ed.) *Cities and Social Change in Early Modern France* (London, 1989).

Berlin, Michael. 'Civic Ceremony in Early Modern London', *Urban History Yearbook* (1986), 15–27.

Bernard, Leon. *The Emerging City: Paris in the Age of Louis XIV* (Durham, NC, 1970).

Bilinkoff, Jodi. *The Avila of Saint Teresa: Religious Reform in a Sixteenth-Century City* (Ithaca, NY, 1989).

Black, Anthony. *Guilds and Civil Society in European Political Thought from the Twelfth Century to the Present* (Ithaca, NY, 1984).

Black, C. E. *The Dynamics of Modernization: A Study in Comparative History* (New York, 1966).

Black, Christopher F. *Italian Confraternities in the Sixteenth Century* (Cambridge, 1989).

Blendinger, Friedrich. 'Versuch einer Bestimmung der Mittelschicht in der Reichsstadt Augsburg vom Ende des 14. bis zum Anfang des 18. Jahrhunderts', in Erich Maschke and Jürgen Sydow (eds) *Städtische Mittelschichten* (Stuttgart, 1972), 32–78.

Bogucka, Maria. 'Entwicklungswege der polnischen Städte vom 16. bis zum 18. Jahrhundert in vergleichender Sicht', in Marian Biskup and Klaus Zernack (eds) *Schichtung und Entwicklung der Gesellschaft in Polen und Deutschland im 16. and 17. Jahrhundert: Parallelen, Verknüpfungen, Vergleiche* (Wiesbaden 1983), 174–91.

Bogucka, Maria. 'Nationale Strukturen der polnischen Städte im 17. Jahrhundert', *Die alte Stadt*, 14 (1987), 240–53.

Bolland, Jürgen. *Senat und Bürgerschaft: Über das Verhältnis zwischen Bürger und Stadtregiment im alten Hamburg* (Hamburg, 1977).

Borsay, Peter. *The English Urban Renaissance: Culture and Society in the Provincial Town, 1660–1770* (Oxford, 1989).

Bothe, Friedrich. *Frankfurts wirtschaftlich-soziale Entwicklung vor dem Dreissigjährigen Kriege und der Fettmilchaufstand (1612–1616)* (Frankfurt, 1920), vol. 2 (vol. 1 not published).

Bothe, Friedrich. *Geschichte der Stadt Frankfurt am Main* (Frankfurt, 1913; repr. 1966).

Boulton, Jeremy. *Neighbourhood and Society: A London Suburb in the Seventeenth Century* (Cambridge, 1987).

Brady, Thomas A., jr. *Ruling Class, Regime and Reformation at Strasbourg, 1520–1555* (Leiden, 1978).

Brandi, Karl. *The Emperor Charles V*, trans. C. V. Wedgwood (London, 1939, repr. 1965).

Brodsky, Vivien. 'Widows in Late Elizabethan London: Remarriage, Economic Opportunity and Family Orientations', in Lloyd Bonfield, Richard M. Smith and Keith Wrightson (eds) *The World We Have Gained: Histories of Population and Social Structure* (Oxford, 1986), 122–54.

Brown, Frank E. 'Continuity and Change in the Urban House:

Developments in Domestic Space Organisation in Seventeenth-Century London', *Comparative Studies in Society and History*, 28 (1986), 558–90.

Brucker, Gene A. *Renaissance Florence* (New York, 1969).

Brunner, Otto. 'Das "ganze Haus" und die alteuropäische Ökonomik', in Otto Brunner, *Neue Wege der Verfassungs- und Sozialgeschichte*, 2nd edn (Göttingen, 1968), 103–27.

Brunner, Otto. 'Souveränitätsproblem und Sozialstruktur in den deutschen Reichsstädten der früheren Neuzeit', *Vierteljahrschrift für Sozial- und Wirtschaftsgeschichte*, 50 (1963), 329–60.

Buck, Lawrence P. and Zophy, Jonathan W. (eds) *The Social History of the Reformation* (Columbus, Ohio, 1972).

Burke, Gerald. *Towns in the Making* (London, 1971).

Burke, Peter. *Popular Culture in Early Modern Europe* (New York, 1978).

Burke, Peter. *Venice and Amsterdam: A Study of Seventeenth-Century Elites* (London, 1974).

Burke, Peter. 'The Virgin of the Carmine and the Revolt of Masaniello', *Past and Present*, 99 (May 1983), 3–21.

Butlin, R. A. (ed.) *The Development of the Irish Town* (London, 1977).

Calvi, Giulia. *Histories of a Plague Year: The Social and the Imaginary in Baroque Florence*, trans. by Dario Biocca and Bryant T. Ragan, jr (Berkeley, Calif., 1989).

Carter, Francis W. *Dubrovnik (Ragusa): A Classic City-State* (London, 1972).

Chabert, Alexandre R. E. 'More about the Sixteenth-Century Price Revolution', in Peter Burke (ed.) *Economy and Society in Early Modern Europe: Essays from 'Annales'* (New York, 1972), 47–54.

Chamberlin, E. R. *The Sack of Rome* (London, 1979).

Chambers, David and Pullan, Brian (eds) *Venice: A Documentary History, 1450–1630* (Oxford, 1992).

Chandler, George (ed.) *Liverpool under Charles I* (Liverpool, 1965).

Chrisman, Miriam Usher. *Strasbourg and the Reform: A Study in the Process of Change* (New Haven, Conn., 1967).

Cipolla, Carlo M. *Clocks and Culture, 1300–1700* (New York, 1978).

Cipolla, Carlo M. *Cristofano and the Plague: A Study in the History of Public Health in the Age of Galileo* (Berkeley, Calif., 1973).

Clarendon, Edward, Earl of. *The History of the Rebellion and Civil Wars in England, Begun in the Year 1641* (Oxford, 1732).

Clark, Peter. 'The Civic Leaders of Gloucester, 1580–1800', in Peter Clark (ed.) *The Transformation of English Provincial Towns, 1600–1800* (London, 1984), 311–45.

Clark, Peter. 'The Migrant in Kentish Towns, 1580–1640', in Peter Clark and Paul Slack (eds) *Crisis and Order in English Towns, 1500–1700: Essays in Urban History* (London, 1972), 117–63.

Clark, Peter (ed.) *Country Towns in Pre-Industrial England* (Leicester, 1981).

Clark, Peter (ed.) *The Transformation of English Provincial Towns, 1600–1800* (London, 1984).

Clark, Peter and Slack, Paul. *English Towns in Transition, 1500–1700* (Oxford, 1976).

Clark, Peter and Slack, Paul (eds) *Crisis and Order in English Towns, 1500–1700: Essays in Urban History* (London, 1972).

Clasen, Claus-Peter. 'Armenfürsorge in Augsburg vor dem Dreissigjährigen Kriege', *Zeitschrift des historischen Vereins für Schwaben*, 78 (1984), 65–115.

Clasen, Claus-Peter. *Die Augsburger Weber: Leistungen und Krisen des Textilgewerbes um 1600* (Augsburg, 1981).

Cochrane, Eric. *Florence in the Forgotten Centuries, 1527–1800: A History of Florence and the Florentines in the Age of the Grand Dukes* (Chicago, 1973).

Cohen, Elizabeth S. and Cohen, Thomas V. 'Camilla the Go-Between: The Politics of Gender in a Roman Household (1559)', *Continuity and Change*, 4 (1989), 53–77.

Cohen, Thomas V. and Cohen, Elizabeth S. *Words and Deeds in Renaissance Rome: Trials before the Papal Magistrates* (Toronto, 1993).

Corfield, Penelope J. *The Impact of English Towns, 1700–1800* (Oxford, 1982).

Corfield, Penelope J. 'A Provincial Capital in the Late Seventeenth Century: The Case of Norwich', in Peter Clark and Paul Slack (eds) *Crisis and Order in English Towns, 1500–1700: Essays in Urban History* (London, 1972), 263–310.

Coudy, Julien (ed.) *The Huguenot Wars*, trans. by Julie Kernan (Philadelphia, Pa., 1969).

Cowan, Alexander F. 'Urban Elites in Early Modern Europe: An Endangered Species?', *Historical Research*, 64 (1991), 121–37.

Cowan, Alexander F. *The Urban Patriciate: Lübeck and Venice, 1580–1700* (Cologne, 1986).

Craig, Maurice. *Dublin, 1660–1860: A Social and Architectural History*, 2nd edn (Dublin, 1969).

Cramer, Johannes, 'Zur Frage der Gewerbegasse in der Stadt am Ausgang des Mittelalters', *Die Alte Stadt*, 11 (1984), 81–111.

Davis, James Cushman. *The Decline of the Venetian Nobility as a Ruling Class* (Baltimore, Md., 1962).

Davis, Natalie Zemon. *Society and Culture in Early Modern France* (Stanford, Calif., 1975).

Davis, Natalie Zemon. 'A Trade Union in Sixteenth-Century France', *Economic History Review*, 19 (1966), 48–69.

Davis, Robert C. *Shipbuilders of the Venetian Arsenal: Workers and Workplace in the Preindustrial City* (Baltimore, Md., 1991).

Deiseroth, Wolf. 'Fürstliche Stadtgründungen aus der Sicht der Baugeschichte und Denkmalpflege', in Wilhelm Wortmann (ed.) *Deutsche Stadtgründungen der Neuzeit* (Wiesbaden, 1989), 45–80.

DesBrisay, Gordon R. 'Authority and Discipline in Aberdeen: 1650–1700' (Ph.D. thesis, University of St. Andrews, 1989).

De Vries, Jan. *Economy of Europe in an Age of Crisis, 1600–1750* (Cambridge, 1976).

De Vries, Jan. *European Urbanization, 1500–1800* (Cambridge, 1984).

Deyon, Pierre. *Amiens, capitale provinciale: étude sur la société urbaine au 17e siècle* (Paris, 1967).

Diefendorf, Barbara B. *Beneath the Cross: Catholics and Huguenots in Sixteenth-Century Paris* (New York, 1991).

Diefendorf, Barbara B. *Paris City Councillors in the Sixteenth Century: The Politics of Patrimony* (Princeton, NJ, 1983).

Dinges, Martin. *Stadtarmut in Bordeaux, 1525–1675: Alltag, Politik, Mentalitäten* (Bonn, 1988).

Dirlmeier, Ulf. 'Die kommunalpolitischen Zuständigkeiten und Leistungen süddeutscher Städte im Spätmittelalter', in Jürgen Sydow (ed.) *Städtische Versorgung und Entsorgung im Wandel der Geschichte* (Sigmaringen, 1981), 113–50.

Dolan, Claire. 'The Artisans of Aix-en-Provence in the Sixteenth Century: A Micro-Analysis of Social Relationships', in Philip Benedict (ed.) *Cities and Social Change in Early Modern France* (London, 1989), 174–94.

Domínguez Ortiz, Antonio and Aguilar Piñal, Francisco. *El Barroco y la Ilustracion: Historia de Sevilla, IV* (Seville, 1976).

Dorner, Friedrich. *Die Steuern Nördlingens zu Ausgang des Mittelalters* (Nuremberg, 1905).

Dreher, Bernd. *Vor 300 Jahren: Nikolaus Gülich* (Cologne, 1986).

Duchhardt, Heinz. 'Frankfurt am Main im 18. Jahrhundert', in Frankfurter Historische Kommission (ed.) *Frankfurt am Main: Die Geschichte der Stadt in neun Beiträgen* (Sigmaringen, 1991), 261–302.

Dugan, Eileen T. 'The Funeral Sermon as a Key to Familial Values in Early Modern Nördlingen', *Sixteenth Century Journal*, 20 (1989), 631–44.

Dülmen, Richard van. *Theatre of Horror: Crime and Punishment in Early Modern Germany*, trans. by Elisabeth Neu (Oxford, 1990).

DuPlessis, Robert S. *Lille and the Dutch Revolt: Urban Stability in an Era of Revolution, 1500–1582* (Cambridge, 1991).

Dyer, Alan D. *The City of Worcester in the Sixteenth Century* (Leicester, 1973).

Earle, Peter. *The Making of the English Middle Class: Business, Society and Family Life in London, 1660–1730* (Berkeley, Calif., 1989).

Elliott, J. H. *Imperial Spain, 1469–1716* (New York, 1966).

Elliott, Vivien Brodsky. 'Single Women in the London Marriage Market: Age, Status and Mobility, 1598–1619', in R. B. Outhwaite (ed.) *Marriage and Society: Studies in the Social History of Marriage* (London, 1981), 81–100.

Endres, Rudolf. 'Sozialstruktur Nürnbergs', in Gerhard Pfeiffer (ed.) *Nürnberg: Geschichte einer europäischer Stadt* (Munich, 1971), 194–9.

Erdmannsdorfer, Karl. *Das Bürgerhaus in München* (Tübingen, 1972).

Euler, Friedrich W. 'Wandlungen des Konnubiums im Adel des 15. und 16. Jahrhunderts', in Hellmuth Rössler (ed.) *Deutscher Adel, 1430–1555* (Darmstadt, 1965), 58–94.

Fairchilds, Cissie C. *Poverty and Charity in Aix-en-Provence, 1640–1789* (Baltimore, Md., 1976).

Farr, James R. 'Consumers, Commerce and the Craftsmen of Dijon: The Changing Social and Economic Structure of a Provincial Capital, 1450–1750', in Philip Benedict (ed.) *Cities and Social Change in Early Modern France* (London, 1989), 134–73.

Farr, James R. *Hands of Honor: Artisans and their World in Dijon, 1550–1650* (Ithaca, NY, 1988).

Fiennes, Nathaniel, *Colonell Fiennes letter to my Lord General, concerning Bristol* (London, 1643).

Finlay, Roger, 'Debate: Natural Decrease in Early Modern Cities', *Past and Present*, 92 (Aug. 1981), 169–74.

Finlay, Roger. *Population and Metropolis: The Demography of London, 1580–1650* (Cambridge, 1981).

Flandrin, Jean-Louis. *Families in Former Times: Kinship, Household and Sexuality*, trans. by Richard Southern (Cambridge, 1979).

Flynn, Maureen. *Sacred Charity: Confraternities and Social Welfare in Spain, 1400–1700* (Ithaca, NY, 1989).

Forbes, Thomas Roger. *Chronicle from Aldgate: Life and Death in Shakespeare's London* (New Haven, Conn., 1971).

Ford, Franklin L. *Strasbourg in Transition, 1648–1789* (Cambridge, Mass., 1958).

François, Etienne. *Koblenz im 18. Jahrhundert: Zur Sozial- und Bevölkerungsstruktur einer deutschen Residenzstadt* (Göttingen, 1982).

François, Etienne. *Die unsichtbare Grenze: Protestanten und Katholiken in Augsburg, 1648–1806* (Sigmaringen, 1991).

Fremantle, Katharine. *The Baroque Town Hall of Amsterdam* (Utrecht, 1959).

Friedrichs, Christopher R. 'Anti-Jewish Politics in Early Modern Germany: The Uprising in Worms, 1613–17', *Central European History*, 23 (1990), 91–152.

Friedrichs, Christopher R. 'German Town Revolts and the Seventeenth-Century Crisis', *Renaissance and Modern Studies*, 26 (1982), 27–51.

Friedrichs, Christopher R. 'Immigration and Urban Society: Seventeenth-Century Nördlingen', in Etienne François (ed.) *Immigration et société urbaine en Europe occidentale, XVIe-XXe siècle* (Paris, 1985), 65–77.

Friedrichs, Christopher R. 'Politics or Pogrom? The Fettmilch Uprising in German and Jewish History', *Central European History*, 19 (1986), 186–228.

Friedrichs, Christopher R. *Urban Society in an Age of War: Nördlingen, 1580–1720* (Princeton, NJ, 1979).

Fudge, John D. 'The Supply and Distribution of Foodstuffs in Northern Europe, 1450–1500', in W. Minchinton (ed.) *The Northern Seas: Politics, Economics and Culture* (Pontefract, 1989), 29–39.

Furger, Fridolin. *Zum Verlagssystem als Organisationsform des Frühkapitalismus im Textilgewerbe* (Stuttgart, 1927).

Gascon, Richard. *Grand commerce et vie urbaine aux XVIe siècle: Lyon et ses marchands (environs de 1520 – environs de 1580)*, 2 vols (Paris, 1971).

George, Dorothy M. *London Life in the Eighteenth Century* (London, 1925; repr. New York, 1964).

Gerteis, Klaus. *Die deutschen Städte in der frühen Neuzeit: Zur Vorgeschichte der 'bürgerlichen Welt'* (Darmstadt, 1986).

Girouard, Mark. *Cities and People: A Social and Architectural History* (New Haven, Conn., 1985).

Glamann, Kristof. 'The Changing Patterns of Trade', in E. E. Rich and C. H. Wilson (eds) *The Economic Organization of Early Modern Europe (The Cambridge Economic History of Europe*, vol. 6, Cambridge, 1977), 185–289.

Goldthwaite, Richard A. 'Local Banking in Renaissance Florence', *Journal of European Economic History*, 14 (1985), 5–55.

Goldthwaite, Richard A. 'The Medici Bank and the World of Florentine Capitalism', *Past and Present*, 114 (Feb. 1987), 3–31.

Goldthwaite, Richard A. *Private Wealth in Renaissance Florence: A Study of Four Families* (Princeton, NJ, 1968).

Goubert, Pierre. *The Ancien Régime: French Society, 1600–1750*, trans. by Steve Cox (London, 1973).

Goubert, Pierre. *Beauvais et le Beauvaisis de 1600 à 1730: contribution à l'histoire sociale de la France du XVIIe siècle*, 2 vols (Paris, 1960).

Gross, Hanns. *Rome in the Age of Enlightenment: The Post-Tridentine Syndrome and the Ancien Regime* (Cambridge, 1990).

Grubb, James S. *Firstborn of Venice: Vicenza in the Early Renaissance State* (Baltimore, Md., 1988).

Gruber, Karl. *Die Gestalt der deutschen Stadt: Ihr Wandel aus der geistigen Ordnung der Zeiten*, 3rd edn (Munich, 1977).

Guillerme, André E. *The Age of Water: The Urban Environment in the North of France, A.D. 300–1800* (College Station, Texas, 1988).

Gutmann, Myron P. *Toward the Modern Economy: Early Industry in Europe, 1500–1800* (New York, 1988).

Hagel, Jürgen. 'Mensch und Wasser in der alten Stadt: Stuttgart als Beispiel und Modell', *Die alte Stadt*, 14 (1987), 126–39.

Hajnal, J. 'European Marriage Patterns in Perspective', in D. V. Glass and D. E. C. Eversley (eds) *Population in History: Essays in Historical Demography* (London, 1965), 101–43.

Häuserbuch der Stadt München (ed. by Stadtarchiv München), 5 vols (Munich, 1958–77).

Hibben, C. C. *Gouda in Revolt: Particularism and Pacifism in the Revolt of the Netherlands, 1572–1588* (Utrecht, 1983).

Hildebrandt, Reinhard. 'Rat contra Bürgerschaft: Die Verfassungskonflikte in den Reichsstädten des 17. und 18. Jahrhunderts', *Zeitschrift für Städtegeschichte, Stadtsoziologie und Denkmalpflege*, 1 (1974), 221–41.

Hilger, Marie-Elisabeth. 'Umweltprobleme als Alltagserfahrung in der frühneuzeitlichen Stadt? Überlegungen anhand des Beispiels der Stadt Hamburg', *Die alte Stadt*, 11 (1984), 112–38.

Hill, J. W. F. *Tudor and Stuart Lincoln* (Cambridge, 1956).

Hilton, R. H. 'Capitalism: What's in a Name?', *Past and Present*, 1 (Feb. 1952), 32–43.

Hiltpold, Paul. 'Noble Status and Urban Privilege: Burgos, 1572', *Sixteenth Century Journal*, 12 (1981), 21–44.

Hirschmann, Gerhard. 'Das Nürnberger Patriziat', in Hellmuth Rössler (ed.) *Deutsches Patriziat, 1430–1740* (Limburg/Lahn, 1968), 257–76.

Hitchcock, Henry-Russell. *German Renaissance Architecture* (Princeton, NJ, 1981).

Hoffmann, Friedrich Wilhelm. *Geschichte der Stadt Magdeburg*, ed. by Gustav Hertel and Friedrich Hülsse, 2 vols (Magdeburg, 1885–86).

Hofmann, Hanns Hubert. 'Nobiles Norimbergenses: Beobachtungen zur Struktur der reichsstädischen Oberschicht', in Theodor Mayer (ed.) *Untersuchungen zur gesellschaftlichenStruktur der mittelalterlichen Städte in Europa* (Constance/Stuttgart, 1966), 53–92.

Hohenberg, Paul M. and Lees, Lynn Hollen. *The Making of Urban Europe, 1000–1950* (Cambridge, Mass., 1985).

Hook, Judith. *The Sack of Rome, 1527* (London, 1972).

Houston, R. A. *Literacy in Early Modern Europe: Culture and Education, 1500–1800* (London, 1988).

Howell, Martha C. *Women, Production and Patriarchy in Late Medieval Cities* (Chicago, 1986).

Howell, Roger, jr. *Newcastle-upon-Tyne and the Puritan Revolution: A Study of the Civil War in North England* (Oxford, 1967).

Howell, Roger, jr. 'The Structure of Urban Politics in the English Civil War', *Albion*, 11 (1979), 111–27.

Hsia, R. Po-chia. 'Münster and the Anabaptists', in R. Po-chia Hsia (ed.) *The German People and the Reformation* (Ithaca, NY, 1988), 51–69.

Hsia, R. Po-chia. *The Myth of Ritual Murder: Jews and Magic in Reformation Germany* (New Haven, Conn., 1988).

Hsia, R. Po-chia. *Society and Religion in Münster, 1535–1618* (New Haven, Conn., 1984).

Imhof, Arthur E. 'Die nicht-namentliche Auswertung der Kirchenbücher von Giessen und Umgebung: Die Resultate', in Arthur E. Imhof (ed.) *Historische Demographie als Sozialgeschichte: Giessen und Umgebung vom 17. zum 19. Jahrhundert*, 2 vols (Darmstadt/Marburg, 1975), 1: 85–77.

Imhof, Arthur E. 'Demographische Stadtstrukturen der frühen Neuzeit: Giessen in seiner Umgebung im 17. und 18. Jahrhundert als Fallstudie', *Zeitschrift für Stadtgeschichte, Stadtsoziologie und Denkmalpflege*, 2 (1975), 190–227.

Irsigler, Franz and Lassotta, Arnold. *Bettler und Gaukler, Dirnen und Henker: Randgruppen und Aussenseiter in Köln, 1300–1600* (Cologne, 1984).

Irvine, Frederick M. 'From Renaissance City to Ancien Régime Capital: Montpellier, c.1500–c.1600', in Philip Benedict (ed.) *Cities and Social Change in Early Modern France* (London, 1989), 105–133.

Israel, Jonathan. *European Jewry in the Age of Mercantilism, 1500–1750*, 2nd edn (Oxford, 1989).

James, Mervyn. 'Ritual, Drama and the Social Body in the Late Medieval English Town', *Past and Present*, 98 (Feb. 1983), 3–29.

Jeannin, Pierre. *Merchants of the Sixteenth Century*, trans. by Paul Fittingoff (New York, 1972).

Jones, E. L., Porter, S. and Turner, M. *A Gazetteer of English Urban Fire Disasters, 1500–1900* (Norwich, 1984).

Jones, Emrys. *Towns and Cities* (New York, 1966).

Jütte, Robert. 'Die Anfänge des organisierten Verbrechens: Falschspieler und ihre Tricks im späten Mittelalter und der frühen Neuzeit', *Archiv für Kulturgeschichte*, 70 (1988), 1–32.

Jütte, Robert. 'Household and Family Life in Late Sixteenth-Century Cologne: The Weinsberg Family', *Sixteenth Century Journal*, 17 (1986), 165–82.

Jütte, Robert. 'Nepper, Schlepper und Bauernfänger im frühneuzeitlichen Köln', *Rheinische Vierteljahrsblätter*, 51 (1987), 250–74.

Jütte, Robert. *Obrigkeitliche Armenfürsorge in deutschen Reichsstädten der frühen Neuzeit: Städtisches Armenwesen in Frankfurt am Main und Köln* (Cologne/Vienna, 1984).

Jütte, Robert. 'Das Stadtviertel als Problem und Gegenstand der frühneuzeitlichen Stadtgeschichtsforschung', *Blätter für deutsche Landesgeschichte*, 127 (1991), 235–69.

Kähni, Otto. 'Die Reichsstädte der Ortenau', *Jahrbuch für Geschichte der oberdeutschen Reichsstädte*, 11 (1965), 43–61.

Kalinowski, Wojciech. *City Development in Poland up to Mid-19th Century*, trans. by Agnieszka Glinka (Warsaw, 1966).

Kaplow, Jeffry. *The Names of Kings: The Parisian Laboring Poor in the Eighteenth Century* (New York, 1972).

Karant-Nunn, Susan C. *Zwickau in Transition, 1500–1547: The Reformation as an Agent of Change* (Columbus, Ohio, 1987).

Kastner, Sabine. 'Bürgerliches Wohnen und Bauen in Göttingen', in Hermann Wellenreuther (ed.) *Göttingen, 1690–1755: Studien zur Sozialgeschichte einer Stadt* (Göttingen, 1988), 175–251.

Kendrick, T. D. *The Lisbon Earthquake* (London, 1956).

Kent, D. V. and Kent, F. W. *Neighbours and Neighbourhood in Renaissance Florence: The District of the Red Lion in the Fifteenth Century* (Locust Valley, NY, 1982).

Kettering, Sharon. *Judicial Politics and Urban Revolt in Seventeenth-Century France: The Parlement of Aix, 1629–1659* (Princeton, NJ, 1978).

Keysler, John George [Johann Georg]. *Travels through Germany,*

Bohemia, Hungary, Switzerland, Italy and Lorrain, Giving a True and Just Description of the Present State of Those Countries, 4 vols (London, 1756–57).

Kindleberger, Charles P. 'The Economic Crisis of 1619 to 1623', *Journal of Economic History*, 51 (1991), 149–75.

King, Walter. 'How High is Too High? Disposing of Dung in Seventeenth-Century Prescot', *Sixteenth Century Journal*, 23 (1992), 443–57.

Kintz, Jean-Pierre. *La Société strasbourgeoise du milieu de XVIe siècle à la fin de la guerre de trente ans, 1560–1650: essai d'histoire démographique, économique et sociale* (Paris, 1984).

Kirchhoff, Karl-Heinz. *Die Täufer in Münster, 1534/35: Untersuchungen zum Umfang und zur Sozialstruktur der Bewegung* (Münster, 1973).

Klaits, Joseph. *Servants of Satan: The Age of the Witch Hunts* (Bloomington, Ind., 1985).

Konnert, Mark. 'Urban Values versus Religious Passion: Châlons-sur-Marne during the Wars of Religion', *Sixteenth Century Journal*, 20 (1989), 387–405.

Konvitz, Josef W. *Cities and the Sea: Port City Planning in Early Modern Europe* (Baltimore, Md., 1978).

Konvitz, Josef W. *The Urban Millennium: The City-Building Process from the Early Middle Ages to the Present* (Carbondale, Ill., 1985).

Kracauer, Isidor. *Geschichte der Juden in Frankfurt a.M. (1150–1824)*, 2 vols (Frankfurt, 1925–27).

Krekić, Bariša (ed.) *Urban Society of Eastern Europe in Premodern Times* (Berkeley, Calif., 1987).

Krüger, Eduard. *Schwäbisch Hall: Ein Gang durch Geschichte und Kunst*, 2nd edn (Schwäbisch Hall, 1967).

Kubinyi, András, 'Städtische Wasserversorgungsprobleme im mittelalterlichen Ungarn', in Jürgen Sydow (ed.) *Städtische Versorgung und Entsorgung im Wandel der Geschichte* (Sigmaringen, 1981), 180–90.

Lahrkamp, Helmut. 'Das Patriziat in Münster', in Hellmuth Rössler (ed.) *Deutsches Patriziat, 1430–1740* (Limburg/Lahn, 1968), 195–207.

Lake, Jeremy. *The Great Fire of Nantwich* (Nantwich, 1983).

Lane, Frederic C. *Venice: A Maritime Republic* (Baltimore, Md., 1973).

Landes, David S. *Revolution in Time: Clocks and the Making of the Modern World* (Cambridge, Mass., 1983).

Lange, Nicole. '"Policey" und Umwelt in der Frühen Neuzeit: Umweltpolitik in Hamburg als Sozialdisziplinierung', *Zeitschrift des Vereins für Hamburgische Geschichte*, 76 (1990), 13–39.

Latimer, John. *Annals of Bristol in the Seventeenth Century* (Bristol, 1900).

Le Goff, Jacques. *Time, Work, and Culture in the Middle Ages*, trans. by Arthur Goldhammer (Chicago, 1980).

Le Roy Ladurie, Emmanuel. *Carnival in Romans*, trans. by Mary Feeney (New York, 1979).

Le Roy Ladurie, Emmanuel. 'A System of Customary Law: Structures and Inheritance Customs in Sixteenth-Century France', in Robert Forster and Orest Ranum (eds) *Family and Society: Selections from the Annales* (Baltimore, Md., and London, 1976), 75–103.

Levack, Brian P. *The Witch-Hunt in Early Modern Europe* (London, 1987).

Lottin, Alain. *Chavatte, ouvrier lillois: un contemporain de Louis XIV* (Paris, 1979).

Ludolf, Hiob. *Allgemeine Schau-Bühne der Welt, Oder: Beschreibung der vornehmsten Welt-Geschichte, so sich vom Anfang dieses Siebenzehenden Jahr-Hunderts . . . begeben*, 4 vols (Frankfurt, 1699–1719).

Lynch, Michael. 'The Crown and the Burghs, 1500–1625', in Michael Lynch (ed.) *The Early Modern Town in Scotland* (London, 1987).

Lynch, Michael (ed.) *The Early Modern Town in Scotland* (London, 1987).

MacCaffrey, Wallace T. *Exeter, 1540–1640: The Growth of an English County Town* (Cambridge, Mass., 1958).

McGrath, Patrick. *Bristol and the Civil War* (Bristol, 1981)

Mackenney, Richard. *The City-State, 1500–1700: Republican Liberty in an Age of Princely Power* (Atlantic Highlands, NJ, 1989).

Mackenney, Richard. *Tradesmen and Traders: The World of the Guilds in Venice and Europe, c.1250–c.1650* (London, 1987).

McLaren, Angus. *Reproductive Rituals: The Perception of Fertility in England from the Sixteenth to the Nineteenth Century* (London, 1984).

McLynn, Frank. *Crime and Punishment in Eighteenth-Century England* (Oxford, 1991).

McMullan, John L. *The Canting Crew: London's Criminal Underworld, 1550–1700* (New Brunswick, NJ, 1984).

McNeill, John T. *The History and Character of Calvinism* (Oxford, 1967).

Marshall, Dorothy. *Dr. Johnson's London* (New York, 1968).

Martz, Linda. *Poverty and Welfare in Habsburg Spain: The Example of Toledo* (Cambridge, 1983).

Maschke, Erich. 'Die Unterschichten der mittelalterlichen Städte Deutschlands', in Erich Maschke and Jürgen Sydow (eds) *Gesellschaftliche Unterschichten in den südwestdeutschen Städten* (Stuttgart, 1967), 1–74.

Mathis, Franz. *Zur Bevölkerungsstruktur österreichischer Städte im 17. Jahrhundert* (Munich, 1977).

Meckseper, Cord. *Kleine Kunstgeschichte der deutschen Stadt im Mittelalter* (Darmstadt, 1982).

Mentzer, Raymond A., jr. '*Disciplina nervus ecclesiae*: The Calvinist Reform of Morals at Nîmes', *Sixteenth Century Journal*, 18 (1987), 89–115.

Meuvret, Jean. 'Demographic Crisis in France from the Sixteenth to the Eighteenth Century', in D. V. Glass and D. E. C. Eversley (eds) *Population in History: Essays in Historical Demography* (London, 1965), 507–22.

Meyn, Matthias. *Die Reichsstadt Frankfurt vor dem Bürgeraufstand von 1612 bis 1614: Struktur und Krise* (Frankfurt, 1980).

Midelfort, H. C. Erik. *Witch Hunting in Southwestern Germany, 1562–1684: The Social and Intellectual Foundations* (Stanford, Calif., 1972).

Miskimin, Harry A. *The Economy of Later Renaissance Europe, 1460–1600* (Cambridge, 1977).

Moeller, Bernd. *Imperial Cities and the Reformation: Three Essays*, trans. by H. C. Erik Midelfort and Mark U. Edwards, jr (Philadelphia, 1972).

Monter, E. William. *Calvin's Geneva* (New York, 1967).

Monter, E. William. 'The Consistory of Geneva, 1559–1569', *Bibliothèque d'Humanisme et Renaissance*, 38 (1976), 467–84.

Monter, E. William. *Witchcraft in France and Switzerland: The Borderlands During the Reformation* (Ithaca, NY, 1976).

Montias, John Michael. *Artists and Artisans in Delft: A Socio-Economic Study of the Seventeenth Century* (Princeton, NJ, 1982).

Morhard, Johann. *Haller Haus-Chronik*, introd. by Wilhelm Dürr (Schwäbisch Hall, 1962).

Mörke, Olaf. 'Der gewollte Weg in Richtung "Untertan": Ökonomische und politische Eliten in Braunschweig, Lüneburg und Göttingen vom 15. bis ins 17. Jahrhundert', in Heinz Schilling and Herman Diederiks (eds) *Bürgerliche Eliten in den Niederlanden und in Nordwestdeutschland* (Cologne, 1985), 111–33.

Morris, James. *Venice*, 2nd rev. edn (London, 1983).

Muir, Edward. *Civic Ritual in Renaissance Venice* (Princeton, NJ, 1981).

Muller Fz., Samuel. *De Dom van Utrecht: Dertig Platen met Tekst* (Utrecht, 1906).

Mumford, Lewis. *The City in History: Its Origins, its Transformations and its Prospects* (New York, 1961).

Nader, Helen. *Liberty in Absolutist Spain: The Habsburg Sale of Towns, 1516–1700* (Baltimore, Md., 1990).

Naujoks, Eberhard. *Kaiser Karl V. und die Zunftverfassung: Ausgewählte Aktenstücke zu den Verfassungsänderungen in den oberdeutschen Reichsstädten (1547–1556)* (Stuttgart, 1985).

Newman, Karin. 'Hamburg in the European Economy, 1650–1750', *Journal of European Economic History*, 14 (1985), 57–93.

Norberg, Kathryn. *Rich and Poor in Grenoble, 1600–1814* (Berkeley, Calif., 1985).

Nussdorfer, Laurie. *Civic Politics in the Rome of Urban VIII* (Princeton, NJ, 1992).

Orme, Nicholas, 'The Reformation and the Red Light', *History Today* (March 1987), 36–41.

Österberg, Eva and Lindström, Dag. *Crime and Social Control in Medieval and Early Modern Swedish Towns* (Uppsala, 1988).

Ozment, Steven. *Magdalena and Balthasar: An Intimate Portrait of Life in Sixteenth-Century Europe Revealed in the Letters of a Nuremberg Husband and Wife* (New York, 1986).

Ozment, Steven. *The Reformation in the Cities: The Appeal of Protestantism to Sixteenth Century Germany and Switzerland* (New Haven, Conn., 1975).

Ozment, Steven. *When Fathers Ruled: Family Life in Reformation Europe* (Cambridge, Mass., 1983).

Ozment, Steven (ed.) *Three Behaim Boys: Growing Up in Early Modern Germany* (New Haven, Conn., 1990).

Palliser, D. M. *Tudor York* (Oxford, 1979).

Parker, Geoffrey. *The Dutch Revolt* (Ithaca, NY, 1977).

Parker, Geoffrey. *The Military Revolution: Military Innovation and the Rise of the West, 1500–1800* (Cambridge, 1988).

Parker, Geoffrey (ed.) *The Thirty Years' War* (London, 1984).

Partner, Peter. *Renaissance Rome, 1500–1559: A Portrait of a Society* (Berkeley, Calif., 1976).

Patten, John. *English Towns, 1500–1700* (Folkestone, 1978).

Pearl, Valerie. 'Change and Stability in Seventeenth-Century London', *The London Journal*, 5 (1979), 3–34.

Pearl, Valerie. *London and the Outbreak of the Puritan Revolution: City Government and National Politics, 1625–1643* (Oxford, 1961).

Pehl, Hans. *Als die Frankfurter noch hinter der Mauer lebten: Die mittelalterliche Befestigung der Freien Reichsstadt* (Frankfurt, 1977).

Pepys, Samuel. *The Diary of Samuel Pepys*, ed. by Robert Latham and William Matthews, 11 vols (London, 1970–83).

Perrenoud, Alfred. 'La Mortalité à Genève de 1625 à 1825', *Annales de démographie historique*, 1978, 209–33.

Perrenoud, Alfred. 'L'Inégalité sociale devant la mort à Genève au XVIIe siècle', *Population*, 30 (1975), num. spéc. 221–43.

Perry, Mary Elizabeth. *Crime and Society in Early Modern Seville* (Hanover, NH, 1980).

Perry, Mary Elizabeth. *Gender and Disorder in Early Modern Seville* (Princeton, NJ, 1990).

Phillips, Carla Rahn. *Ciudad Real, 1500–1750: Growth, Crisis, and Readjustment in the Spanish Economy* (Cambridge, Mass., 1979).

Phythian-Adams, Charles. 'Ceremony and the Citizen: The Communal Year at Coventry, 1450–1550', in Peter Clark and Paul Slack (eds) *Crisis and Order in English Towns, 1500–1700* (London, 1972), 57–85.

Phythian-Adams, Charles. *Desolation of a City: Coventry and the Urban Crisis of the Late Middle Ages* (Cambridge, 1979).

Pike, Ruth. *Aristocrats and Traders: Sevillian Society in the Sixteenth Century* (Ithaca, NY, 1972).

Polišenský, J. V. *The Thirty Years War*, trans. by Robert Evans (Berkeley, Calif., 1971).

Poni, Carlo. 'Norms and Disputes: The Shoemakers' Guild in Eighteenth-Century Bologna', *Past and Present*, 123 (May 1989), 80–108.

Porchnev, Boris. *Les Soulèvements populaires en France de 1623 à 1648* (Paris, 1963).

Pound, John F. *Poverty and Vagrancy in Tudor England* (London, 1971).

Pound, John F. 'The Social and Trade Structure of Norwich, 1525–1575', *Past and Present*, 34 (July 1966), 49–69.

Power, M. J. 'East London Housing in the Seventeenth Century', in Peter Clark and Paul Slack (eds) *Crisis and Order in English Towns, 1500–1700: Essays in Urban History* (London, 1972), 237–62.

Prior, Mary. 'Women and the Urban Economy: Oxford, 1500–1800', in Mary Prior (ed.) *Women in English Society, 1500–1800* (London, 1985), 93–117.

Pullan, Brian. 'The Occupations and Investments of the Venetian Nobility in the Middle and Late Sixteenth Century', in J. R. Hale (ed.) *Renaissance Venice* (London, 1973), 379–408.

Pullan, Brian. *Rich and Poor in Renaissance Venice: The Social Institutions of a Catholic State, to 1620* (Cambridge, Mass., 1971).

Rabb, Theodore K. 'The Expansion of Europe and the Spirit of Capitalism', *Historical Journal*, 17 (1974), 675–89.

Rabb, Theodore K. *The Struggle for Stability in Early Modern Europe* (New York, 1975).

Raberg, Marianne, 'The Development of Stockholm since the Seventeenth Century', in Ingrid Hammarström and Thomas Hall (eds) *Growth and Transformation of the Modern City* (Stockholm, 1979), 13–26.

Raeff, Marc. *The Well-Ordered Police State: Social and Institutional Change through Law in the Germanies and Russia, 1600–1800* (New Haven, Conn., 1983).

Rammstedt, Otthein. *Sekte und soziale Bewegung: Soziologische Analyse der Täufer in Münster (1534/35)* (Cologne, 1966).

Ranum, Orest. *Paris in the Age of Absolutism* (New York, 1968).

Ranum, Orest and Ranum, Patricia (eds) *The Century of Louis XIV* (New York, 1972).

Rappaport, Steve. *Worlds within Worlds: Structures of Life in Sixteenth-Century London* (Cambridge, 1989).

Rasmussen, Steen Eiler. *London: The Unique City*, rev. edn (Cambridge, Mass., 1967).

Rasmussen, Steen Eiler. *Towns and Buildings* (Cambridge, Mass., 1969).

Rathgeber, Julius (ed.) *Colmar und Ludwig XIV (1648–1715): Ein Beitrag zur elsässischen Städtegeschichte im siebenzehnten Jahrhundert* (Stuttgart, 1873).

Rausch, Wilhelm (ed.) *Die Stadt an der Schwelle zur Neuzeit* (Linz, 1980).

Rausch, Wilhelm (ed.) *Die Städte Mitteleuropas im 17. und 18. Jahrhundert* (Linz, 1981).

Reddaway, T. F. *The Rebuilding of London after the Great Fire*, 2nd edn (London, 1951).

Rice, Eugene F., jr. *The Foundations of Early Modern Europe, 1460–1559* (New York, 1970).

Richet, Denis. 'Aspects socio-culturels des conflits religieux à Paris dans la seconde moitié du XVIe siècle', *Annales, E.S.C.*, 32 (1977), 764–89.

Roberts, Michael. *Gustavus Adolphus: A History of Sweden, 1611–1632*, 2 vols (London 1953–1958).

Rödel, Walter G. *Mainz und seine Bevölkerung im 17. und 18. Jahrhundert: Demographische Entwicklung, Lebensverhältnisse und soziale Stratifikation in einer geistlichen Residenzstadt* (Stuttgart, 1985).

Roeck, Bernd. *Bäcker, Brot und Getreide in Augsburg: Zur Geschichte des Bäckerhandwerks und zur Versorgunsgspolitik der Reichsstadt im Zeitalter des Dreissigjährigen Krieges* (Sigmaringen 1987).

Roeck, Bernd. *Elias Holl: Architekt einer europäischer Stadt* (Regensburg, 1985).

Roeck, Bernd. *Eine Stadt in Krieg und Frieden: Studien zur Geschichte der Reichsstadt Augsburg zwischen Kalenderstreit und Parität*, 2 vols (Göttingen, 1989).

Romano, Dennis. 'The Regulation of Domestic Service in Renaissance Venice', *Sixteenth Century Journal*, 22 (1991), 661–77.

Roper, Lyndal. *The Holy Household: Women and Morals in Reformation Augsburg*, rev. edn (Oxford, 1991).

Rossiaud, Jacques. 'Prostitution, Youth, and Society in the Towns of Southeastern France in the Fifteenth Century', in Robert Forster and Orest Ranum (eds) *Deviants and the Abandoned in French Society* (Baltimore, Md., 1978), 1–46.

Rublack, Hans-Christoph. 'Political and Social Norms in Urban Communities in the Holy Roman Empire', in Kaspar von Greyerz (ed.) *Religion, Politics and Social Protest: Three Studies on Early Modern Germany* (London, 1984), 24–60.

Rudé, George. *Hanoverian London, 1714–1808* (Berkeley, Calif., 1971).

Sabean, David W. *Property, Production, and Family in Neckarhausen, 1700–1870* (Cambridge, 1990).

Sacks, David Harris. *The Widening Gate: Bristol and the Atlantic Economy, 1450–1700* (Berkeley, Calif., 1991).

Schama, Simon. *The Embarrassment of Riches: An Interpretation of Dutch Culture in the Golden Age* (Berkeley, Calif., 1988).

Schilling, Heinz. 'Aufstandsbewegungen in der stadtbürgerlichen Gesellschaft des Alten Reiches: Die Vorgeschichte des Münsteraner Täuferreichs, 1525 bis 1534', in Hans-Ulrich Wehler (ed.) *Der Deutsche Bauernkrieg, 1524–1526* (Göttingen, 1975), 193–238.

Schilling, Heinz. *Civic Calvinism in Northwestern Germany and the Netherlands: Sixteenth to Nineteenth Centuries* (Kirksville, Mo, 1991).

Schilling, Heinz. 'Wandlungs- und Differenzierungsprozesse innerhalb der bürgerlichen Oberschichten West- und Norddeutschlands im 16. und 17. Jahrhundert', in Marian Biskup and Klaus Zernack (eds) *Schichtung und Entwicklung der Gesellschaft in Polen und Deutschland im 16. und 17. Jahrhundert: Parallelen, Verknüpfungen, Vergleiche* (Wiesbaden 1983), 121–73.

Schneider, Robert A. 'Crown and Capitoulat: Municipal Government in Toulouse', in Philip Benedict (ed.) *Cities and Social Change in Early Modern France* (London, 1989), 195–220.

Schneider, Robert, A. *Public Life in Toulouse, 1463–1789: From Municipal Republic to Cosmopolitan City* (Ithaca, NY, 1989).

Schoenwerk, August. *Geschichte von Stadt und Kreis Wetzlar*, 2nd edn, rev. by Herbert Flender (Wetzlar, 1975).

Schraitle, Egon. 'Die Bevölkerungsentwicklung Esslingens in der Spätzeit der Reichsstadt', *Esslinger Studien*, 10 (1964), 78–105.

Schramm, Percy Ernst. *Neun Generationen: Dreihundert Jahre deutscher 'Kulturgeschichte' im Lichte der Schicksale einer Hamburger Bürgerfamilie, 1648–1948*, 2 vols (Göttingen, 1963–4).

Schulz, Knut. *Handwerksgesellen und Lohnarbeiter: Untersuchungen zur oberrheinischen und oberdeutschen Stadtgeschichte des 14. bis 17. Jahrhunderts* (Sigmaringen, 1985).

Schuster, Peter. *Das Frauenhaus: Städtische Bordelle in Deutschland, 1350–1600* (Paderborn, 1992).

Schütz, Armin. *Handwerksämter in der Stadt Schleswig: Altstadt, Lollfuss und Friedrichsberg, 1400–1700* (Schleswig, 1966).

Schwemmer, Wilhelm. *Die Schulden der Reichsstadt Nürnberg und ihre Übernahme durch den bayerischen Staat* (Nuremberg, 1967).

Schwerhoff, Gerd. *Köln im Kreuzverhör: Kriminalität, Herrschaft und Gesellschaft in einer frühneuzeitlichen Stadt* (Bonn/Berlin, 1991).

Scott, Tom. *Freiburg and the Breisgau: Town–Country Relations in the Age of Reformation and Peasants' War* (Oxford, 1986).

Seaver, Paul S. *Wallington's World: A Puritan Artisan in Seventeenth-Century London* (Stanford, Calif., 1985).

Sharlin, Allan. 'Natural Decrease in Early Modern Cities: A Reconsideration', *Past and Present*, 79 (May 1978), 126–38.

Shesgreen, Sean. *Engravings by Hogarth: 101 Prints* (New York, 1973).

Shorter, Edward. 'The History of Work in the West: An Overview', in Edward Shorter (ed.) *Work and Community in the West* (New York, 1973), 1–33.

Sieh-Burens, Katarina. *Oligarchie, Konfession und Politik im 16. Jahrhundert: Zur sozialen Verflechtung der Augsburger Bürgermeister und Stadtpfleger, 1518–1618* (Munich, 1986).

Slack, Paul. *The Impact of Plague in Tudor and Stuart England* (Oxford, 1985).

Slack, Paul. 'Metropolitan Government in Crisis: The Response to Plague', in A. L. Beier and Roger Finlay (eds) *London, 1500–1700: The Making of the Metropolis* (London, 1986), 60–81.

Slack, Paul. *Poverty and Policy in Tudor and Stuart England* (London, 1988).

Slack, Paul. 'Poverty and Politics in Salisbury, 1597–1666', in Peter Clark and Paul Slack (eds) *Crisis and Order in English Towns, 1500–1700* (London, 1972), 164–203.

Slack, Paul. 'The Response to Plague in Early Modern England:

Public Policies and their Consequences', in John Walter and Roger Schofield (eds) *Famine, Disease and the Social Order in Early Modern Society* (Cambridge, 1989), 167–87.

Soliday, Gerald Lyman. *A Community in Conflict: Frankfurt Society in the Seventeenth and Early Eighteenth Centuries* (Hanover, NH, 1974).

Soom, Arnold. *Die Zunfthandwerker in Reval im siebzehnten Jahrhundert* (Stockholm, 1971).

Souden, David. 'Migrants and the Population Structure of Later Seventeenth-Century Provincial Cities and Market Towns', in Peter Clark (ed.) *The Transformation of English Provincial Towns* (London, 1984), 133–68.

Specker, Hans Eugen. *Ulm: Stadtgeschichte* (Ulm, 1977).

Spielman, John P. *The Crown and the City: Vienna and the Imperial Court, 1600–1740* (West Lafayette, Ind., 1993).

Spiess, Werner. *Geschichte der Stadt Braunschweig im Nachmittelalter*, 2 vols (Braunschweig, 1966).

Starn, Randolph. 'Historians and "Crisis"', *Past and Present*, 52 (Aug. 1971), 3–22.

Stone, Lawrence, *The Family, Sex and Marriage in England, 1500–1800* (London, 1977).

Stone, Lawrence. 'The Residential Development of the West End of London in the Seventeenth Century', in Barbara C. Malament (ed.) *After the Reformation: Essays in Honor of J. H. Hexter* (Philadelphia, Pa., 1980), 167–212.

Stoob, Heinz. 'Die Stadtbefestigung: Vergleichende Überlegungen zur bürgerlichen Siedlungs- und Baugeschichte, besonders der frühen Neuzeit', in Kersten Krüger (ed.) *Europäische Städte im Zeitalter des Barock: Gestalt, Kultur, Sozialgefüge* (Cologne, 1988), 25–54.

Stow, John. *Stow's Survey of London*, introd. by H. B. Wheatley (London, 1956).

Stoye, John. *The Siege of Vienna* (London, 1964).

Strauss, Gerald. *Luther's House of Learning: Indoctrination of the Young in the German Reformation* (Baltimore, Md., 1978).

Strauss, Gerald. *Nuremberg in the Sixteenth Century* (New York, 1966).

Stürmer, Michael (ed.) *Herbst des alten Handwerks: Quellen zur Sozialgeschichte des 18. Jahrhunderts* (Munich, 1979).

Subrahmanyam, Sanjay. '"Um bom homem de tratar": Piero Strozzi, a Florentine in Portuguese Asia, 1510–1522', *Journal of European Economic History*, 16 (1987), 511–26.

Supple, Barry. 'The Nature of Enterprise', in E. E. Rich and C. H.

Wilson (eds) *The Economic Organization of Early Modern Europe (The Cambridge Economic History of Europe*, vol. 6, Cambridge, 1977), 393–461.

Swanson, Heather. 'The Illusion of Structure: Craft Guilds in Late Medieval English Towns', *Past and Present*, 121 (Nov. 1988), 29–48.

Teisseyre-Sallmann, Line. 'Urbanisme et société: l'exemple de Nîmes aux XVIIe et XVIIIe siècles', *Annales, E.S.C.*, 35 (1980), 965–86.

Terpstra, Nicholas. 'Piety and Punishment: The Lay Conforteria and Civic Justice in Sixteenth-Century Bologna', *Sixteenth Century Journal*, 22 (1991), 679–94.

Tittler, Robert. *Architecture and Power: The Town Hall and the English Urban Community, c.1500–1640* (Oxford, 1991).

Turrel, Denise. *Bourg en Bresse au 16e siècle: les hommes et la ville* (Paris, 1986).

Underdown, David. *Fire from Heaven: Life in an English Town in the Seventeenth Century* (New Haven, Conn., 1992).

Valentinitsch, Helfried. 'Die innerösterreichischen Städte und die Türkenabwehr im 17. Jahrhundert', in Kersten Krüger (ed.) *Europäische Städte im Zeitalter des Barock: Gestalt, Kultur, Sozialgefüge* (Cologne/Vienna, 1988), 169–94.

Van Deursen, A. T. *Plain Lives in a Golden Age: Popular Culture, Religion and Society in Seventeenth-Century Holland*, trans. by Maarten Ultee (Cambridge, 1991).

Verschuur, Mary. 'Merchants and Craftsmen in Sixteenth-Century Perth', in Michael Lynch (ed.) *The Early Modern Town in Scotland* (London, 1987), 36–54.

Villari, Rosario. 'Masaniello: Contemporary and Recent Interpretations', *Past and Present*, 108 (Aug. 1985), 117–32.

Walker, Mack. *German Home Towns: Community, State and General Estate, 1648–1871* (Ithaca, NY, 1971).

Wallace, Peter G. *Communities and Conflict in Early Modern Colmar, 1600–1730* (Atlantic Highlands, NJ, 1994).

Walter, John. 'The Social Economy of Dearth in Early Modern England', in John Walter and Roger Schofield, *Famine, Disease and the Social Order in Early Modern Society* (Cambridge, 1989), 75–128.

Walter, John and Wrightson, Keith, 'Dearth and the Social Order in Early Modern England', *Past and Present*, 71 (May 1976), 22–42.

Wandel, Lee Palmer. *Always Among Us: Images of the Poor in Zwingli's Zurich* (Cambridge, 1990).

Warmbrunn, Paul. *Zwei Konfessionen in einer Stadt: Das Zusammenleben von Katholiken und Protestanten in den paritätischen Reichsstädten*

Augsburg, Biberach, Ravensburg und Dinkelsbühl von 1548 bis 1648 (Wiesbaden, 1983).

Weber, Max. *The City*, trans. by Don Martindale and Gertrud Neuwirth (New York, 1958).

Wehrmann, Martin. *Geschichte der Stadt Stettin* (Stettin, 1911; repr. Frankfurt, 1979).

Weinstein, Donald. *Savonarola and Florence: Prophecy and Patriotism in the Renaissance* (Princeton, NJ, 1970).

Wensky, Margret. 'Women's Guilds in Cologne in the Later Middle Ages', *Journal of European Economic History*, 11 (1982), 631–50.

Westrich, Sal Alexander. *The Ormée of Bordeaux: A Revolution during the Fronde* (Baltimore, Md., 1972).

Whaley, Joachim. *Religious Toleration and Social Change in Hamburg, 1529–1819* (Cambridge, 1985).

Wheaton, Robert. 'Family and Kinship in Western Europe: The Problem of the Joint Family Household', *Journal of Interdisciplinary History*, 5 (1975), 601–28.

Wiesner, Merry E. *Working Women in Renaissance Germany* (New Brunswick, NJ, 1986).

Willax, Franz. 'Bürgerausschuss und Feuergehorsam im Nürnberg des 17. und 18. Jahrhunderts', *Mitteilungen des Vereins für Geschichte der Stadt Nürnberg*, 75 (1988), 109–82.

Wissell, Rudolf. *Des alten Handwerks Recht und Gewohnheit*, 2nd edn, 6 vols (Berlin, 1971–88).

Woehlkens, Erich. *Pest und Ruhr im 16. und 17. Jahrhundert: Grundlagen einer statistisch-topographischen Beschreibung der grossen Seuchen, insbesondere in der Stadt Uelzen* (Hannover, 1954).

Wrigley, E. A. *Population and History* (New York, 1969).

Wrigley, E. A. 'The Process of Modernization and the Industrial Revolution in England', in E. A. Wrigley, *People, Cities and Wealth: The Transformation of Traditional Society* (Oxford, 1987), 46–74.

Wrigley, E. A. 'A Simple Model of London's Importance in Changing English Society and Economy, 1650–1750', *Past and Present*, 37 (July, 1967), 44–70.

Wunder, Gerd. *Die Bürger von Hall: Sozialgeschichte einer Reichsstadt, 1216–1802* (Sigmaringen, 1980).

Zagorin, Perez. *Rebels and Rulers, 1500–1660*, 2 vols (Cambridge, 1982).

Zimányi, Vera. *Economy and Society in Sixteenth and Seventeenth Century Hungary (1526–1650)* (Budapest, 1987).

Zimányi, Vera. 'Die wirtschaftliche und soziale Entwicklung der

Städte Ungarns im 16. Jahrhundert', in Wilhelm Rausch (ed.) *Die Stadt an der Schwelle zur Neuzeit* (Linz, 1980), 129–141.

Zschunke, Peter. *Konfession und Alltag in Oppenheim: Beiträge zur Geschichte von Bevölkerung und Gesellschaft in einer gemischtkonfessionellen Kleinstadt in der frühen Neuzeit* (Wiesbaden, 1984).

Map

Europe in 1600.

Tallinn
Stockholm
Moscow
SWEDEN
RUSSIA
BALTIC SEA
Danzig
POLAND
Warsaw
Breslau
Cracow
Prague
BOHEMIA
Vienna
HUNGARY
Munich
AUSTRIA
BLACK SEA
OTTOMAN
Dubrovnik
Constantinople
Naples
NAPLES
EMPIRE
Palermo

Index